2 W9-ATP-832
A12902 037572

WITHDRAWN

DOING TIME FOR PEACE

DOING TIME FOR PEACE

RESISTANCE, FAMILY, AND COMMUNITY

Compiled and Edited by
Rosalie G. Riegle

Vanderbilt University Press ■ NASHVILLE, TENNESSEE

© 2012 by Vanderbilt University Press
Nashville, Tennessee 37235
All rights reserved
First printing 2012

This book is printed on acid-free paper.
Manufactured in the United States of America

Segment by Joan Cavanagh, copyright Joan Cavanagh.
Words of Jim Douglass, copyright Jim Douglass.
Lyrics for "There's a Train," copyright Jim Strathdee.
Reprinted by permission of Desert Flower Music. Copy
license 03262011 P1.

Library of Congress Cataloging-in-Publication Data on file

LC control number 2012029830
LC classification number JZ5584.U6R54 2013
Dewey class number 303.6'6--dc23

ISBN 978-0-8265-1871-2 (cloth)
ISBN 978-0-8265-1872-9 (paperback)
ISBN 978-0-8265-1873-6 (e-book)

To Johannah Hughes Turner,
for making this book possible

Protest that endures . . . is moved by a hope far more
modest than that of public success: namely, the hope
of preserving qualities in one's own heart and spirit
that would be destroyed by acquiescence.
—Wendell Berry, "A Poem of Difficult Hope"

CONTENTS

PREFACE
Coming to the Project

Ever since the Vietnam War, when I walked in candlelight vigils and visited draft boards with Catholic Workers and Quakers and students and friends, I've been a protester working for peace in the world, like many other people. One day I found myself crossing the line from protest to nonviolent resistance, from saying no to "acting no," as Jim Wallis characterizes the direct action that disobeys the law and has consequences in jail or prison time. In 1984 Wallis wrote, "To protest is to say that something is wrong; resistance means trying to stop it. To protest is to raise your voice; to resist is to stand up with your body."[1]

I decided to stand up with my body and walk through an open gate onto a military base near Omaha, kneel down, say an Our Father, and refuse to leave when asked, in order to send a message, that STRATCOM, the Strategic Air Command, was endangering the world.[2]

Then I thought, "Whoa! What will my grandchildren think if their granny is in jail?" Then, "Can their granny take it? Can she give up her creature comforts, her computer, her glass of wine at 5:00?"

Well, I didn't have to go to jail. After three court visits and a bench trial, I received only a fine and a scolding from a judge who said I was "old enough to know better." But this brush with prison—I could have "done time" for six months—was the genesis of this, my third oral history project.[3] I wanted to know why people would take that risk, why they would make what many of us see as huge sacrifices, and what it was like for them when they did.

Civil disobedience that results in prison is not new: the most significant victories for justice issues in the last one hundred years have been achieved at least partially because nonviolent resisters have stood up with their bodies and spent time in jail for doing so—Mahatma Gandhi, Nelson Mandela, Martin Luther King Jr., and countless others, known and unknown. From India to Poland to Egypt to the United States, citizens have taken pacifist Barbara Deming's advice and moved from "words of dissent to acts of disobedience." From these nonviolent actions, the world has been changed. The "peace people," as they sometimes call themselves, stand up with their bodies to change our foreign policy to one of peace instead of endless war and preparations for war.

Now, I must have always known that peace resisters were connected to someone—were mothers and fathers and grandparents and aunts and uncles and members of communities. But before I started to interview for this project, I'd never thought of the implications of that connection, both for those who did the actions and went to prison and for those in the family and community left behind. Barb Kass of Luck, Wisconsin, explains: "The person at home does the time. Absolutely. For instance, in a family, he or she makes up emotionally for the other parent being gone. And also, that person is always answering to the larger community who says, 'Why don't you just write letters?' I volunteered a lot at school and people *do* look at you and try to figure out what resistance means. So if you have relationships with them, they can't write you off quite as quickly."

The people I interviewed call nonviolent direct action by several names— civil disobedience, divine obedience, and lately civil resistance—because they feel it is their government that disobeys the law, especially international law, not they. Although they see the web of connections between war and oil and caring for the earth and for the poor of the world, they speak here about their peace resistance.

These narrators are mainstream in many ways (white, mostly college educated, and from the political Left) but they are people who have come to see resistance as normative for a moral person. While diverse in lifestyle, motivation, and experience, they are alike in another important aspect: their resistance decisions spring from a Christian or Jewish faith. Often, but not always, they evidence a profound commitment to that faith. In fact, one hears them called "faith-based activists." Because their religious and moral choices run counter to the well-funded waving of flags and teabags, they provide a strong counterpart to the current conception of religion as the fundamentalism of the Right.

A few are known throughout the nonviolent peace movement, like Jesuit priest John Dear and Kathy Kelly of Voices for Creative Nonviolence, but many have been unheeded and unsung. They come from metropolitan areas and from family farms, from Seattle and San Francisco, from Baltimore and Boston, and from Duluth in the North to Norfolk in the South. Some strive to be macroscian—that is, to influence the future. Some show a surprising humility, taking their lives and actions for granted. Their jail and prison experiences range from the notorious Los Angeles County Jail to Alderson Federal Prison, the latter with buildings originally modeled after those of Bucknell University. Some have spent years in prison, some just a few days in jail. Some served "easy time," some carry lasting scars.

Some speak of broken marriages caused by long separation, troubles in the communities left behind, the loneliness of children while their parents are imprisoned, the fears of rape, the failures of communication between prisoners, and the frequent exasperation at the prisons' failure to address injustices. Some narrators now question the value of their resistance, some continue to make it a part of their lives. Many evidence a sardonic or wry introspection, and there's a surprising amount of humor, which I hope readers will see without the "stage directions" transcribers traditionally insert.

Today one hears little about the resisters' arrests and trials in mainstream media. Unlike newspapers and television of the Vietnam era, which reported dramatic stories of draft file burnings and the resultant trials, contemporary media seem bored with nonviolent actions, so the voices have been muted. This book seeks to remove the mute and with it I hope to show readers that resistance is a normal and necessary response in today's perilous world.

After you've read the stories, I hope your understanding will have grown as mine has in the listening and in the writing. You will have heard that each person's experience is different and realized that sometimes these differences bump up against each other and beg for more analysis, more introspection, more searching for the right way. I hope they bump up against your own preconceptions, jostle them out of any comfortable positions, and invite pondering and questions. If the voices encourage analysis, and particularly if that analysis leads to action, the words will work.

Collecting and Shaping the Stories

From 2004 to 2007, I interviewed 173 people who had been imprisoned for resistance actions, or like me, had participated in such actions with the expectation of prison. This book presents insights from sixty-eight of these unlikely jailbirds, their families, and their communities. It also includes selections from twenty people interviewed for my first oral history project. In selecting the interviews, I chose those that most clearly answered the main question that plagued me— what was it like to risk arrest as a member of a family and a community?

I started with people I knew from Catholic Worker houses and from peace actions in which I had participated. Everyone was happy to help with additional contacts within the web of nonviolent resisters. I could have kept going for years; in fact, good leads kept surfacing, even as I finished the editing process. One group of people was hard to find, though—those who had left the peace people because of ruptures in personal relationships. As Stephen Kobasa of New Haven told me, "Sometimes the rhetoric of our nonviolence has a kind of perfection that our relationships don't have. Some people who were involved in the movement at some point no longer are, because they were burnt so badly."[4]

I used an unobtrusive MP3 recorder with a lavalier mike, only occasionally resorting to a telephone conversation. Each interview lasted approximately an hour. I sent narrators the first edit of their interviews for their correction and emendation, and the expectation of that collaborative process, explained before we began each interview, further put the narrators at ease.

Following the lead of the early Studs Terkel, my original inspiration, I edited more heavily than some oral historians, using only about 25 percent of the words collected from the narrators, partly to eliminate repetition but also to remove the embolalia we all use when we speak (a wordiness that can hinder readability). I was thus more present than it may seem from the number of my words. Removing many of the interview questions has also masked my presence. The audio files and both the verbatim and edited transcripts of all the interviews in the project have been deposited in the Catholic Worker Archives at Marquette University in Milwaukee. The edited interviews of the Plowshares activists were also placed in the Berrigan Archives at DePaul University in Chicago and those of the Ground Zero Trident campaigners in the archives at the University of Washington.

Some readers may be baffled by resistance language: "confronting the powers," "redemptive suffering," "personal disarmament." These words, common to faith-based resisters, can sound alien to those not a part of this loosely knit but somehow coherent community. I've defined these phrases when I could without spoiling the syntax, but please bear with unfamiliar terms, knowing that the concepts may be repeated in a different form and that understanding will grow.

These years of collecting and editing and shaping have been richly rewarding, even happy, in spite of the sometimes disturbing subject matter. They have been made easy by the friendly cooperation of the narrators, by the sheer fascination of their stories, and by the fantastic help I've received from Johannah Turner and others. The narrators have been generous with their words, generous with their time, generous with their lives. Thank you, all. I couldn't ask for better work than to be the one who unclicks the mute button so the voices of these courageous resisters can be heard.

ACKNOWLEDGMENTS

So many people helped me on this book: my daughter Meg, who cheerfully read drafts of my original proposal; the people who gave me leads to the narrators and ideas about crafting the book; the friends who offered hospitality on my travels, often on short notice; the folks who wracked their brains and raided their scrapbooks for photos. You all remain in my thankful heart.

Particular thanks go to Felton Davis for his bibliography on prison conditions; Felice and Jack Cohen-Joppa of the *Nuclear Resister* (*www.nukeresister. org*), who document antiwar arrests and support for prisoners; and Carl Bunin, whose online publication, *This Week in History* (*www.peacebuttons.info/E-News/ thisweek.htm*) provided me with a rich compendium of actions for peace and justice.

Luke Hansen, SJ, helped with important connections; Karen Skalitsky gave perceptive suggestions as a reader; and Jeanne and George Schaller of the Helen Casey Center for Nonviolence in Midland, Michigan, offered retreat space at their poustinia.

Without careful transcribers, the mass of interviews would never have seen print. In addition to the super-professional Johannah Hughes Turner, who was much more than a transcriber, Hillel Arnold, Fran Fuller, Kate Hennessy, and Maura Conway performed expert and timely transcribing work. Catholic Workers Frank Cordaro and Art Laffin frequently assisted me in tracking down crucial details, as did Liz McAlister and Ardeth Platte, OP of Jonah House. No one can write about Catholic Workers without the expert assistance of Phil Runkel, the Catholic Worker archivist at Marquette University's Raynor Library. I thank Phil more than he'll ever know.

I thank also the many photographers cited. Their work helps the stories to come alive. I thank most especially the people who helped me to find them: Marcus Bleech of the Jesuit Conference; Wendy Chmielewski, Swarthmore Peace Collection; Morgen MacIntosh Hodgetts, Berrigan Archives at DePaul University; Nicolette Bromberg, archivist for Ground Zero at University of Washington; Tod Ensign, Citizen Soldier; Bob Smith, Brandywine Peace Community; Lewis Randa, Peace Abbey; Leonard Eiger, Ground Zero Center for Nonviolent Action; Ethan Vesely-Flad and Richard Deats, Fellowship of Reconciliation; Jonah House; Voices for Creative Nonviolence; Nukewatch; the Sisters of St. Francis of Tifton, Ohio; Anthony Giacchino, director of the documentary *The Camden 28*; Joe

Tropea, director of the documentary *Hit and Stay*; Dede Smith, *Florida Times-Union*; John Admian, *Hartford Advocate*; Robert Drew, *Los Angeles Times*; Priscilla Lord Faris; Charles Jenks; Oona DeFlaun; Bob Graf; Terra Lawson-Remer; John Schuchardt; Erin Stieber; Molly Rush; Frank Hudson; and Chrissy Nesbitt. In addition, a number of narrators gave help over and above what one could ask, especially Kim Wahl, whose persistence in locating photos and photographers of the Trident submarine and White Train actions finally paid off.

I appreciate mightily the support and encouragement of my family and friends, both in Michigan and in my new home of Evanston, Illinois. Of course the most heartfelt thanks go to the 173 people I interviewed especially for this project and to the others I interviewed for my earlier oral histories. I wish I could have used all your stories. I acknowledge also the resisters like Phil Berrigan and Elmer Maas who joined the "the cloud of witnesses" before I was able to interview them. Your lives inspire us all.

Thanks go, too, to Michael Ames, director of Vanderbilt University Press, to Joell Smith-Borne, managing editor, and to Peg Duthie, Susan Havlish, and Dariel Mayer for their help in bringing together this publication. I also thank Temple University Press for permission to reprint selections that originally appeared in a different form in *Voices from the Catholic Worker* (1993).

In conclusion, I hope all the people I forgot to thank will forgive me. The community of peace people remains close to my heart and always in my mind. All mistakes and misjudgments are, of course, my own.

INTRODUCTION

Doing time for peace is nothing new. For as long as rulers have ruled by violence, peacemakers and justice seekers have found themselves on the receiving end of that violence. More than 2,600 years ago, the prophet Jeremiah was thrown into a dungeon for his words of prophetic witness against the Israelite monarchy, while Daniel was thrown to the lions by a Babylonian king. Socrates was imprisoned and then killed for his gadfly bites into the Athenian social order. John the Baptist and Jesus met similar fates at the hands of the Romans and their proxies, and their example inspired thousands of subsequent Christian martyrs. Saint Paul's practice of writing letters from prison inaugurated a literary tradition that has been carried forward by authors as diverse as the medieval Catholic Boethius, the Puritan John Bunyan, the Quaker George Fox, the German patrician Dietrich Bonhoeffer, and the Black Baptist preacher Martin Luther King Jr. The individuals featured in this book, nearly all of whom did their prison time within the past fifty years, can claim as fellow convicts most early Christian bishops as well as their "heretical" adversaries; founders or major leaders in virtually every strand of Christianity, from Eastern Orthodoxy (Maximus Confessor) to Lutheranism (Martin Luther) to Mormonism (Joseph Smith); and heroes of national liberation from South Africa (Nelson Mandela) to Myanmar (Aung San Suu Kyi).

It is true that not all of these predecessors "did time for peace" in the strict sense of suffering imprisonment as a direct consequence of efforts to end war. Many were imprisoned for preaching a new and controversial religious message—a message that included opposition to war in the cases of Jesus and George Fox, but not Martin Luther or Joseph Smith. Others were imprisoned for refusing to serve in the military or to participate in a particular war. One early model for such refusal was Martin of Tours, who withdrew from the Roman army shortly after his baptism, declaring that "I am a soldier of Christ. I cannot fight." But the witness of the so-called military saints was as much against Roman idolatry as against warfare as such, and many have been claimed as patrons by subsequent Christian armies. Similarly, many persons who have been imprisoned for their pursuit of justice were also willing to use limited violence for their cause. Dietrich Bonhoeffer plotted to assassinate Adolf Hitler; Nelson Mandela's African National Congress used sabotage as well as nonviolent direct action to undermine apartheid. Still, the solidarity of suffering runs deep, and virtually all of these predecessors have helped to inspire the imprisoned resisters featured in this book.

Representing just one strand of an enormous tradition, the individuals featured in this book are relatively homogeneous in their practice and motivation. They are war *resisters*—people who oppose war as such, as well as particular wars, and who do not merely refuse to participate in war but take positive action in hopes of ending it. Most are also deeply committed to struggles against imperialism, racism, poverty, sexism, homophobia, and the abuse of the environment, but the acts of resistance featured here are primarily against war. Other, similar books might well be written about activists who have gone to prison as a result of their involvement in Greenpeace or Earth First, the Clamshell and Abalone Alliances (against nuclear power), the animal liberation movement, the sanctuary movement, Central American and South African solidarity movements, the global justice movement of the 1990s, or even the pro-life movement. Like those activists, but unlike many pacifist prisoners, the people featured in this book generally took deliberate action—burning a draft card, trespassing at a military installation, sabotaging a nuclear weapon—that they anticipated would result in their imprisonment. They sought to bring the violence of the state onto themselves, in hopes that this would expose underlying injustices and lead to change. On the other hand, it is worth noting that most of these resisters took action in contexts where they could be reasonably confident that resistance would not result in their death. In this, they differ dramatically from war resisters in some other times and places.

The people featured in this book are also united in the fact that their resistance took place within the context of vital activist networks. Virtually all were personally acquainted with others who had "done time for peace" before taking their personal action. This mentoring made it easier for them to face the isolation and psychological burdens intrinsic to prison life. Recognizing the value of ongoing support, most have spent a significant portion of their lives living in intentional community with other war resisters. What's more, nearly all participate in networks shaped by Roman Catholic spirituality. These networks are by no means exclusively Catholic, but the influence of Dorothy Day, Dan Berrigan, Phil Berrigan, and Liz McAlister outweighs that of Quaker, Mennonite, mainline Protestant, Buddhist, neopagan, or Jewish resisters. Non-Catholic spiritual traditions inform their own activist networks, with their own distinctive but overlapping patterns of resistance.

The community of resisters featured here—intentional, communally rooted, American, and at least vaguely Catholic in its underlying spirituality—has a particular genealogy within the larger history of "doing time for peace." At the risk of omitting some important antecedents, I will try here to trace a bit of that genealogy.[1] Among the first Americans to deliberately court imprisonment for the sake of peace were the Transcendentalists Bronson Alcott and Henry David Thoreau, along with their British friend Charles Lane. Thoreau's night in the Concord jail in July 1846 is best remembered, in part because it occurred just weeks after the outbreak of the Mexican American War. But Alcott began refusing to pay his poll tax in 1842, on the grounds that the federal government was using violence to protect slavery, and he was very briefly jailed for this resistance in 1843. (Lane barely had time to write a letter to the abolitionist *Liberator* explaining Alcott's motives before a wealthy sympathizer paid Alcott's tax.)[2] The principle underlying Alcott and Lane's action was "nonresistance," a particularly strict version of pacifism that grew out of the abolitionist critique of the violence inherent in slavery. Abolitionism had already engendered significant experiences of righteous imprisonment: William Lloyd Garrison wrote letters from prison during his incarceration for libeling the owner of a slave-trading ship, and his allies Abby Kelley and Stephen Foster were frequently arrested for disrupting church services with the abolitionist message. A bit later, Frederick Douglass was arrested for claiming the right to sit in a whites-only train car. Recognizing the ways communal support could facilitate such actions, many nonresistants participated in intentional communities during the 1840s. The most enduring of these, Hopedale, played host to the New England Non-Resistance Society, and its founder, Adin Ballou, wrote the most comprehensive guide to pacifist action published in the nineteenth century. But it was Thoreau—neither a pacifist nor a committed member of any organization—who coined a more descriptive term for deliberate action intended to change society without violence. "Civil disobedience," he declared, was the best response to injustice, for "under a government which imprisons any unjustly, the true place for a just man is also a prison."[3]

Just as the term "civil disobedience" emerged from a struggle against both slavery and war, so the idea of "war resistance" was developed by early twentieth-century activists who opposed both World War I and the underlying economic injustices that, in their view, gave rise to war. After the United States entered the war in 1917, thousands of young men were sent to prison for refusing to serve in the military. Most were members of historic peace churches who had not sought out imprisonment and had no expectation that their imprisonment would contribute to peace. Very different were Harold Gray and Evan Thomas, who as YMCA relief workers in Europe were exempt from conscription and out of the reach of the federal government. But after becoming pacifists, they deliberately resigned their positions and sailed home to face the punishment for refusing conscription. Sentenced to military prison, they continuously experimented with hunger strikes and other forms of resistance to their jailers. Ultimately they were sentenced to life in prison, though they were pardoned after the war.

Thomas's and Gray's prison experience was shared not only by other conscientious objectors, but also by women's suffrage activists who refused to suspend their agitation during the war and by Socialist presidential candidate Eugene

Debs, who was convicted of sedition after encouraging young men to resist the draft. These inspiring examples led to the formation of two enduring pacifist organizations, the Fellowship of Reconciliation and the War Resisters League, both of which fostered networks of activists with a fervent desire to refine their practice of nonviolence. In the 1920s, these activists—along with African American freedom advocates, some of whom were themselves members of the Fellowship or the League—introduced the Gandhian practice of *satyagraha* to the United States. Following Gandhi, they began to dream of extended, nonviolent campaigns against racial segregation and economic injustice, as well as war itself. Gandhi's influence also made it easier for them to break out of their Protestant and post-Protestant roots, forging a particularly important alliance with the circle of Roman Catholic radicals around Dorothy Day and Peter Maurin's *Catholic Worker* newspaper.

The Great Depression and World War II dramatically reorganized the community of war resisters in the United States. Some leaders, notably Norman Thomas and Reinhold Niebuhr, renounced absolute pacifism on the grounds that force was sometimes needed to defend socialism and democracy from fascism. Even A. J. Muste, who led the Fellowship of Reconciliation during the war years and beyond, was a Marxist militant during the height of the Depression. As one of the few consistently pacifist leaders, Dorothy Day took on a more central role in the community of resisters, effectively drawing Catholics to pacifism and non-Catholics to the Catholic Worker. Prominent in the latter group was Ammon Hennacy, one of the young socialists who had spent World War I in jail as a conscientious objector. Prodding Catholic Workers to stress "resistance" as much as "hospitality," Hennacy helped knit together traditions that might seem ideologically incompatible.

World War II also saw the emergence of a new generation of conscientious objectors. Though federal policy was much more accommodating than it had been a generation before, many felt called to go to jail rather than participate in service camps for conscientious objectors. Among them were the "Union Eight"—idealistic students from Union Seminary—and Bayard Rustin, an African American Quaker with a special flair for resisting segregation in prison. After the war, these energies flowed into the racial justice work of the Congress of Racial Equality; intentional communities such as Koinonia, Macedonia, the Harlem Ashram, Glen Gardner, and Skyview Acres; activist campus ministries; and concerted campaigns against nuclear proliferation. Anchored by its houses of hospitality in New York City, the Catholic Worker movement remained an integral part of this network—and grew steadily once the Second Vatican Council affirmed nonviolence as a valid path of Catholic spirituality.[4]

By the early 1960s, in short, war resistance was a vital tradition with a heroic history, a rich repertoire of practices, a mix of underlying spiritualities, and an interconnected network of practitioners. The tradition was available to Americans in general and to Roman Catholics in particular. Of course, many Americans and many Roman Catholics had never heard of it. This book tells the story of the new generations of resisters who joined the tradition since 1960, bringing their witness of peace to the warmakers and the prisonkeepers alike. Their voices, and the voices of their families and communities, have much to teach us all.

—Dan McKanan
Harvard Divinity School

1

Precursors to the Plowshares Movement

Like most, I was taught US history with an emphasis on wars and westward expansion. Only as an adult did I learn that there have always been citizens opposing war and actively living their lives in opposition to armed conflict.[1] The few conscientious objectors (COs) to World War I received harsh sentences and little institutional support. The founding of the Women's International League for Peace and Freedom (WILPF) in 1914 and the US Fellowship of Reconciliation (FOR) in 1915 was a start, and in 1923 the War Resisters League (WRL) began supporting COs who signed a pledge renouncing participation in war, regardless of religious affiliation. After the debacle of World War I, groups such as these made the 1930s a decade where peace seemed respectable; they were aided by socialists and others on the left as well as the traditional peace churches—Quakers, Brethren, and Mennonites—and some mainline congregations. Their parades, prayer services, and protests against war toys helped a nation to remember the carnage of the supposed "war to end all wars."

Pacifists saw the dangers of Nazism early on and protested vigorously when President Franklin D. Roosevelt refused to lower immigration barriers to allow escaping Jews into the country. But when the draft was reinstated and war fever swept the land, almost all the peace groups except the WRL and the Catholic Worker at least temporarily buried their pacifist ideals.[2] Fifty-two thousand men were classified as COs during World War II and 6,086 men refused to cooperate with the draft and went to prison. (Over 75 percent of the latter were Jehovah's Witnesses.)[3] David Dellinger and seven other ministerial students at Union Theological Seminary received wide publicity for refusing to register for their draft deferment and going to prison.

Dick Von Korff, 2011. (Photo courtesy of Dick Von Korff.)

Dick Von Korff went by himself, unheralded and unknown. A man who knows his own mind, Dick was born in 1916 and decided "war was stupid" when he was in high school. After going to Sandstone Prison for refusing induction into the army in World War II, he completed his education with a PhD in chemistry. His research career finally took him to the Michigan Molecular Institute in Midland, Michigan. He was eighty-nine when I interviewed him in 2004, with a mind still going a million miles a minute. We looked at his scrapbooks as we talked.

Dick Von Korff

> "I pled guilty and I was guilty because my draft orders came and I disobeyed them. There was no way around it, I violated the law. But wars are wrong. The only way we're going to stop them is to refuse to participate."

My wife, Jane, convinced me. This was in 1944 and we lived in Peoria, Illinois. I was working in a lab, doing top secret work on penicillin, without a graduate degree, even. I told the people at the lab I wouldn't go, and they said that I was crazy, that I'd ruin my career. [*Reading his refusal statement.*] "I am unable to report because of my religious belief." That's not right. I should have said, "I *will* not report." Sure, I was *able* to, I just wasn't going to do it.

After I didn't report, the lab tried to make me quit, and I said, "Oh, no no no! In this country you're innocent 'til you're proven guilty." So I went on working until the FBI said they had a warrant for my arrest. Then I went in immediately, with Jane, who was pregnant at the time. Got out on bail and was able to start graduate school in Minnesota before finally being sentenced to eighteen months at Sandstone, the federal penitentiary.

I was treated very nice. I never encountered any nastiness, ever! Nowhere. In prison, I found that if you respect the other guy, they'll leave you alone and respect you, no matter what. My problem was being away from my wife and child. He was four months old when I went in, and he and Jane came up every month. But I got my revenge because once Jane accidentally left a diaper full of BM under the bench. And it served them right.

Oh, I used to live for those visits! No one else came, though. My parents were probably 550 miles away. My dad had been working on the [Long Island] Arsenal making gun sights, and [my refusal] was hard on him, but he backed me a hundred percent. So, loneliness—that's what I remember most about Sandstone.

Ro: What were the other prisoners like?

Dick: They were mostly COs but not all. Two fellows next to me were in for six months for stealing alcohol from the college pharmacology department for parties. Six months! Men who were in there for taking women across the state line for immoral purposes got less than the COs, by far. I remember two CO brothers, whose father had been a CO in World War I. They were sentenced to five years. Served the five years—or less, because you get a day a month good time—were released, drafted again, and sent back for another five years.

Ro: Do you keep in contact with any of the COs you met there?

Dick: A few. I remember Bill Schulz. He was a Unitarian leader, and he's now president of Amnesty International.[4] Oh, and Art Weiser. He was the son of a minister, and his son was a CO who talked to the soldiers in Iraq.

Now, these other guys that were in the Sandstone CO group—they called themselves "The Sandstone Amnesty and Recreation Society" and had walked out of a Civilian Service camp because they felt they'd become part of the war effort. They felt their integrity [would be compromised] if they became part of the prison system—part of the *war* system—by working in prison. So they refused to work and got locked up for while and couldn't participate in the regular freedoms of the prison. Now, I didn't feel that way. Whether it was fear, I don't know. It's hard to analyze your own motives.

I will say one thing I learned in prison. Don't ever sacrifice your integrity. Because if you do, you have nothing left.

Ro: Did you practice any religion while you were in prison?

Dick: All the while I was there, Jane and I tried to read the New Testament together.

We read the same sections at the same time and wrote back and forth about it. I still have the little pocket Bible that I used.

I've bounced around a bit as a Christian. When I was growing up, I was first nothing, really. And then a Presbyterian after my first wife died, then a Quaker, and then a Methodist, and then I went to Unity, and now I go to the Unitarian Universalist fellowship. I can say now that I'm rather unsympathetic with [all this going to different churches]. It's not logical. I used to say I was an atheist, and then I'd say I was a nontheist. (That's less irritating.)

Now I say I define God in a different way. I now believe that what others call God, for me is embodied in all the good, the kindness, the love in humankind. Yes, people are doing God's work, but it comes from within them, not from a supernatural source. I feel that the great prophets, Jesus and Mohammed, were keen observers of human nature, and they saw what worked and what didn't work. That's what their teachings are about.

Ro: When you tell people today why you are a pacifist, what reasoning do you give?

Dick: Well, war is a dead end. It just leads to more wars. I've always felt that war was wrong, ever since high school. I pled guilty and I *was* guilty because my draft orders came and I disobeyed them. There was no way around it, I violated the law. But wars are wrong. The only way we're going to stop them is to refuse to participate.

Ro: Did you serve the whole eighteen months?

Dick: I served six months and got out on the first day I could be paroled. Didn't have any trouble adjusting, none whatsoever. I'm not an easy guy to get along with, you know? I have a problem of always wanting to be in control, so I was just as glad as hell to get out.

Went right back to school and also worked. My wife got me an orderly job at University Hospital. This was the year of the big polio epidemic, and I was the only orderly for the entire hospital on the second shift. I'd bring one kid in the front door, take him up to one of the nineteen iron lungs, take another kid to the morgue.

Hey, wanna know something? Our younger son got a CO from the "Berrigan board" in Catonsville, when we were living in Maryland. (This was after Vietnam was over.) I volunteered as a witness for him and was allowed to hear part of the hearing. After I came out, I heard the clerk say to two young kids, "You have to register, but the war's over so you won't be called." After they left, she said to me, "I wish I could [have told] all the boys that! These wars are caused by nothing but greed."

Woot! That was the Berrigan board, where they poured the blood on the draft files. And my son got the full CO!

Ro: How did going to prison affect your later life?

Dick: Oh, I think it was great. It had a tremendous effect. I've always told people I went to prison, just like I tell people I was in a special hospital for depression. It used to bother my wife. I said, "What the heck! It's a fact. I was."

Ro: Did you put being in the penitentiary on your résumé?

Dick: You *have* to say, even if you're pardoned. They ask you, "Were you ever arrested?"

"Yes."

"What was the disposition?"

"Penitentiary. Pardoned by President Truman in 1948." I have the pardon letter right here. [*Looking at scrapbooks.*] And I'm proud of it all.[5]

While Dick continued his career as a research chemist, other COs, such as Dellinger and his companion George Houser, became professional civil rights and peace activists. The Catholic Worker (CW) movement, founded in 1933 by Dorothy Day and Peter Maurin, had successfully lobbied for Roman Catholics to be accepted as COs and remained staunchly pacifist throughout the war, to the horror of many liberal Catholics who had previously welcomed its threefold program of houses of hospitality, agronomic universities where workers could become scholars, and clarification of thought to address the ills of society.

Day, a convert from a secular socialism, became a complete pacifist when she saw how the teachings of Jesus fit her ideals for a world where "it would be easier to be good." After the bombing of Hiroshima, the *Catholic Worker* wrote that the nation should "put on sackcloth and ashes, weep and repent."[6] The nation didn't, but instead built more and more nuclear weapons and perfected both surveillance techniques and the methods of delivering larger and more lethal bombs.

People in the small peace movement went to work. Using Gandhi as a touchstone, they defined and refined nonviolent resistance, learning to live and work together in both nationwide organizations and small intentional communities. An alphabet of new groups such as CNVA (Committee for Nonviolent Action) and SANE (Committee for a Sane Nuclear Policy) joined the WRL and the American Friends Service Committee (AFSC) to forge alliances and plan sometimes theatrical actions to alert the public. A responsible and responsive press got the message out and people listened, but government policy rarely changed as we fought a very, very Cold War.

Communities such as the New England CNVA and the Catholic Worker demonstrated that nonviolent direct action was able to succeed only if buttressed by communities who themselves "studied war no more" and attempted to live peaceably both within their small communities and with those in disagreement.

Brad Lyttle says he was "born a pacifist," taking his lead from a Unitarian mother who was also a socialist and a feminist. Born in 1927, he decided as a young man that peacework would be his profession. After serving an apprenticeship prison sentence for draft refusal, he worked first with the AFSC and later with CNVA and other groups. Brad's skill with logistics helped with dramatic actions at the Nevada nuclear test site, Mead (now Offutt) Air Force Base in Nebraska, and the submarine works at New London, Connecticut. (These sites remain targets of contemporary peace activists.) He also coordinated several long peace walks, including one from San Francisco to Moscow, and one through the southern United States, attempting to get to Guantanamo and to protest its use as a US base. After a hiatus to care for his aging parents, Brad returned to resistance, and in 2010 he was arrested both at Creech Air Force Base in Nevada, protesting the drones, and at the Oak Ridge, Tennessee, nuclear weapons research facility.

Bradford Lyttle

"I found I had a natural talent for logistics. . . . But five thousand miles in ten months! Madness!"

My father was a minister and we lived a comfortable middle-class life here, near the University of Chicago. The summer I was eighteen, I heard the news about the atomic bomb on Japan, and I said to myself, "Either the human race has to end war or war is going to end the human race."

At Earlham College, I was thinking about making the peace movement my life's work, and I knew that would mean spending some time in jail, so I decided to refuse alternative service in the draft, partly to get the experience of jail.

My sentence was a year and a day at Springfield, but I only served nine months. Saw a great deal of racism and segregation and I couldn't cooperate with that, so they transferred me to something called "the Honor Ward." Much less crowded. And not segregated. You had a separate cell and room for a little desk.

I met some extraordinary people there and learned a lot. The library was excellent, and the librarian told me why. He was a famous Communist—I've forgotten his name now—who'd been put in prison under the Smith Act.[7] He told me, "We got control of the libraries at some of the military bases and brought in all these books on sociology and politics and psychology. After the war was over, these books were sent to the federal prison system."

Brad Lyttle leafleting with Bayard Rustin, circa 1955. (Gamble Brothers, Fellowship of Reconciliation Records, Swarthmore College Peace Collection.)

When I got out, I had to decide whether to be a doctor or to work in the peace movement and I decided on the latter because it was more difficult. I knew there'd always be large numbers of highly trained people in medicine, and the research would go forward, but the field of peace and social change—that was different. It didn't have the social support—the pathways—that medical research did.

Now, I wouldn't change that decision, but . . . I had a talent for the medical stuff—had done research before I went to prison—but I had no talent for peace work. I'm not a politician; in fact, I was rather asocial as a young person. I had to develop the skills I needed for peace organization.

Nothing has been easy, but I found I had a natural talent for logistics. So if it came to creating a project which involved complicated setups, I could do that. Easily. I could set up the context within which other people would act.

[Before he started on his life's work, Brad spent a year making enough money to travel, and then went around the world, studying the Gandhian movement and other peace organizations and spending only $2,500 in eighteen months.]

Brad: I saw the way most of the people in the world live, and I realized very, very deeply that I was a privileged minority. When I came home and walked into a supermarket, I burst into tears because there was more food in that one supermarket than in a city of thirty thousand people in India.

San Francisco to Moscow peace walkers in Pennsylvania, May 1961. (Theodore Hetzel, Theodore Hetzel Photograph Collection, Swarthmore College Peace Collection.)

After some time at AFSC, I began to work for the Committee for Nonviolent Action in nonviolent demonstrations against nuclear weapons—the Nevada Project, and then at the SAC [Strategic Air Command] headquarters on Offutt Air Force Base near Omaha. We drew people from all over the country. Took a whole offset printing press with us to print our leaflets. The television stations in Omaha came out and showed pictures of our demonstrations on their news program. Later we'd send them our own pictures and they'd use those, but then the air force got wind of that and had the news director fired and so forth. I did civil disobedience there, too, and got six months and I was shipped back down to Springfield.

After I got out, there were the demonstrations against Polaris subs out in Connecticut. This was the summer of 1960, and it's still the action closest to my heart. It was extraordinary! The day we began up at Electric Boat on the Thames River was the same day as the Yale-Harvard Boat Race, with an audience of over ten thousand. A lot of young people walked from New London across the river on the I-95 bridge and over to Electric Boat. It was just wild! One of the Electric Boat workers took our leaflets away and then knocked me cold—the only time I've ever been knocked out.

We got tremendous publicity, as you can imagine, and more people came. The research director at Electric Boat resigned and joined us. We went all over the East Coast to talk and demonstrate and eventually we committed civil disobedience.

See, they'd launch one of these submarines with great fanfare—bands and champagne against the bow of the ship. Our people would dive into the water and

Brad Lyttle speaking with Russian villagers, with Patrick
Proctor translating, 1961. (Photo courtesy of Scott Herrick.)

swim out and climb up onto the submarine. The demonstration became the news, not the launching. We got tremendous coverage all over the country.

The young people were incredibly courageous. I remember when one of our people climbed up on the tail fin of the *Ethan Allen* and the navy knocked him off with a high-pressure hose. Millions of people saw that on NBC. The government is much more sophisticated about this now, and they pressure the networks to prevent this type of publicity, but then the media was just eating it up!

Except that they kept building the submarines. The shipyard workers would yell at us, "Go tell it to the Russians! We're not the cause of the problem. Just try to do over in Russia what you're doing here. They'll shoot you!"

One day I said to some guys in a restaurant, "Let's walk to Moscow." So we did. We decided to walk from San Francisco to Moscow. That's the kind of thinking that people in their twenties and thirties engage in.

Ro: Holy cow! That's one long march! How many people did it?

Brad: Oh, various numbers at different times. I don't think more than maybe five or six went the whole way. I was with the project, especially at the end in Russia, but I didn't walk the whole way. It was madness—absolute madness—to even try to consider walking 5,900 miles in ten months. Madness! But it was a remarkable experience.

None of the governments liked us; France wouldn't even let us in. But then the US put the word out to the Western European nations: "Let these fools through. They'll get to Russia, but they'll never get in, and that'll be the end of that."

The governments of Poland and East Germany didn't like us, either, but word came down from Moscow to let us through. So we had the peace committees of these Communist countries sponsoring us, providing our logistical support and big feasts and concerts, organizing rallies, and things like that. It was one of the major political events of western Russia at that time. The American press, of course, reported it only in a small way. We had this big meeting with professors and students at the University of Moscow, and the Western reporters were absolutely amazed. Khrushchev was at the time interested in moderating tension, and they wanted to create the impression that there was a little bit of civil liberty in the Soviet Union. But maybe the main reason was that they respected us. Otherwise, how would they have let people distribute 150,000 leaflets that advocated nonviolent resistance and unilateral disarmament? And let us talk to thousands and thousands of people?

Sure, they were using us for public relations, but they were also risking the possibility of dissent. When I look at what happened later in the Soviet Union—the Velvet Revolution—I'm not going to say the march was the cause of that, but all the ideas that we were advocating in the course of that march you could find later in the Velvet Revolution.[8]

That walk to Moscow was the most exhausting experience I've ever had. The government cut our time there by 50 percent, so we had to walk fifty kilometers a day. We'd start at two o'clock in the morning and stop walking at ten at night, walking in shifts. Only three hours of sleep a night. Afterwards, I was totally wiped out, and it was two years before I could really do any organizing.

Then they got me to work on the Nashville to Washington March for Peace, which was very dangerous during the civil rights period because we had with us young white women and young black men. We were threatened with death many times as we went through the Allegheny Mountains.

Then we did a Quebec to Guantanamo Walk for Peace, integrating civil rights issues with opposition to nuclear weapons and our government's repressive Cuban policies. This was eighteen months in '63 and '64. We got thrown into jail in Albany, Georgia, and we right away began to fast.

It's Albany, Georgia, run by Police Chief Laurie Pritchett, who arrested all the demonstrators who came in with King and kept them indefinitely. He tried to do the same thing to us. When you face that kind of situation, you have to adopt extreme methods of resistance, and the only resistance you can really do in jail is to fast. Nobody completely fasted—we drank water, I guess—but it went on and on and on. I was so weak when they let us out after two months that I could hardly walk.

We finally got to Miami, but then we had all sorts of trouble, and when we tried to leave for Cuba, the coast guard stopped us. Key West wouldn't even let us into the city. Then back in Miami, we were beaten up by Cubans, and after that, we were just too tired, so we stopped.

[For seventeen years during the Vietnam era, Brad organized war tax resistance and cared for his parents in Chicago.[9]]

Brad: My father made it to age ninety-six and my mother was just days short of a hundred. Of all the things I've done in my life, taking care of my parents was the most satisfying. People don't believe that, but it's true. At the end, they couldn't walk and were incontinent; everything was gone to pieces physically. Except their minds—they were both good companions straight up to the end. My mother and I . . . she and I were just the same person, really, so it was wonderful to have her as a companion.

> [Brad went back to school during this time of caretaking, getting an MA in political science at the University of Illinois and taking a year of political philosophy at the University of Chicago, where he wrote a history of the Chicago peace movement. He also published a three-page paper in *Harvard Magazine*, showing with a stochastic equation that nuclear deterrence is scientifically irrational and shouldn't be used as a basis of national security. Every four years, he runs for president as a candidate of the Pacifist Party.]

Brad: See, quite a few people within our movement are personal pacifists, but not too many project pacifist ideas into political activity. I do. I think military power is morally wrong as an institution, and if continued, it's going to lead to the destruction of the human species, and I proved that statistically in my graduate work. The basic principle of the Pacifist Party is to substitute nonviolent resistance for military defense. But my four campaigns so far have been incredibly unsuccessful.

> [Brad continued to walk the walk, and in 1993 joined a large contingent of internationals heading into the war zone in former Yugoslavia. Kathy Kelly, who was with him, remembers that Brad strongly advised the group to proceed on foot.]

Kathy Kelly: He told me, "Buses don't communicate. People do." People marching unarmed, distributing fliers, communicating through loud speakers, carrying signs, and clearly proceeding unarmed have a tremendous potential to communicate a message on behalf of saving lives and ending war.[10]

> [When the city of Chicago refused to let peace activists march down Michigan Avenue on the anniversary of "Shock and Awe," the bombing that began the Iraq War, Brad walked alone down the street.]

Brad: I was the only one! Of course I was arrested. The National Lawyers Guild took up my case and after two years, we won. In a very amusing way, actually. It was really hot in the courtroom and somehow I fell asleep. Well, the judge put it in the record that the defendant fell asleep, and of course I thought my goose was cooked. But then he said, "We have here a seventy-nine-year-old man who was only given five minutes to disperse. He may not even have heard the order. Case dismissed." Ever since then, the city has let people walk down Michigan Avenue in the parade. So I think people in the peace movement should understand that going to sleep in the courtroom could be a key tactic! [*Laughs heartily.*]

[In his latest trials, Brad didn't fall asleep. At his sentencing for the Y-12 antinuclear action at Oak Ridge, he gave a clearly reasoned rationale for his civil disobedience. The judge sentenced him to one year probation and one month home confinement.[11]]

The sixties saw the civil rights movement, well documented and cataclysmic in the social change it fostered. The United Farm Workers and their supporters campaigned for a living wage and better working conditions for the migrants and others who fed America. Many nonviolent peace activists joined in these campaigns, but as the war in Vietnam became "hot," moving from the military advisers to South Vietnam in the fifties to increasing troop involvement in the early sixties, David McReynolds and others at the WRL began calling for not only negotiation but withdrawal. They were joined by thousands in the first large demonstrations in New York and around the country in December 1964.[12]

It grew from there. 1965 was declared "The Year of Vietnam" by CNVA, and peace groups urged civil disobedience to resist the war. They called for tax resistance and escalated their activism, thronging to the streets in large protests.[13] Students joined the fray, with draft counseling, draft refusal, campus teach-ins, and national moratoriums. And a fray it became, with Students for a Democratic Society (SDS) moving away from the nonviolence of the more traditional peace groups. By force of personality, A. J. Muste of FOR and CNVA forged alliances between disparate groups and developed models for nonviolently mobilizing dissent, but the decade saw the United States becoming increasingly polarized. Draft resistance and draft card burnings said "Hell No! We Won't Go!"

One who said no to the draft was the Honorable Robert Wollheim. In 1968, he was sentenced to eighteen months for refusing induction, although a Supreme Court decision shortened his stay. Later he went to law school, was admitted to the Oregon bar, and finally became a state appellate judge.

Robert (Bob) Wollheim

"People did what they could. . . . Not everybody could go to jail. When mass movements are good, you don't have to have people marching in lockstep."

When I ran for judge in the nineties, my opponent tried to make my Vietnam conviction an issue, but he didn't succeed. I've always been up-front that I refused induction and went to prison.

Ro: I thought you couldn't be admitted to the bar if you had a felony conviction.

Bob: Well, it depends on the nature of the felony. The legal phrase is, "If you've been convicted of a crime of moral turpitude." I usually say "moral turpentine." (For example, there's a fellow here who was involved in blowing up a building back at the University of Wisconsin, where I think someone died—unintentionally. He asked to be admitted to the bar and was found "not of good character.") For what I did, it's a nonissue. When you apply to take the bar exam here, you have to fill out this very long questionnaire. List all your addresses. "Did you ever bounce a check?" All these things. So I even listed my jaywalking tickets! See, I'd been living downtown in Portland in the early seventies, and the police at that time were giving jaywalking tickets to folks with long hair. Like me. That's the only question the board of bar examiners had for me—my jaywalking tickets.

Ro: Oh, those long-haired hippies! Can we go back now to those early days?

Bob: Sure. I came out here in 1966 to start college at Reed. Grew up in Chicago, in Roseland on the South Side. So segregated Chicago was then! The first demonstrations I went to were Dr. Martin Luther King Jr.'s open housing marches in Chicago.

Ro: Were your folks involved in that?

Bob: No. Not at all. But certainly ideas about fairness came from them, as well as from my religion, being Jewish. But anyway, I came out here for college. I was opposed to the Vietnam War by that point, but I wasn't involved, and I had a student deferment.

> [Bob heard about a nationwide protest where people would turn in their draft cards and would then be declared 1-A delinquent. After thinking about the consequences over the summer, he decided to join the protest.]

Bob: I believe it was on October 7, 1967, when about five of us went down to the induction center, turned in our draft cards, and went home. They wouldn't open the doors to accept them, so we just left them on the sidewalk. Had a little bit of coverage in the local paper, but it was all pretty quiet. Sometime later I got a notice from my draft board that they were classifying me 1A delinquent. By that time, I'd gotten somewhat more involved with the resistance, as it was called. You know, I probably called myself a resister back then, but I say "draft dodger" now because I don't want to be pretentious. It drives my wife crazy!

I learned what the average sentence was, here in Portland, and what the average sentence was in Chicago, where my draft board was located, and that I could transfer my induction out here because I was living here. (Later, the Selective Service [cracked down] about transferring. Everybody had been transferring to Oakland, for instance, because the doctors who performed the physical examinations there were refusing [to certify] people as physically fit to serve.) But my parents . . . if I was going to do this stupid thing, they wanted me to do it in Chicago.

Ro: Would your parents have really wanted you to go to Vietnam?

Bob: No. "Go to college. That's what's important." But this was at the height of the generational divide about the war, and some of the information that was being put out . . . Well, in the spring of '68, I flew back to Chicago. It was the very weekend Martin Luther King was assassinated. The west side of the city was in flames. Mayor Dick Daley had given the "shoot to kill" order to the police.

My parents had arranged for me to have a private, off-the-record meeting with a judge—Abraham Lincoln Marovitz—in his chambers. (I've always thought part of the purpose of this meeting was to talk me out of refusing induction. Abraham Lincoln Marovitz was well known as being a tough but liberal judge. He was also famous because [in] World War II, at the age of thirty-nine—way past the age of being inducted into the Armed Forces—he *enlisted* in the Marines.)

I'm just *so* scared. All these big desks and . . . but at least he wasn't wearing his robes. Anyway, he unbuttons his shirt and brings out his mezuzah. (The mezuzah is the thing that some Jews wear around their neck. It has the Ten Commandments rolled up inside.)

The judge says, "Do you know what this is?"

I go, "Yeeeeeeesssssss" [*in a stuttering voice, humorously mimicking nervousness*].

"Do you know the fifth commandment?"

"Yeeeeeeesssssss."

"Are you honoring your mother and father?" Well, I couldn't answer that.

So after scaring the . . . the everything out of me, he says, "Well, if you were to come before me—and I'm one of the most liberal judges—I'd give you the full five-year sentence." End of meeting. Now, in Portland, the judges were only sentencing to eighteen months. Eighteen months versus five years? My parents got it. "If you're going to refuse induction, refuse in Portland." So I did, in May of 1968.

I got to the induction center and they bring me into the back of this big room, all by myself. They read a statement to you and you step forward, and that means you're in the military. This guy in the front reads me the thing, doesn't even look up, and says, "I see you have not stepped forward," reads it again, and they take me out.

To this day, sometimes I think, "Should I have stepped forward?" I could've tried to talk antiwar stuff from inside [the army]. And certainly after I got out of prison, the Vietnam Veterans Against the War were very active. But in any case, I did what I did because that's what I could do.

They actually had me write up why I wasn't serving. I never was a pacifist. (Sometimes I say jokingly, "I don't think you can grow up on the South Side of Chicago and be a pacifist.") I was certainly opposed to that war, so I put down stuff about that, and I probably mentioned something about race. Then I said goodbye and finished out the year at Reed.

I spent part of the summer in Chicago—this was 1968, now—and I went to some of the demonstrations, but I made certain that I wasn't arrested, because I didn't think that'd be real good. Sometime during [that time], I got a notice of my arrest and trial.

My folks came out for the trial. A group of lawyers had agreed to represent draft dodgers. The one I got was very paternalistic and didn't prepare me at all. The judge was Gus J. Solomon. Very liberal, had a tough time getting on the bench. He also had gone to Reed College, and I was the first Reedie he'd had on the draft stuff, and I think the first Jew. All of which don't mean anything.

I cleaned up and cut my hair and wore a suit 'cause I was a good middle-class kid. (I'm willing to stick a knife in myself, but I'm not going to twist it.) Actually, the assistant US attorney made some comments about us cleaning up. "But look at the pictures in the file, Judge. You'll see what they're *really* like!"

Judge Solomon said something like, "There were guys at Reed who wore togas for four years, and they were fine. So move on to other stuff." Then the trial is set to start, and my lawyer gives me this form and says, "Gus gave me the signal; he doesn't want a jury trial. Sign here."

"Huh?" Well, I signed the form, because I didn't know what else to do. Then it's my turn and I want to say my bit. Again, it's "Gus gave me the signal. He doesn't want any witnesses." I didn't get to say a word! *Nobody* said a word! Trial over, we all go home. I would've had more time to say something with a traffic ticket! They called me up for induction, I refused, I'm going to jail. Oh, my naiveté! And my total lack of any understanding of the legal system.

That was in November of 1968, and the judge didn't find me guilty until the next July. So I could have gone to school, but my head was nowhere close to it. My life was totally on hold, even though I stayed involved with draft resistance stuff.

I reported for sentencing in September, and *finally* had a chance to talk. I talked about Nuremberg and choice and . . . [Judge Solomon] came back with the federal marshals during desegregation in the South and I said, "Yeah, but I'm much more like the Alabama state troopers." You know, I'm the one who's disobeying the law.

Afterwards, once I became a lawyer, I knew what I should have said: "I broke the law. Find me guilty, sentence me to probation, and let me go out there and do draft resistance stuff." But I didn't say it, and I was sentenced to eighteen months in prison.

Told to report to the US marshal's office in Portland on a certain day. (Later on, they started making people self-report at the prison because it saves them money.)

Anyway, I have this big goodbye party and then go to the marshal's office. "Go home. The marshals aren't here to transport you."

I come back the next day and this time there are these two marshals to transport three of us, well trussed up and hitched together. Takes us three days to get to LA and they never do tell us where we were going. I'm booked into what was considered the highest security place of the Los Angeles County Jail system, and I am just scared beyond belief. Luckily, prisons back in 1969 were not the prisons now.

The bed in the cell's just a mattress on a steel frame. Steel sink and toilet and the lights were never totally out. We spent about twenty-three hours a day in there, with no clue of time passing. When they'd take me out for a meal, I wouldn't know if it was breakfast or lunch until I saw the food. I was there for a couple of weeks, and it was somewhat intense. You know, no contact with anyone. Then I'm on the road again and they drop me off in Sanford, Arizona.

I see a three-foot wall in front and some one-story buildings, and nothing, nothing, in the back but desert. A prisoner tells me, "Do whatever you want, just don't go too far." This is after being in total confinement. Disconcerting, that's for sure.

There were about three hundred people there, and half of them were Mexicans. For border crossing. There were maybe about a hundred draft dodgers, but they broke up into very different camps: the Jehovah's Witnesses, who kept totally to themselves, and then at least three groups, although there was interaction between those groups. Of course we all had to label ourselves. There were "the hippies" who did a lot of drugs and weren't very political, but somehow didn't think it was right to fight a war. Then there were a bunch of activists from California— David Harris, with all that very strong nonviolent direct action. Then there was us—political, but not into their kind of activism.

You know, when I talk about this stuff now, I do it in a humorous way, because some of it *was* really funny, but it was a prison, and I think most of us were trying to make the best of a bad situation. There was always an intense loneliness. Coming from the sixties, we had all the hugging and touching, and that was a no-no in prison, so that was part of the isolation.

People had different work assignments. We were building a road up in the national forest, with supervised drilling and dynamite. The prisoners were laying the cord—the stuff that explodes—and of course they'd put as much down as they could, to make the explosion bigger, you know? The story was that before one of the explosions the road was 17 percent complete and afterwards, it was 15 percent complete. My whole job was just to set out stuff for lunch and then clean up afterwards. Lots of make-work.

I was able to get some newspapers sent in, but the underground papers would have a lot cut out. I tried to subscribe to the *Guardian* out of New York City and they said, "Oh, no. Maybe *The Guardian* from England, but not that."

There wasn't much TV and certainly no radios, so it was hard to figure out what was happening with the war, but we watched them draw the first lottery numbers on TV. Now, all of us had chosen to be there, but you'd hear, "Oh, man, I could have had three hundred!"

Also, we knew the moratorium was going on. On the first day of the moratorium, a bunch of guys refused to work. Nothing happened to them. At the next moratorium, the prison officials decided to let us skip work and watch the World Series. They had a bunch of different activities, like trying to grab a greased watermelon—you know, all this stuff to let us run around.

Ro: They gave you a party so you wouldn't resist.

Bob: Right. Then they didn't have to ship people out for not working. I made some good friendships at Sanford. There was definitely loneliness and isolation, but . . . You hear people talk about when they felt they became an adult. For me—to the extent I am an adult—it was probably that experience.

At the time, I thought that all this stuff was going to come together and overthrow the government. I thought that if enough of us went to jail, we'd gum up the works, and people would see that as the first step [toward] the end of the government. Nonviolence made the most sense, tactically. You'd gum up things and then other people would say, "Wow! They're not shooting at us, they're not killing us, and we can change things." In retrospect, I don't think we've had the revolution. [*Chuckles ironically*.]

But I was part of a movement that eventually led towards ending the war in Vietnam. My perspective is that people did what they could, at all different places in their lives. Not everybody could go to jail. When mass movements are good, you don't have to have people marching in lockstep.

Ro: What about when you were released?

Bob: Well, I remember one incident in particular. We had three sets of clothes in prison, all khaki and all the same. They also gave us army boots with a deep cut on the heel and a little circle. (That was for tracking us in the desert if we walked away.)

Anyway, after I get out, I walk into this store to get some clothes. The guy takes me over to a whole wall of folded pants. "These are all your size and they're all different." Well, I just broke into a cold sweat. Had to leave 'cause it was just too much of a decision. This reaction scared me tremendously. I'd heard about folks becoming institutionalized, but hey, that wouldn't be me! And I was!

When I got back to Portland, I was going to take it easy. I'd done my time, so I could just play around. Drove a cab and washed windows and stuff like that. But I wound up getting into some antiwar activities after all, and then stuff with an ex-prisoner group. At that point, I was thinking we shouldn't have any prisons, that they were counterproductive and they didn't do . . . But I was also aware that there was a bond with people who'd been inside that I didn't share with others. After a while, though, I stopped being involved with them, partly because I was afraid that I'd make some really stupid decisions, you know, get too much into their life.

This led into what I do now. Getting out of prison made me think about law. Because the short story is I got out early. My lawyer had appealed, and while I was in prison the US Supreme Court decided a case of a ministerial student who had been called up out of the normal order, like me, because we'd turned in our draft cards. You see, pre-lottery, they were calling up people based on age, oldest ones first. I was nineteen or twenty at the time, and both I and the divinity student got brought to the head of the line. The Supreme Court said we were denied due process and I got out in less than five months.

Ro: Wouldn't that have affected a lot of others who had refused induction?

Bob: Well, that's one of the horrible parts of law. The way the law works, if your attorney didn't have an appeal in, you didn't get out. That made me see the power of law. I became a legal assistant with Legal Aid, working on prison conditions lawsuits and taking classes at the local community college. Then I went to work with the National Lawyers Guild [NLG] in Portland.[14]

One day I decided that what the world really needed was another white male Jewish lawyer. So I got a degree in general studies at Portland in 1979. A perfect degree for a lawyer. I had a fair amount of money saved up, so I traveled around the US for a year while I applied to law schools. Worked for a while at the National Lawyers Guild office in New York and also worked with them in law school and afterwards.

> [Bob graduated from law school in 1982, and as a lawyer, he did workers' compensation law and served on the board of Legal Aid, with what became the United Farm Workers union and with an AFL-CIO group helping displaced workers. He became a judge on the Washington State Court of Appeals in 1998.]

Bob: What I find probably the most difficult thing in being a judge is . . . When I was a lawyer, I took an oath to follow the law, but I never thought much about it, because I had to zealously represent my clients. As a judge, I think of that all the time, because now my only obligation is to follow the law—follow what those words say, follow that precedent, not what I think is the best social policy. I try to be very faithful to that oath of office, but I dissent when I think dissent is appropriate, if I don't think something is right. I think that's why I'm one of ten [judges on the appellate court] and that's part of what I'm paid for. But there may come a day when the law

The Honorable Robert Wollheim, 2011. (Photo courtesy of Andy de Gues.)

requires me to do something I don't feel I can agree with. I would just hope that I would resign rather than do that. Now, it hasn't happened yet and maybe that's just because I'm in my mid-fifties and old and a sellout. The whole thing for me is going with my gut and being able to look myself in the face in the morning. If I can do that, that's enough.

———————

The numbers of draft resisters and draft card burners grew. Then some of those in what came to be called the "Catholic Left" or the "Ultra Resistance" moved to actual draft file destruction.[15] These actions and the resulting trials received wide publicity in an increasingly frenetic decade, but some segments of the nonviolent peace movement saw them as divisive and eroding of mass support. Patriotic Catholics were horrified that priests would be so against the war as to break the law. Others worried that such actions were violent. The "actors," as they called themselves, pointed out that it was the draft files themselves that were violent. Others objected that the necessary secrecy violated the Gandhian goal of alerting one's adversary. The larger peace movement, becoming increasingly more radical, more violent, and more fragmented, didn't understand a Christian theology of redemptive suffering and thought the draft file destroyers were simply crazy to stand around waiting for arrest. The actors in these draft board raids believed otherwise; they saw going to jail as redemptive for a nation gone mad.

The first draft file defilement, rarely mentioned then or now, was a lonely one in 1966 by Barry Bondhus of Minnesota. Son of a machinist passionately against the war, Barry dumped two buckets of human feces on draft board records, calmly waited for arrest, and served eighteen months in Sandstone Prison.[16] On October 27, 1967, Father Phil Berrigan, John Hogan, George Mische, and

Tom Lewis burned draft files in Baltimore, followed a short time later by a larger group who poured blood on Catonsville files.[17]

Tom Lewis was in both actions. A strong and gentle soul with an activist's heart and an artist's eye, Tom didn't stop resisting after the Vietnam War finally ended, but continued his nonviolent activism. He told me he'd spent about three years in prison during his forty-five years of resistance. This segment combines three interviews we had over the years, the last one in June 2005, three years before he died.[18]

Tom Lewis

> *"As we picked the files out of the cabinet and dropped them on the floor with the blood dripping, it showed very much what those files are about."*

I was a young artist, quite successful, winning some prizes. Then the war and Phil Berrigan intervened. I met Phil at one of the meetings of the [Baltimore Interfaith Peace Mission]. We went to a little beer hall [afterward] and drank a beer and ate some pretzels. I was quite touched by that, that a priest would be so open and interesting and involved. I became connected to his parish in Baltimore, a black parish, and Phil and I became increasingly active in antiwar work, organizing a group in Baltimore called "Clergy and Laity Against the War."

Ro: As I remember, it was "Clergy and Laymen" when it was started.

Tom: Well, yeah. The young resisters were saying no to Vietnam by burning their draft cards or refusing induction and were being sent to prison. So how to connect with these young men? We tried burning our own draft cards, but the FBI didn't care 'cause we'd already been in the army and were too old to go, anyway. Then we said, "If they're destroying their draft cards, then it makes sense for us to destroy draft *files.*" So Phil and I put together the first draft board witness—the Baltimore Four. Besides the two of us, there was Jim Mengel, a United Church of Christ minister, and a young poet named David Eberhardt.

Ro: Did you confront the question of violence when you did your planning?

Tom: Oh, very much so. We both had a history of nonviolence through the civil rights movement, but we realized that destroying a draft record would be a little different, certainly, than sitting in at a lunch counter. We struggled with it and explored what that would mean, in the sense of responsibility during the action, and . . . and knowing that perhaps others would follow us.

Also, we realized there's a fundamental difference between violence to property and violence to people, and the two can't be associated as one.

Ro: Well, some people do.

Tom: I think this shows how people worship *things* in our culture. I recall a very interesting letter from Thomas Merton where he raised questions about destruction of property, especially the destruction of buildings that the young political radicals were talking about. How you would be responsible for anybody in the building. He made it very clear that he was not ruling out destruction of property as such, and of course we ruled out any kind of property destruction that might harm a person. We were quite clear about taking responsibility for everybody's safety. Not like the red groups. We very clearly said no to "Burn, baby, burn!" So, in a way, both Catonsville and Baltimore set the limits for destruction of property in [subsequent nonviolent actions].

But how would we safely destroy the draft files? Phil came up with the symbol of blood. I personally liked the idea of fire as a symbol, but . . . one thing about these actions over the years, especially ones where there's a lot of risk involved, is that a community develops, and we learn to listen and adjust, so the action combines everyone's vision. As a community, we struggled with symbols, and I adjusted and felt good about choosing blood for that first action.

As we picked the files out of cabinet and dropped them on the floor with the blood dripping, it showed very much what those files are about. They weren't about justice. They were sending draftees to Vietnam to face a bloody death.

Ro: Weren't you just absolutely scared to death?

Tom: Well, you know, it's interesting. Fear is a healthy thing. When you proceed with a witness like this, my experience is that fear is replaced by a kind of . . . I would say it's a spirit of hope. And as a Catholic, I think that has something to do with divine help or intervention.

We essentially did as much planning as we could. We contacted several press people ahead of time, people we could trust. Didn't tell them exactly what we were doing 'cause we were careful not to exploit them for a potential conspiracy indictment. A support person gave them a packet of information which they were to open only after we went into the building.

The main draft office was across the street from my art studio, which made it convenient. I was to go upstairs first to check that there was no [armed] security guard. We didn't want anyone . . . we didn't want any kind of overreaction. If there was a guard, I was to come back down and wave my handkerchief, and the action was off. Otherwise I was just to walk down the steps and stand there. There wasn't a guard, so that's what I did. But a truck was blocking the way and the others couldn't see me, so I went back up and did it all again.

So then the other three came across the street. We knew where the 1-A files were because we had checked ahead of time, so we went right to the files and poured our blood, destroying six hundred records. We didn't try to leave.

We prepared the best we could as human beings and then basically left it in the Lord's hands. There's some kind of inner strength—I think it's spiritual—that you get in these kinds of actions. It's a combination of doing the best preparation you can and then really being willing to give that up and put it in the Lord's hands.

Ro: A skeptic might call that adrenalin.

Tom: Well, to me it feels spiritual. Of course we were found guilty and had a sentencing date in May, a couple of months away. We were facing, I think, about twenty years with all the charges that we'd been found guilty on.[19] Then a short time before our sentencing date, Phil suggested that we do another draft board action. So we proceeded to search for other people.

Ro: Wasn't there a time when it didn't look like there were going to be very many others? A lot of people who thought about it and said no, that it wasn't for them?

Tom: Yes. That's correct. But people emerged. Dan Berrigan, of course. I remember Dan one morning up at Cornell. He came over with two cups of coffee, handed one to me, and said, "Well, I'm in." I knew then that it would happen. I found out later that Dan and Phil had sat up all night talking about it. That led to the Melvilles, the two missionaries from Guatemala, and John Hogan and David Darst, who were Christian Brothers. Mary Moylan and George Mische. It involved some real discerning with people because of the risk. By the time the nine of us came together, it was just a week before the action.

We met at my mother's house [the day of the action], and I made the phone call to the press from there, so they knew we were leaving and didn't open the envelope we gave them until the set time. That also saved them from the indictment the FBI tried to bring. They were there within minutes of the witness . . . of our going into the Catonsville draft office and taking the files out in big wire trash containers and burning them on the parking lot. We picked Catonsville partly because we were able to take the records outside and have an open and safe place to burn them.

Dan Berrigan says it very well about the fire.

> Our apologies   good friends
> for the fracture of good order   the burning of paper
> instead of children   the angering of the orderlies

The Catonsville Nine at the police station, minutes after the action, 1968. From left to right, standing: George Mische, Philip Berrigan, Daniel Berrigan, Tom Lewis; seated: David Darst, Mary Moylan, John Hogan, Marjorie Melville, Tom Melville. (Photo courtesy of Jean Walsh/Baltimore County Library.)

> in the front parlor of the charnel house
> We could not   so help us God   do otherwise
> For we are sick at heart   our hearts
> give us no rest for thinking of the Land of Burning Children
> and for thinking of that other Child of whom
> the poet Luke speaks[20]

We used homemade napalm. Father Dick McSorley found it for us at the George-town Law Library, in the *Special Forces Handbook*, which told the soldiers how to make their own napalm in case they ran out of the professional stuff.[21] I think that just shows the sickness of the military.

Five of us went into the offices; the rest were lookouts. I read a statement about why we were there, and the clerks just ignored us, so we started unloading the 1-A files into the containers. (I think over three hundred records.) Then they got upset. One woman put her hand out to try to stop us, and her hand got scratched. That was resolved later, and she actually supported us twenty-five years later at a remembrance of Catonsville. We sent her flowers from jail.

Phil and I were to be sentenced on Friday from the Baltimore Four witness and we did Catonsville on Tuesday. Needless to say, [the Baltimore police and the FBI] were quite upset, especially with Phil and me. We were both held without bail because we [had violated probation. At the trial] they'd bring us back and forth from jail to court in handcuffs.

And that's where I met Dorothy for the first time—Dorothy Day. We were sitting up in front and someone tapped me on the shoulder. "Look around! Dorothy is here to see you." And there was this beautiful face, almost like it was surrounded by sunshine. . . . [The] white hair and great smiling face of Dorothy in the courtroom.

Ro: Tom, I think there are different perceptions on how Dorothy felt about Catonsville. Did you ever talk to her about that, particularly about the fire aspect?

Tom: No, I've never personally spoken to Dorothy. She came to support us, and she writes about Catonsville as being a liturgy and a very proven way. And certainly getting that sense from [how she supported] the draft resisters who were in jail and also those in prison for destroying their draft cards. So my understanding and my experience is certainly one of Dorothy's approval.

Ro: What about the press?

Tom: Well, it's a mistake to do it for the press, but we got an awful lot of press for Catonsville. Once again, the root of the action is its moral correctness. Many in the general peace movement did not support Catonsville. Some asked why we didn't burn the building and some asked why we stayed to get arrested. They couldn't understand the idea of a spiritual witness and its continuance in prison. This kind of action doesn't really have a political rationale. It *does* have a spiritual rationale. The political rationale calls for publicity. Ours was the doing itself, the rightness of our action.

Phil and I were initially sent to jail for six years, with the three and a half years for the Baltimore action running concurrently. But for about nine months after the Catonsville trial, both of us were out on appeal. That was a remarkable time because we'd been in jail for close to a year already. I'd been sent to the big pig farm in Lewisburg. Phil had been sent to the Wall, the main complex at Lewisburg, which is more high security. It's literally a wall. [*Here Tom showed me an ominous painting he did of that prison.*]

Ro: Did you really farm pigs?

Tom: Yes. They were training prisoners to be farmers, and they liked to put the resisters out there, scraping all the pig stuff away, washing the place down with hoses. One day we decided to run a pig for president. We put a sign up in his pen and would bring him extra cookies from lunch. A couple days later, the prison hack came around and ripped the sign off. No sense of humor at all.

Tom Lewis, 2005.
(Photo courtesy of Rosalie Riegle.)

I also did my woodcuts, in the little prison arts and crafts room. Other resisters were there—draft resisters and people burning draft cards and then other draft file burnings. You'd connect with them and form a little community. You'd share books. You'd share stories and organize prayer meetings—Bible study, certainly—and just some good, healthy talk.

Ro: Did you ever do any prison protest?

Tom: That's a very serious matter, and I really respected people who did that in prison because the authorities took it very seriously. There was a wonderful series of protests in Danbury where Dan and Phil Berrigan were for a while together. Flags turned upside down and things like that.

Ro: Now, you're the only person I've talked to who was involved in property destruction during the Vietnam War and is still doing it, with the Transfiguration East Plowshares.[22] What differences do you see?

Tom: Well, in my experience, there's far more discernment and preparation in the Plowshares than with the draft board witnesses in the sixties. Maybe that's why there's not so much personal trauma anymore. In fact, the building of community really becomes more important than the action, so that may be what we're learning, actually. And that may be helpful in the future. 'Cause you certainly do live on the edge when you're preparing for a Plowshares—live on the edge spiritually, psychologically, and physically.

Ro: Are the trials different now?

Tom: Trials are always new and different. I average about one a year, and I've experienced judges telling us to continue the good work and judges throwing us in jail for trying to quote the bishops on civil disobedience. But the fear never wears off. I personally believe in preparing what you're going to say, and then trusting the Spirit. For instance, I had written about three different sentencing statements for our Transfiguration East Plowshares and ended up referring to none of them and just speaking from the heart. Very much caring about the judge, who was a black woman. I said that someday we'd all be joining hands and protesting these weapons together—all of us, including the judge and the prosecutor—but that I knew from experience in the civil rights movement that in order for this to happen, some of us had to go to jail.

The judge didn't have anything to gain politically by going against the government's recommendation, but she did, and I respect her for that. We got six months probation and community service, one of the lowest Plowshares sentences ever, and she . . . it was really an act of courage on her part.

Many Catholic Workers pretty much distanced themselves from the draft file burnings. Two exceptions were Willa Bickham and her husband, Brendan Walsh, founders of Baltimore's Viva House Catholic Worker in 1968.

Willa Bickham

Our first houseguests were the Catonsville Nine folks. . . . And we had lots and lots of visitors when the trial started. The theme for the support work during the trial was "Come to Agnew country!" It was the biggest antiwar demonstration ever held in Baltimore. People came from all over, and it was a real focus of attention for the antiwar movement.

Dorothy Day came down for the trial and stayed at the house a couple of nights. Then she took us aside and asked Brendan and me if our feelings would be hurt if she stayed at the local convent 'cause it was too noisy at the house. So many people! I mean, we packed them in every room. I remember her coming over and doing dishes, though.

Even after the trial, the house was filled with folks who were working very hard against the war. We had no trouble at that time getting money or volunteers. There was a lot of enthusiasm and we even named our newsletter *Enthusiasm*. Anything people could do to end the war in Vietnam, they were willing to do. And they knew that we were involved in the works of mercy as well as resisting the works of war. We did a soup kitchen for, oh, about a hundred, a hundred fifty people a day every day.

When Tom Lewis got out of prison, he came back to live with us. In one of the front rooms, we have some huge etchings that he's done: four panels that portray the entire Catonsville Nine and Baltimore Four time. Yes, Tom was a very great influence on our lives.

Just before they were to report to prison, five of the draft file burners went underground—David Eberhardt from the first action, and George Mische, Mary Moylan, and the two Berrigan priests from the Catonsville action. David and Father Phil were picked up in ten days, and Mische the following month, but the FBI apparently didn't think it worthwhile to look for Mary Moylan. She lived underground until 1978, using an assumed name, dyeing her beautiful red hair, and moving frequently. When she finally turned herself in, she served a three-year prison term, one year longer than her original sentence.[23] Dan Berrigan eluded the FBI for months, occasionally surfacing theatrically and then sneaking away again. He was finally captured on Block Island by FBI agents masquerading as bird-watchers. Some of the public had difficulty reconciling renegade anti-war priests with the generally unblinking patriotism of the Catholic Church as a whole, but draft board raids spread across the land.

The next of the two dozen or so draft board raids was the Milwaukee Fourteen on September 16, 1948.[24] After a few weeks of planning, fourteen men burned one hundred thousand draft files, hauled out from draft board offices to a nearby square in large burlap bags. Lay and religious, single and married, they all had different duties. Some entered the building shortly after closing time and took the keys from the cleaning women; some bundled the draft files into the bags and hauled them out of the building; some were lookouts as others poured homemade napalm and lit the fire. Then they stood together in prayer and waited for the police to arrive.

Michael Cullen was one of the family men in the group. A native of Ireland, Michael had come to the States to study for the priesthood, but left the seminary and married Annette Rhody, a Wisconsin nurse. Together they started the Casa Maria Catholic Worker house of hospitality in Milwaukee and became active in antiwar efforts, which culminated in the Milwaukee Fourteen draft file burning. After serving a hard prison sentence, Michael and his family were deported to Ireland. I was able to interview them there in 1987 and again in Wisconsin in 2005 after they were finally allowed to return to the States. This segment includes material from both interviews.

Michael Cullen

"I've carried the wounds of it and others have, too."

The Irish scene was different than the Vietnam War time in the States. It was hard to know how one confronts the violence in your own culture—a violence resulting, I know, from the violence done to us. In Ireland it was done in secret—in masks, you know. There was no place to demonstrate, no focus. So you realize it's very much within us all and can only be healed by being reconciled in our faith history, and that's what we tried to do at Camp Jesus, and in the walks to Belfast, and in other ways.[25]

Our approach to the Vietnam War tended to be more political than religious. It had a religious base, but not enough, so by 1973 when I was deported, I was exhausted spiritually. I hadn't the resources to confront my deportation trial, and I caved in and went back to Ireland. We were many victims in that war. [*Pause.*] But it is behind me now. I've carried the wounds of it and others have, too. I wouldn't . . . although I still say yes—yes to nonviolent action, yes to conscience.

The Vietnam times . . . We started with a fast, at the cathedral. It catapulted me into a position I was unprepared for. Unprepared in the sense of how wide the screen was, you know. I thought it was just a simple thing, and I was amazed that people paid so much attention.

Casa Maria became a kind of focus where people would gather. I guess people saw me as the leader. It was accidental leadership, I think, but once I understood intellectually the truth of Christian nonviolence and the truth of resistance, it took my whole passion. Christian nonviolence has my passion still but now I'm living it out another way, in ministry as a deacon.

In the second century, they said if you're a Christian in the military you cannot kill, and Dorothy [Day] and the CW brought us back to that, helped the Catholic Church restore its loss of memory about Christian nonviolence. Today you still have people going to war and thinking they're killing in the name of Christ. If a Roman Catholic Council adopted the position of the early church, we'd be a billion people and it would change the world!

But you can't act without suffering. Obviously, when people are in power, they want to stay there. When someone's making millions of dollars off of weapons of death, they don't want to hear you speak that truth.

Ro: Now, you were one of those who actually took the files out and threw then on the fire. How did it feel then when you realized you had actually done it?

Michael: I'm not sure if I can get into what my feelings were then. It . . . it was really weighty . . . and it was very prayerful, actually, waiting for arrest, because it was a witness, a stand-around action. For me, that's where it takes on its real meaning. But it brought suffering from then on. If I had known the price you have to pay in isolation, confusion, difficulties with the family . . . The big bail, the defense fund, the long waiting, the extended period of separation . . . Mine was the only federal trial. And then lawyers coming into play and all the media and all the big heavies.

It was still the civil rights days. Today we're starving for hope, but then we were the children of hope. But certainly not looking for the purification and the purging and the fire we had to endure. In prison, and being separated, and realizing that I had brought this on them. I think it's miraculous that we weren't destroyed as a family. That's all I can say. Nothing had prepared us for this.

Milwaukee Fourteen draft file burning, 1968.
(Gary Ballsieper/Marquette University Archives.)

But for me in prison, there was the companionship of other resisters and conscientious objectors. It was certainly good times in jail with some of those brothers, if you will. There was comfort in that, and once Annette got settled on the farm with her parents, that was a comfort, too.

Ro: Michael, I have to ask this. Do you regret having done the Milwaukee Fourteen action?

Michael: Well, everybody . . . maybe people think I do because I didn't want to do another one. If I had regrets for anything about the action, it was this: Violence could have happened. Something could have gone wrong. The risk of that happening—that's where I have the problem. And the sense of . . . the heat of the excitement getting into it. Also the secrecy. Now, it took my history to be able to speak this way. I'm more reflective now, these years later.

Dorothy helped me see that, too. Afterwards, I shared a lot with her, and she shared a lot in a private way. She told me, "The suffering redeems the action." It's behind me now. I've carried the wounds and others have, too. I wouldn't advocate it for anybody again. Now, tax resistance—that's really nonviolence to my mind. Yes.

Ro: Which was worse, the prison or the deportation?

Michael: I think the prison was big, but the deportation was humiliation. I was just blessed to be in a country that was welcoming, to be in Ireland. It was fruitful for us, but we knew we were in exile. That was evident in Annette and in the children, but I, too, was an exile. I didn't realize how much this country—the United States—was part of me. I think the miracle is that we're here again.

Ro: Everybody got prison terms, but you got prison terms plus deportation.

Michael: Yeah, plus the eighteen years of exile. Eighteen years of exile. We'd come back to the US embassy every five years, because in some way, we were being called back to the States. And always refused. Then the miracle, and that's the incredible piece. I'm a citizen now, too, you know. I'm proud to be a part of the American story.

I think I've come a long way. A key for me was forgiving, forgiving, forgiving when interior wounds would come up. Forgiving prisoners, forgiving prison staff. Forgiving is part of the healing, too. If we live in regret, then we haven't gone anywhere. But, yeah, the suffering was real. The state is very powerful in its way of imposing serious suffering on people. I think those who resisted the Vietnam War experienced the totality of it.

We need diplomacy and new thinking about how we can make peace. As for going to prison, people can go for right reasons and wrong reasons. And the right reason: if the occasion calls you and that's the only choice you have, pray you have the courage to do it.

Therese Cullen, one of Michael's daughters, told me: "People are still intrigued about the action, but often it's all to do with Dad, and then you realize that they're more interested in the ego part than in the spirituality. Now, certainly Dad has his ego. He wasn't somebody who sits up on a pedestal, even though people looked up to him. But our family always makes sure no one gets too high and mighty. I suppose that made mentors real to me, because you understand what it's like for people to be just normal, to make mistakes, and to sometimes do stupid things. But to also be provocative."[26]

———————————

Annette (Nettie) Cullen

> *"You have to trust when you say yes to any marriage because you*
> *don't know the whole of it. You give yourself fully to this person,*
> *but who knows what the future's to be?"*

The night Michael asked me to marry him, he was talking again about his dreams, talking about doing missionary work in China. And here I'd been thinking I'd be a nurse and then marry a Wisconsin farmer. So when I said yes to him, it *was* a big yes, a yes to the challenge, a yes to the whole thing.

Ro: But when you said that big yes, did you think he'd be going to prison?

Nettie: Well, no. [*Laughs.*] We had a normal married life in the beginning. Lived in the suburbs. I worked as a nurse and he was an insurance salesman. We'd have these weekly discussions in our little apartment about articles in the Catholic Worker paper. We'd talk about it and talk about it. And finally it was, "All right! Let's stop talking and do it!"

So we opened a Catholic Worker house of hospitality. Will, our first child, was just a new baby. The night we moved into the rectory of Our Lady of Guadalupe, our first guest arrived. From Colombia, South America, and she had not a word of English. That was September 24th of 1966. Our house very quickly got very full. Single men in the basement, families in the first and second floors. Later we got evicted 'cause of too many people but we found another house on 21st, where Casa Maria is now today: Casa Maria—House of Mary.

The Vietnam War was foremost. Michael was not an American citizen, but he was given a draft card, too. As the war went on, he felt he needed to do something, but he always checked with the bishop before he did anything big. He felt loyalty to the church.

Ro: Did he tell the bishop about the Milwaukee Fourteen action?

Nettie: Um . . . I'm not sure. I'm not sure he told him exactly what he was going to do. I don't think anybody really knew. He started with a Lenten rice fast in the cathedral. Stayed there night and day for one week, praying and fasting for an end of the war. I'd bring him a bowl of rice once a day.

I was expecting our third child in 1968, when the big action took place. Michael had wanted to be part of the Catonsville action, to have a louder voice, if you will. But because I was pregnant with Brigid, our third child, he said he'd respect it if I said no. I didn't say no, but I said "Wait." So after she was two weeks old, we went on the retreat for the Milwaukee Fourteen, and I said I would give him my yes. Of course, I was thinking he was a hero, you know? And if we hadn't had three children, I probably would have done the action, too. I remember when it happened. September 24th, 1968. The phone call—"The hot dogs are burning."

But then, the reality hit. He's in prison and I have this month-old baby and two other wee ones and I'm taking them all down on the bus to visit him in prison. "How am I going to be able to do this?" We still had the support of people around us, of course, and they'd help with the children, too, at times. My own family, they were totally against it, and, you know . . . Michael's family wasn't supportive, either, and basically didn't know about it over in Ireland.

Ro: So how *did* you cope? Did you close the house of hospitality?

Nettie: No, we didn't. We had the support of the community living [nearby]. I kept on with the cooking, and we had young people from Marquette [University] coming up to help out, too.

Then it looked like maybe ten years in prison. That's when I kind of broke down. But they got the bond reduced and he got out and after a while we had the trial and he was sentenced to prison up in Sandstone for ten months. Got out early on good behavior and we went to live with my parents on the farm.

But before the trial, he was giving a lot of interviews and going around the country and our marriage was starting to drift apart. It was. Basically, for frivolous reasons. I mean, I was very busy with the children; he was very busy giving talks. Same after prison. I was on the farm, and my parents would babysit, and he continued the very same, going around the country giving talks. Then when he heard that he was going to be deported, he . . . he went underground, or what he considered underground.

Ro: Dan Berrigan did that, too.

Nettie: But Dan Berrigan wasn't married! Michael didn't tell me *anything*! One day he didn't come home, and I had no idea where he was. He didn't come home and he didn't come home, and it was two weeks, and I was so devastated. I just totally felt rejected and abandoned. I couldn't eat and was just totally in shock, even though I continued to work.

Our marriage . . . It was just really ruptured. It's . . . it's still hard to talk about. Well, eventually, he called. He had gone out to Wounded Knee and had been taken in by the Native Americans, and had gotten pneumonia and had to have the last rites, as they called it then.[27]

When he eventually came back—it was a couple of weeks, at least—he had the bedroom down the hall, thank you very much. I was just hard.

Then he went to Notre Dame and had an experience that turned his life around, if you will. Now it's the charismatic movement, you know?[28] First we have the peace movement, then we have the civil rights movement, and then the Wounded Knee movement, and now all of a sudden it's the Charismatic Renewal.

So when he came home, I was thinking, "How long is *this* movement going to last?" So I was sittin' on the fence with this one, just waiting. But there was a difference. First of all, he was very interested in the kids again, and he wasn't going off all the time. He was also trying to include me. At first I wouldn't let myself be included. We went to some prayer meetings, and it just felt strange. He was going to be deported and I had already told him I wasn't going to go to Ireland with him.

But he was looking at me again. He saw me as a person again. Like before, it was come home, get clean clothes, and off he'd go again, you know? Sometimes not even a meal. My dad was always after him and I heard myself trying to change him, too. One day, Michael was so frustrated that he shaved off all his hair.

I looked at him with his bald head, and I said, "Oh my God, what am I doing to this poor man?" And the words that were coming to me were, "What right have you to change a person, to change his values?" I was trying to change him into

Mike and Nettie Cullen in Ireland, 2010.
(Photo courtesy of Therese Cullen.)

the kind of husband the good German wife is supposed to have. Molding him into what my parents would have liked.

Finally, I'm having a thought in the back of my head. "Forgive. Forgive seventy times seven." I started seeing myself, and what I saw wasn't all good. I'm blaming him, right, but I started looking inside my own life and started seeing my negativity, my hardness to his ways. I was going to stay here with the kids and not go off to Ireland. I had a job—night supervisor at a hospital. If we go off to Ireland, he'll be with Bernadette Devlin, you know?[29] Just another cause.

So all these thoughts are coming through my mind. But I saw myself and what my life would be like. I saw a cold and barren and lifeless dark road. If I said yes, it felt good. Hope and sunshine. But I'd try to justify not going: he's done this and this and this on me [*speaking softly, indicating her inner voice*]. Then "Forgive seventy times seven" would come into my head. I also had the sense of Our Lady next to me, and her "Yes" to be the Mother of God and all that it meant to her.

So finally it was, "Okay! I'll say yes to Michael, I'll say yes to being his wife again, I'll say yes to going to Ireland." Also, I knew it was going to be yes to God in a way that hadn't been in my life. Before, I had been kind of doing things on my own terms. Now it was a yes to the unknown.

I suppose even the first yes was into the unknown. You know, you have to trust when you say yes to any marriage because you don't know the whole of it. You give yourself fully to this person, but who knows what the future's to be? But you walk the walk and it's not an easy one, it's work. I wasn't a mild little creature who just said yes all the time, believe me. But once I said that yes, it was like . . . I just felt lighter and younger and joyful and . . . So the whole deportation became more of a joyful adventure than a punishment. When Dorothy Day carried the baby onto the airplane, it was a going forth.

I'd get homesick in Ireland, be fierce homesick at times. But just when it would get really intense, I'd have a dream that I was home with my mom and dad and sitting at the kitchen table, having a cup of coffee and a chat. I think that was really a grace that I was given, so I would be able to carry on again.

Not all the resistance marriages of the 1960s and early 1970s survived the times, however, especially given the challenges of imprisonment and of changing gender roles and identities. In contrast to the Cullens, who finally made their marriage work, here are three stories of dissolution.[30]

Tom Lewis, Chuck Quilty, and Marcia Timmel

Tom: I married between the Catonsville Nine trial and the time we were to go to jail. Married a beautiful woman who was actually working with the Catonsville Defense Committee. Quite simply, the marriage did not survive the three-year prison sentence. She started to understand herself as a lesbian woman during that time. We talked about it and suffered with it.

For me, personally, it was giving up the sense of power. Even though I was in jail, I certainly had a sense that I could demand that the marriage stay together. "How could you do this to me?" et cetera. I didn't insist, so for me it was really a beginning of learning to give up power as a male in our culture. So the marriage did not last [beyond] prison. We met once after I got out and haven't seen each other since.

Chuck: I was living a very unquestioning sort of existence in the '60s—just doing my job, you know, but getting socked by racism and then by the war in Vietnam. Martin Luther King did it for me—spoke some long truths, and if I hadn't read him, I may not have heard the message of Catonsville.

I didn't know anything about the Catholic Worker movement and certainly knew diddly about Gandhi, Tolstoy—any of the great writers on CD [civil disobedience] and nonviolence—but Baltimore and Catonsville got to me. Then Mike Cullen pushed me over the edge. He came down here [to Rock Island] and by the time he got done talking, tears were rolling down my cheeks.

My wife said later, "I took one look at you and knew it was all over. It was never going to be the same." Within five months, I had resigned at the [Rock Island] Arsenal and started Omega CW house. We had two kids and one on the way when I left the company, and there was no question my wife was going through a lot of turmoil when we started the house.

That's when the problems in our marriage began, for sure. Some of them maybe we worked through, but not ultimately, I guess. At the Worker house, we were wall-to-wall, up to a hundred people a night. My wife and my mom were doing all the cooking while I was running around, organizing peace demonstrations and helping people at the house get jobs, things like that.

I remember when Dorothy Day came to visit us. She chewed us up one side and down the other for being involved in resistance and hospitality and being married. I've always disagreed with her, and talked about this with a whole lot of people, including guys who've done heavy jail time. We all came up with the same answer: she was wrong, you know, but at the same time, she was calling a spade a spade.

Even though our breakup means I can't deny what she said, I think there's a deeper issue. Jim Douglass wrote an essay about it, "Marriage and Celibacy."[31] He wrote that most married folks are into what he calls a "bungalow marriage." Raising their kids and getting two cars in the garage and the nice little bungalow. And if somebody within one of those marriages starts taking the Gospel seriously, there's going to be a problem.

I don't want to reduce everything that happens in every marriage to that, even my own, but I think that's a large part of it. Let's face it. We all grow and mature at different rates. (I mean, even leaving radical politics out of it, people still change and grow in different ways.) That's always a source of conflict, and it's obviously even more intensive and seems more drastic when you're talking about divorcing yourself from the values that your culture's all about.

[My wife and I] ended up fighting to save the marriage, fighting for twenty-four years. Some times were real happy and others were full of conflict. It was when I was on trial or when I lost a job again that the conflict came up. You know, I don't want to reduce it to that—we had other problems, too, and probably never learned to communicate as well as we should have. I've seen a daughter die and my dad die, and I think divorce is probably the most painful thing I've ever dealt with. And yet I wouldn't change it.

I finally said, "We've gone through this before. It's time for me to let her go." I mean, that was the only loving thing to do, you know. It hurts, but . . . Jim Douglass also said that people who do the kind of nonviolent resistance that results in jail will go through long periods of celibacy within their marriages. I think it really makes a difference when people enter into it *knowing* the shape their life's [going to take], *knowing* they've got a radical commitment to social change and outreach to the poor. Knowing that's in the equation has got to make a difference!

[Marcia Timmel was married to Paul Magno at the time of our interview. They have since divorced.]

Marcia: I was the person on the outside when Paul was incarcerated in Florida for the Martin Marietta Plowshares. That was a horrible time of life for me. It put a lot of stress on our marriage. Paul was in jail for our first wedding anniversary, and counting the time I was in for my own Plowshares [Plowshares Number Four in 1982], we were together only about eight months in the first three years of our marriage.

When you go to jail, your life goes on hold and nothing . . . is . . . supposed . . . to change. When Paul came out, he was expecting that everything would be the way it was [when he went in], and I saw it as my responsibility to make that happen for him. (This is where the whole "good wife" syndrome comes in. It was not a whole lot different than Harriet Nelson wanting to have a nice meal for Ozzie. I mean, it's just drilled into women. Whatever our husbands want is what we're supposed to deliver.)

When I got back from his trial and was living in community again in DC, the community was crumbling—personal and financial and . . . just everything. It was a real mess. I kept feeling that if I could just give a little more and be a little bit more competent, I could fix it up and not let Paul down while he was in jail. Finally, I told Paul that I just didn't know if I had the strength to hold it together any longer. And that was devastating to him. He said, "You've got to. If you don't, I won't have any home to come home to. If you go somewhere else, it will be your home, but it won't be *our* home."

I felt, "Great! If this community falls apart, I've failed in marriage, too." I talked to my spiritual director and he told me I simply had to take time off. Paul didn't understand at first but finally he heard how all of this was killing me and we worked it out that time.

Ro: So you think it's easiest to be the one in jail.

Marcia: Before we had children, I definitely would say it was easier inside. Now, when I think about being separated from the kids for longer than a few days, I just take a deep breath. I don't know now which would be more painful.

In September 1988, a month after I interviewed her, Marcia *did* risk a long jail term by pouring blood and hammering on a weapon at the Air Force Association's Arms Bazaar at the Sheraton-Washington Hotel in DC. The statement she left at the scene gave her own creed of "faith and love for the human family." A jury convicted her of property damage but she only had to serve seven days.[32]

Those who acted in the last big draft board raid, in Camden, New Jersey, on August 22, 1971, did so without telling their wives and children. Mary Anne Grady Flores, one of mastermind John Grady's five children, remembers finding out about the action.

Mary Anne Grady Flores

I was fourteen. We were living in the Pine Barrens of New Jersey, in a campground, waiting for this thing to happen, but not really knowing a whole lot. My uncle Jack came in from Chicago to be with us. He was a priest. We were there for almost two months, in the rain and storm and hurricanes and everything else. The whole family in a six-person tent, with the dog.

We were living under an assumed name—Fagin. Anyway, finally the action happened, and my brother John, who was ten, went down to the local—you know, the little place where you could buy a quart of milk for the morning breakfast— and he saw Dad's picture on the front page of the paper. Dad was in handcuffs, be- ing led away by the feds. And he [squealed], "Dad!" Then the kids who played with him heard him and said, "Hey! What's your name?" And he forgot he was a Fagin.

So we went into town and heard that they were sent to the county jail, not in the Camden Jail, because the Camden riots were happening. That was the first time I ever saw my dad in jail. Behind a real thick glass. Boy, that was a hard mo- ment. And then to hear that he was facing forty-seven years in prison! Seven felony counts.

Ro: Why so many?

Mary Anne: I think it was because they hadn't been able to catch him. There'd been [a lot] of draft board actions on the East Coast as a result of all this organizing. His code name was Quicksilver, and J. Edgar Hoover was really pissed that they couldn't catch him.

The one thing that really ticked them off was the action at Media, Pennsylva- nia, when the FBI offices were raided. Dad "would neither confirm nor deny," using John Mitchell's words, whether he'd done it or not. Because they couldn't get him on the other stuff, they compounded the charges [for the Camden action].

In the March 1971 Media action, more than one thousand documents were stolen.[33] These FBI files revealed tactics designed to suppress dissent, such as wiretapping, infiltration, and media manipulation of peace groups. Within a few days, newspapers and politicians began receiving these documents from an anonymous group calling themselves "The Citizens' Commission to Investigate the FBI." On March 24, the *Washington Post* broke the story, and later the War Resisters League's *WIN Magazine* published many of the actual papers. To this day, no one has claimed responsibility for the break-in and the FBI has made no arrests.

After what they thought was careful planning and practice, the Camden Twenty-Eight group broke into the Federal Building in Camden, New Jersey, in the middle of the night and destroyed hundreds of draft records. As they finished shredding the files, they were arrested on the spot by FBI agents who had learned about the action through an infiltrator. That infiltrator was Mike Giocondo's good friend Bob Hardy; Mike had asked him to join the group.[34] Mike had been a Franciscan brother who taught for several years in Costa Rica. After he returned, he opened a storefront center for Puerto Rican immigrants in Camden, New Jersey, and started attending peace demonstrations.

Mike Giocondo

"All of a sudden I hear, 'FREEZE! It's the FBI!' Just like on radio programs when I was a kid."

Mel Madden told me about it—the group that later became known as the Camden Twenty-Eight. I thought it was terrific, you know, and wanted to be involved, too, and I had left the Franciscans by that time, so . . . There'd been a number of stand-up draft board actions, as they were called, since Catonsville Nine, like the Milwaukee Fourteen and others. They did their thing and waited for the police to come, but we weren't going to do that. We'd go into the draft board and close it down by destroying records, and *not* wait around to be arrested.

I guess I thought it was kind of romantic—romantic in the sense of adventure. Somehow the risks didn't come across my mind. We were going to do an action to protest the war—protest the draft—and not be caught. We had to be careful but we were going to be safe. At first, they were planning to do it in Trenton but they changed to Camden because they thought maybe the FBI was on to them in Trenton. Ironic, eh? John Grady seemed to be the leader. It was a cooperative kind of thing as far as the logistics and all the planning, but I think he took most of the burden himself.

[At first more than the final twenty-eight were involved in the planning, but eventually it became just twenty-eight men and women. Mike recruited one of his good friends, Bob Hardy, who was extremely helpful in the actual planning and in getting the group all the equipment they needed.]

Mike: For several months we planned and practiced and cased the federal building, which also housed the post office and other federal offices. We'd track the night watchman's rounds and so forth. The draft board was on the top floor, kind of set in the roof with a parapet around it. To get into it we had to somehow get over that

Ridolfi and Reilly on Post Office fire escape on entry
(Taken in darkness)

FBI telephoto of Kathleen Ridolfi and Joan Reilly on fire
escape, 1971. (Public domain.)

wall. Eventually, we decided to use a fire escape to bring an extension ladder up to
the fourth floor level, and then use it to go over the wall and into the draft board
through the window.

We used a glass cutter to cut a hole in the window, reach in, and unlock the
casement latch. It was really pretty easy. Only a few of us were in the draft board
itself. The rest did surveillance around the building. I knew I wanted to go in, not be
on a watch.

We communicated with the people on the street with these little walkie-talkies
Bob Hardy got us from a hardware store. Some were across the street in the Presbyterian church courtyard and another group was at the Reverend Milo Billman's
home, then some were just on the street, walking around to monitor the activity.

The night we'd originally planned the action, we were [stymied]. The police
had arrested a Spanish-speaking man, and he died after the beating they gave him.
That . . . it just turned the town upside down and there was a real riot the night
after he died. So we decided to do it the next night, and even then, the air was still
filled with tear gas.

Of course, we had no idea we were going to be caught red-handed! The FBI
was already in the building when we went in, stationed in an unlit room on the
floor below the draft board. But they let us do everything we wanted and in fact,
we were ready to leave. We had torn up all the draft records we could get a hold of,
and put some of them into post office mailbags to destroy later.

All of a sudden I hear, "FREEZE! It's the FBI!" Just like on radio programs when I
was a kid. I thought at first it was some kind of joke. But there they were! I was tearing up records and they came up and grabbed me. I . . . I couldn't get any sense of
what had happened. The FBI *here*? I mean I just couldn't believe it!

Ro: Did they rough you up?

Mike: Maybe I was just too nerved up to feel anything but I don't think they did. I remember being forced to lie down and having them handcuff me behind my back. And sitting on a chair with my hands over the back of it for an hour or two while they separated us and tried to ask us questions. Most of us didn't say anything.

We were in jail close to two weeks, waiting for people to raise the bail money. All of us had pretty high bail, especially John Grady and the ones who'd been inside the draft board.

Ro: How did it feel when you realized you had seven felony charges and were facing a possible forty-seven years in prison?

Mike: I hate to say this but I'm not much of a worrier about what's going to happen tomorrow. Even now, and it sometimes drives my wife crazy!

Ro: Now, your friend Bob Hardy. Did he go into the building with you?

Mike: No, no. I guess he hadn't planned to. Then he gave some excuse the night of the action, that he was going to get some sandwiches or coffee for those who were on watch. Said he'd come back, but he didn't. We didn't notice that he wasn't with us until we started to count noses when they were booking us. "Where's Bob?" He wasn't there. We didn't get the full story until after we got out.

Everybody had trusted Bob! I know I certainly did—and just found it hard to believe that he'd gone to the FBI [and agreed to become an informant]. Went right after I'd asked him to join us! I felt incredibly guilty, and I felt that others thought it was my fault, too. I had nightmares about what I was going to do to Bob Hardy and the family. I mean, I even thought of firebombing his home. (I still can't believe that those thoughts were going through my mind.)

I was known as a peace-loving guy, and his betrayal had to be the most cataclysmic thing that ever happened to me. I mean, there was several months where I couldn't . . . Those first nights, while we were in jail, were the hardest, because I experienced not only guilt, but . . . I had asked him because I thought he could help us out. And he *did* help us. Took care of getting all the equipment, which we found out the FBI paid for.

I tried to see him a couple of times after the trial, when his son was mortally wounded from falling on a spiked fence. I went over to the funeral service for his son, and I wanted to talk to him then, but I just couldn't . . . couldn't put the words together, even though I'd visited him briefly in the hospital while his son was still alive, and told him that I was sorry about the accident.

You know, you've stirred up a lot of things I haven't thought of lately. See, it really wasn't until when we were filming the reunion, the [Anthony] Giacchino movie, that I actually spoke to him. But still . . . there is that feeling. Emotions so kind of ripped apart can't really be put back together.

[During the trial, in a dramatic turnaround from his position as an infiltrator, Bob Hardy became a witness for the defense, claiming the FBI had misled him. He told the jury that when he had gone to the FBI with his misgivings about the action, they promised him that if he cooperated by infiltrating the group, no one would be threatened with jail time. Most participants think his identification of the equipment used in the break-in, all purchased by the FBI, made a dramatic impression on the jury.]

Ro: Even his recanting and turning to the defense didn't . . .

Mike: No, no. That didn't seem to do anything to how I felt. Time really hasn't done much, either. It's like people say: when you break something like a piece of china, you might glue it together but you can always see the crack. It's that kind of thing. Our friendship can never be one again. We had worked together and I knew his family. It had used to be that we could trust each other, you know, and say we were sorry . . . But you know, saying it still doesn't make it right. It somehow doesn't. [*Long silence.*]
    At the trial, they offered us a plea bargain, to drop the felonies and make it just a misdemeanor. I didn't agree. We did the action to let others know that the war was not right, and a trial would highlight that thousands were being killed—not only our soldiers but Vietnamese and others in that part of the world. And also people in Camden dying because there was no money for the cities.

[The jury found the Camden Twenty-Eight not guilty on all charges—the first legal victory for the antiwar movement in five years of draft board actions. One of the defense strategies was jury nullification, a little-used legal precedent where the jury could nullify the law by refusing to convict in instances where the law would punish someone for doing the morally right thing. Juries in the nineteenth century used it when they refused to convict those who helped runaway slaves, but judges in most civil disobedience cases refuse to instruct the jury on nullification. Because they were afraid the jury wouldn't all agree about the immorality of the war, the defense lawyers also brought in the concept of entrapment or "overreaching government participation." The judge charged the jury to decide if this was a case in which the government went too far in helping to instigate and commit a crime.]

Mike: The jurors just thought it was too much for the FBI to let us go to the point that we could do what we planned. They had actually supplied us with everything we needed. But I think our lawyers went overboard a little bit, too, because we *could* have gotten all that stuff without Bob. But what the FBI did was just amazing! I remember Bob saying things like, "No problem. I know where I can get a drill and I'll have it the next day." Then we find out that FBI agents gave him all this stuff!

The jurors! Oh, my! A sociologist told us how to do the voir dire, and how we'd select people who would be most likely to support our action. He coached us to record everything, even our gut feeling about someone. Then at the end, when we could actually talk to the jurors and hear their thinking . . . Oh! Mrs. Anna Bertinni. She owned a clothing factory down in Hammonton, New Jersey. She was against the war and thought we did a terrific job in making our reasons clear during the trial. I think she was able to convince some of the jury herself, and then another juror was also very much supportive of us. As it turns out, they all were.

Ro: When you think back on your eventful life, where do you put the Camden Twenty-Eight?

Mike: Oh, it's number one. It really expressed the way I was feeling. And *am* feeling even now. We were tearing up papers, that's all, and they were destroying lives, actually killing people. But now—I don't know. During the Vietnam times, you felt you were making some kind of progress.

Mary Anne Grady Flores: The trial was an amazing historical thing. A couple years later, I met Justice William Brennan on the back porch of my cousin's house in Nantucket. I was introduced as the daughter of John Grady from the Camden Twenty-Eight and the judge said, "That was one of the great trials of the twentieth century!"

2

"Let's Do It Again!"

The Berrigans and Jonah House

At the end of the Vietnam War, the two now-famous Berrigan brothers didn't go back to teaching and parish work but remained in the forefront of peacework. While I was unable to interview either of them, we can learn of Dan through his poetry and of Phil through the words of his wife and children.

Father Dan Berrigan, SJ

Father Dan Berrigan was released in 1972 from Danbury Federal Correctional Institution for his Catonsville Nine prison term. In 1980 he participated in the first Plowshares action. Even today, he continues to pastor the nonviolent peace movement, to write and speak out for peace, and to practice his Jesuit calling. Dan declined to be interviewed for this book but gave me permission to use anything he's written, so I've chosen two poems that hold special meaning for me.[1] Today, "The Trouble With Our State" speaks even more loudly than when I first marked it in a book Dan gave me in the late '90s. It reminds me of Catholic Worker founder Peter Maurin's pithy "Easy Essays." At that time, I also marked "Less Than" as being perhaps uncharacteristically autobiographical.

The Trouble With Our State

The trouble with our state
was not civil disobedience
which in any case was hesitant and rare

Civil disobedience was rare as kidney stone
No, rarer; it was disappearing like immigrants' disease

You've heard of a war on cancer?
There is no war like the plague of media
There is no war like routine

There is no war like 3 square meals
There is no war like a prevailing wind

It blows softly; whispers
don't rock the boat!
the sails obey, the ship of state rolls on.

The trouble with our state
—we learned it only afterward
when the dead resembled the living who resembled the dead
and civil virtue shone like paint on tin
and tin citizens and tin soldiers marched to the common whip

—our trouble
the trouble with our state
with our state of soul
our state of siege—
was
Civil
obedience

Less Than

The trouble was not excellence.
I carried that secret,
a laugh up my sleeve
all the public years
all the lonely years
(one and the same)
years that battered like a wind tunnel
years
like a yawn at an auction
(all the same)

Courage was not the fault
years they carried me shoulder high
years they ate me like a sandwich
(one and the same)

the fault was—dearth of courage
the bread only so-so
the beer near beer

Father Dan Berrigan, SJ, at an anti-Iraq war vigil in Manhattan, 2003. (Photo courtesy of Vivian Cherry.)

I kept the secret under my shirt
like a fox's lively tooth, called
self knowledge.

That way
the fox eats me
before I rot.

That way I keep measure—
neither Pascal's emanation
naked, appalled
'under the infinite starry spaces'
nor a stumblebum
havocking
in Alice's doll house.

Never the less!
Summon
courage, excellence!

The two, I reflect, could
snatch us from ruin.

A fairly modest urging—
Don't kill, whatever pretext.
Leave the world unbefouled.
Don't hoard.
Stand somewhere.

And up to this hour
(Don't tell a soul)
here I am.

Priest, renegade, exile. Prophet and poet still. Dan's memorable line at the Catonsville trial, "The burning of paper instead of children," seared my brain in 1969. The scar remains.

———————

Phil Berrigan

Dan's younger brother, Phil Berrigan (1923–2002), was the rock on which the movement I chronicle grew. I used to see him at peace protests in DC, but frankly he scared me, so big and craggy and famous in the small circle of peace people. So I never introduced myself and missed being personally influenced by his rapier-sharp mind, his steadfastness, and his uncompromising moral allegiance. Instead, I know him through the people he has formed in their faith, through the continuing work of Jonah House and the Plowshares movement and through his family, his wife, Liz McAlister, and his children, Frida, Jerry, and Kate—all following him, but in their own way, and all living examples of his vision.

Awakened by his exposure to violence and racism as a combat soldier in World War II, Phil entered the seminary and was a Josephite priest for eighteen years, with his first arrests as part of the civil rights movement. When the Vietnam War came to the fore of his conscience, he was increasingly compelled to the peace movement and participated with Tom Lewis in the first two draft board actions. Shortly before their sentencing hearing for the first action, he said to Tom, "Let's do it again."

Thus a movement was born, first in the draft board actions of the Vietnam War and then through the worldwide Plowshares movement, with its concentration on symbolically unmasking and disarming nuclear weapons. The name comes from the Bible—Isaiah 2, with its prophecy of beating swords into plowshares and spears into pruning hooks.[2] While each group contemplating Plowshares actions does so independently, the inspiration and much of the impetus comes from the Jonah House community founded after Phil left the priesthood and married.

Phil Berrigan, 1986. (Photo courtesy of Frank Cordaro.)

Liz McAlister: We asked, "How do we deepen community enough to be able to sustain us in a life of resistance?" So we began hatching a vision and in 1973, six of us started Jonah House. When you start living it, some say, "Nah, this isn't what I imagined it was going to be," and several of the initial community quickly came to that conclusion. "On paper and in meetings it's fine, but living it, no." Also, the whole women's movement was becoming stronger and we grappled with that.

At Jonah House, we started with this vision of developing communities of resistance all over the place, beginning with weekly meetings in small groups. Then we realized we were working so hard on this that we weren't doing resistance ourselves, so over time these meetings morphed into the [biannual] Faith and Resistance Retreats, which always include actions.[3]

[This concentration also gave them time to do the Plowshares actions with which Jonah House is identified. I asked Liz if she and Phil ever talked together about their courtship and she answered: "We didn't talk about it, and I won't talk about it, either. There is so much of our life that's public that I will keep some of it . . . it's ours."

Jonah House has evolved over the years, but the focus has always been on nonviolently resisting war. For the first twenty-three years, a large community—including the three Berrigan children—was crammed into a narrow row house on Park Avenue in West Baltimore, and the community supported its resistance activities by painting houses. In 1996, it moved to St. Peter's Cemetery, and some of the income now comes from maintaining the old cemetery the community members cleared. Phil is buried there, surrounded by berry bushes and flowers. Vegetables grow nearby, and in the distance one sees llamas, goats, guinea fowl, and donkeys. The animals help with bugs and invasive vegetation and provide entertainment for visitors.

The community now has many guests, as it has enough space to hold meetings, liturgies, and educational programs and to accommodate overnight visitors, including the student groups who come for retreats on nonviolence, community, and resistance. It's a member of the Atlantic Life Community, which holds frequent resistance retreats that result in nonviolent actions, primarily against the might of the Pentagon. Additionally, it coordinates the larger Faith and Resistance Retreats mentioned above. These gatherings provide opportunities for prayer, education, reflection, and entry-level resistance actions for peaceworkers from across the country. They also give coherence and provide fellowship to the movement.

I interviewed the Berrigan family a few years after Phil had died and asked Liz how the community had managed after Phil was gone, particularly with two community members—Sisters Ardeth Platte and Carol Gilbert—then serving long prison terms for a Plowshares action.]

Liz: We lost Phil about the same time the nuns went to prison. All huge losses. We *did* wonder about our ability to keep going, so we [asked ourselves] what we needed to focus on. Through that process, the last discourse in John's Gospel became central to us, especially the statement on Phil's tombstone, "Love One Another." We realized that if we couldn't realize that, we should just fold. So now we work on that more than ever, and the community has stayed strong and committed, even with Phil gone.

By linking the words "Catholic" and "radical," Phil Berrigan and Jonah House changed the US peace movement, changed American Catholicism, and perhaps changed the way some of the world sees Catholics.

His daughter Frida points out that both his seminary training and his personality enabled him to survive, even to thrive, in prison. Well that it did, for he spent more than eleven years incarcerated for his two Vietnam actions, six Plowshares actions, and numerous other resistance arrests in Baltimore, Washington, and elsewhere.

In a final statement written just days before his death, Phil was still fighting strong: "I die with the conviction, held since 1968 and Catonsville, that nuclear weapons are the scourge of the earth; to mine for them, manufacture them, deploy them, use them, is a curse against God, the human family, and the earth itself."

I regret that my timidity kept me from knowing Phil Berrigan. Frida shares this memory of her father:

Phil Berrigan stood before the court. It was October 1968. He was on trial with eight others for burning and pouring blood on the paperwork of war, the draft files that send young men off to Vietnam. He would be sentenced to three and a half years in jail. He told the judge: "From those in power we have met little understanding, much silence; much scorn and punishment. We have been accused of arrogance. But what of the fantastic arrogance of our leaders? What of their crimes against the people, the poor and powerless? Still no court will try them, no jail will receive them. They live in righteousness. They will die in honor. For them we have one message, for those in whose manicured hands the power of the land lies, we say to them, 'Lead us. Lead us in justice and there will be no need to break the law.' Let the president do what his predecessors failed to do. Let him obey the rich less and the people more. Let him think less of the privileged and more of the poor. Less of America and more of the world. Let lawmakers, judges, and lawyers think less of the law, and more of justice; less of legal ritual, more of human rights. To our bishops and superiors we say, 'Learn something about the Gospel and something about illegitimate power. When you do, you will liquidate your investments, take a house in the slums, or even join us in jail. . . .'"

Again and again, for the next thirty-four years, in courts all over the country, Phil Berrigan would stand resolute and righteous before power. He would accept the consequences without flinching. My brother and sister and I watched him walk into jail and prison fearless and full of joy more times than we can count.

Phil Berrigan was a fearless activist, but he was also a father who made fearsome oatmeal—flavorless, hot muck designed to "stick to your ribs." In the battle of the bowls, we played the impassioned activists and he was the heartless and impassive judge. But, rather than be late for school, we ate the oatmeal and pulled our stocking hats low over our ears before leaving the house. He watched us for two blocks to make sure the hats stayed on. Try telling the man who does not blink at a five-year prison sentence that only geeks wear winter hats.

The folk troubadour Charlie King sings, "Count it all joy, for a life well lived is well worth living." My dad loved that song. He would hum it as he painted houses, washed dishes, made soup, pumped gas, and cleaned paint buckets.

He would also reference it when community life and the dramas of others dragged on him. "Count it all joy" took on a whole different meaning if accompanied by a wagging of the eyebrows and a world-weary wave of the hand. It was a compelling combination of self-mockery and seriousness—if we believe that we find meaning and some sort of solace in suffering, then "bring it on." He would sort of grin and add, "Don't forget the locusts and plague." And he meant it. I miss that voice—gruff and gentle at the same time. I miss his fearlessness—born out of practice and prayer rather than bombast or machismo. I miss his impatience with formality and decorum, with how things are "supposed" to work.

My dad was born in 1923. He turned six two weeks before Black Tuesday in 1929. The youngest of six brothers, he watched his mother welcome in the travelers who crowded the roads, looking for work far from their families. My dad's own family was poor but they shared what they had.

These early experiences of poverty, of seeing a nation unravel and whole communities forced onto the open road, marked my father and informed his approach to life. To us kids—my brother and sister and I—the shadow of the Great Depression was manifest in the nightly ritual of washing out the white plastic bags that held the day's "garbagio" and hanging them on the clothesline. Every night we'd replace the used bag with a dried, smelly, still-greasy one, until it wore through. Dad rotated through three or four outfits, repairing his own work pants umpteen times. He even reused his dental floss.

I did not know my father as a priest. The photos of the handsome, well-dressed cleric do not fit neatly next to the grizzled house painter and working man who was my father . . . but I did understand my dad as a person struggling to be faithful, as one whose considerations and deliberations were studded with biblical insights.

My dad's advice—in every situation—was drawn out of his faith: a lived, applied, practiced and practical discipline. Never taken for granted. A tool to use, again and again and again, to carve hope out of despair, light of darkness, community out of alienation.

(1) Matthew 6:34: "Take therefore no thought for the morrow: for the morrow shall take thought for the things of itself. Sufficient unto the day is the evil thereof." He proffered this line in response to my "what-do-I-do-with-my-life?" agonizings.

(2) Luke 12:48: "From everyone who has been given much, much will be required." You and your brother and sister are gifted with love, talent, and strong family. Use your gifts.

(3) John 15:12: "Love one another." Always.

One of my most enduring memories of my dad is singing the Lord's Prayer at St. Lucy's Parish in Syracuse, New York. The whole congregation—which includes L'Arche members who are deaf and developmentally disabled—stood close together. Our hands were clasped tight and raised high. As we prayed "the kingdom and the power and the glory," I looked over to see tears streaming down the planes and creases of my father's face—big, fat, shameless tears of joy and communion and recognition of the presence of God in the circle.

Count it all joy.

Dad died on December 6, 2002. He died at Jonah House, and more than thirty friends and family and community members were there—we had walked the last weeks with him. Each of us wept, probing the hole his absence would leave in our lives. There was gratitude, too—that his long, painful journey was over—and there was expectant hope that we had gained a powerful advocate in heaven.

I think of all the friends who have died since, and I feel so lost . . . but a friend reminded me that the stars we see twinkling in the night sky are millions of miles away. Their light travels all that way. Long after the stars have died, we continue to be guided and inspired by their light.

Count it *all* joy, *all* the same.[4]

In spite of or maybe because of his eleven years in prison, Phil Berrigan was an unforgettable presence in the faith-based peace movement. His uncompromising stance and vivid personality provided strong moorings for many—on the Catholic Left, in the Jonah House community, and particularly in his own family.

Elizabeth (Liz) McAlister

"We would structure each [prison] visit so that I'd spend one-on-one time with each of the kids."

Raising family in community was a great gift and it was also difficult. Because you had other people interacting with them, other people being harsh with them, other people being lenient with them. And then trying to help them figure out

Liz McAlister, 2005.
(Photo courtesy of Rosalie Riegle.)

their own way with each one. There were people they loved deeply, and people they found pretty obnoxious. Different kids with different people. They also had a bigger field of role models than most children.

Phil was certainly the one who was gone the most, but he was such a powerful presence when he was there. His talks with them went very deep. I remember after his death, Jerry told me, "You know, I would call Dad and he'd always be straight with me." I remember another time when Frida needed to talk to him alone, but he was in prison in Maine, and she had to share the visit with other people. But he later asked her, "What's your ten-year plan? If what you're doing right now is good and human and decent, what you do next will become obvious." I'm not saying that as well as he said it, but it was very, very beautiful. He had that kind of relationship with each of them, and that was even better than his being around all the time.

Ro: What about when you went to prison, especially after the Griffiss Plowshares?

Liz: It was very hard. Very, very hard. Kate was two and a half, and there's a level in which that was the hardest. But the others were like eight and nine. Kate was just lovable and outgoing and absolutely beautiful, and her needs were right out there. A classic was one night when Ellen [Grady] was cooking dinner, and she comes to her and says, "Ellen, I need you to read me a story right now." She was clear with her needs, whereas with the older kids, it was harder to see what they were needing, so I think there were levels on which it was harder on them than on her. I got wind of that as time went on, and did a great deal in terms of letter writing. And then we would structure each visit so that I'd spend one-on-one time with each of the kids. Then in the evening, they'd do something with someone else in the community, and I'd have time alone with Phil. That pattern helped and so did daily letter writing.

Ro: I've heard that some of the movement families have troubles with their children being teenagers because their families aren't like anybody else's.

Liz: I think they would have had a much, much harder time in a suburban school. In an inner-city high school, they were already a minority. Everything about them was different. Kate went through all of middle school as the only white kid in her class, so the fact that she had parents who did this resistance and went to prison wasn't outstanding in that regard. But the big difference between the way our kids came through it and the way other kids don't is the relationships they have with other adults. Those relationships were always central.

Frida Berrigan and her two younger siblings are quintessential "resistance kids." Recently married to another child of the resistance, Patrick Sheehan-Gaumer, Frida writes and takes leadership roles in both the War Resisters League and Witness against Torture.

Frida Berrigan

"We saw each other as our only outlets for being honest about how hard it was when Dad was in prison. We were sort of encouraged—or maybe expected—to present a brave face to everybody else."

Oh, I hold a ton of memories. A couple of years ago, we got back a packet of letters that Mom had written to us when she and Dad were both in jail at the same time. (That was something they'd tried to avoid doing but, you know, at a certain point you just can't control it.) Mom was in jail for six months, and I think Dad was in jail for two separate periods during that time. I was too young to actually remember, but reading through these letters as an adult, I got a sense of how difficult it was for them to be away from us, particularly for my mom.

Two or three people in the community were very consistent in taking care of us while they were gone. We'd get daily letters from Mom, and somebody in the community would read them to us, and then we'd sort of dictate a letter back. We pasted their letters in a book of wallpaper samples, and I've been told that whenever anybody came to visit, I'd make them sit and look at all the letters from Mom and from Dad.

They were very colorful. Mom did lots of drawings, and I think she did the letters of the alphabet and illustrated little Bible stories. You could tell when she'd be transferred because her art supply would dwindle to nothing, [she'd send] just pencil drawings, and then she'd build [the supply] back up. From pencil to pen and ink, and then to pastels and watercolors. Then later she'd have to start all over again with just pencils and white notebook paper.

I do have one vivid memory from when I was very young of sitting on the sofa in the living room at Jonah House and having somebody read to me a letter from my dad, and really believing that he was speaking out of the letter—you know, that the letter was somehow really him.

I think that as I got older, the pain of missing us that was expressed when we were young got a little bit mitigated, and we'd hear more that prison was "no big deal, things are fine, da, da, da." And of course, when we were older, we knew they'd come back.

Ro: Any times when you missed them particularly?

Frida: Oh, yes! On my birthday, which is April first, so it's often around Easter. It's in this holy season, so lots of things happen at my birthday. When I was seventeen, Dad did an action on my birthday, which was on Easter that year. (I think it was the Aegis Plowshares up in Maine.) We weren't supposed to know what was happening ahead of time, but I was kind of a little eavesdropper and loved knowing things, so I knew exactly what was going on.

I was so upset! So sad! I was a big journaler—still am, you know—and I spent all day long in my room, just writing and writing and writing. I'd done all this reading about the weapons system, and I read the Bible—which is something I don't do all the time—and I totally understood why they were doing it and was totally in agreement with the whole Plowshares thing. But why did it have to happen on this day?

I remember my mom came *this* close to buying me a puppy to make me feel better. I'm really glad she didn't, you know, because I needed to work through it myself and not be *made* to feel better. And I don't even like dogs! Mom and I ended up having a real good conversation, but we never . . . [being home for our birthdays] was never anything that we children insisted on, you know.

Ro: Did you and your sibs talk about this among yourselves?

Frida: Yes, we did. I think we saw each other as our only outlets for being honest about how hard it was. We were sort of encouraged—or maybe expected—to present a brave face to everybody else, but amongst ourselves, we were resources for each other.

I can remember one trip Jerry, Kate, Mom, and I took up to Maine—maybe it was for Dad's resentencing—and I remember just being in a total funk and making the trip a real living hell for everybody. I wasn't a two-year-old then, I was in my early twenties, and I was *so* frustrated! Because we weren't talking about what this meant—not talking about how hard it was. "Who else am I gonna talk to? I really need you guys, really need *us* to be talking about this."

Finally I just pulled over and cried, and we had this sort of "moment" in a gas station and that was really good. We'd been putting out all of this stuff about how we could handle everything. Putting a pretty face on it. It's easy to internalize that as well, and I think all of us struggle with that.

Ro: So it was good for you to lance the wound.

Frida: Yes, yes. I was being very emotional because Dad had finished his prison sentence for another Plowshares action—maybe that was the Plowshares versus Depleted Uranium—and we'd had a month or two with him and then he was going back to Maine because he'd violated the terms of his probation by doing the action, so it was just . . . uh, it was just a very hard time.

Ro: Did you ever ask him, "Is it ever gonna end?"

Frida: Yeah. We really encouraged him not to do the Plowshares versus Depleted Uranium. I remember coming home from New York to ask him to reconsider and he didn't, as usual. He was adamant. "I'm not gonna be put out to pasture. If younger people were stepping up to do this kind of thing, maybe I'd feel comfortable about it, but they're not." That last one was really hard.

Ro: Now he had some illness the last time he was in prison, I think, but was he ill before he came in?

Frida: No. He had a cataract operation in prison, and then found out that he had cancer in September of '02. The doctor said it was level four, and it probably had been in there for two years or more. He died that December. When he'd gotten out of jail in December of 2001, he definitely wasn't very peppy. His hips were bothering him, too, so he'd say things like, "I'm just gonna be stretching more and taking more walks and I'll be fine." Then he had hip surgery.

But getting back to your question, I worry when other people go to jail, but I really didn't ever worry about Dad because he was just so comfortable there. He was just so singular and so sort of easy with the whole thing. After September 11th, I started worrying more about him. He was put into isolation right away and I worried about him being in his seventies and not being able to get exercise, not being able to do this or that.

The worst thing about that time is that we didn't know until . . . See, he wrote Mom every day and . . . and the letters suddenly stopped. (He wasn't so good about calling. Jonah House doesn't have an answering machine, and they're not there all the time, so a call could get missed, and he didn't like to worry them, so he didn't call.) It took her days to figure out what had happened and it was only because she was so dogged that we even found out where he was.

I remember sitting here in my office in Manhattan on September 11th and writing Dad a letter about what was happening and telling him I really wish we . . . could . . . talk.

I posted this letter in the mailbox on the corner, and of course it never went anywhere— never got there, you know. I was just so needing him and so terrified that maybe he'd be in solitary for the rest of his time there—that maybe there'd be a whole new level of imprisonment. I had sort of taken it for granted that my dad would be accorded a certain degree of respect in prison—not abused or scapegoated or punished in extra ways. After September 11, all of that was thrown away. So that was very, very troubling, and I don't think I got over it.

He got out that December and then maybe there was one month before he was down in Maryland or in Virginia. That was a tough place to visit because there's a barrier and you can't lean across it except to hug at the beginning and the end.

Everyone is in a big, loud, open room and the prisoners are mostly like young guys from Washington and it's a . . . it's tough. I hated that but, you know, you just sort of live with it.

Ro: Story of your life. [*Laughs wryly.*] Can we talk a bit about your growing up? Did you all go to public school with kids who were living a very different life than you were?

Frida: Yes. What was interesting is that prison in and of itself wasn't so remote to lots of folks that we went to school with. Other people's dads or uncles or older brothers would be somehow connected to the system. I remember . . . I think I was in seventh grade and a boy named Roy said, "Your mom's a drug dealer." And I said, "No, no, no! She's a peace activist," and he's like, "No, only drug dealers go to jail and your mom is in jail, so she's a drug dealer."

Kate had a different sort of experience because she went through school by herself and my brother and I were together all through elementary and middle school. We didn't work all that hard to educate people. It wasn't something that we put out there, although it was known. We would have preferred it if people just sort of forgot, you know, and our teachers were aware of that.

Ro: Now, where did you go to college?

Frida: I went to Hampshire College in Amherst, Massachusetts. The self-directed curriculum was really, really great, and I really dug into the academics. Eqbal Ahmed was a professor there, and they'd had this extraordinary antiwar campaign during the first Gulf War.[5] I'd been very, very active in that kind of thing in high school, and I wanted to go someplace where I could sort of dig into that. By the time I got to Hampshire, though, there was a different dynamic, a sort of weird identity politics that I just couldn't wrap my head around. I'm not really comfortable being "I, too, was oppressed" or "I was called a honky," but I also didn't feel like a guilty white girl. So I found Hampshire really . . . I didn't graduate with a peace house or a peace community. Instead, I worked for Frances Crowe in the AFSC office and brought a lot of people with me to Faith and Resistance Retreats and stuff like that.

Ro: Have you ever gone to jail?

Frida: Well, I've been arrested. I haven't spent any overnights except at the [2004] RNC [Republican National Convention], which doesn't really count. I don't know. One thing I've been thinking about a lot recently is that . . . the decisions that both Mom and Dad made cost us a lot, cost each other a lot. And we all agreed to shoulder those costs, but I think I'd have a very, very hard time asking the people that I love to pay that cost. I've been with Mom when Jerry's been on trial, or when Kate was on trial, and Mom was so kind of beside herself. Worried and anxious. I'd have a hard time making her feel that way. Although I *have* made her feel that way really regularly.

Ro: Well, isn't worry endemic to being a mother?

Frida: I suppose so. But I'd have to think long and hard about doing anything serious. A true resistance action upsets the apple cart in such a way that . . . In America we have such a tenuous sort of existence anyway that the last thing we want to do is leave it and go to prison. Now, I don't really consider getting arrested at the RNC or at the recruiting station in Manhattan or anything like that to be real.

Ro: That's really just protest, not resistance.

Frida: Exactly. That's a nice distinction. I struggle a lot, though, and feel pulled to do a lot more than I *am* doing, and I definitely feel a tension there.

Ro: This brings me to something I think about a lot, which is the idea of a hierarchy of resistance, with a Plowshares action at the top. I remember Rachelle Linner saying, "In the olden days, we used to get plenary indulgences. Now we get prison sentences."[6]

Frida: [*Pause.*] That's a tough one. Because I think it leads to people doing a Plowshares action without being emotionally, psychically, and spiritually prepared, and not having the time to prepare or [develop the] type of community that's going to walk with them through all of it. Or the experiences with smaller actions, like at the recruiting centers or the Pentagon. Those all seem prerequisites to being able to go into a Plowshares action with a disarmed heart that makes it a genuine . . . a genuine transformative action. Then it really does turn spears into plowshares.

Ro: Maybe the hierarchical thinking that isn't the best is when people think that the only action that's worth anything is a Plowshares action. So maybe the prereq idea is separate from the hierarchic one.

Frida: Right, right.

Ro: Now, when your dad was alive, he definitely was a leader. So many people who decided that nonviolent resistance was going to be the center of their lives had intimate contact with Jonah House, and routinely it was your dad who they went to for advice. How do you think that's going to play out now?

Frida: Dad could give real clear advice. And he would listen, too. But he wanted people to make the same kind of commitment that he had made. I think somebody like my mom would be a lot more careful about that. Because everybody that Dad led along, you know, didn't pan out or didn't, at the end, take it all the way. I think my mom might be a bit more—what's the word? Uh . . . reserved. Taking more of a wait-and-see attitude. Dad got excited about a lot of people.

Ro: Maybe, particularly at the end, your dad was working to ensure the continuity into a new generation.

Frida: Yes. Right. I think Carol and Ardeth could maybe fill in the role that Dad played, but with . . . with a sort of tenderness that maybe Dad didn't necessarily have. They have definitely said to me, "Hey, if you ever get the call, let us know." That's something I can't easily dismiss. That doesn't mean I wouldn't consider everything, but I just trust them and trust their sensibility. I . . . I just trust them.

Ro: Oh, good! Frida, how have the family dynamics changed now that your dad is gone?

Frida: I . . . I don't know. We spent a fair amount of time together without him when he was alive, and we were able to knit a family life out of letters and calls. I think all of us still feel in communication with him, even if it's pretty unidirectional. He was the one who was in jail more than anybody else, so we had plenty of moments when we were together, without Dad. Like my sister's graduation from college, he wasn't there. My graduation from college, Dad wasn't there. Jerry's graduation from college, Dad wasn't there. So we would always mark significant moments without him.

Ro: I'm wondering . . . is your Catholicism an important part of your life, as it was to your parents?

Frida: Actually, I've been thinking about their faith while we've been talking. It was most visible to me when they were in prison. I have this image of my dad's time in jail, in particular, as a ritualized time of deep and fervent faith. I remember his saying to me at one point . . . I was in high school and wanted to go to a movie or something. He's like, "Kiddo, you really have to work on what's in your head and what fills your mind. When you're in jail and you're away from all these distractions, what's there? What's inside your head?"

Whoa! I thought a lot about that during my one short experience of jail. (At the RNC, when there was nothing to do at all.) What can I just sort of sit and think about? What's going to keep me calm and keep me friendly but not . . . uh, needing people. Whether it's twenty-four hours or forty-eight hours or seven days, what's going to keep me centered? And being totally confident that there *was* a lot in there, you know. But remembering Dad's discipline of prayer and the physicality of that. And the resource he had in the Bible. Having that tradition and that wealth of inspiration and groundedness in their heads and in their hearts. That comforted me because I knew they weren't going to lose themselves in jail. They weren't going to despair because they were being held up by faith.

When I think about my own faith, I worry that it's never really been tested, in any sort of fundamental way. I think about myself as someone who's been, uh . . . graced maybe. It's like I have this little guardian angel. I really can feel like there's something watching over me, saying, "So maybe she's done a lot of really stupid and dumb things in her life, but . . ."

I go to church but not often enough. I definitely find solace and some inspiration in going to church, but I don't feel as biblically literate or as well-versed in things theological as my brother and sister are.

Ro: But you have a different kind of knowledge base. You do really good work on statistics and policy analysis and get so much out there with your writing. How do you see all that fitting into the family and the Jonah House community?

Frida: [*Pause.*] There are lots of ways to answer that. When Dad was alive, we had what I always thought of as a trusted source of information from him. I remember he had the statistics from Rosalie Bertel about how many people have been killed by nuclear weapons throughout the nuclear age. I'd say, "You know, I'm not really sure, Dad. That sounds really, really huge." Of course any number is too big, but you know . . . Then a little while later Rosalie came and we did the math, and it came out a much more modest figure. Still shocking and criminal, but it fit other statistics better.

We'd have these conversations about the relationship between information and analysis and action. I think I was a little bit more naive than I am now, thinking that all people need is the facts—to have it all lined up for them—and then action would be unavoidable. Now I'm more aware of the blinders and filters and the strength of the denial reflex.

I struggle with things differently now than I used to but I guess I see myself as becoming a trusted source. Like, Dad was saying for a while that depleted uranium is a "new nuclear holocaust." And I said, "Okay, rhetorically that's very powerful, but . . ." I would be more careful. I would say, "Depleted uranium can be insidious and lasting and worthy of Plowshares actions. It could be all of these things without being on the scale of Hiroshima." It's really, really awful, but different. As lasting in effect, but not as dramatic.

So we'd have these really good conversations, and I continue to play the sort of cautionary function, which I don't particularly like because I don't want to be the conservative Berrigan on anything. But I think things are so bad that we don't have to move into the realm of hyperbole to describe the situation accurately and in a grounded sort of way.

Ro: We used to think that the words would work, that they had meaning, and that the facts would change people. And with the world today, those ideas seem thrown to the winds. How do you justify continuing to work with words?

Frida: Well, one reason is that words last a long time. So much is ephemeral and so sad and so fleeting but, you know, words actually stick around. And they damn people. For example, we have what Bush said three years ago and what he said two years ago and things just don't match up. It's because they committed words to paper or said things out loud that we *can* damn them with their own rhetoric.

Ro: But the good logic, the kinds of things that you do so well in our writing, will it change things?

Frida: [*Long pause.*] I don't know. I think we *are* making a difference—the rapidity with which the lies of the Bush administration about Iraq have been refuted, for example. The research that shows there were absolutely no weapons of mass destruction, no hidden mushroom clouds, no stockpiles of chemical weapons. It was all bullshit! But will it make a difference in the long run? The easy gut sort of thing to say is that it's too soon to tell. I keep coming back to that—that in the long arc of history, the words and the actions are in this . . . this strengthening dynamic. I just hope they are.

Several years after graduating from Kalamazoo College, Jerry and his wife, Molly Mechtenberg, founded Peace House with fellow K College alumni Jen and Mike DeWaele. Between their families, they have six toddlers, and they now live in two houses that together serve as an oasis and a resource for neighborhood children on the east side of Kalamazoo. A large shared yard is the site of a community garden, a summer camp, and many neighborhood parties. The middle Berrigan and the only boy, Jerry speaks cogently about what it was like to be Phil Berrigan's son.

Jerry Berrigan

> *"When Mom did that Plowshares in 1983, and they told us her plans, our first reaction was 'No.' And then we watched The Day After, which just very graphically depicted what would happen, and after that, we said, 'Okay, whatever it takes to stop that. We support you. We send you forth.' So those are moments of clarity."*

As I became a teenager, I certainly felt different from the other kids, no question about that, because our parents were doing unorthodox things like getting arrested and going to jail and then they'd show up in the papers. And like all kids, we were much more self-conscious, much more insecure, than we had been earlier. To complicate matters, we were almost the only white kids in our class, all through middle school. Then in high school it was about 85 percent black and 15 percent white. Our college-prep, pretty selective school represented the racial makeup of Baltimore quite accurately. So we were a minority to begin with.

We had a lot of black friends, but we were also victims of reverse racism. I'd tell my parents I got bullied more than I would have if I were black, and Dad'd say, "That *is* hard. But when you experience reverse racism, it gives you a sense of what black people have had to go through. I wish it weren't that way, but it's the cross."

So those difficult things . . . uh . . . it's a lot to put on a kid, I think. But the love was always there and always unquestioned. Mom and Dad could be strict, but they always had time for our real needs, always had time to talk and to walk us through stuff.

Nuclear war was always a possibility discussed around the dining room table. "It could end at any time. We wish it weren't that way, and we're trying to make it different, and that involves a lot of hard work, but at least we're trying." When Mom did that Plowshares in 1983, and they told us her plans, our first reaction was "No." And then we watched *The Day After*, which just very graphically depicted what would happen, and after that, we said, "Okay, whatever it takes to stop that. We support you. We send you forth." So those are moments of clarity.

I will say, though, that Dad and I . . . You know, he was a very strong father. I had to put up with a lot of . . . Like if I'd ask him for five bucks to go to the movies: "Why do you want to give those shysters five dollars of your money? Just to watch stuff that's going to indoctrinate you into the culture? You could be reading a good book, you could be doing math!"

It was like, "Oh, my God! I just wanted to go to the movies!"

There was a willingness to debate, though, especially when we got to college. Dad, in particular, was intensely focused on war and the bomb and on his own kind of brand of Catholic . . . uh, I don't want to call it morality, because Catholic morality is . . . But he was intensely disciplined. Discipline is the root word for disciple, right? So he didn't have time for crazy-wavy ideas, you know? It was always, "What are we here for? The warmakers are busy and people are dying, so what is our duty?" Kind of always calling us back to that. And then we had all of these people coming through Jonah House. I sought many of them out to study with when I was at Kalamazoo College.[7] And, frankly, it's because they were right and because they were loving that Frida and Kate and I do what we do.

I couldn't jump into Dad's shoes, though, and it'd be false to even try. He was a product of his times and of his Catholic upbringing and . . . of his priesthood, certainly. The fierce discipline of the 1930s Catholic Church. The Depression, growing up on a farm, being the youngest of six boys—all those things formed him. There's a lot in who Dad was that I've tried to emulate and I'll continue that. His fearlessness and his clarity—those were great gifts for me. And I can always go back to his writing and learn more. In one part of his prison journal, he says, "So-and-so visited me and they asked, 'Does it have to mean this, all these years in prison?'"

He replied, "You know, either the Gospel means what it says or it doesn't. If it doesn't, it's not worth anything and we shouldn't waste our time on it. But if it does, this is what it means. It means sacrifice and endurance. It means the cross."

I read something like that and it's like, "Yes!" But I'm not him. And he wouldn't want me to be.

Kate, the youngest of the Berrigan children, found a peace community at Oberlin College in Ohio and graduated with a major in peace studies. Today she lives in Oakland, California, and works with adults with developmental disabilities. She is currently finishing prerequisites for a degree in physical therapy.

Kate Berrigan

"Jonah House always stressed to us the importance of using conscience as a basis for action, conscience as something that needs to be cultivated and followed."

I was only two and a half when my mom did the Griffiss Plowshares, but I have memories of visiting her in prison. People say that I'd cry when I had to leave her—lots of tears all around. But I don't remember that part; I just remember playing in the nice yard at Alderson. I think in some ways my siblings had a harder time with it than I did because they were older.

Lots of people were there to take care of us. Our dad was there pretty much the whole time and Ellen Grady and Peter DeMott were around a lot. John Heid was there. Lin Romano, Dale Ashera-Davis, Andrew Lawrence, Jim Reale, Greg Boertje-Obed—they were all really involved with our lives and played with us all the time. Sometimes people at school would ask about all the different people who picked us up, but actually, everyone thought Mom and Dad were my grandparents, anyway.

Ro: Was it all wonderful at Jonah House?

Kate: No, it wasn't. It's hard when there's a lot of people in a relatively limited space. For twenty-three [years], the little house that was Jonah House was fourteen feet wide, with a ten by twenty back yard or something like that, and at times there were a dozen adults and several children there. Just a lot of people! Personalities can clash and people need space and time to be alone.

The Berrigan family, 2011. Liz McAlister (seated), Frida, Jerry, Kate. (Photo courtesy of Patrick Sheehan-Gaumer.)

So the biggest problems come from disagreements over people's individual needs. Jonah House tries to work those disagreements out, as opposed to agreeing that everybody's welcome to do their own thing. Because obviously we don't agree on everything. Ever. I guess that's the biggest problem in *any* community.

We moved to the bigger house when I was fourteen. I had all my friends over for a big housewarming party, and we sort of played hide-and-seek in the cemetery. I had expected to feel slightly strange about living in a cemetery. (Maybe all teenagers would.) But immediately it was super-comfortable, and I loved being able to spend so much time outside and mow the grass and watch the birds and the sunsets.

Ro: How did growing up at Jonah House give you a basis for your life?

Kate: Ummm. [*Pause.*] I think growing up . . . Jonah House always stressed to us the importance of using conscience as a basis for action, conscience as something that needs to be cultivated and followed. Because it tells you how to live your life, it needs to be listened to and maybe even struggled with. It's hard to live by one's conscience, and I don't have illusions about doing it well, but it's what I've been given as a value and what I look to as a goal.

3

Beating Swords into Plowshares

Plowshares Communities and Their Actions

> And they shall beat their swords into plowshares, and
> their spears into pruning hooks: nation shall not lift up
> sword against nation, neither shall they learn war any
> more.
>
> —Isaiah 2:4

These are the nuclear abolitionists, the people who make nuclear resistance the compelling center of their lives, those who risk long prison terms and sometimes even death for their actions of symbolic disarmament. It's a big step to go from crossing a line, sometimes with hundreds of others, to sneaking into a fenced military installation in the dark of night to hammer and pour blood on a target in order to dismantle a weapon, to symbolically turn it into a plowshare or a pruning hook. Yet over 150 people have been moved to this type of "divine obedience." The numbers differ depending both on who does the counting and what one counts.[1] Perhaps in the end, numbers don't matter as much as the commitment each represents.

The term "Plowshares actions" originated in 1980, coined by the peace activists affiliated with Jonah House.[2] They took the promise of Isaiah to heart and used it to unite a continuing series of actions against the US nuclear arsenal, a threat to the world they call the "taproot of violence." The actions began in the United States, but soon spread to other countries, with Plowshares or similar disarmament actions occurring in Germany, Australia, Ireland, Scotland, England, Sweden, and Holland.[3]

Targets include the plants that make weapon components, the planes and ships that carry them, and the silos that store the missiles, ready to strike. During the eighties and early nineties, when 450 underground silos dotted the Midwest, sitting fenced but unguarded in out-of-the-way cornfields, silos were frequent actions sites. Under the provisions of the Strategic Arms Reduction Treaty (START), the missiles in the Minuteman II system were deactivated, with the last of these missiles removed in 1995.[4]

Plowshares actions are united by their process and their symbols. Unlike conventional Gandhian direct action, secrecy is essential, but participants always either wait for arrest or turn themselves in. For various reasons, people involved in the early planning don't always stay. Those who provide support but don't want to "risk arrest," as the phrasing goes, may meet in community with the group at first, but Plowshares people are careful that these helpers—those who serve as media contacts, raise money, drive to the site, and perform other tasks—don't expose themselves to a conspiracy indictment.

The group chooses symbols and props, mostly from biblical narratives. Blood—their own, usually carried in a baby bottle—remains a primary symbol. Hammers are an obvious choice from the biblical plowshares verse; other instruments have included a jackhammer and air compressor, spray paint, saws, hatchets, and wire cutters. Kathleen Rumpf told me that blood-pouring is actually more damaging than hammering because the blood corrodes engine parts.[5]

They eliminate the potential for violence to persons, including themselves, by taking great pains to avoid contact with military personnel until after they've performed their actions, and only infrequently do they choose targets within a "shoot to kill" high security zone.

They usually act at dawn, often simply cutting a fence to enter a site and sometimes walking long distances to reach their target. Then they hammer on the weapons, pour their blood, hang photos and artwork, and sometimes spray-paint peace slogans on the planes or other equipment. They pray and sing and have even said complete Roman Catholic Masses on the sites. Many leave statements explaining their rationale or banners with slogans such as "Disarm and Live" or "Choose Life for the Children and Poor." They also leave documents they hope to have presented as evidence during the trials—codes of international law, the Nuremberg principles, disarmament treaties. Often they have ample time to complete the planned actions, and several times they've had to alert security personnel before they were arrested and charged.

Later, one or more state and/or federal trials occur, although very occasionally charges are dismissed. Plowshares people regard the trial and the prison sentence as part of the action, as more chances to "speak truth to power." Prison sentences range from the rare acquittal to seventeen years, although no one in this collection has served that long at one time.

In the trials, the rhetoric becomes complicated, as the charges vary by jurisdiction, prosecutory whim, and judicial temperament. It seems to me that police officials, federal agents, and judges show little consistency on severity of the charges, type of prosecution, admissible testimony, and length of sentence.

The resisters make both individual and group decisions about the type of defense, and if they're not allowed to be together to plan their trial, this period can cause disharmony in a once-united Plowshares group. Most Plowshares activists represent themselves, sometimes assisted by legal advisers. They often at least try to use "necessity" as a justification, attempting to prove that "the actions are morally and legally justified and that their intent was to protect life, not commit a crime."[6] Judges vary in what they allow as testimony, with some using contempt citations with abandon and issuing long lists of forbidden words, and some going so far as to allow videos and songs as evidence.

Most often, a wide support community forms around the Plowshares group. Some of these supporters attend the trials themselves, sometimes gathering for a "Festival of Hope" the night before a trial starts. Others provide financial and moral support, conduct public relations campaigns, and raise funds to support the families of resisters.

Felice and Jack Cohen-Joppa maintain a support website and mail a quarterly newsletter, the *Nuclear Resister* (*www.nukeresister.org*), that chronicles the activities of Plowshares and related groups. Each year it tabulates the number of arrests for nuclear resistance and distributes this information to the mainstream media. But unlike the journalists who covered early faith-based protesters, mainstream media personnel today are bored with trespass, petulant about property destruction, and prosaic about prison terms. So the orchestrated and clandestine actions of the Plowshares movement have dropped out of public sight and receive scant publicity, except on the e-mail lists and newsletters of the Catholic Left. Few are looking and yet the hammering continues.

While most Plowshares are done by groups, Art Laffin notes that seventeen Plowshares actions took place with only one participant.[7] In fact, the second Plowshares disarmament was accomplished by one man, the late Peter DeMott. In December 1980, he was protesting with a group in the General Dynamics Electric Boat (EB) shipyard in Groton, Connecticut. The occasion was a launch ceremony for the USS *Baltimore* fast attack submarine.[8] Peter saw an empty security van with keys in it, got into the driver's seat, and repeatedly rammed it into another Trident submarine in the shipyard. For this spontaneous action, he was sentenced to a year in prison.

One can see in many of these actions liturgical components common to Roman Catholic Masses: conscious orchestration; an emphasis on community, symbols, and symbolic actions; a sermon in the form of a statement of the group's rationale; and songs, prayer, and artwork such as banners and peace cranes. In a statement with resonance to church bells, Kathleen Rumpf of the Griffiss Plowshares compared "the ring and ping of her hammer" to "bells proclaiming [her] love of Christ and for the people on this planet."[9]

This chapter includes interviews from thirteen Plowshares activists and two short interludes, one on the groups' use of blood and one that critiques the Plowshares concept. Sister Anne Montgomery, RSCJ, describes the first action and provides a planning scenario followed in many other actions. Kathleen Rumpf reminisces about singing new words to Christmas carols during another early action. John LaForge tells of an amazing judge—the Honorable Miles Lord—who recognized the necessity justification and castigated the target of the Plowshares action, Sperry Corporation. Father Carl Kabat, a veteran of the first Plowshares and several more, tells why he's spent almost seventeen years in prison as a resister. Jean and Joe Gump talk about their nuclear silo actions, as does Darla

Bradley, who struggled with paying restitution and now has reservations about this kind of resistance.

Father John Dear, who was in prison with the late Phil Berrigan, and Katya Komisaruk, who did a solitary action in California, describe their lives behind bars. Mark Colville talks about his Plowshares actions in the context of family and community, and three members of the Grand Rapids Dominicans, a community of vowed religious women, show how their antinuclear commitment plays out in complicated trials and long prison sentences.

Anne Montgomery was born in San Diego to a military family. As a Religious of the Sacred Heart (RSCJ), she taught high school before turning to active resistance. In September 1980, she and seven others entered a GE plant in King of Prussia, Pennsylvania, hammered on two missile nose cones, poured their own blood on documents, and prayed for peace. Different permutations of their trial took ten years, and in the final resentencing in 1990, the judge allowed defendant statements and sentenced only to time served.

Sister Anne hasn't stopped. In November 2009, she and four others cut through a fence and entered the vast naval base near Bangor, Washington, in an action they called the Disarm Now Trident Plowshares. Anne was eighty-three.

They walked for hours that night, passing in full view of military personnel engaged in an early morning shift change. They cut through two high security fences and entered the area where nuclear weapons are stored. Finally, some marines stopped them and escorted them off the base. They were released and misdemeanor trespass charges were dropped, but almost a year later, they received federal charges with possible penalties of ten years imprisonment. In March 2011, the group was found guilty on all counts. Sister Anne received the lowest sentence—two months incarceration and four months house arrest.

Sister Anne Montgomery, RSCJ

"As Americans, to break the law—even in a little way—is a big deal. So I don't look down my nose at anybody who finds it difficult."

My first experience with civil resistance was at the UN in 1978, its first session on disarmament. Through that, I came in contact with Jonah House and began to come to their summer sessions. That experience of community and action within a little group impressed me very much, so I kept coming back.

In the early spring of 1980, I was invited by John Schuchardt to be part of an action which would raise the level. It would be actually reaching some component of a nuclear weapon, disarming it, and possibly serving a long jail time. I went away to discern that and wrote down my pros and cons. Finally I just tore them all up and said, "In the end, this is an act of faith." So I decided to go ahead.

I wrote my provincial. "I'm going to do a more serious action and it might involve more jail time." She really didn't connect on how serious. Because you don't give people information that might get them a conspiracy charge, bring them up before a grand jury. We have to be very careful about that.

So we did it. We called ourselves the Plowshares Eight, and it was sort of a shocker to many people, both outside the peace movement and in, because it was the first time we'd actually taken hammers to something. Some people considered destruction of so-called property "violent." I think Dan Berrigan gave the best one-sentence definition of property: "Property is what enhances human life." If it kills human life, it's not true property, because it's not what's proper to human life.

When we were sentenced, our superior general in Rome, a woman from Spain, sent me a telegram of support. Both the international [RSCJ] community and my local communities have been very supportive, which is wonderful, because I know other sisters who've done even simple acts of civil resistance and not had that support.

Ro: You were really a pioneer.

Anne: In that respect, yes. I mean, there have been plenty of sisters involved in demonstrations or in crossing the line onto a military base, but I don't know of any before us who received felony charges. In this country.

We went to jail right after our arrest, awaiting trial. The six men were together in Norristown.[10] Molly [Rush] and I were the only women. We were put in another county jail because the women's jail in Norristown had been condemned as unhealthy for human life, I guess. Then everybody was separated and shipped around to five different county jails. We had a very difficult time communicating, even with the lawyers. The men could plan things, but then they'd have to write us through a lawyer.

At first we were going to just let them do whatever they wanted with us, but our supporters said people needed to understand and that we needed to speak up in court, so when the bond came down, my congregation paid my bond and part of Dean Hammer's so we got out. Then the other men were put out of jail because they were organizing too much in there and weren't welcome anymore. So, in the end, we could all make decisions together.

[The Plowshares Eight were convicted of burglary, conspiracy, and criminal mischief and given sentences of five to ten years. After a complicated ten-year appeal process, their terms were reduced to time served. In the

The Plowshares Eight, 1981. From left to right: Father Carl Kabat, Elmer Maas, Philip Berrigan, Molly Rush, Father Dan Berrigan, Anne Montgomery, John Schuchardt, Dean Hammer. (Photo courtesy of Charles Bauerlein.)

final sentencing, Judge James Buchanan "listened attentively to statements by the defendants, attorney Ramsey Clark, Dr. Robert J. Lifton, and Professors Richard Falk and Howard Zinn, placing the 'crime' in the contest of the common plight of humanity, international law, America's long tradition of dissent, and the primacy of individual conscience over entrenched political systems."[11] Such judicial consideration rarely happens in Plowshares trials today.]

Anne: Actually, by the time our sentence was changed to "time served," Carl and I and Elmer were in prison for other Plowshares actions. I've been in six or six and a half actions altogether. See, there were two Kairos Plowshares, because we didn't make it to the Trident [in Groton, Connecticut] in the first one, so Kathy Maire, a Franciscan sister, and I decided to finish that one, and went back to Quonset Point and hammered on parts of the Trident submarine.

Ro: How do people plan Plowshares actions?

Anne: It's a long process. I've helped with several Plowshares preparations, during the eighties especially, and we've learned that many things should be worked out before an action, because the action is more than one moment. There's a before and especially an after, when people are often separated in prisons and often can't communicate very well. Maybe you've made an agreement that you won't put up bond or sign things. But what about family emergencies? People have to be able to support people who decide to bond out, for instance, and all that stuff has to be worked out ahead of time so there are no bad feelings and people don't feel betrayed. You don't want a breakup of community. So now the process is—or should be—that there are very serious times for retreat.

First, a community forms, but they don't pick a site right away. They do research and get input on different weapons systems. They learn about biblical resistance and learn about building community and praying together, so the preparation is both spiritual and political. Also, they get to know each other—life-sharing and feelings.

Then there's a whole list of questions about how much legal stuff you want to participate in. Do you represent yourself or have a lawyer? What about bond resistance? Cooperating in prison? These things need to be talked out ahead of time and you make agreements, but you also allow for trusting each other if an emergency arises.

Most of us like to speak for ourselves in the trials. Often, generous lawyers will offer their time free of charge, to advise us and help people write briefs. You have to know all these legal technicalities, and decide if you want an opening statement and who's going to make it. And whether you'll take the stand or not, because that means you'll be questioned by the prosecutor. Are we going to question jurors or are we just going to let the first twelve be selected?

And then there's always a planning discussion on fear. What if somebody gets hurt or killed? You don't act in such a way that some young soldier or policeman is going to shoot because they're afraid, because that puts a burden on them as well as on you.

Now, this preparation has sometimes gone on for a year. People come and go. There is a point, somewhere about two-thirds of the way into the planning, where the community decides who's in and who isn't. You don't want people just deciding at the last minute. Although at the last minute, everyone is still free to say, "I'm sorry, I can't do this."

Somewhere in the process, people choose the kind of weapon they want to target. Is it depleted uranium, is it nuclear weapons, is it nuclear weapons in space? Then we scout the places where these things [are housed]. Sometimes the actual actors will go and sometimes someone who's supporting us and willing to take the risk. You get information about security and so forth. Toward the end, when the site has been decided on, a few people will offer to be support, to drive us to the site and so forth. They're willing to risk the conspiracy charge—because it *is* a risk. But not many, you know, just a couple.

Ro: Have there in fact been conspiracy charges?

Anne: Prosecutors have tried, over and over again. People just refuse to speak, even though they're threatened with contempt. Usually, the actors get a conspiracy charge for each felony, because it ups the ante. Prosecutors try to force plea bargaining and all that stuff. They've learned that Plowshares people will talk to international law and to justification and refer to spiritual matters, so they present pretrial motions saying these things shall not be allowed, and the judge always goes along with it. It really limits our court witnesses.

More and more, we try to argue from our heart instead of bothering with all the legal briefs. You know, you don't want to play lawyer. You have to be human about it. The courts always insist that you need a lawyer because you don't understand, you're not expert enough, or not bright enough, or something.

That's not right. Because how can you keep a law if you can't talk about it? If you can't express it in your own language? So to change the language rather than play lawyer, which we can't do, we put it in our own words, and talk about life.

Ro: If you're thinking of guiding—or shining a light, I guess—on people who might be coming along on this kind of thing, what would you say to them?

Anne: I think if they don't have a community already, they need to find others of like mind and begin talking with them, praying with them, forming a little community. We have Kairos in New York City which meets twice a month. People are free to come who've never been there before. There are no papers to sign. You pray together, you discuss what you're doing. You see, there's a principle: if we want the world to be in community, we'd better be able to act in a community ourselves and to *be* a community.

So find a community of support—others who think alike—and work with those who've had some experience. And maybe before thinking about serious action, watch people in action, so you're not so afraid anymore of the police. Then get involved in less risky things first. As Americans, to break the law—even in a little way—is a big deal. So I don't look down my nose at anybody who finds it difficult. Sometimes the hardest work is being part of a support community, because they have to keep going with their own work and do all the support work, too. And then, you know, somebody may not be called to this kind of resistance at all. They may not feel they can handle prison.

Ro: How do you know whether you can handle it?

Anne: Well, I think that's part of doing something a little less risky at the beginning. When we did it, I said, "This is it. I may be in for years." And we might have. I wouldn't recommend that as a general plan of action, but I trusted the people I was with.

I think faith is important to us. When I think of the French Resistance and Camus, whose love of human beings was so great that he could do the things without the sense of support from a faith, I really admire him. It doesn't really matter what faith tradition a person comes from; if a person has that, it's a great support. Otherwise, it takes great heroism.

[In addition to her high-risk arrest actions, Sister Anne has worked abroad with Christian Peacemaker Teams, in Palestine and in Iraq, where she lived with the people, not in the Green Zone.[12]]

Anne: I was in Sarajevo in 1993 when it was being bombed very heavily, and I saw the UN "peacekeepers" in white tanks, with guns, flak jackets, military equipment. I became convinced that nobody would believe there could be real nonviolent intervention—people risking themselves the same way soldiers do but for peace— unless people actually *did* it. I'm not an organizer, but I could do that, so in 1995, I joined the Christian Peacemaker Teams. I think these two forms of resistance are two sides of the same coin.

Kathleen Rumpf has been serving long prison terms for resistance since the Griffiss Plowshares action in 1983, which she describes here.[13] She also works tirelessly for improved prison conditions, both in Syracuse, New York, where she lives, and at Federal Medical Center Carswell in Texas, where she has been incarcerated.

Kathleen Rumpf

"One of the military personnel said, 'You've done a million dollars' damage.' And I'm thinking, 'Oh, come on! How could we?' Then I remembered they spend $400 on a hammer."

I was living at Tivoli, the Catholic Worker farm on the Hudson, helping with the nursing and the old folks. I think Vietnam did it for me. Finding out about the tiger cages, and then learning that they'd been made in the United States.[14]

It had always been fun being arrested at nuclear plants—Seabrook or Indian Point—and getting a few days in jail. It was really good compared to the reality we were living at the Catholic Worker. We'd say it was time to go "on retreat" again. You'd have a jail cell to yourself, and you have time to read. It *was* a retreat, really! But then I started reading about nuclear weapons and the Berrigans and started educating myself and realizing that the problem with all the poverty we saw at the Catholic Worker was the money spent on wars and weapons. It was slow, and the more I started understanding, the harder it got. I finally realized that a lot of what I'd been raised to believe was a lie.

In 1980, I went to the Pentagon for the first time. Went with a vanload of Catholic Workers, and we were all to be arrested. Well, one by one, everybody backed out. Here I am alone at the Pentagon. This is the evil empire and I'm saying, "I can't not do this! I just can't *not* do it." So I went to look for another affinity group. I wanted to do something big and symbolic.

Finally, I came upon this back room. I walked in, a total stranger, and found out they were doing blood and ashes—big-time symbolism—so I asked to join them. I saw this hesitation. (I had no way of knowing then that these were all the heavies, the so-called resistance heavies.) They're looking at me and, at that point . . . I don't know if I want this in the book, but . . . I weighed over four hundred pounds. But a few real good souls spoke up right away, and I was able to join.

We had all our actions synchronized. All these wonderful plans. I decided to do ashes. I didn't know what I thought about blood, but ashes . . . it was an easy choice. I was very moved by the Vietnam veterans at this protest. They vigiled all night long out in the bitter cold and then they did a die-in on the front steps of the Pentagon. Well, some of these guys really know how to die! They really caught my eye. I'm supposed to be on the steps with them and throwing the ashes, but instead I'm watching everybody die.

And then I see the blood go up on the pillars of the Pentagon. (This is before they put the plastic on the pillars to keep the blood from staining.) It was another conversion! I thought, "Oh my God! The blood's already there! We just refuse to see it." Meanwhile, I'm holding this bag of ashes and gaping at the pillars.

Well, I finally make it up to the steps and I'm pouring my ashes out of a bag, and this policeman taps me on the shoulder. I look at him, expecting him to drag me away, you know, but he's just pointing at the ground. There at my feet is a veteran who had "died," and I'm throwing the ashes right in his mouth. When I finally got arrested that time, I told the police that if they weren't nice to me, I'd go limp. I always say that now and I always seem to get my way.

After that, I decided to move to the Baltimore Catholic Worker. Lived there for two years, so I could be close to Jonah House, close to Washington. Resistance became really, really important to me—that whole tradition within the Catholic Worker.

We started planning for the Griffiss Plowshares. By that time, I'd been arrested many, many times and had been in court and listened to some of the Plowshares trials. I have many contradictions in my life. I watch war films on TV and have these funny little quirks, so who am I to speak the truth? But I was in and out of jail so much. Liz described me in court as a one-woman crime wave. Cute, but . . .

I was seeing people literally freeze in the streets. It wasn't so much what's going to happen if the bomb drops because I know we're loved by God. The real sin is to not speak out now while children are starving and people are dying in the streets.

I really expected life in prison for our action. That's what I was trying to prepare myself for because we were the first ones to go onto a military base. Then there's this problem I have with depression. If I don't find hope, I have to make some. There's no hope if people aren't doing anything. The only hope is if we try.

The night before . . . I was having fun and joking around and couldn't really sleep. I kept convincing myself that I wasn't scared. But once I got over the fence at Griffiss, I couldn't breathe. I mean, talk about a bunch of klutzes! Vern Rossman

Bloody handprint on B-52 bomber, Griffiss Air Force Base, New York, 1983. (Public domain.)

drops his hammer and his goggles and we had to go back over the fence to get them. I'm trying to get everybody into the woods before the security car comes around. Meanwhile, we hear alarms going off someplace.

It was quite a long walk to the airplane hangar—over the fence, through a field, then through the woods and across a golf course. When I'd been on the base before, there were people all over the place. (I'd been almost caught, actually.) But this was a holiday, and no one was working.

And then the doors were open and all the lights were on and we went [into the hangar] and saw the B-52 and began hammering. My little hammer would ping and then almost fly in my face without even leaving a mark. I painted on the plane: "This is our cry, this is our prayer of peace in the world." And the symbols we brought with us—the pictures of the children, the indictment that we put on the plane, the blood we poured . . . I hung paper peace cranes on the different engines. (The FBI kept calling the cranes "paper airplanes" like they call blood "red substance.")

We had decided we'd do twenty minutes of hammering and putting our stuff around, no more. In reality, we were there for about two and a half hours. We didn't want to do more destruction, and we kept wondering what to do next. We phoned the press from their top security lines. We sang and prayed out on the tarmac. We went back in to go to the bathroom. Went up into a B-52 and looked around. Now, we were charged with sabotage. Had we been about that, we certainly would have had time to do it. Anyway, finally we were able to wave somebody down to arrest us. They were going to take us to the Burger King and drop us off, like they usually do for protests at Griffiss. I said, "Well, gee! You might want to check Hangar 101 before you release us."

So they go to the hangar and then they get on the walkie-talkies, and then we had about sixteen or eighteen guys with forty-inch necks, marching double time with M-16 rifles. They made us kneel in the sand, holding rifles on us.

Then sitting on that bus . . . we were on the bus for eight, nine hours, and they wouldn't let us talk, and they had us handcuffed behind our backs. Waiting for the FBI to come from Albany, which was quite a trek. But certainly I could understand where they were coming from. That's a gift I've had, raised as I was. I could really understand people and their fears and what they are raised to believe. So it's easier for me to be patient, but still, it was a hard eight hours with my hands behind my back and hearing this constant, "Shut up! Shut up!"

We'd say, "Well, we didn't join the military, you did."

Ro: Did you try to pray?

Kathleen: Oh, I never stopped.

Ro: I mean out loud.

Kathleen: No. Because at that point, we were all too scared, I think. They'd taken Karl Smith off the bus and they were kind of punching him. He was talking about the Gospels, and they told him that the Bible didn't exist on Griffiss Air Force Base.

I didn't expect so many hours of that. I couldn't be . . . I couldn't feel very funny at that point. They kept telling us to shut up, and they wouldn't let us go to the bathroom. I have arthritis, and it was getting very painful, and they said, "If you're not quiet, we're going to put you out in the mud."

It was sleeting and snowing and raining all at once, but finally I'd had enough, and I stood up. "Well, do it! Put me out in the mud." And they did. They picked me up by my handcuffs and kind of pushed me off and set me down in the mud outside. I got some relief then 'cause I could move around a little more. And the next thing I knew, Vern Rossman and Liz McAlister were out there, too. Cars were driving by, and we're out there like prisoners of war. Finally, the FBI arrived and started interrogating us, and we got our bologna sandwiches.

One of the military personnel said, "You've done a million dollars' damage." And I'm thinking, "Oh, come on! How could we?" But then I remembered that they spend $400 on a hammer. We got the sabotage charges about two days later.

I'd been born in Syracuse, left there at the age of five, and here I was home again, sitting in this jail. The conditions were horrific. I'd been in some of the worst . . . I mean, there's really no such thing as a good jail, but there was an oppressiveness about the Syracuse jail that I'd never experienced anywhere else. All you'd hear was banging metal bars, and the TV was on all the time.

One thing we could do, though, was go on the roof every day for exercise. It was the only time the four were us were all physically together. We'd laugh and sing and make up words for songs like "We're getting nothing for Christmas." [*Sings it.*] And new words to "The Twelve Days of Christmas," like "The sergeant gave to me two strip searches." You have to have some kind of lightness of heart to go into this, because it's so serious. It's life and death kind of stuff, but you really do need that lightheartedness.

The jail became our community, including the guards. We had one guard named Gloria. She was always kind of hard, but I sensed a real heart in her. We'd be strip-searched every time we'd come down from the roof, strip-searched for everything. One day this tough Gloria was stripping us in the hallway and Jackie Allen and I started singing, "Gloooooooooooooria, please don't touch our bodies." [*Sings it to the tune of "Gloria in excelsis Deo" in the Christmas carol "Angels We Have Heard on High."*]

Well, the guards just cracked up! They really didn't know what to do with us. The bishop visited us one day and of course we were strip-searched after his visit, too, and Jackie quipped, "What do you think we've got, Bibles up our orifices?" There was a great spirit amongst us, despite the oppression and meanness of this place.

We got kicked out at three and a half weeks. I was never so surprised in all my life. Here I was expecting life in prison, and we go into the courtroom and the judge brings up bail. Well, we don't pay bail. There are too many people sitting in jail who don't have any resources, and we are in solidarity with them, so we never expected to see the outside, but they released us [into the custody of different people]. I stayed in Syracuse for the six months before our trial, to start the support work going.

The trial: I stated in court that I wasn't afraid of the bombs dropping, but that I had come across bodies frozen in the streets, and I was more afraid of not speaking. The people who are dying are real faces and real names to me. I talked with the jury about my years at the Catholic Worker. When I was finished, there was dead silence. And the two prosecutors . . . there was nothing they could come back at me with, so I didn't get cross-examined that time.

We were sentenced to two years and I did eighteen months at Alderson. Before, I had only done thirty days here, sixty days there, ten days another time, but I knew what I was getting into. And then to have only the eighteen months when we had expected much more because of the sabotage charge. It . . . it was a valuable time.

I still get arrested sometimes at Griffiss but I haven't done any more Plowshares there.[15] I had one judge I really loved a lot. He's dead now. I went to his funeral and wake. His wife put her arms around me and told me that I was her husband's favorite defendant. Once I got a personal letter from the prosecutor: "If anything, I wish that there were more of you getting arrested. I'm no better than a hypocrite because I don't believe in the policies, and I'm here just to get a paycheck."

What we do is very little, we know. People ask me all the time about effectiveness, and I just don't know. I could go nuts if I asked myself if I'm effective while I'm in a jail cell. I *want* to be effective. God knows I want to be effective! All of us want to be. But I also have to let go of that. This is a witness that goes beyond being effective, that goes into what I believe we should be doing. Into faithfulness.

John LaForge is codirector of Nukewatch, a nonprofit peace and environmental action group with headquarters in Luck, Wisconsin.[16] He was influenced to make resistance his life by two conscientious objectors who taught him at Bemidji State University in Minnesota—one from World War II and one from Vietnam.

John LaForge

> *"Sometimes you have to do something you're not sure you can handle."*

My first arrest? The Des Moines Worker was doing their first actions at Strategic Air Command [SAC] in Omaha, so I hopped in a van with Father Carl Kabat and some folks from Bemidji and drove down there. My first action was to sit on a live runway on the most important air base in the country. Guess we didn't know how risky that was. But it was a lot of fun, and they did their song and dance with the police.

Then in 1981, I was arrested at the White House, protesting aid to El Salvador. All the men were thrown together and Howard Zinn was in the group. Howard immediately launched into a lecture. Carl had just done the Plowshares Eight, and that was a huge shock to us, because we knew him personally. (When I say "we," I mean my partner, Barb Katt, and myself.) That action really spoke clearly to us. We decided then, "If we were prepared enough, we'd have to do that, too."

> [During the eighties, the couple was jailed several times for actions in DC and also closer to home—at the SAC base, at Bemidji State University, and at Grand Forks Air Force Base in North Dakota. In 1987, John and Barb visited all one thousand nuclear missile sites in four months, double-checking their locations for a map published by Nukewatch in *Nuclear Heartland*.]

John: Once we came across a silo with the hatch wide open. They were obviously doing repair or replacement. It was a Sunday, and no one was around. Any disarmament activist could have thrown a concrete block in there, and done a million dollars' worth of damage in a blink.

Ro: Did you ever do Plowshares?

John: Yes, one. In 1984. For that, we served one day. Yeah, $37,000 damage and the judge let us go. We had the most incredible judge in the country—Judge Miles Lord.

We went into Sperry Corporation in Eagan, Minnesota—East St. Paul. We dressed up like corporate executives. Heels and suits and a haircut. Carried brief-cases for the hammers and a banner and some blood in a baby bottle. Funny . . . I just cut my hair short again, the first time since that action. And my mom said, "You're not going to do another action, are you?"

The Sperry computers were for guiding missiles from the submarines to the targets. We found two of them, and we smashed them and poured blood on them. At our jury trial, we decided we weren't going to put on a big evidentiary trial, because of what had just happened out west. A couple months before, an Arizona judge had decided he was going to let all this evidence in—international law, treaty law—and that the jury could hear the defense of necessity. The prosecution appealed to the Ninth Circuit in California, which rules over Arizona, for a writ of mandamus, which is to stomp on this judge, shut him up, so he can't let the jury hear this. And they granted it and shut that judge down.

This was just prior to our trial, so we thought, "Why pretend that we're going to get any fairness out of this system by putting on evidence?" So we didn't. We presented our whole case without lawyers, although we had two really good law-yers as advisory counsel, and it went about as well as a *pro se* trial can go in federal court. We told the jury about our motive and intent.

The witnesses the prosecutor put on the stand were interesting. One said that she'd heard the word "Trident" but didn't know what it meant. Which was our point

The Honorable Miles Lord, 1981.
(Photo courtesy of Dwight Barnes.)

in doing the action. So many people who work in factories don't know the outcome of what they're doing. They don't even know what the computers they build are designed to do. In fact, a few people told us they quit their jobs after they found out what they were working on.

The jury was out for two and a half hours or so, but we did get convicted and the sentencing was in November. The maximum penalty was ten years, and we felt we might get four and a half. Worked really hard on our sentencing statements.

Then at sentencing Judge Miles Lord first read out the most anticorporate, antimilitary critique of the Reagan administration we'd ever heard from the bench. Then he talked about a Sperry case in his own courtroom. He had presided over a plea agreement between Sperry and the government where the company pled guilty, basically, to defrauding the government out of three and a half million dollars by fixing time cards. And the government was going to fine them *ten percent* of that. They'd get to keep the rest of the money.

Miles Lord just went through the roof about this. He said, "Why is there one kind of justice for the rich, who are making weapons to bring down the earth, and a totally different kind of justice for these two, who have very few resources and just want to prevent nuclear war?"

"Now if you're *making* the bomb, you get this"—and he rattled off the plea agreement between Sperry and the government—"but if you're protesting the bomb, you get indicted, you get charged, you get tried, you get convicted." He said that if you're making the bomb, none of the corporate officials are named or indicted. They're making money even as they're pleading guilty. Well, because of this blatant disparity of rich and poor getting different justice, he said, "I'm going to take the sting out of the bomb."

He gave us unsupervised probation for six months, which is nothing at all. Nobody could believe it. Here we are, walking out with no sentence at all.

Ro: Oh, what a wonderful shock! What advice would you give to young people who are thinking they might like to live a life like yours?

John: [*Long pause.*] Well, for one thing, I'm pretty sure they can handle more than they think they can. They don't know that until they risk, and that's why it's called a risk, I guess. So sometimes you have to do something you're not sure you can handle. When Barb and I did that Plowshares action, you know, we weren't very far into our relationship. We had lived together for only three years, and we realized that a ten-year prison term might end it. We thought we might be sacrificing the relationship, and even so, in the end we said, "Yes."

I think jail time was a way for me to figure out what I wanted to do, actually. I remember clearly a Christmastime in Douglas County Jail in Omaha. I was maybe one of ten white guys out of eight hundred people. All the rest were African American. On Christmas Eve, or the day before, they brought in this church choir, and they put all the inmates on the bleachers in the gym. This church choir was so

John LaForge entertaining at a Midwest Catholic Worker
gathering, 2005. (Photo courtesy of Frank Cordaro.)

scared of us as they marched in. They stood in the middle of the gymnasium floor,
looking at a bleacher full of toughs.

Then the choir started singing and the men in the bleachers started singing
along with them. That was just a moment for me. I remember thinking so clearly,
"This is where I'm supposed to be. I'm going to keep doing this." [*Pause in memory*.]
It's hard to believe it's been twenty, twenty-two years, because that memory is like
ringing a bell.

One thing I ask young people to do is to read Albert Camus, who wrote in part
during the Nazi occupation of France. He asks the question, "Would you oppose
a tyranny without hope of success?" And I think that's a question young people
have to face. We *all* have to face it. Albert Camus answers it in the affirmative. He
ultimately convinces us that if you don't oppose tyranny—even if there's no hope
of success—you're going to forget that you're a human being.

Father Carl Kabat, OMI, has spent nearly seventeen years in prison for protesting nuclear weapons. Today, he lives with Carolyn Griffeth, Terry McNa-
mee, and their two children at Carl Kabat House, one of the houses in the St.
Louis Catholic Worker community.

When I interviewed him in 2004, he was only three weeks out of prison
from a Plowshares action. "Give me a little time," he said. "I'm getting older
and I don't bounce back as fast as I used to." But bounce back he did. Dressed
as clowns, Father Carl and two Catholic Workers from Duluth entered another silo in North Dakota in 2006, an action that earned him fifteen months
in prison. Then in 2009, on the fiftieth anniversary of his ordination as a
priest and again vested in his clown costume, he went into another Minute-

man III nuclear missile silo, this time in Colorado, hung banners, and then knelt and prayed. After his arrest, he refused to post bail and was kept in jail until his trial in December where he was sentenced to time served.

Father Carl Kabat, OMI

"We have to be fools for God's sake. And for humanity's sake because if we're not, the world won't be here."

I'm an order priest: the Oblates of Mary Immaculate, OMI. From 1965 to 1968, I was in the Philippines, and when I came back to the States, I realized I didn't fit in, kinda like, so I went down to Brazil. My little parish down there had like forty thousand Catholics. When I came back here in 1973, I still didn't fit into the ordinary box, so I began running all over the country—Pax Christi, Bread for the World, all those kinds of groupings.

In '76, I guess it was, the World Day of Peace was going to be held in Baltimore. Well, old Carl figured that maybe he'd be able to talk to one of the bishops. Twelve of us from Jonah House participated with the bishops at this World Day of Peace, and then we all went down to Plains, Georgia, to let the new president know how we felt about nuclear arms and that was my first arrest.

I felt real, real good, about it. I remember somebody asking me, "Are you okay?" and I said, "Oh, yeah!" And I was, from the neck up. I guess my body from the neck down was shaking so hard it was making the metal bunk rattle! But after all the yakety-yak, I'd finally taken a stand, had done something.

After that, the antinuclear movement became my total focus, and it's still the number one problem facing humanity, all these years later. So my life of crime began. From '78 to '80, it was the Pentagon and the White House. Then the Plowshares Eight, the first one we called Plowshares. Et cetera, et cetera, et cetera.

Ro: What does the order think about this?

Carl: Well, you'll have to ask them. In about '98, I think, I was grounded, I guess you'd call it, at St. Henry's in Belleville, Illinois. Treated like a thirteen-year-old who has to be in by ten o'clock! At that time, I'd been doing restitution—four or five thousand dollars—by working at the Catholic Worker house in Wisconsin, calling it ten bucks an hour, for forty hours a week. Then in 2000, they wrote that they were beginning the process to expel me from the order. But it hasn't happened yet. Individually, some support me.

I'm not exceptional. I'm just me. But I personally feel that if we don't take a public stand as Christians, we're not living like Jesus did. When I see something I think needs doing, I'll do it. I can recall that as a young priest I was assigned to two little places in Minnesota—Kinmount and Kabetogama. Some guy had just moved into town, had a wife and three kids, and I loaned him five hundred bucks from the church funds. After he brought the money back, the pastor said, "Oh, my goodness, what did you do?" It didn't even enter my mind to ask. I sensed the person was trustworthy and knew he needed to make a down payment on an apartment. I'm an activist, a doer, not a real verbal person.

With the Silo Pruning Hooks, Helen [Woodson] got eighteen, I got eighteen, Paul [Kabat, my brother] got ten and Whitefeather [Larry Cloud Morgan] got eight. Our times were all reduced, but basically I did ten years—six and two-thirds at that time and the rest later on [because of] a parole violation.

Ro: How does this doing what needs doing play out when you're in jail?

Carl: Well, I get along real well. These are broken people, and I'm very, very comfortable with them. I've had a few bad experiences, but I was even very comfortable in the DC Jail. I'll be honest with you, for me it's a little more difficult in the camps where you have the white collar. They don't understand, but the poor really do. Certainly the black population does. "This bomb could kill six to ten million people." They get that.

Ro: Any sad or bad experiences in jail?

Carl: Well . . . yes. [*Pause.*] It happened in Missouri. I was in Lafayette County Jail and assigned to an upper bunk. A young man offered me his lower bunk, and he moved into the next pod, and that night, about midnight, some men tried to rape him. (The word was that he was there because of child molestation.) He fought like a tiger. I heard him and woke up. Yelled, "Cut that out!"

Then I heard, "We'll get you in the morning, old man!"

I was moved the next day and I think he was, too. But that was . . . If I had known what'd happen, I wouldn't have taken that lower bunk.

Ro: How do you feel about supervised release?

Carl: See, it's like a game, unfortunately. The supervised release this last time was three years, so every time I'd go across the Mississippi, here [in St. Louis], I'd have to check with my parole officer, even though the river's only four blocks away. The first six months were like house arrest, and then for two and a half more years I'd have to constantly be checking. Would it be okay for me to go to Belleville for a meeting [with my order]? If it had only been six months, I'd probably have said yes. But for three years! That I could only see as harassment.

I finally told them I would noncooperate and the next week they came for me at Karen House [Catholic Worker]. Someone told me later that there were nine marshals surrounding the place.

Ro: Sounds like a bit of overkill. Have you ever been in a maximum security prison?

Carl: Yeah, after the Plowshares Eight, in 1980. For a work stoppage. Six months in the hole, but then they moved me to Huntingdon, which is the max-max joint for the State of Pennsylvania. Of the 400 of us in the cell block, 350 were there for homicide. In that place, you had to be very, very careful. I'm a little bit streetwise 'cause I worked in the slums overseas. When you walk in a max security, for instance, you're very careful not to bump anybody, even by accident.

Now, Huntingdon . . . that was a special max-max-max. In many of the other places I was well known and really respected, honestly. I have to say in a certain sense, I was, ah . . . treated a little . . . uh, with kid gloves. Like this last time: they checked my teeth and my heart and gave me a complete physical. Now, the ordinary prisoner isn't going to get that. I think they were being extremely careful because I'm a bit higher profile.

You know, my basic theme is do what you can, then you sing and dance. Once I've tried to make a statement—a clear statement, an honest statement, a truthful statement—I just relax and enjoy it. I'll be honest with you, I'm nice to Carl after an action. Everybody who goes in for peace or justice shouldn't beat themselves to a frazzle in prison. Otherwise, you can burn yourselves out, because it's an inhuman place!

Do what you know how to do, take the punishment—if you want to use that term—and then just relax and try to get as much enjoyment—if you want to use

Greg Boertje-Obed, Father Carl Kabat, and Mike Walli, entering a nuclear missile silo enclosure, 2006. (Photo courtesy of Susan Crane.)

that term—as you can. In prison, I play basketball, play cards, just hang out. This pure business, like Ivory Soap, 99.9 percent pure—aw, forget it! (At least for me.)

You know, in some ways I'm more free in than out. As Victor Frankl said, "If you have a reason, you can put up with anything." We have to get rid of these damnable things. Symbolic is fine, but it has to be . . . somehow, I guess, violence to "improperty."

What would we do if there was a gas chamber and a crematorium on the corner? If we had a Caterpillar, we'd run the thing through it, wouldn't we? I'm joking but again, I'm not joking. Even though we had the jackhammer for the Silo Pruning Hooks action, it was still symbolic because we would've had to work there day and night for a month to really do anything. The Plowshares Eight destroyed two Mark 12A nuclear bombshells, and that was kind of the same thing.

I don't know what the answer is. If you're kind of bounded and based in faith of some sort, faith in yourself and in God and in brotherhood and sisterhood, you do what you have to do and then you sing and dance.

Jean and Joe Gump were propelled into political action by the Catholic Family Movement when their twelve children were young. After they all left home, both Jean and Joe participated in separate Plowshares actions and served overlapping prison terms.

On Good Friday of 1986, Jean symbolically disarmed a Minuteman missile silo near Holden, Missouri. Acting with Catholic Workers Darla Bradley, Larry Morlan, Ken Rippetoe, and John Volpe, she waited forty minutes for an arrest that was filmed by Mike Wallace of *60 Minutes*. Her action merited her four years and one month in Alderson, one of the longer terms served by a resister. Joe followed her on the Feast of the Transfiguration in 1987, again pouring blood and hammering on a Minuteman silo controlled by Whiteman Air Force Base, in an action with Jerry Ebner. Plowshares prisoner Helen Woodson acted as "coconspirator" from a prison in Minnesota. For this action, Joe was sentenced to thirty months, so he was released before his wife.

I interviewed them separately during the summer of 2005 in their Michigan retirement home, where they live simply and participate in local peace vigils. In 2010, Jean was jailed again, with thirteen other resisters, in an action at the Nuclear Security Administration weapons plant in Oak Ridge, Tennessee. After a time in a privatized jail, she was released and sentenced only to a fine and with time served. For that action, Judge H. Bruce Guyton gave wildly disparate sentences, and some resisters served eight months or more for a simple federal trespass charge.

Jean and Joe Gump in their
Michigan garden, 2006.
(Photo courtesy of Rosalie Riegle.)

Jean and Joe Gump

*"That's part of what you do as a Christian. We take it for
granted that you go to jail."*

Jean: We were involved first in the civil rights movement. Morton Grove [Illinois]
had no black families, and we were concerned about that, so we picketed real
estate companies and stuff like that. Then around 1965—the year Dr. King went to
Montgomery—I was fixing dinner one night and my son said, "Mom, come look at
what's on television."

See, with a big family, sometimes, you have a hard time giving individual
attention, so we'd have "community talks." I'd say to all of them, "At school some
bully will be picking on people, and it's kind of fun to gather around that bully, but
it's absolutely critical that you stand up for the individual who's being picked on. If
we're going to be kind people, we have to do this."

So anyway, on the TV, we saw the civil rights people sprayed with all sorts of
stuff by the police. Joey looked at me. "Well, Mom, what are you going to do about
that?"

What do you mean, what am *I* going to do about that?

"Didn't you tell us we had to stand up against bullies?"

And of course, that *is* what I'd said! There was a bus leaving from [nearby]
Evanston for Montgomery, and Joe said he'd babysit for the weekend, so I hopped
on that bus, and it was quite an experience! Dr. King said at that time that he'd be

coming to Chicago, "the most racist city in the country." So when he came, I got some of the kids—and Joe, certainly—and we went down there to march with him.

We did things like, uh . . . we sent little notes out to everybody in the block saying, "What would you do if a black family were to move into the neighborhood? We're having a meeting at 7:30 on such-and-such a night."

Well, we'd have the whole neighborhood out. They just absolutely knew we were going to move and sell our house. Of course we'd talk instead about the horrors of that kind of discrimination. This was Catholic Family Movement in action. "Observe, judge, act." Yep, that was it. It started out very simply; if somebody got sick, everybody'd bring over meals. Then we got around to politics. We were Republicans when we first came to Morton Grove, and I even had a coffee for a fellow by the name of Don Rumsfeld, the first time he ran for public office. My dad had said, "There's so much corruption in Chicago politics, we really can't afford to be Democrats." But later, we changed.

Ro: Did you protest during the Vietnam War?

Jean: Oh, yes! That was a hard time for me, because both my younger brothers were draft eligible. One went and one went to Canada. Except for my brothers, though, my birth family felt kind of like, "A war is a war."

Ro: Just taking it for granted.

Jean: Yeah. Like we do about going to jail, but on the other side. That's part of what you do as a Christian. We take it for granted that you go to jail.

Ro: How did you move from going to marches to going to jail?

Jean: I guess it was vigiling every Thursday with Eighth Day.[17] We'd go to the building where Morton Thiokol had their corporate offices because they made rocket fuel. On certain days of the year—like on Good Friday—we'd go into the building and kneel in prayer, and they'd call the police.

The cops would tell us to leave or we'd be arrested, and we'd say, "Well, we're not done praying here. You do what you have to do." So they'd arrest us. One day, a cop was carrying me out, and he bent the back of my arm way up on my back.

I said, "Heavenly days! You're hurting me! Do you realize that I have twelve children, officer? How can I take care of them with a broken arm?"

Then he kind of released my arm. "My mother has eleven."

I said, "God bless your mother." And he gently moved me into the police car. There's always a way to reach the officers.

Ro: Now, would you get convicted for these actions or would they just let you go?

Jean: They put us in 27th, a terrible precinct police station, [that day,] but just for a while. I can remember one woman said to us, "What you honkies doing in our jail?" [*Laughingly imitates a dialect.*] We didn't have any trials then. Although we did have a trial when I went out to Motorola in Schaumburg. (They made electronic equipment used by the military.) We blockaded so the employees couldn't get in and the police came, of course, but they didn't do anything at first. So we started singing Irish songs.

When the cop told us to leave, this time I said, "We're not through *singing* here." We started to sing "My Wild Irish Rose" and suddenly *he* broke into song! With a lovely tenor. Then he hauled us off, of course, but we had a lovely time with some of "Chicago's finest."

Ro: When was the first time you went to jail for any length of time?

Jean: Um . . . I really didn't go for a long time, except for the Plowshares.

Ro: No kidding! So you didn't practice?

Jean: No. No. I'd been arrested seven or so times but not spent much time in jail. I'd heard that Helen Woodson had gotten eighteen years for just sitting on a missile silo, and I figured we had to tell people that it's not just Helen, that a *lot* of us are here! So we met with a group from Rock Island that was planning a Plowshares. I thought, "They won't want my kind. I'm a . . . what? A suburban housewife." But it didn't happen that way.

I was there to learn, and I learned a lot. From Phil Berrigan, Elmer Maas, Peter DeMott from Ithaca—lots of good people. They told us it takes a long time to decide because there's a whole lot at stake. "Can you give this up?" "Can you give that up?" We'd started out with maybe ten or twelve people, and it wound up to be five of us.

It was a very interesting experience, because it's not always as harmonious as you would like. There's a lot at stake. My baby was twenty-one years old, so my kids didn't necessarily need me. My mother was elderly, and I thought if she were to pass away when I'm in the prison, would I be able to go to her funeral? I thought about the years in jail. Would I get eighteen years for going into a silo like Helen did? You just want to think of every possible thing. Could I live with this, could I live with that? I decided I probably could, on all counts.

It was very tense. It was the first Plowshares action for all of us, and the planning process went on for a whole year. Of course, you can't tell anybody about it, because that would make them complicit in a crime. So even Joe was left out in the cold, and my kids, of course, were out there with him.

Finally we went onto the silo. It was Good Friday. A beautiful day, and the fellows cut the fence so we could get in, and then we put a beautiful banner on the side of the silo. I was pretty excited and nervous, and we were there such a long time—probably forty-five minutes—before anybody came. I cut the wires on the sensors and painted the sign of the cross on the silo with our blood. Mike Wallace was filming us for *60 Minutes*.

When the authorities finally came, they roared up in an armored vehicle with a machine gun up on the top—the whole kit and caboodle—and it just made me . . . I felt giddy because they looked so silly, barreling down on these nonviolent people.

We had to come out with our hands up. Then they patted the guys down, but they couldn't do that to me and Darla [Bradley] because we were girls and there weren't any women in the [arrest] vehicle. So the army guy said, "Well, take off your coat and keep your hands up in the air."

I did that for a while but then I put them down, and he said, "Now wait a minute, ma'am! You've got to keep your hands up in the air."

"I've got arthritis and it hurts, so I'll just put them down for a while to rest them and then I'll put them up again."

But he said again that I had to keep them up in the air.

I finally just said, "Okay, then shoot me."

He chose not to. He hadn't been told to shoot, so I guess that would have been against the rules. They put me in one of the vehicles, and on the side it said "Peacekeeper." I asked one of the guys if he'd ever read Orwell's *1984*. He said, "No, I didn't, ma'am, and I'm not allowed to talk to you."

I said, "Well, I'll just talk to you, then."

Then they took us to a jail in Kansas City, but we got out without posting bail and I was home for Easter. My son read about our action in the *Chicago Tribune*. One daughter, who was an attorney, was very angry, but if the rest of them had reservations, they didn't say so, and some of them were very supportive and came to the trial. You weren't allowed to sass your mother in those days. And they didn't.

At the trial, we defended ourselves, and I think judges really don't like that because they have to explain things to you. The trial lasted five days and we were found guilty, and then I served an extra week there for contempt of court because I wouldn't talk about the folks who had helped us.

At the sentencing, Darla was the first one, and when I heard him say "eight years," I . . . I was just *so* disgusted! Here she was, you know, just a young person. So I turned my back to look out at the audience, and the judge hollered at me, "You don't turn your back on me, Mrs. Gump!"

I just sat there like a lump. Didn't turn around. You know, if you're not afraid of prison, there isn't anything else they can do to you. My original sentence was eight years, too, but later the judge reduced it to six and I served actually four years and one month, because at that time there was still what they call "time served" and also "good time."

I self-reported to Alderson. Joe came to the gate with me, and there were eight or ten officers waiting for us, including the warden. They wanted to see who I was, I guess, because I'd had a lot of press at that point. I was what they call "a high profile," so people came to interview me, and of course there was always a staff person there with us. One day the three of us saw a prisoner coming into the prison from the warden's garden with two men guards, and they'd been patting her down. I said to the reporter, "This is just one of the perks of men working in the prison. The boys get the chance to pat the ladies down."

Well! The staff person who was with me was just enraged that I should call attention to that. So about a week later, they ordered me to "give a urine."

I refused. "This is ridiculous. I'm not here on drug charges and you know it." Refusing was a number five violation. (You know, if you sass an officer, it's a one or something. If you put a bullet in the warden's head, that's a five.) So I went immediately into solitary confinement.

I was in there for sixty-three days. [*Voice drops.*] It was a . . . a long time. Some of the prisoners got the word out, and the press picked that up, too. In solitary, I could write and read and I had my Bible, but the days got awfully long. I'd do exercises, but the room was so tiny—just about seven feet across—so for some of my yoga stuff, I had to keep my head underneath the bed. And no window. Couldn't see a thing. They let us out for an hour each day, though, and three days a week I'd get a shower.

Ro: What was the worst thing about being in prison?

Jean: The hardest time was when my brother, Tommy, died. He was only forty-one, and he died of Agent Orange that he got in Vietnam. To go to the funeral . . . someone on the staff would have to be with me, and I'd be kept in a jail and just come out for the wake and the funeral. It would cost me over $3,000 for the guard's hotel and our plane tickets, and depending on how I or he behaved, he could have me going in handcuffs to my brother's funeral. I thought my family had enough pain with Tom dying, and they didn't need to have this kind of a show at the funeral. So I didn't go. But the people were so kind, even the staff. I really had a three-day mourning period. Didn't have to work, and I was able to just stay in my room.

When they let me out of prison, we had a big celebration, and I got to see all my new grandchildren. But that was really the hardest time, because I was on probation for *five* years. They took that time very seriously, so I wasn't allowed to leave the state, and I missed some family weddings. Because I wouldn't pay my fine, which was $429.

Finally I wrote to the judge and asked if I'd still owe the money after my five-year probation. A lawyer in Kansas City—Henry Stover, such a sweetheart—wrote to the judge about all the things that had happened since I hadn't paid the fine, missing the weddings and all. "Don't you think she's suffered enough?"

The judge agreed and took away both the probation and the fine. I said, "Thank you, sir. Would you put that in writing, please?" And he did. So that was that.

Ro: Since that long stretch at Alderson, have you done much protesting?

Jean: Well, up in the Upper Peninsula with the Michigan Faith and Resistance group. They took us to this local jail and I was with Ardeth [Platte] and Carol [Gilbert]. We're in this glass room, and they could see our heads over this little wall. Carol had to go to the bathroom. I said, "For heaven's sake! The toilet's sitting right in plain sight!" So we asked for a blanket and held the blanket up around Carol. Carol was going, and Ardeth and I were singing, "Peace is flowing like a river, flowing out of you and me." [*Sings the song.*]

Ro: Jean, what advice would you give mothers who feel called to start risking arrest?

Jean: Well, it's a decision you have to make on your own and with some planning. You need to know the ramifications. Um . . . It's got to be a prayerful decision. You're doing it for your children, your grandchildren. We are all made in the image and likeness of God, and to kill somebody is totally inappropriate, I don't care who it is. There's no country and no individual that we can dare to say God doesn't love. And so, if we are Christians, we have to say no to all killing.

I think gradually everybody will begin to just say no. Because what our government is doing is criminal. Against international law. Even to think of using a nuclear weapon—at that time, I think they called it "MAD"—Mutually Assured Destruction. And it *is* mad!

I think of people going into the service. They could die. They *do* die! They don't go into the service thinking they *will* die, but they certainly have to go with the idea that they *could*. If we peace people really wanted peace enough, we'd all take the same kind of risk.

Joe: We did things together at first, especially during the civil rights days, but later I backed off because I figured somebody had to support the family. But after her Plowshares trial . . . I was close to retirement age then, and it was a different story. I'm someone who asks questions and will satisfy my own sense of understanding before I believe anything that's told to me. If I hear something said by the government that's blatantly false, I will speak out against it. I will resist it, and I will suffer the consequences. So that's what I did.

[On August 5, 1987, at 5:15 p.m., corresponding to the exact moment when the United States dropped the first atomic bomb on Hiroshima in 1945, Joe and Jerry Ebner entered a Minuteman missile silo site controlled by Whiteman Air Force Base in Missouri.[18] They locked themselves in the fenced-in area with a Kryptonite bicycle lock, poured blood, took a sledgehammer to the tracks used to open the silo lid, cut electric wires with a bolt cutter, hung disarmament banners, and sang and prayed while waiting for the arrest. They named themselves the "Transfiguration Plowshares" to commemorate the Christian feast celebrated on August 6 that recalls the revelation of Christ to his disciples.]

Joe: I remember when we poured our blood on that silo cover, just like Jean did. It fried right off because it was so hot. We even used the same banners and bolt cutters as their action. Somehow they disappeared after our trial, though, which was too bad. We wanted to start a Plowshares museum with 'em. [*Chuckles.*] See, we wanted to carry on the momentum, so we felt it was important to repeat exactly what Jean had done and hopefully before the same judge.

He very quickly found out I was Jean's husband, though, and came out with a wild statement in the newspaper. In response, I wrote a letter saying he should recuse himself because he was obviously prejudiced, and then we got a different judge who was much better. We had the same two felony indictments as the other folks, but had a more open trial. Were able to show a video of the action and Jerry even got to sing one of his songs to the jury. I got a shorter sentence than Jean— only thirty months—so I was out before she was.

First, I went to Oxford Camp, in Wisconsin, but I refused to do some work there—build a horseshoe pit for the guards' country club. My rule was simple: If it was for the benefit of the guys, I'd do it. If it was to benefit the administration in any way, I wouldn't. For that refusal, I was immediately put in solitary in the [maximum security] prison next to the camp, and a month later, they shipped me up to Sandstone.

Jerry [Ebner] and Father Carl Kabat were at Sandstone, and they welcomed me with a party. In fact, we had lots of parties. We called ourselves "KEG Caterers"— Kabat, Ebner, and Gump. "We will do your going-away parties or your birthday party!" Carl achieved nacho fame with a bucket of hot water. Take a plastic bag, put all the ingredients in it, and dunk it in hot water to melt it. We'd leave the lunchroom with our pockets stuffed with stuff—cheese in coffee cups, things like that. (I guess we *were* criminals!) You could get caught, but Carl would stash the contraband in the bottom of his laundry bag. No one'd be willing to go through that laundry bag to find anything! I'd say to him, "Carl! Remember we're gonna eat that!"

The staff gave us porterhouse steaks one Fourth of July. How rough was that? (Conditions today, I understand, are quite a bit different.) And later we'd have great visiting days, because Father Jerry Zawada and Sam Day were there for the Missouri Peace Planters action, so we'd have big get-togethers in the visiting room.[19] The guards didn't really approve, but they never interfered too much.

The only time I remember having any problem was when several of our support people from Kansas City planned to visit and Jean Huebner was put on my visiting list. My counselor told me she couldn't be on without my wife's written permission because I was married, and she wasn't. So Jean had to write the letter. It was a scream! One thing she said was, "You people worry so much about destroying marriages, but you do it regularly."[20]

When I got out, I was at Alderson most of the time. I could see Jean all day, at any time, five days a week. We'd play Russian Bank, and even bridge, especially when some of our kids came down.

You know, we were in a unique position to do what we did. Our children were raised, so that was no problem. Jean didn't know what my reaction to her action would be, so there was a little bit of a risk there, but for all of our married life, I've had a great respect for her thinking and for what she has done. Great respect.

At twenty-two, Darla Bradley was the youngest member of the Silo Plowshares. She was sentenced to eight years plus five years probation and $1,680 restitution. I interviewed Darla on July 5, 1989, when I was preparing to write *Voices from the Catholic Worker*.[21] In 2007, when I was interviewing for the project on war resisters, I contacted her, and she e-mailed a thoughtful postscript. This segment includes selections from both texts.

Darla Bradley

> *"The more intellectual type would see just a right choice; I saw two wrongs, a wrong choice of staying in with all the pain and suffering or the wrong choice of getting out and violating both my conscience and the conscience of the community."*

I'd heard about Plowshares actions in college, and they appealed to me because they concretely do what you want to have happen—disarmament. Oh, there were so many factors in deciding to do it! I don't think you can make a decision like that from just one thing. Part of it was the idea of defining the law by a higher standard than our government. Part of it was making a concrete life choice to stand for peace. It was also a response on behalf of the homeless women I worked with at Ruth's Shelter [in Chicago]. I wanted to show the disconnect between the care and protection we give to weapons and the care we give to people.

Not going to jail right away was hard, though, because we knew the long sentence was hanging over us. We had trouble getting along in community because of all the pressure and . . . and it was just really hard. Definitely the hardest time I've ever had in my life. Like, how many times do you say goodbye to somebody?

My sister was pretty bad. Said that I was killing my parents. She was . . . she was bad. She lived near Fort Worth Women's Prison. It was like, "Oh, God! Anywhere but

Fort Worth!" And then, of course, that's where I was sent. She would visit a lot, and it was hard at first because we weren't getting along at all, but she's very loyal to the family, so we kind of developed a relationship out of that, I guess.

I didn't like visits at all. They were weird, some sort of twilight zone between . . . In prison, I felt very separated from the outside world. There's an inside world and then the world out there. When you go into the visiting room, it's in between.

Ro: What else was bad about being in prison?

Darla: Probably feeling powerless was what got to me most. Realizing that the system is so huge and awful. I'd always known the system from a position of no power, but I still felt I controlled my own life, you know. Even things you'd think of as not important would really get to me, and that's when I realized I wouldn't hold up to torture. I'd be a mess in no time.

I think they try to break down everyone at some point or another, usually right when you get in. New people tend to get a lot of extra duty to make sure they realize who's in charge. Then when people are leaving, they kind of like to give you a shot or harass you.

Ro: What's a shot?

Darla: An incident report. You've done something wrong and you might get days [added to your sentence]. Parole boards were horrible. Every three months the whole prison would go into depression. You have such high expectations. Even if everybody talks like they don't believe it, they really get all built up for getting out and then end up being depressed when they don't.

It was kind of like when I got sentenced. Even though I knew intellectually [that] I'd get a lot of time, I wasn't ready for it. And the same thing with the parole board. It's usually not good news, at least the first time.

[Darla was granted parole in June 1987 after her sentence had been reduced to one year and she agreed to pay restitution.]

Darla: I had a real hard time when I first got out. First, I was feeling guilty because I'd agreed to all the things. Violated what I thought were absolute principles. I'd think, "Jean [Gump] would never do this." It was hard to come to terms with what I decided, but I finally realized that whether it was right or wrong didn't really matter because it was done.

Ro: Looking back on the whole thing after a couple of years, would you do it again?

Darla: Oh, I hate that question! I knew it was going to come.

Ro: Well, would you? After you pay the money back, for instance?[22]

Darla: I . . . I . . . It's still a big question. Not in Missouri, that's for sure. People have been getting up to two years just for trespassing. I like Plowshares actions, like the idea of disarming the weapon, like everything about them, but I . . . I haven't decided whether the price is too high and whether you can do just as much good in another place or not. That debate inside of me will probably go on for a long time.

I still believe in doing resistance. On a lot of levels, Plowshares are very . . . you're choosing to follow your conscience and what you believe in over [your relationships]. When I decided to get out of jail, I had to call a lot of things into play to analyze everything. On the one level, there were the effects of violating my conscience and also the conscience of the resistance community to a degree. Because whether you choose to resist the state or cooperate with it, it has some sort of ripple effect.

But in my own life—the idea of eight years with no parole, when you're twenty-three or twenty-four . . . to be thirty when I get out! That blew my mind! Then all the mixed feelings about what happened after the action and how that flavored the action and the bad human relationships that developed. Maybe someone who comes from a more ideological perspective can separate these things better than I do. The more intellectual type would see just a right choice; I saw two wrongs, a wrong choice of staying in with all the pain and suffering or the wrong choice of getting out and violating both my conscience and the conscience of the community. I think, though, that even though it was a hard choice, it was the right choice for me.

[Darla and I corresponded via e-mail in August 2007, and her answer to my direct question is below.]

Darla: I would not do it again. I think Plowshares actions are very misunderstood as a symbol. When I was young I thought it was straightforward, the idea of actually pounding swords into plowshares in a symbolic way. However, since spending time with others in the peace community, I find it's pretty much perceived as a bit of a borderline action. Not everyone sees the dismantling aspect the same way as those who do it.

Today, I would only be willing to face such an extreme consequence—eight years in prison—for actions that are directly saving a life. Or perhaps to aid our [undocumented] brothers and sisters who live in such fear of deportation. I think the government is doing a good job of keeping the level of deportations out of the media, so building awareness of their plight is important to me.

I also believe that if we really want to have an impact, we have to be better at communicating what we do to the indifferent majority. We have to build human connections. We have to help people see the faces of those who are suffering and not isolate ourselves.

When I made the decision to get out, I truly felt it betrayed everything, and it took me many, many years to feel okay about it. I felt like a fake and I couldn't face [the other people in the group]. Our split decision on the restitution was the end of our connection, I guess.

I've spent many years struggling with the inconsistencies that can exist between the personal and the prophetic. To me compassion is the center, but for many in the peace movement, it seems the ideological issues are at the center. Our community became a mini-example of how difficult peacemaking is, and I quit believing that what we were doing meant anything because the interpersonal conflict was so intense. I became disillusioned and was then unprepared to be strong in prison.

You know, those six months we were out before we went to prison were worse than being in jail. I realized for the first time that being an activist doesn't make a person a peacemaker. Since that time I have been on more of an internal journey of peacemaking, and I don't know if that can lead back to activism.

I also believe that there are seasons in life. Currently I am in the season of nurturing my kids. I also participate in justice work by giving to my husband's family who live in poverty in Guatemala, assisting immigrants to navigate this complicated society, and participating in smaller ways in the struggle for peace and justice. As I have matured, I have found that compromise is part of my life and that it's okay. I can now be more forgiving of my younger self who chose a path of compromise.

I believe the most important aspect of my faith is compassion. This is what Jesus exhibited most clearly in his life. So I continue down a path that is filled with compromise and compassion. Perhaps when I reach the end of this life, some truth will be revealed to me. Until then, I must do the best I can to be faithful to our calling to love our neighbor as ourselves.

An Interlude: Michele Naar-Obed and Joe Gump on the Use of Blood

Michele: Blood brings home the bloody nature of war. Most people who fight in wars drop bombs from the air, and they don't see the blood, they don't hear the screams, they don't feel the violence. It's like a video game to them. So we use blood to make that bloodshed real.

Another aspect is that it's a small and symbolic gesture of our willingness to pour out our own blood so that others' blood may not have to be shed. And it's following the example that Jesus gave us in the Eucharist when He gave His body and blood.

Sister Carol Gilbert, OP, arrested after throwing her blood on the wall at the Pentagon, 1997. (Photo courtesy of Joe Gump.)

When we receive that Eucharist, they say, "This is the blood of Christ, the blood that was shed for you so that sins may be forgiven." We sing the song "Given for Our Freedom." And say we do this "in remembrance of Him." That means that we need to be willing to shed our own blood, to lay down our own lives. The ultimate example would be to have your life taken in order to save another, and this giving up of a few vials of blood is nowhere near that, but it's a symbol and a gesture.

Joe: Pouring blood turns many people off, at least initially. I remember once we were out with Ardeth [Platte] and Carol [Gilbert] at the Pentagon and they threw blood up on the side of the building. I can still see that blood coming down the walls. And then, of course, the big concern with all the security guys is whether the blood is contaminated.

[The courts seem to have a particular aversion to calling it blood, using a euphemism such as "a red substance," even after tests show it's the resister's own blood, usually drawn the night before the action by friends trained in medical procedures. Blood was used first in the 1967 Baltimore Selective Service raid. Phil Berrigan wrote in his "Letter from a Baltimore Jail," "You showed an odd fascination with blood, my friends. You worried the point as a puppy worries a rubber bone, with as much profit."[23] But as a Pentagon security officer once told Liz McAlister, "It really makes its point."[24]]

Father John Dear is a Jesuit who has authored and edited over twenty-five books, writes a weekly column for *National Catholic Reporter*, and is in demand as a retreat leader and speaker, all the while continuing his life of protest. Like other priests, he sometimes has conflicts with the superiors in his community. In this interview, he speaks frankly about the difficulties he faced while imprisoned for a Plowshares action in 1993.

Father John Dear, SJ

"I think there's an inverse proportionality. The more you try to make a difference and be successful and bring the dramatic change yourself, the less happens. And the more you let go and go forward into the darkness and give up your life for peace and justice, like the great martyrs did, like Dan and Phil did with their Plowshares actions, the more happens."

I entered the Jesuit Order [in 1982], and from the beginning, I wanted to follow Jesus by crossing the line and engaging in nonviolent civil disobedience. When I said that to my novice master, he said, "You do that and you're dismissed immedi-

Father John Dear, SJ, arrested at the White House, July 2000.
(Photo courtesy of Father John Quinn, SJ.)

ately." But in the end, I did. I went to the Pentagon and got arrested. I thought God wanted me both to be a Jesuit and to work publicly for peace and justice, so I said, "It's your problem, God. You resolve it." Well, the novice master dismissed me, but the provincial overruled him. "I'll let him stay in, but he's never to tell this story to anyone ever again."

It's been like that ever since. They've moved for dismissal against me six or seven times, simply because of some public act of organizing against war. Dan Berrigan's my great friend and mentor, and I can't complain at all, because he's been through so many terrible things and he's just as committed to peace as ever.

[John served as director of the Fellowship of Reconciliation for several years and after September 11 became involved as a chaplain at Ground Zero.]

John: And then the Church abuse scandal broke in Boston, and I wrote a piece saying that the US bishops' support of the bombing of children in Afghanistan is child abuse. This didn't go over well. The New York provincial called me in. "Who do you think you are? What do you know about peace?"

I should have said, "I don't know anything about peace. Help me! I want to work for peace and justice." Instead I didn't say a word, and he ordered me immediately out of New York. I decided on New Mexico. It's the bleakest place in the country, and I was a pastor of four parishes and five missions covering over a hundred and fifty miles. A circuit rider, that's what I was. I finally stepped down from the four parishes, though. I had gone there to have one little parish, so I could travel and speak and write, but they're so desperate for priests that the archbishop gave me this huge operation, which had lovely people and no money. I had many invitations to speak around the country, and it just became too much. I still get a lot of speaking invitations, and I'm always writing, so now writing and traveling and protesting are my full-time jobs.

I started Pax Christi New Mexico, and we've been having annual protests at Los Alamos. In my first year, the archbishop forbade me to pray publicly for peace at Los Alamos. This is while the pope was blasting the US against the war on Iraq. Our Pax Christi group went there for the first time, and the media showed up and asked for me, and the Pax Christi group said I was banned from praying for peace, so the headline in the state paper the next day was "Archbishop forbids priest to pray for peace." After that, I've been going [to the Los Alamos protests].

Ro: You've been arrested, what? About seventy-five times?

John: Something like that, yeah.

Ro: What's the longest time you've ever served?

Pax Christi Spirit of Life Plowshares, 1993. (Photo courtesy of Bruce Friedrich.)

John: Well, I faced twenty years in prison for a Plowshares action with Philip Berrigan, Lynn Fredriksson, and Bruce Friedrich on December 7, 1993 [at Seymour Johnson Air Force Base] in my home state of North Carolina. We thought we'd get four to five years, given the judge and the climate in that state. Phil said at the time it was the most horrific courtroom experience he'd ever witnessed, and he'd seen hundreds of trials. But Judge [Terrence W.] Boyle was Catholic. I was a brand-new, newly ordained Catholic priest, and my guess is that Judge Boyle felt guilty. So I got released with time served—about eight months and then nine months under house arrest—because I was a new priest. Phil got out as a former priest, but Bruce and Lynn did a further year in prison and we'd all done the same thing.

Ro: Would you do another Plowshares? Or is prison the best place for you to be?

John: The best place for me to be is where the God of peace wants me to be.

Ro: How do you tell?

John: That's the thing. And that's the heart of Ignatian spirituality. The best part about the Jesuits was St. Ignatius, who was way ahead of his time. He said, "I want people who are going to be on the forefront for the revolution of the Gospel of peace and justice. I want them to live like Jesus and do what He wants."

So the real question is, "Where is that place, and how do you discern it?" That's what prayer and reflection are about and what community is about. I've tried a lot of different things. I've given thousands of speeches and press conferences, published twenty books [as of the time of the interview], and traveled the world and met everybody.

Father Richard McSorley was very upset with me when I was in jail. He said I needed to be out there, speaking against war, and not in prison. But my take is that there's an inverse proportionality. The more you try to make a difference and be successful and bring the dramatic change yourself, the less happens. And the more you let go and go forward into the darkness and give up your life for peace and justice, like the great martyrs did, as Dan and Phil did with their Plowshares actions, the more happens.

I've done all those different actions and organized hundreds of demonstrations and been arrested in so many places, and knew the Jesuits who were killed in El Salvador and have been close friends to Philip and Daniel Berrigan for many years. I always knew that I wanted to do what they had done, because they were my teachers as well as my friends. So I knew I was going to do a Plowshares action, and I'd been preparing for it for years during my annual Jesuit retreat.

When I was in that tiny county jail cell with Phil, we never went outdoors for eight months. It was really horrible. But we were inundated with mail! I got five thousand letters in five months. I count it as the most difficult experience of my life and, at the same time, the holiest experience of my life, the most profoundly spiritual experience, because it was like God was right there with us. And the greatest mystery.

This is what the cross means, I think—nonviolent resistance to the structures of war. You have to go up to Jerusalem, like Jesus, turn over the tables of the war-making culture, and suffer the consequences. If you do that, there are profound blessings. So maybe jail *is* the best place for me, but it's a matter of discernment and prayer and talking with my friends and trying to decide what God wants me to do.

I have lots of communities. I've traveled so much now that I have friends in the peace and justice movement everywhere in the United States. I've become friends with so many of our heroes. My core community is the West Side Jesuit Community in New York, but across the country—in the churches, in the Jesuits, in the peace movement—they're all my community. The main thing is to have people you can pray with, and walk with, and laugh and cry with.

Ro: No wonder you got so much mail in jail. Can you talk about your prison experience?

John: We were in rural North Carolina county jails, which are as bad as they come in the United States. The Robeson County Jail, for instance, was built for seventy-five, but it had four hundred prisoners, and the four of us were the only white ones there, of course.

We took the civil disobedience into the courtroom and disrupted the first trial, so a mistrial was declared, and we went back to the county jails for another four months. The second time, we had four separate trials. Now, most people are in a county jail for a short time and then they go to a prison camp. We never did that. I don't know anybody else in the movement who had an experience like Phil and I did.

For the first two weeks after our arrest, we were separated, too, in this big horrible county jail. I didn't think I'd see Phil and Bruce again for twenty years, and it was a terrible experience for me. I thought I was used to jail, but this was something new. People were knocking each other unconscious, and I was sitting in the middle of it. Very scary. I wrote to the warden and asked if our group could be put together, and he agreed, so just before Christmas I was brought in with Phil.

Then we were transferred to the Edenton County Jail, where we spent the seven months. That was like Mayberry RFD. Built for four people and it had twenty-eight. One big room, and the men were sleeping on the floor, because there were only two little private cells. Now, the warden was worried about us, because we were attracting attention. Phil was a celebrity, and Martin Sheen was coming to see us, and there was so much press. _20/20_ came down to do a show on us. So [the warden] put Phil and me in our own private cell and kept us separate, and Bruce was in the cell next door and could come in and spend the day with us.

It was like he locked Phil and me in a bathroom together for seven months. Now, at first, I was happy about that, but it became very hard. We never went outdoors, never went outside, and I . . . it got to me. I was very, very hurt.

The walls were caving in. Every day got worse, and there was no getting out. When we had visitors, I'd be brought out in chains for a ten-minute visit, maybe once a week. That's my impression; I wrote all about it in the book.[25]

Phil said it was the worst experience he'd ever been in, and he'd been in a lot of jails. He was kind of an old ex-con. Unflappable. Used to the routine. But I'm a Jesuit, and I guess you could say we're high maintenance. I was trained to have quiet time and private time—a couple of hours of private reflection every day.

Now, I know a lot of folks would say that was a great blessing, to be with Phil, and it was, but it was also very hard. We got on each other's nerves. To be locked in a tiny room is . . . It's . . . It's inhuman. We suffered. I'll tell you what we did, though. Phil was a big one for getting up early and being monastic, so we were up at five or six o'clock. Bruce would come in and we'd start our little Bible study. We would read three or four verses of the Gospel and talk for three hours. I learned more about scripture than in my four years of theology school.

At the end of this sharing, we got a piece of Wonder Bread. And once a week we got a little plastic cup with grape juice in it, which we hid and fermented over time into something like wine. We'd break the Wonder Bread and pass the cup and have Eucharist. It was like Jesus was right there, a powerful experience of God and grace. But hard, too, you know, because we were so lonely and tired.

After Eucharist, the mail would come, and each of us got sixty or so letters every day, and we'd have an hour to go through the mail, which was our salvation. And then lunch and a brief little prayer afterwards, and then—now, I was big on this—we had a one-hour timed writing session. Phil was rolling his eyes at first, but in the end he loved it, because we churned out many, many articles between the two of us. No talking, just writing.

We wrote an article a week. And our friends and Dan got them published all over. Then Phil would sleep from two to six, and I had a quiet afternoon. Then dinner would come, and afterwards sometimes they'd let us go out in the hallway to watch the TV. And every single night after dinner, Phil wrote a letter to Liz.

One day, we were sitting around, and I said, "Phil, I want you to tell me your entire life story. We've got nothing but time." So Phil talked to us for one week. Told us everything. That was a great, great experience. He had a hard time with me, though, I'm sure; I mean, it was not easy for Phil to be with me, for a variety of reasons. We both suffered and tried to remain nonviolent, but our nerves were shot.

I know that if I did another Plowshares, I'd get three years. And I don't know if I can do it. It was very hard on my family, first of all. They were scared when my brother called them and said I was facing all these years in prison. They came to see me weekly. Drove six hours and had ten minutes.

Ro: Your mother would see you in chains.

John: Yes, she's a PhD professor at Johns Hopkins and it was very, very hard on her. My provincial called her and said, "We're so proud of him; he's just like St. Ignatius." So it was confusing. Nowadays, though, she talks to my Irish relatives in New York, and she'll say, very straight-faced, "Well, during the Troubles . . ." But you know, they've learned a lot, too, and they've now become friends with Liz McAlister, and they've met everybody from Bishop Tom Gumbleton to Martin Sheen. So it's opening up their lives, and I think they're probably proud of me. But it was hard. The papers said I was the ringleader of this movement of terrorists.

Ro: Amazing! John, why do you do it?

John: Because I want to follow Jesus, who was civilly disobedient, who engaged in criminal activity through active nonviolence. Jesus was arrested, jailed, and tortured. He went a specific way, and He was executed. Now, they haven't executed me, and they probably won't. But, wow! They sure will arrest you and imprison you. And you can suffer. So for me, the best thing about going to jail is feeling like you're sharing in the story of Jesus.

Gandhi called nonviolence "conscious suffering," and he also said Jesus was the most active nonviolent resister in the history of the world. The Holy Spirit is going to work through us and change many people's hearts. Through our suffering love, the Spirit will touch and melt other hardened hearts.

The only way I survive, in jail and out—and it's the only way Phil and the other Plowshares people have survived—is to spend serious quality time, each day, in silent contemplative prayer. Ultimately it's not a duty, not an obligation. We're in love. We've been touched by Someone who loves us, so we want to spend time with the God of love and peace.

But you also need a community of friends, and through my crazy life, I've met some of the greatest peacemakers in the world. Maybe all of them, actually. I know them and they keep encouraging me. And, you know, my family and my friends try to help me. They put me in my place and care for me and try to keep me centered.

It's not brain surgery. We're just being human here. I saw this in the refugee camp in El Salvador, when I lived there in '85. There were survivors who'd lost all their loved ones, yet they were taking care of each other, with more deep faith and joy than I've ever witnessed since. How did they do it? Because they were compassionate and concerned with one another. *And* very devoted to God.

More and more of us are learning to do that in North America. I actually don't spend a lot of time studying the bad news, the newspapers and all, because it's too horrible, but I'm always studying the Gospel, and the lives of Dorothy Day, Gandhi, Dr. King, and the great peacemakers. Mahatma Gandhi laughed! He was lots of fun to be with. He was way beyond anger and burnout. I want to be like that. I want to live life to the fullest while I'm resisting death.

On June 2, 1987, after five years of activism around the country, Katya Komisaruk walked alone through an unlocked gate and entered a satellite control facility named "NAVSTAR" at Vandenberg Air Force Base in Santa Barbara County, California.[26] She used a hammer, crowbar and cordless electric drill to damage an IBM mainframe computer and a satellite dish on top of the building. On the walls, she spray-painted "Nuremberg" and "International Law" and taped statements on disarmament. She left undetected and turned herself in later that morning. She was charged with sabotage as well as destruction of government property. After doing her time, she went to Harvard Law School and became a member of the California bar.

Katya Komisaruk

"I'd gotten the idea that people who did Plowshares actions were Bodhisattva-types, so evolved and calm that deprivation and distress just sort of flowed by them. [Sister] Pat corrected me on that. People who do Plowshares actions necessarily have a faith that supports and insulates them, but she taught me that really, anybody could do a Plowshares action."

I didn't even know the term "direct action," but I saw this little poster about a demonstration down at Livermore.[27] In my mind I had mental images of a riot—the sort of things I'd seen on TV during the Free Speech Movement—tear gas and helicopters and dogs. It sounded scary, but it was time to do something.

The poster also said that you had to go to a nonviolence training, which I thought was probably a lot of religious mumbo-jumbo that I had no interest in, so I was going to pass that up. Then it hit me that there was no public transportation to Livermore because it's way the heck out in Contra Costa, so I actually went to the nonviolence training to get a ride to the riot.

It was a great training! At least sixty people, with two very good facilitators, and it lasted eight hours. When they asked if people were going to risk arrest or just support, I found myself saying I was getting arrested. So I was guided into an affinity group, and a month or so later I got arrested, along with 1,400 other people. This was in June of 1982. The preceding week, 1,800 people had been arrested at the five embassies of the then-nuclear nations in New York City.

Ro: What happened at your first arrest?

Katya: The usual. We negotiated, using solidarity tactics, and got all the charges dropped to infractions—to jaywalking, basically. They tried to give heavier charges to some people and that was negotiated against, again using solidarity tactics. A great lesson for me in all sorts of things—the power of nonviolence and of solidarity tactics, plus the exhilaration of doing direct action.

And also the sexism in the movement! The women were detained in a gym of some sort on military property, and it came to light that there might be toxic contaminants there, so the men decided that the women needed to be released immediately because "their eggs were at risk." The women said, "Actually, we're planning to make up our own minds about our eggs."

I got arrested another thirty times between then and actually doing a Plowshares action. Went all over the country, in both large and small actions. My original affinity group was called "Noah's Ark." Then there was a really nice affinity group called "BAG LADIES," which was "Big Affinity Group with Lots of Activists Denying the Impending End of Society." Somewhere in all of this, I finished an MBA and got a job with the Graduate Theological Union [GTU]. My undergraduate degree is in classics. I thought about sticking with that and specializing in medieval Latin, but the prospects for employment were dim.

> [It was while Katya was at GTU, directing a strategic planning project, that she heard about Sister Pat Mahoney, who was in prison for protesting at the Rocky Flats nuclear weapons plant.]

Katya: I got Sister Pat's address and we started a correspondence. I'd gotten the idea that people who did Plowshares actions were Bodhisattva-types, so evolved and calm that deprivation and distress just sort of flowed by them. Pat corrected me on that. People who do Plowshares actions necessarily have a faith that supports and insulates them, but she taught me that really, *anybody* could do a Plowshares action.

And of course the moment that popped into my head, I started thinking along those lines. Another thing I learned from her was that you don't need to have all the answers to your spiritual or ethical questions before you do a Plowshares action, but it's good to have the questions at least lined up. So I thought of a lot of questions I wanted to answer and made a nice reading list. Got that all together before I did the action, so I'd have things to do while I was in prison.

Other Plowshares activists said the right way to do this was to get in a group and spend about a year having meetings, going on retreats, engaging in those processes of reflection and discernment.

"No, I think not. I've attended too many meetings already in my short political career." So I decided to do a Plowshares action alone in order to avoid more meetings. Which turned out also to be a bit of a misconception, because after the action, I ended up having *lots* of meetings.

I'd originally planned to do it pretty low profile, thinking of it as just a personal dialogue between me and the state. I was just going to go before the judge and speak truth to power and see what happened. I mean, I expected the usual to happen, but I wasn't planning a lot of publicity.

Well, three days after I was arrested, when I was sitting in the San Francisco Jail, a deputation of friends came to me. They said, "Looks like you're going to prison. To get the most bang for your buck, you should get out and do a lot of public speaking until you're sentenced." So, although I hadn't planned to do this, at this point I'd been eating San Francisco Jail food for three days, so getting out seemed a really good idea. They came up with $15,000 and bailed me out. I got wonderful guidance and turned out to be reasonably mediagenic, so [there were] lots of press and speaking engagements.

Ro: When did you name your action?

Katya: Somewhere in the planning stage. I learned about the White Rose group when I was thirteen and studying German.[28] I remember thinking I hadn't translated it right because at the end these people were executed for distributing leaflets. Growing up as a Jew, I've always been very conscious of the Holocaust. It disturbs me, as it disturbs most people, to think that an entire nation could let its neighbors and friends and business associates be disappeared and executed. You wonder why people didn't sit on the train tracks, didn't do *something*! What I perceived was that the people's news was very distorted. They were very heavily propagandized and very xenophobic, and by the time they *did* realize how bad things were, it was too dangerous to act. The risk got too high.

What was important, though, was to know that there were people who *did* act, even though they knew they were risking their lives and probably wouldn't stop Hitler.

When I first became politicized in 1982, it took probably a year before I realized how very far in the wrong—how evil—the United States has been internationally. It finally became clear to me that people doing Plowshares actions were very similarly situated to the White Rose group—doing something as a marker to people in subsequent generations. For me, the White Rose group was in some way redemptive for the German nation as a whole, that there was a vestigial humanity there. It seems to me that in some ways the Plowshares actions do that for our generation. That sounds really high-falutin'. I don't mean to say that the Plowshares activists are taking anywhere near the risk that the White Rose group did, but symbolic actions can have a real and lasting effect.

Ro: The potential is always there, though, because when you're cutting the wire or hammering in a lethal force zone, the military is authorized to shoot to kill.

Katya: One of the Plowshares activists so advised me, before my action. Mind you, I did the action alone, but naturally I sought the advice and consent of the elders, so to speak. I went to Jonah House and had the traditional walk around the block with Phil, and he thought I should work with a group and go on a lot of retreats. But I didn't. I'm part of the community and receive support from it and try to give support back. I imagine some people don't want to be lumped with the Roman Catholics, but considering the scripture they're using is from my part of the Bible anyway . . .

Another person who was a big influence on me, aside from Sister Pat, was Jean Holladay.[29] She reminded me that it was important to be safe—that just because *we* know we're nonviolent doesn't mean the soldiers do, and that it would not enhance the impact of my Plowshares action if I got myself shot. She suggested that I wear hippie clothes or put flowers in my hair or do something to indicate that I wasn't a terrorist. So I left a big bouquet of red, white, and blue flowers at the front gate, and a box of cookies and a poem.

Ro: Did you have much contact with the soldiers when they were arresting you?

Katya: Well, mind you, the soldiers never did arrest me. I walked out. Spent the whole night trashing this computer installation and a big satellite dish. Then it just seemed sort of undignified to wait there. Most of the Plowshares people simply kneel and pray until the authorities come, but I couldn't really swallow that notion, so I walked out to the edge of the property, got several rides, and turned up in San Francisco.

"Hi, I'm a fugitive. What's for breakfast?" I was really hungry by then, and I wanted a shower. So my friends helped me. They wrote a press release and distributed it, and then I held a press conference at the Federal Building. The FBI showed up partway through and eventually got it together to arrest me.

Ro: How did you manage your trial?

Katya: I was represented by Lennie Weinglass.[30] He's one of my role models, a really amazing lawyer, and a great and compassionate person. But the trial was a bit of a nightmare. It lasted a week and the judge forbade any mention of anything even remotely relevant. The day before the trial started, I got the laundry list of forbidden words like "first strike," "nuclear weapon," "Geneva Convention"—a big list of bad words. It was even forbidden to refer to children.

Because we weren't able to give any evidence of intent, in the jury's eyes it must have seemed like mindless vandalism. They submitted the original press release with half of it blanked out, and that was entered into evidence and termed my confession. And of course the stuff they took out of the press release were the reasons I did it and the international law. Everything was all out of context. At the end, I was sentenced to five years.

Ro: How did you feel when you heard the verdict?

Katya: Oh, a bit wobbly, I suppose. My friends and legal team were watching, so I sure wasn't going to crumple in public. I didn't need to crumple that much in private, either. I'd looked at the Plowshares sentences before mine and they'd ranged from six months suspended to [eighteen] years for Helen Woodson; on average, people got about two years, so . . .

I spent the first forty days and forty nights in the LA County Jail for Women, which is a ghastly place. Then I went to a medium security institution in Spokane, Washington, called Geiger Corrections Center.

Ro: Did you have any trouble in the LA jail, being such a little bit of a thing?

Katya: Not really. Well, I did one time, and only one time. I'd once spent an entire day thinking and writing about my conception of nonviolence. What it entailed and whether it was a good idea. I'm not a pacifist, and like many people, I came to the conclusion that it would be reasonable, under certain circumstances, for me to use violence to defend myself or the people I'm connected to. Of course, "the people I'm connected to" gets bigger, the more you think about it; it's not just your immediate family and friends. It's your community and . . . In any case, I practice martial arts and . . . On exactly one occasion in jail, I had to fight to defend myself and I did so successfully.

Everyone was impressed. I guess they thought that my stature and my mode of speech and the fact that I'm an activist protester . . . My nickname in prison was "Snow White," probably because I have dark hair and a prissy voice and they thought I was idealistic.

So on one occasion I was challenged and had to fight back. I won, and after that everyone was *so* nice to me and so proud of me. Gave me candy and did my hair, and . . . Because they all thought it was funny that I could fight at all. And having done so once, I never had to again.

I didn't tell many of my activist friends about it, though, because some of them would say that there's always another option, always something else that I could have done. And, in fact, I could have backed down when I was challenged, but then I would have been the pecking chicken for all the other prisoners. One of the lessons we learn from the Holocaust is that there are moments when fighting back is particularly important. Discerning that moment can be very tricky, but one has to acknowledge that they exist. I still wrestle with the whole thing, but I'm pretty comfortable about it now.

Ro: Even Gandhi said it's better to fight back than to do nothing at all.

Katya: And that you should choose to be nonviolent from a position of strength. If you're behaving nonviolently because you are weak and afraid and passive, it doesn't work.

Ro: Was it a sexual challenge?

Katya: Oh, no. That's a myth, at least on the women's side. I've written about that, and it's on my website [*www.lawcollective.org*]. I've spent time in over a dozen jails, and in no place did I ever hear about, let alone see, women being sexually exploited by other prisoners. I've occasionally seen women get into fights with one another, but this B-movie myth of women raping each other is just that, a myth. In every place I've done time, I've seen male correctional officers screwing women prisoners. Once in the Rhode Island State Penitentiary, I wasn't there thirty minutes before a cop propositioned me.

Did you know I once did an action inside the LA County Jail? Not while I was waiting to go off to Spokane from there, but on a previous occasion. I hung up a banner. It's pretty hard to make a banner in jail. I used a little bedsheet and those little golf pencils they give you to write with. Spent all one evening writing in black letters: "Every human being deserves to be treated with respect." A really puerile phrase, and that's the embarrassing part of the story, but I'd just read the Viking Modern Masters edition of *Gandhi*, and was full of lofty thoughts of that nature.

We were in this cell block with twelve cells, and then there was a walkway and then there were some more bars that went like two stories up. So I climbed up these outer bars and hung up my banner.

Ro: Like on the second story?

Katya Komisaruk at the launch of her book, *Beat the Heat*, 2003. (Photo courtesy of Jeff Foss.)

Katya: Kind of like that. Then there was another walkway beyond that. It took the guards a while to notice it, and they were kind of aghast. They told the first person they saw to go up and take it down, and she said, "Oh, I can't climb way up there!"

Anyway, the other prisoners all kept quiet about it. I'd told them I'd take responsibility for it eventually. When the guards threatened to lock everybody down—no showers, no mail, no commissary—I told them I did it.

They said, "Take it down."

"No, it's the truth. It should be up." So they took me off to the hole. It was very scary. My hands were shaking, so I stuck them in my pockets. We wore these big smocks, sort of jumper dresses with patch pockets, and when I put my hands in the pockets, my whole dress started shaking. I was in the hole for several days. They charged me with insubordination, destruction of county property, and inciting a riot. [*Laughs gleefully*.]

Ro: When you were up in Spokane, did you work?

Katya: I worked. At first I had a job in the prison law library, which was great. I helped initiate a number of lawsuits against the prison. Then the warden told me to stop doing that or else they'd give me a job I didn't like. And they did; I spent the rest of the time cleaning the bathrooms. I wouldn't have worked for UNICOR, for example, or done secretarial work for the administration or anything like that, but cleaning the bathrooms was helping the prisoners, not the prison.

I stayed pretty aloof from the guards and they didn't much mess with me. I have class and skin privilege and an inordinate amount of education—more than most cops, at any rate. They prey on the people for whom English is a second language and whose socioeconomic status creates barriers for them. I reek of privilege, both in credibility and support.

Ro: How did this privilege work with the other prisoners?

Katya: I've gotten along really brilliantly with all the people I've been locked up with, virtually, just because I'm . . . I mean, I got good advice before I ever went to jail, which I've encapsulated in my book. [*Shows me a copy of* Beat the Heat: How to Handle Encounters with Law Enforcement.][31]

You need to treat other people with respect and be very aware of such privacy as people can glean for themselves. Because there's so little of it. The privacy of another person's bunk or Bible or shampoo is to be particularly respected.

But beyond that, the intonation and vocabulary and syntax that I'm exhibiting now, I mitigate to a large degree when I'm in jail. I don't pose, but if I listen for a day or two, I can speak more colloquially, and I do. Most people are perfectly comfortable with my background. As long as I'm not snooty, as long as I don't whine or try to claim a privilege, then most people think I'm a rather advantageous friend to have.

I was a great jailhouse lawyer, and I learned how to do legal research and writing while I was there. I was able to study for the LSAT and do all the practice tests and ended up in the 99th percentile, which got me to Harvard Law School. The other prisoners would time my practice tests for me, and they gave me all kinds of good-luck charms when I went to take the test.

Ro: It was a group effort.

Katya: Yes. They thought of me as the person they were sending in. When I left prison, they made this letter for me—a card that everybody signed—and it said not to forget them, because when I became a lawyer, many of them would still be in the system. So my book is for them.

Ro: How much of your five years did you serve?

Katya: A little over two. At that point, divine intervention occurred. Which happens a lot for me, and I don't necessarily believe in God. On this occasion, my case came up for parole, about a third of my way into the sentence. In part, one's parole-ability was based on the dollar amount of the crime—the amount you stole or the value of the drugs, for instance. In my case, it was the value of the computer that I smashed, which the government said was worth $500,000.

Based on that amount, I would surely have served the usual two-thirds of my sentence and been paroled after thirty-nine months. On the day of my parole hearing, the parole board was just one guy. He's looking at this piece of paper, very closely typed, with all of my data upon it, and he's doing all these calculations. And he misreads it as *fifty thousand*!

"Well, I guess you're eligible about now. It'll take a month or so for the paper-work to go through, but I'd say you'll be going home in about a month and a half."

Now, I didn't think it would really happen, because I figured someone would notice the error. But sure enough, they let me out. Even as they buzzed open the gates of the prison, I was thinking the loudspeakers in the tower would go, "Komisaruk, get back here! You're not going anywhere."

When I got to the airport for my flight home, I hid behind a big potted plant, in case some federal marshal showed up. Often—not often, but occasionally—they let people out of prison inadvertently, and then they just go out and get them again. But once I was actually in Harvard Law School, I felt fairly safe.

Ro: Did somebody come to pick you up?

Katya: Al Mangin, one of the activists in Spokane, who had been taking great care of me. You know, they sent me to Spokane to get me away from my base of politi-cal support. But naturally there were peace activists in Spokane, too. My father and my lover met me when I landed in San Francisco, and we went for Japanese food.

Ro: Did your family generally support you?

Katya: Oh, yeah. Well, my mother was pissed at me, of course. "Self-destructive." "How can you do this to me?" That sort of thing, but she got over it. They certainly have supported me publicly, to the hilt. My mother was rather clever at sending me things I wanted. In fact, I was astonished at how many of my friends turned out to be good at smuggling.

Ro: What kind of things did they smuggle?

Katya: Sewing supplies. A wristwatch. Things like that. One of my friends came to visit me wearing a pair of shoes for me and went out wearing my old shoes. We just traded them under the table. Another friend—my best friend, Jody Lee, a very straightlaced Chinese American woman—brought me a whole bunch of things. I was like, "Jody, I'm shocked!"

She said, "Well, we are inscrutable, you know."

Ro: Oh, she sounds neat! Did you have trouble getting admitted to the bar?

Katya: Oh, yes! Mind you, I got into a bunch of the top law schools—Harvard, Stanford, Cornell—because I had a good GPA and a very high LSAT score. I also passed the California bar exam, which is about the hardest in the country. But the ethics committee of the California Bar Association spent slightly over a year trying to discern whether or not I was moral enough to be a lawyer. First I had to write an essay about what I had done to rehabilitate myself.

Ro: You don't sound terribly rehabilitated.

Katya: I tell you, I'm an officer of the court! If the California Bar Association says I'm rehabilitated, my goodness, I am! [*Laughs merrily.*] The whole process was incredibly long, with about sixty or seventy people as character references, then a private investigator who interviewed friends, employers, and so forth, and then interviewed me. Then the Bar Association held a hearing at which there were seven bar attorneys all cross-examining me, tag-team style, about whether or not I was ready to express remorse and whether I wanted to make restitution to the government.

I was very nervous about all of this, of course. I even had a professional manicure, the first and last one in my life. I felt that if I got a really nice French manicure, it would say, "How could a woman with nails like this possibly disgrace the California Bar Association?"

First they asked about remorse, and I said no. In the first place, I want to be honest: I don't feel remorse. In the second place, if I suddenly said, "Oh, they were just follies of my youth," who would believe me? They asked if I wanted to make restitution, and I said that would be inconsistent since I don't have any remorse.

Then they wanted me to promise that I'd never break the law again, and I said, "Well, it could happen, improbable as it may seem, that we might have some lunatic for president who was embroiling us in one war after another and violating every possible international law."

I said, "If we ended up in a situation where we were moving into a sort of Third Reich of our own, why then I might feel obliged to break the law." But—and this was my offer to them—I told them that I might in the future do misdemeanor civil disobedience, but that if I ever felt obliged to commit a *felony*, I would withdraw from the Bar Association first. And they accepted that and finally admitted me.

Ro: They let you in when you said you'd resign before you disgraced them.

Katya: Before I committed another felony. At least some of them feel that I disgrace them right and left. I hope they do! I've done my best to do it.

My book, for example, I think is certainly consistent with much of my other political work. Social change is not made in the courts, by and large. At best, they codify or affirm changing mores, but they *are* important, at least as some degree of safety net for activists. And one advantage we have here is that I can do the same thing that Sophie Scholl did and not expect to be executed or stuck in a psychiatric hospital and shot full of thorazine.

Since I've become a lawyer, I've been doing a lot of organizing for civil disobedience. I coordinated the legal defense for the WTO [World Trade Organization] protests in Seattle, and in several subsequent large-scale actions. In particular, I've tried to show how solidarity tactics can be used wisely and effectively.

Lawyers can pollute and overreach in organizing, but they can also be effective and use what leverage still exists in the court system. Not to be presumptuous, but Gandhi was a lawyer. Nelson Mandela was a lawyer. Lenin was a lawyer, too. There have been lawyers involved at the planning level in many mass actions and campaigns. If my presence or my availability for support can give people whatever it is that pushes them over the edge into action, it's an honor to provide it.

An Interlude: Karl Meyer, Joan Cavanagh, and Jim Forest Critique the Plowshares Movement

Karl Meyer is a lifelong peace activist who now farms at Greenlands Catholic Worker in Nashville, Tennessee. He says simply, "My philosophy about property damage is the Golden Rule: 'Do unto others as you would have done unto you.'"

Joan Cavanagh lived at Jonah House in the 1970s.[32] Jim Forest was a member of the Milwaukee Fourteen draft board action.

Joan Cavanagh

I drove the "get there" car for just one Plowshares action. For this action, we made a conscious effort to avoid religious symbolism and didn't call it a Plowshares. It was called "Trident Nein." (*Nein* [is] the German word for "nine" and a play on the fact that there were nine people involved.)

I respect religious activism a lot, but I've always had questions about it. Not about people acting out of their religious convictions—I think that's wonderful—but I always feel that the use of specific religious symbolism draws a line in ways that say, "them versus us." Or that "we" (the actors) are part of some kind of a club that requires a secret knowledge or vocabulary to join.

I'm not comfortable with anything that smacks of cultism, but I think we all made mistakes in that direction. I know I kind of bought into that when I was younger. There *is* something compelling about risking your freedom and earning your stripes, so to speak, by going to jail. If you have strong convictions, you have to stand behind them. You've got to take risks. So on one level I understand. But to make it be about some kind of hierarchy . . . I'm not comfortable with that.

I think you just recognize other people's work for its value. Some people don't believe being arrested is effective, so they'll do something else. I say, "Well, good for you! You're living what you believe." It was difficult for me to get [to that point, though], because I was very caught up in the whole civil disobedience drama, among other things. I do see civil disobedience as a way of putting it all out there, a way of making a very strong statement. And I wouldn't want to see that become trivialized or watered down.

That's the other thing that I worried about sometimes with the Plowshares [actions]. They have been repeated and repeated and repeated, and are they really compelling anymore to anyone except to the people who are doing them? And the people in their community of actors? Have the Plowshares actions changed anyone's life like Catonsville did [for me] when I was fourteen? Of course they probably have; I have to acknowledge my own subjectivity here.

But I think there need to be new symbols all the time. For me the symbol of napalm in Catonsville was just right at the moment because it demonstrated clearly what was being done to human beings in Vietnam. And Stephen [Kobasa]'s action with others around the Enola Gay [exhibit] at the Smithsonian. They used blood *and* ashes. It was a great use of symbolism to describe what really happened to human beings when the bomb dropped from the Enola Gay.

During interviews in 1988 and 2007, Jim Forest critiqued the Plowshares movement as well as his own participation in the Milwaukee Fourteen draft file burning.[33]

Jim Forest

I don't have a very romantic idea of most of the things we did during the Vietnam times. People were in a state of fierce alienation, and there was a kind of vandalism. We weren't interested in breaking windows or writing our names on the walls. That was not nearly important enough. We were furious at America. Rightly so. That fury was at the center of much that we did. What we did was good. I'm not sorry I did it, but I wouldn't build any shrines over it. It was one cry of the heart at the time. I think it had some positive aspects and was by no means the worst example of what happens when property is destroyed. Constructive consequences did indeed follow. But it disturbs me to see it become a kind of institution. It was one of the first of a pattern of actions which I think moved further and further away from what I would consider classical nonviolence. I'm a major critic of the Plowshares, for example.

I remember Thomas Merton and Dorothy both being disturbed by our action, even though Dorothy treasured us and supported us. She wrote about us and published our things in the newspaper. [*Pause.*] But she also made it clear that this was not her idea of the best way to bring about the change that we wanted. At the time, I was very annoyed by both Merton and Dorothy because I had my own thing to defend. (Once you've done something, you tend to become annoyed with people who don't agree with what you've done, especially if you admire them.)

Merton said that the root of war is fear. A significant number of peace movement activities, I think, just make people more afraid and so probably do more harm than good. I think people who see the society collapsing—who see everything coming apart at the seams—they're living in fear. Then here come religious people, attacking what they see as the structures of society, like the military. I think that's scary for people.

One thing that's very often missing in a peace movement is a compassion for—a sense of sympathy for—those people who are frightened by change, frightened by divorce rates, frightened by the possibility that their kids are gonna end up gay, all the ten thousand things that they're worried about.

Ro: Are you saying that an act of nonviolent civil resistance makes those people even more afraid?

Jim: I'm saying it *can*. I think if there is a sympathy for people who are afraid and you can work from that, you can do some very good things with an act of property destruction. I don't think it's inevitable that property destruction is bad. But when you decorate it with slogans like "act of disarmament," that's just American hype, straight from Madison Avenue to the peace movement. For me, disarmament is when a person who has a weapon puts it away, gets rid of it, melts it down. If I steal your gun from you, that's not an act of disarmament, 'cause you want every bit as much to have that weapon in the future as you did in the past. Maybe more. So the real question is, how do we change? How do we become a converted people?

Now, I don't want this to come across like some kind of a big attack on the people who do these things, because many of them are my friends. They're spiritually very deep and I admire them greatly.

There's another criticism of the Plowshares, too. It's weapon centered. It's not relationship centered. Sure, the weapons are a problem, but the problem is the relationship. And that means we have to be much less ignorant about the people where these weapons are aimed. We knew much more about missiles and airplanes and numbers of megatons and all these kinds of technical military vocabulary than we do about our enemy. When we were fighting Communism, we could see that it at least wrestled with selfishness. Considered it a moral problem. And the tragedy about capitalism is it doesn't. Capitalism considers selfishness a virtue. It glorifies one of the cardinal sins. And that selfishness is one of the reasons for all the mess we're in now. To be a real peace movement, instead of a complaint movement, we have to do something to get rid of the selfishness. Or at least that's part of it, one part of it.

Catholic Workers, with their choice to live in voluntary poverty in order to be in solidarity with the poor, try personally to address the selfishness of capitalism. One such couple is Mark and Luz Colville, who in 1994 founded the Amistad Catholic Worker in New Haven, Connecticut. Mark has participated in two Plowshares actions, Prince of Peace Plowshares in 1997 when his children were still very young, and Riverside Plowshares in New York City in 2003, for which no charges were brought. He continues to resist in a variety of ways in addition to his work in the house of hospitality. For instance, in 2005 he joined a march to the gates of Guantanamo, asking that the prison there be closed; in 2007 he and other Catholic Workers staged a dramatic witness against Blackwater in North Carolina; and in 2008, he attempted to bring medical supplies into Gaza.

For the Prince of Peace Plowshares action, Mark served thirteen months in prison. He was still refusing to pay the $4,000 restitution when he was released, and the court finally said it would serve no purpose to incarcerate him again because his views still would not be changed.[34]

Mark Colville

"In the long run, taking part in this kind of resistance deepened our [family's] ability to live interdependently. We learned to give up our own personal control over things, a control which gets in the way of community."

I think Catholic Worker connects directly with my Plowshares action, living as we are in a poor neighborhood. The victims of our warmaking come to our table on a daily basis, eating and sharing their stories, so we're able to feel their pain and struggles.

When we first began to consider the Plowshares action, we thought I'd just do support. But along the way . . . Luz was very involved in all the decision making. Together we began to struggle with the question: Does my identity as a parent exempt me from the responsibility of direct disarmament? Is it not even more important for us—as parents—to cry out about the real danger for the future of our children?

For a parent of small children to put oneself and one's family at risk could be a significant statement. The group really challenged me, though, both as somebody who had not been in jail previously and as the parent of three small children at the time. These challenges helped me to clarify my own thoughts about why I was doing this. So in answering [the Plowshares planning] group, I answered myself.

To make it work practically, Luz and I took a lesson from the people in our neighborhood who were living interdependently, who were depending on us in some sense. We started to think, "Could we not depend on our neighbors to take care of us?" In the long run, taking part in this kind of resistance deepened our ability to live interdependently. We learned to give up our own personal control over things, a control which gets in the way of community.

The numbers of people who came forward, both from our extended community and from the neighborhood—you'd be amazed! People would constantly check in with Luz—give her opportunities to get away, to rest, to go on retreat. People helped to care for the kids and they'd drive Luz and the children up to Portland, Maine, where we were in jail, which is about a four-and-a-half-hour trip. In Portland, a circle of people would put them up and Sacred Heart Church gave us a key to the rectory and a whole section where the family could stay. Our family came out of it stronger in relationship, more stable as a family and as a community. That was really the beauty of the whole thing.

In terms of material support, the donations to the house increased a lot. Honestly, we had expected a negative backlash. We were very much connected with parish and with the archdiocese. Certainly there were some ruffled feathers, but the overall effect was that people saw beyond political stance, saw a family in need because they were putting themselves at risk for the Gospel. We were modeling the people who receive, putting ourselves in the position of weakness, and people really responded to that.

Before the action, the Archdiocese of Hartford had been giving us $5,000 a year through the Office of Urban Affairs. We understood that we might be putting that money at risk, and as it turned out, after the action happened, we were. . . . Suddenly they didn't have any money for us. Which is fine. I mean, we were learning not to depend on those things. But interestingly, once people in the parishes found out that our grant had been cut off, they made such an uproar that not only did that funding get replaced the following year, but they put us on the archbishop's annual appeal, which was another lump sum of money. So we ended up getting almost twice as much.

Ro: Amazing! Mark, what was the most emotional time you can remember—the time when you wonder, "How did I get through that?"

Mark: I guess trying to get to sleep at night a couple of nights before the action. Sort of staring into this abyss of the unknown. The unknown . . . that was . . . uh, really scary and emotional. And then the long drive up there in a blinding snowstorm. I'm crunched in the back seat with all these people and thinking, "Where is this going?"

What got me out of the car was . . . My oldest daughter had just turned six. She'd been in the Christmas pageant in the church and they sang a song that was popular at the time: "I believe I can fly, I believe I can touch the sky." That scene of her singing in her little school uniform with all the other kids, that's what got me to untangle my legs and get out. In fact, that's how I got through the whole thing—just putting her right in front of me.

The hardest part, though, was to see her pain because of the separation. (The boy was too young to realize what was happening.) But as a Christian, I know that suffering is redemptive, that it's what's going to turn this whole thing around. It's not the media, it's not getting our political thoughts in order, it's when we try to repeat the sacrifice of Christ. To take the violence on ourselves and to try to participate in that redemptive process in whatever way we can. That's what's going to achieve the change that we're working for. As Phil was always saying, there's a spiritual quality to these acts of resistance, no matter how small they are or how unreported. Every act of civil disobedience against this totalitarianism has a spiritual quality that goes well beyond who hears about it or who is moved or not moved.

Speaking personally, it's not so much about changing the system as it is about changing who I am within it. And these actions have the power to do that, they have the power to set us personally free. And because I'm connected into a suffering neighborhood here in New Haven, the more I can become personally free, the more it has a positive impact on my neighborhood. Society gets transformed through personalism, through changing our own selves, changing our own stance with regard to these things.

Ro: What was it like in jail?

Mark: Well, I learned an awful lot. First of all, reading scripture from the perspective of where much of the New Testament was written—in prison. And doing Bible study with the other members of our group who had such a wealth of experience. Especially Phil [Berrigan].

Becoming his friend. With his sense of humor, living with him day-to-day was just so much fun.

Then there's the spiritual development that goes on in prison when you're there for reasons like this, you know. The constant reminders of why you're there are a joy for the resister, because you stood up against the powers and it's the best thing you ever did. And that's different from most of the other people in there, whose prison time is identified with the worst thing they ever did, and every day they're reminded of it.

I did a year in jail for doing something that was actually *legal* by US constitutional law and by international law. (Our action took place several months after the World Court decision outlawing the building and possession of first-strike nuclear weapons, so their dismantling was a legal act.) I think now, more than ever, we've got to start standing outside the laws that legalize scandals, legalize criminality.

It's not enough to just disagree anymore. Especially now, because of the activism of our right-wing government that's trying to co-opt even the name "Christian" and to twist the Christian message in such a way that it creates a community founded on a bedrock of violence. This kind of thing cannot simply be disagreed with, or spoken out against. It has to be resisted. It has to be resisted by direct

Prince of Peace Plowshares, 1997. (Photo courtesy of Bruce Friedrich.)

action. So, to me, it becomes a question of deciding—like Dan [Berrigan] would say—deciding where you stand, and standing there. You can't avoid breaking the law these days if you really and truly are against this empire ethos and if you really and truly are with Christ.

Of course being in prison and separated from your family and being bossed around by belligerent guards and being treated unfairly all the time and all that . . . I mean, those are the daily indignities that everybody has to bear. Now, I'm not saying that we bore them with joy. In fact, I got in trouble quite a few times.

There were times when I decided I just wouldn't put up with something, so I'd go into noncooperation and be thrown in the hole. For example, my wife was told she couldn't breast-feed the baby in the visiting room. There's been a four-and-a-half-hour drive and only an hour-and-a-half visit, and the baby needs to eat, you know. So because of that, the visit's over? That was just wrong! So it became an issue, and I was punished for that.

In fact, deciding what to put up with was one of the significant struggles that we had in the Prince of Peace Plowshares community. We came from different places in our personal consciences with regard to that, and it was often a struggle to work out the daily stuff. Keeping our group together for the Bible study and for the daily community-building became a high value. So we talked a lot about the need for maybe putting our own personal conscience into submission to the communal conscience. If you resist and are sent to the hole, you won't be able to have community. [*Long pause.*]

Oh, I've got an interesting prison story for you. Its significance didn't hit me until weeks later. This was when we were in the county jail, one of those new jails with electronic locks and monitors everywhere. No outside rec yard because they didn't want the public to see prisoners in orange suits running around outside. So we were basically inside all that time and had an inside gym we could use an hour a day.

You had to all go in a group. You'd follow these guards down the hall, and every twenty yards or so there'd be a metal door with an electronic lock, which a guy in central control would open. Well, there was one prisoner who would try the knob every time he'd come to a door. Like it was somehow going to open for him. Every single door. On the way back, I finally turned to him: "Do you really expect that door to be open?"

He said to me: "I refuse to go through my life expecting every door to be locked." [*Pause, and then laughter.*] That was this guy's personal daily practice of resistance. He was not going to accept the totalitarian control that is prison. And you know? He was right, because eventually, he's going to try a door and it will open. I mean, he'll get out of prison someday. And he won't be bringing locked doors outside with him.

Ro: That simple act of resistance may be the kind of thing that keeps someone going, so they don't fall into a prison stupor.

Mark: Right. And that's . . . Actually, that's what we're trying to say with the Plowshares action. We're resisting the idea that nuclearism is an immovable force, that it's this mountain that nobody can budge, as unchangeable as sun coming up in the morning.

Ro: So why don't we have more resisters going to prison?

Mark: Well . . . I think it's the fear. Fear is nurtured so competently in our society, particularly since September 11th, so it's inescapable that it filters into all levels of society, including our resistance communities and our Catholic Worker communities.

Step one is to realize that. And step two is to get together and find the strength in each other to do something. You can't do it alone. Fear is the opposite of love, as they say. We've got to take up the arms of love and combat this fear. I know there's not a lot of people involved right now, but I really do believe that there's a spiritual movement going on underneath and that it's going to come out.

For years, three Dominican nuns—Sisters Ardeth Platte, Carol Gilbert, and Jackie Hudson—have tried to combat the fear Mark speaks of.[35] Members of the Order of Preachers (OP), they preach with their lives in Plowshares and other peace actions. The support they've received, especially after their Sacred Earth and Space Plowshares action in Colorado, enlarged the meaning of "peace community" to include groups around the world. These are the nuns the Maryland State Police targeted as terrorists, and almost the only contemporary Plowshares activists to make headlines in the mainstream press.[36]

During the Vietnam era, Sister Ardeth and I protested together in Saginaw, Michigan. Ardeth, known then as Sister Richardine and still wearing the habit of her religious order, was principal of St. Joseph Alternative High School and Delta College's Saginaw Center. In the seventies, she served several terms on the Saginaw City Council.

Carol came to Saginaw later, first to teach school and then to work full time with Ardeth on justice issues. In 1979, they formed Advocacy for Justice and later the Home for Peace and Justice, a house of hospitality that became a focal point for peace resisters as well as a haven for poor people in search of support and sustenance.

Jackie, a Saginaw native, served as a sister and participated in resistance actions from a base in Grand Rapids, Michigan, before moving to Poulsbo, Washington. A member of the Ground Zero Center for Nonviolent Action, founded to resist nuclear weapons, she attended the yearly chapter of the Grand Rapids Dominicans whenever she could.[37]

Sisters Carol Gilbert, Jackie Hudson, and Ardeth Platte, OP

"The military has done a magnificent job of programming people into [believing in] their gods of metal."

Ardeth: In 1982, a million people met in New York City to call for nuclear disarmament. We were present. When weapons were being transferred from Seneca Falls in New York to Latin America, we were there and arrested [at the Women's Peace Camp]. While hundreds of women climbed the fences into the arms of the military, twenty-six of us occupied the gate area for thirty hours. In one of the worst rainstorms I can recall, and when the rain cleared, a heat wave set in. We had no protection until the Seneca Encampment folks brought us a tent and food. After that we learned to do better planning. [*Laughs wryly.*]

In October of 1983, seventeen of us [affiliated with] the Home for Peace and Justice entered onto the airstrip of Wurtsmith AFB, home of B-52 missiles on hairtrigger alert. We were young and old, professors, homemakers, business people, students, religious—united together to close Wurtsmith and transform it for civilian use. We wanted no nuclear weapons on Michigan soil and no cruise and Pershing missiles in Europe.

We walked onto the base, entering through strands of barbwire. (Later a twelve-foot fence was constructed around the entire perimeter.) The military surrounded us, armed with attack dogs, placed us on a bus, processed us, and banned us from the base. That was the beginning.

> [In 1985, Ardeth and Carol made a peace pilgrimage across the country, vigiling for "forty days and forty nights" outside nuclear weapons sites. They came to see that all the justice issues they'd been working on—poverty, homelessness, immigrant issues, America imperialism throughout the world—were undergirded by the threat of nuclear Armageddon. They decided to consecrate their ministry to eliminating nuclear weapons.
>
> At first they remained in Michigan, moving to Oscoda, home of Wurtsmith SAC base. They lived there for three years and vigiled daily at the gates. In one action, on the Feast of the Holy Innocents, they hung scores of antinuclear leaflets on the doorknobs of the buildings, including the home of the base commander, before being apprehended at gunpoint. They also organized large local and statewide civil resistance actions, including sit-ins at the offices of their congressional representatives. These actions resulted in several arrests and imprisonments.]

Ardeth: We did some of the Wurtsmith actions alone, and some with others from Michigan Faith and Resistance Retreats. I smile now when I think of my first jailings. People didn't even want to talk about it. "Jail" was treated as a bad word.

I always try to prepare for ultimates, both in the length of sentence and in the conditions in the jail or prison, but it's a mistaken notion that I *want* to be in jail. Never! You know, in the Bible, when Peter and the others preached the Word after Pentecost, they knew if they continued proclaiming Jesus's life, death, and resurrection, they faced arrest and jail. Each of us understands the same possibility, but that's different than saying we *want* to be in jail.

> [Ardeth's been in at least thirty jails or prisons. After sentencing, she and Carol usually don't self-report, as some resisters do, choosing instead to be transported to their prison assignment as the poor are transported, by extremely circuitous routes, in a process resisters call "diesel therapy." Prisoners in transport are denied almost all possessions, sometimes even a Bible. Importantly, they're out of touch with family and community and supporters. Every imprisonment is different.]

Ardeth: Sometimes being in a city or county jail can be a joyful time, like when all the women are in a cell together after an arrest. We care for each other, we sing, we pray, we tell stories, and it's wonderful to have that time after a demonstration. But there are other lockups, like the one I experienced in Wayne County [Detroit]. The cell reeked of urine and was crawling with cockroaches and mice; the walls were covered with graffiti and dung. (On that stay—mercifully short—Carol read to us—fittingly—from the Acts of the Apostles, while I mopped and scrubbed.) Some cells have been so crowded there's no space to lie down. Some holding tanks house women going into convulsions from heroin withdrawal or vomiting from drunkenness. Some women from the streets are filled with body sores and scabs; others cry out day and night in mental turmoil.

But in many instances our entrance into jails has been an interruption of regular life in a cell. Language changes. Generosity abounds. We enter with nothing and in a few moments someone has given us a towel and washcloth, soap, and a toothbrush. The poorest are usually the most generous.

Prison for me is always where I breathe with the people made poorest, with people who have struggled, made mistakes, and are getting up again. Prison strengthens my faith and gives me opportunities for patience, compassion, and humility. My greatest joy is in being able to listen and lend support. In listening to the women who have been through rape and battering and abuse, I watch them begin to see their own worth and their own strengths, and to make new commitments.

Most of the women there require alternatives, not incarceration! There are so few actually violent crimes committed by women, so how is society being protected when women [are] drawn away from their children, their loved ones, and are given no positive assistance in their lives? (In fact, are given more negatives to cope with upon release, negatives which cause recidivism.) Prison just escalates problems, with billions of dollars spent in a failing system.

[The sentences Ardeth and Carol served during their Michigan years ranged from three days to six months, the maximum for federal trespass. When Wurtsmith closed, they moved to the Upper Peninsula, close to K. I. Sawyer Air Force Base. They did the same things there, vigiling and praying and organizing resistance actions against the base and against Project ELF, the low-frequency communication system that linked Trident nuclear submarines. After K. I. Sawyer closed and ELF was dismantled, they moved to Jonah House in Baltimore, joyful to be joining that long-standing peace community.

In 1996, they participated in their first Plowshares action, Weep for Children, along with Sister Liz Walters, IHM, and grandmother Kathy Boylan. In their trial, the prosecutor compared them to "the Oklahoma City bomber. Judge Thomas Smith firmly disagreed, and said they were following a higher law."[38]]

Ardeth: For many years Carol and I had been attempting to find ways, as people of faith, to resist nuclear weapons and to give even more of our lives to peacemaking. That led us to join the Jonah House community in Baltimore. They're the oldest and strongest and most committed and creative community of nonviolent civil resistance in the country.

For about ten months we met and prayed and planned this Plowshares action. We called it "Weep for Children Plowshares," and our invitation is strongly to women to pick up the actions of disarming.

Carol: We worried at first that people might think of weeping as whining. But Sister Joan Chittister's "A Time for Weeping" taught us that it's a sign of hope. As a culture we don't want to feel anything is worth weeping over. Yet the scriptures are full of weeping—Peter wept and Jesus wept over Jerusalem and Jeremiah wept and the daughters of Jerusalem wept and Rachel wept for her children. These are all signs of hope, that a people could weep.

Ardeth: We weep because we love so deeply and feel so strongly and the weeping calls us to action. As women, maybe this will be our greatest gift to men.

When one stops to think that millions of children have been killed in war, millions of children suffer starvation and hunger, millions of children are blown apart by land mines, millions of children orphaned and separated from their parents when they go off to war . . . So we weep not only for them but *with* them. Their cause becomes our cause. They have no voice and Weep for Children Plowshares gave them one.

As women, we also connect with the Mothers of the Disappeared [in Argentina and elsewhere] and the Russian mothers who marched off to Chechnya to ask their sons to stop killing their own brothers and sisters in the Soviet Union.

We decided on July 27th, 1996, the day the eighteenth Trident submarine would be launched at New London, Connecticut. So we went up there. These huge submarines are lined up on the Thames River. They're built there at Electric Boat; then after they're launched and under government ownership, they go across the river to the underground war center.

In the middle of all this is a museum, the first nuclear-powered submarine ever built. It's now an idol where people come to worship and to learn about the navy's preparation for war. Thousands of people go through this submarine, programming their children into the power and glory and the supposed security of these weapons of mass destruction. We went through it, too, and watched the children playing at computer weapons games and marveling at the gigantic weapons.

The military has done a magnificent job of programming people into [believing in] their gods of metal. They even use biblical terminology. One of the fast attack submarines is called "Corpus Christi," the body of Christ, and they "christen" Tridents when they launch them. As Christians, we believe it's really important for us to reclaim these words, to reclaim ritual, to reclaim symbols, to reclaim liturgy. So when we act, it's always in the form of a liturgy.

Our liturgy in Connecticut began at 3:00 a.m., as we processed down the railroad track and into the dock area of the naval submarine base. We knew at this point in the walk that we could give our life. We found out later that all military bases were on highest alert, yet we four walked openly and publically into the pier. Amazing!

When we entered, it was lit up as if the sun was out. We had with us household hammers on which we had tied children's pictures and our signs of peace: "In the name of our God, swords into plowshares." "Thou shalt not kill." "Love your enemies." We carried baby bottles filled with our own blood. We had lots of documentation: the Nuremberg principles, which is a substantiation of all the laws and treaties that show that nuclear weapons are illegal; the military budget and all the data which shows how poverty-stricken the world is; the World Court decision which says nuclear weapons are illegal and cannot be used or be threatened to be used for first strike by any nation, including our own.

Our objective was to get to the submarines and to mark the god of metal for what it is. Then to hammer it—resist and reject it—and then, using the hammer as symbol, to convert it . . . symbolically transform it into plowshares. Our ritual included those three elements—mark, reject, transform. It was all in the form of prayer and song. Prayers from scripture, prayers from our heart, our own joint statement, our own proclamation of the Word, and then Eucharist itself.

Carol: We danced one of the Universal Dances for Peace on the way in and didn't speak at all until we got inside. I won't say that we didn't enter with fear and trembling, even though we had placed our safety in God's hands and were prepared for whatever might happen. Because clearly it seemed an impossibility that we would ever be able to do this, even though we know with God all things are possible.

For me the dancing and chanting were really important. We just kept repeating the words *Bismillah*, *Ir-rahman*, and *Ir-rahim*, over and over and over as we worked out way into the base. Knowing that for centuries people had been repeating this. *Bismillah* means "We begin in the name of our God." *Ir-rahman* is the word for "all mercy" and *Ir-rahim*, "all compassion."[39]

Then we got to the pier, where it was *so* bright with huge lights! It became clear that we weren't going to make it onto the submarine but then we saw a heavy metal cylinder. We weren't sure what it was, but we said, "This is it. This is where we're going to enflesh the prophecy of Isaiah."

What struck me was how quiet everything was. There were four submarines surrounding us, including the one called USS *Corpus Christi*. Men were standing at the rails of these subs, but they just watched silently. We could clearly feel the presence of cars behind us, but they didn't stop us.

Very quietly, very prayerfully, we opened the baby bottles and poured our blood and it dripped down as we hammered on the cylinder. We pasted on the cylinder both our statements and a banner that said "Weep for Children Plowshares." Then we all knelt down and one of the security officers arrived and radioed back that we were Plowshares, nonviolent protestors. So they allowed us to finish the reading of the statement and to sing a song.

It was almost like being in a monastery. There was this silence and yet people were all around us. Ardeth spoke afterwards about it being the closest that we could feel to actual disarmament. Finally, of course, one of the security people said, "Something very serious has happened here. Put your hands on your head." Then the processing began.

We found out the next day that we had hammered on a cylinder used to test the Seawolf torpedo missiles. It was ready for an open house at Electric Boat. A newspaper article quoted a father whose four-year-old had pushed a button to make the torpedo come out of the cylinder. "What four-year-old child wouldn't be excited about that?"

And that was what we had symbolically disarmed! We were trying to stop war with the very same metal that the military folks were using to program children into being excited about it. Truly, God was present in all of this.

Ardeth: You see, we have come to believe that liturgy isn't just at church. It's not separated from our lives. Every liturgy has two parts. The first is proclaiming the Word. All the way through our action, we were conscious of proclaiming the Word, proclaiming truth. Secondly, we were entering into the second part, the Eucharist. In this action, we began to understand deeply that Eucharist really is our own lives. That we—our body, our blood—must be given for peace in the world. We knew there could be grave consequences.

When the military came over to us and asked if it was animal or human blood on the cylinder, each one of us said, "This is my blood." All the sailors who stood there watching us and all the security people who surrounded us—they all became part of the liturgy. They may not be totally believing at this time, but God can work within their souls and their lives may be changed by our action. As we were taken in, every person we saw gave us another opportunity to communicate the Word. In the courtroom, too, with all the military, the judge himself, the bailiffs and everyone else, and then all the people when the consequences came. So it flows outward to all the people who come in contact with us.

Carol: We don't do it for the publicity or for the media. Hearts are disarmed one by one. With the military and the courts, and also in the churches and homes where we're able to speak, and with the Festivals of Hope held before the trial starts. See, it's not about impact on the government as such, it's about living our faith. We never know what the effects of our actions are going to be, but we try to make holy what needs to be said. Maybe somebody in the government is changed and maybe they're not, but that's not really what we're about.

We're never surprised when a reporter writes these [actions] off as not being relevant or effective. As a culture, we're into effectiveness and success, and the reporters buy into that and try to dismiss us. Others try to portray us as off-the-wall or crazy. We look at ourselves as ordinary people who are trying to live the Gospel but often the media tries to paint [what we do] as something no one can possibly participate in. Not true, as you know, Rosalie.

Ardeth: You know, we don't expect anything from the media. We don't even have great expectations from our own writing and talking. It's God who plants the seed, nourishes the soil, cultivates the heart. And people do hear. After this action, I was interviewed on Pacifica Radio and from that show, maybe some hearts were opened, so someone is motivated to do other positive actions.

For me, that's important, but even if it doesn't happen, I believe that every time we vigil anyplace, God hears the prayer and truth is proclaimed. Every person who sees or hears us is challenged to consider whether warmaking will ever secure God's people on planet Earth.

We know it never has and it never will. And maybe some of those who see us or hear us will also enter into that. Even if they don't, we've disarmed our own hearts and severed ourselves from complicity and followed our conscience. For us, that's a gift to future generations.

[Their second Plowshares action was Gods of Metal in 1998, along with Kathy Boylan again, Father Frank Cordaro of Des Moines, Iowa, and Father Larry Morlan. As Ardeth said, "Our God is in heaven. . . . Their gods are made of silver and gold, formed by human hands." Acting on this theme, they chose an open house at Andrews Air Force Base in Maryland. Hundreds of spectators looked on as they distributed explanatory leaflets and poured blood and hammered on the missile hatches of a B-52 bomber. Kathy received a sentence of ten months because of her long previous record; the rest received four months.

Their next Plowshares action, Sacred Earth and Space Plowshares, was in Colorado, where nearly 50 percent of the income comes from military pursuits. Carol and Ardeth were joined by three other nuns—Jackie Hudson, Liz Walters, and Anne Montgomery. They acted at an air show at Peterson Air Force Base in Colorado Springs.]

Jackie: When I first learned about Hiroshima and Nagasaki and saw the pictures—the complete devastation and horrendous slaughter of the Japanese people—I . . . I just couldn't believe that our nation could do something like that. You know, those pictures were hidden away in a vault in Washington for years and years. Once you know, you can't just sit back and do nothing. I wasn't afraid of prison, and I am not afraid of prison to this day. The military leave their family and friends to fight and if we're too timid to leave our family and friends and creature comforts for prison, who are we as peace-based people?

For this Colorado action, we'd meet for three or four days at a time to retreat and study. We read *Vision for 2020*, the official US Air Force document that calls for the exploitation of outer space and domination of other nations from there. I was just abhorred! Space is the newest frontier, so of course they say we've got to control it. Colorado Springs is the center of all that's happening in the militarization of space—Peterson AFB, Schriever AFB with NORAD, the Air Force Academy, and then on the outskirts of Denver, there's Buckley AFB, which has several radomes (they look like huge golf balls) to receive communications from our satellites in space.[40]

So we decided we'd ring the bell to wake the nation to what's happening in the militarization of outer space. All in violation of the Outer Space Treaty. We did the first one at the air show at Peterson AFB on September 9, 2000. We found a display area that showed all the bombings they'd done in Iraq and I started hammering on the bomb rack under the wings of an F-18 plane. An officer asked us, "Ladies, what are you doing?" But we continued our hammering.

The others found the Milstar satellite dish, which receives the communication from the newest satellite. It was the most highly guarded display, sectioned off with a yellow ribbon with air force personnel stationed around it. The other three got under the yellow ribbon and poured their blood and hammered on the Milstar receiver. (By the way, the air force denies that this happened.)

We were arrested for trespass, but where was the trespass? It was a show for the public, and we were part of the public, so we didn't sign that we had trespassed. After a week in the county jail, they released us late, late one Friday evening. The media had done a couple of interviews, and the head of the jail finally said he "couldn't have nuns in his jail!"

So we were out, with no money. (They give you the money you come in with in the form of a check, and there's no place you can cash it so late.) But we found out where the homeless people stayed in Colorado Springs, and we went to that underpass. A fellow was there with a pickup truck, so we piled in the back and he took us to the Benedictine sisters in Colorado Springs. All the state charges were dropped and the feds never brought any. I guess they just didn't want to deal with us that time.

The next one was different. The people at the air show learned about the fighter planes, but they didn't know about all the missiles in Colorado, so we chose a missile site for Sacred Earth and Space II. There were only three of us this time as Anne opted to return to Iraq and Palestine and Liz had family commitments. We bought white protective jumpsuits online and painted them with "Disarmament Specialist" on the front and on the back "Citizens Weapons Inspection Team." The acronym for that is "CWIT"—quit! We wanted to be very visible and we were.

[On October 6, 2002—the first anniversary of the US bombing of Afghanistan—the sisters traveled to Site N8, a concrete rocket silo that houses forty-nine rockets, each with twenty-five times the explosive force of the Hiroshima bomb. They cut a lock to the gate, opened it wide, hung a banner announcing their action, cut down three panels of fence to expose the site to public view, and laid on the ground near the missile documents pertain-

Sacred Earth and Space II Plowshares entering the site, 2002.
(Photo courtesy of Joe Gump.)

ing to nuclear law and the US plans for exploiting space. Then they banged
with small hammers on the railroad tracks used to open the silo if the missile
were launched, and poured their own blood in the form of crosses on the
110-ton cement cover. For nearly an hour they prayed and sang before the
authorities came thundering in, ignoring the wide-open gate.[41]]

Jackie: It was practice for them—a military exercise. As they were coming up the
highway, we heard them say on their walkie-talkies: "They're singing religious
songs." First, they stopped traffic and assembled on Highway 14. One Humvee
entered the farmer's field and personnel pointed M16s at us from behind a hill.

Finally, all these vehicles came roaring in like Rambos, making a huge racket.
Broke through one fence and then the other, even though we had the other side
open. It was just a den of noise, like a high school basketball game in a small gym!
They were all screaming and shouting, with a machine gun and their M16s, and
grenade launchers aimed right at us.

When they saw that we were women, they had to call back and bring women
in to search us. They marched us outside the silo area, handcuffed us, and had us
lie face down in the dirt until the women came. Then the bomb squad came in by
helicopter and looked in our small bags, finding our water and energy bars. The FBI
was there and the air force military police and the sheriff of Weld County, and there
was a lot of coming and going and waiting in all of this, so we didn't get to the
Weld County Jail in Greeley until late afternoon.

We were arraigned by TV and then early one morning the FBI took us to Denver to face federal charges and then out to Clear Creek County Jail, and then back once again to Denver for [another] arraignment. That's when we heard that it was a sabotage charge and that we were facing a possible twenty years. It was kind of a shock to the system. [*Weak laughter.*]

Clear Creek is a rent-a-cell jail. The county makes money by renting out cells to the federal government. It was kind of hard to prepare for trial when all you've got are pencils and a child's notepad. But finally we put together a wonderful pro bono defense team—Walter Gerash, Susan Tuborsky, Scott Poland, and Anabel Dwyer.

Ardeth: God led us into the site; we had not intended to go there. It was the right moment, it was the right action, and with the movie and our public forums, it's still going on.[42]

The trial was a farce, with the sabotage charge. So extreme! I was looking at 92 to 115 months in prison and it looked like there wasn't going to be any mercy at all, so people just congregated around. You know, there are times in history when you're led to do something that blossoms into something important and good. Now Jackie, Carol, and I would simply say it was the "right moment." It's been good. So many, many people have written and told us that they did an action for the first time because of what we did.

We feel strongly about having a support team in each area when we do a Plowshares action. Though they're never involved directly in planning, we know we can contact them from jail and that they'll begin the process for media, funding, family and community updates, legal help, et cetera. Some support roles are more direct, such as driving to the site, taking photos or videos of the action, coordinating the press release, holding our possessions during the action. These persons must either prepare for a possible arrest or remain unaware of what we're doing. When we're in prison, our close network of friends and communities—our wonderful supporters—they're imprisoned with us, also.

[The sisters were together for seven months in the Clear Creek County Jail, where they organized the other prisoners to make afghans for area seniors and to knit items for the inmates' families. During their trial in Denver, they weren't allowed to call expert witnesses, to present as evidence the documents left at the site, or to use sixty words listed as off-limits to them, including the word "God." On April 7, a jury found them guilty of two felonies.]

Ardeth: When probation officers met with the FBI and the prosecutor, they suggested guidelines spelling out six years for Jackie, eight years for Carol, and nearly ten years for me. But with the excellent help of lawyers and more than a thousand letters to the judge, it was reduced to thirty months, thirty-three months, and forty-one months respectively. Jackie went to Victorville in California, Carol to Alderson in West Virginia, and I to Danbury in Connecticut.

Sister Jackie Hudson, OP, arrested at Ground Zero, 2009. (Photo courtesy of Leonard Eiger.)

Jackie: We were separated right away after the trial, but were able to spend one last overnight together in the Pueblo County Jail. In black-and-white jail suits, just like in the old movies. We said we were back in Dominican jail suits.[43] Then we were flown together to the collection point in Oklahoma City. Just like any other airport, you walk down a walkway, but now you're struggling with leg irons and a belly chain, and the inside of the airplane is very simple. Then when you get to the next airport, you strip, and you're put in various holding areas. We stayed overnight in Oklahoma and when we woke in the morning, Carol and I were taken out and given this little breakfast.

My name was called out, and I didn't think much about it because, you know, names are called out all the time. But suddenly I realized I was leaving—for good—and I didn't even have a chance to say goodbye to Carol. I went west and Carol went east and Ardeth stayed behind. (We were able to say goodbye to her the night before.) Very emotional for all of us as we went to our own individual experience. You know, when you do an action, you have such unity and such spirit together, but once you start your jail time, you're each in your own space and experiencing life entirely by yourself.

Our camp at Victorville was small, with just one building for women, and it's overcrowded, so newcomers stay in the recreation room that had been converted to a dorm. But that's where I spent my entire time because I didn't agree to pay restitution. If you don't sign that paper, you're allotted the least desirable housing and also limited to $25 a month for commissary, no matter how much money [is] in your account, as opposed to $100 or so for the other prisoners. And that $25 included everything—shampoo, laundry soap, all the necessities. Prices in commissary are as high or higher than on the outside, and salaries for prison work begin at twelve cents an hour, so that's over three hours of labor for a postage stamp!

At one of my sessions, they said I needed to take a class about "accountability" to my victim. I said, "My victim is hurting? The United States Air Force is hurting?"

[In Danbury Federal Prison Camp, Ardeth refused to cooperate in any way with restitution or to receive pay for her work; however, the chaplain made arrangements for her to be an unpaid chaplain clerk and Ardeth was strengthened in her long stay by planning and attending services in many faith traditions. She celebrated her jubilee year—fifty years in the Dominican order—while in Danbury. Much of Ardeth's time was spent ministering to prisoners, but at one crucial point they and prison staff ministered to her.]

Ardeth: I had a giant reaction to an antibiotic. My body was red hot, just one huge red beet. I was clearly near death, but three prison nurses went into action. Rosalie, you should've seen it! They unpacked a whole ice machine into plastic bags, and packed me tightly in ice. That's what saved my life.

The women would come in and take care of me and people would advocate for me, which was a lifesaver because that reaction lasted for hundreds of days. It was always like circulating [in] my body, attacking it. All of a sudden you'd see this spreading rash, red as a beet. So people ministered to me then. Women know how to take care of each other.

Carol: That community . . . You know, I think my best experience was learning from the women. The sharing about their lives was so deep. From women at Alderson like Martha Stewart—there were others, too—who were very wealthy, very highly educated, very together women, to those who have grown up abused and literally have absolutely nothing.[44]

To be part of that whole circle of women's lives, and hear their deep sharing—it's very, very humbling, and it's a great thing, but it doesn't make up for the you-know-what that comes your way. The first couple of weeks I was there, they wanted me to take something called an anger management class, and I refused to do that.

And the job . . . Normally, for the first ninety days you work in the kitchen, so that's where I was put. Luckily, I was only there for two days. I wouldn't have survived it, because there were too many women and not enough work, so basically you'd sit there and do nothing for six hours. It was driving me bats, so the first day I went outside and was walking around. One of the officers bangs on the windows, "What are you doing?"

I said, "I'm praying my rosary. There wasn't anything to do in the kitchen."

"Get in here!" So then everybody had to do all these make-work jobs, and of course the women hate you because you're getting them this extra work. Thankfully, there was an opening to clean bathrooms, and that's when I became "the Bathroom Queen."

Oh, my God! You can't believe the condition of some of these toilets! Sometimes right after you'd cleaned them! But you know? One of the best things about my time in Alderson was making sacred the cleaning of these God-awful bathrooms. I don't do well with bugs and dirt and smells, sorry to say. That I could actually go in every day and clean so many toilets and showers, that was a special change for me.

[Jackie had severe asthma. The dry air at Victorville helped her but the altitude didn't, and the nearby forest fires also exacerbated her breathing problems. Then she had pneumonia and ongoing difficulties with her required medications not being on the protocols for the prison system.]

Jackie: This was a work camp and they stressed over and over again that you had to work, but I was so short of breath that I had difficulty even walking any distance. I hadn't been able to lift anything for quite some time because of a back problem. Many of the prisoners were out in the hot sun raking rocks or lifting heavy equipment for a new men's penitentiary they were building, and I knew I couldn't do that. Also, I refused to do anything to enhance a facility that was going to be such a punitive setting for the men, so I didn't work for the first six months, except for sometimes cleaning the bathrooms. I had to carry these temporary work permits with me all the time; otherwise they'd nab me and make me rake designs into the sand. Finally I was able to work part time in the library, and it was pretty well organized by the time I left.

You know, a prisoner is not a person. A prisoner is a number. A prisoner is a thing. And so, contaminated water, contaminated food . . . none of that matters because you're not a human being. But it was a great educational experience, and I met some beautiful women at Victorville and formed friendships which continue to this day.

[Resisters are also supported by friends on the outside who visit when they can and also send mail, much more than the average prisoner gets.]

Ardeth: Hundreds of people wrote from all over the world. We got buckets and buckets of mail, and it was awesome! All three of us would sometimes get communications signed by lots of people. Some days we'd receive five hundred names at a time—from every part of the world—like from a conference in South America. South Africa, Taiwan, Japan, every country in Europe, Iraq. The Iraq nuns. Dominicans. Taiwan, Australia . . . every continent. Countries, cities I'd never heard of. Countries in the midst of turmoil. It just . . . I mean, communications like this would bring tears to my eyes. Because I know they're in the heart of it and they're caring about me, sitting in prison. You're only supposed to keep twenty-five letters at a time, so when it got to be a big pile, I'd put them in a big envelope and send them out. I had to throw away thousands of letters, though.

[After their long incarceration for this action, federal probation officers at first refused to let them return home for the three years of supervision after release, or to let them travel; however, after much negotiation, all three were able to go home and eventually to travel.

Jackie was released in March of 2003, returning to her Ground Zero community in Poulsbo, Washington. Liz McAlister drove to Alderson to get Carol on May 23, 2005, bringing her to a huge welcome-home celebration in Baltimore, attended by friends from across the country. Carol was her usual gracious self that evening, but the large crowd of well-wishers was surely a shock to someone who had slept the night before in prison. She told me the next day that when she finally got to her room in Jonah House, she couldn't fall asleep because it was so quiet and dark, unlike Alderson. She also said she was looking forward to "nesting"—just lying low and getting her things in order.

Ardeth was released the next December, and according to Stephen Kobasa, came dancing into the restaurant where the Kobasa family took her to meet with well-wishers.[45] "This is the day the Lord has made," she sang. Since their release and the end of their probation, the sisters travel whenever they can, speaking to groups about their action and showing the documentary *Conviction*.]

Ardeth: We also do a lot with student groups who come here to Jonah House for retreats. Usually about fifteen groups a year, and they're amazing! They come in with laptop computers, cell phones, iPods. I mean, it's a whole different world. They choose to come here, though, instead of going to the Bahamas or someplace glamorous. Their teachers do the motivating and make the arrangements. Sometimes they think, before they come, that Jonah House is a cult—that we're "way beyond." (Because of what they've heard from others, not the person who brought them here.) But here their lives turn upside down!

Many of them haven't heard of the Berrigans. Or Dorothy Day. *Any* of what we take for granted, like the struggles over Vietnam, the civil rights movement. I mean, they might know Martin Luther King's name, but as far as what other people did in the movement, they don't hear much in their schools.

Carol: We try to instill in them three practices: resistance, community, and nonviolence. If a person is going to resist the empire and live a life of nonviolence, it has to be done in community, so we talk about what it means to be part of a community in a culture that's anti-community.

We talk a lot about nonviolence and what it means. Not only the nonviolence that's part of any nonviolent action but living nonviolence in our own hearts. And then the idea of resistance. Yes, it's resistance against the evil of empire and to weapons of destruction, but it's also growing our own food, combining trips to use less oil, raising children nonviolently. We try to show the young people how they've already plugged into resistance. Because it has to come from ordinary people, like me. I'm a part of the circle, and the students who come here are, too. We help them to think about their next step and the next step and the next step.

Ardeth: We urge them to be observers, and to find out what their passion is by study and discernment, and to concentrate on that, as we concentrate on the taproot—nuclear arms. They simply aren't able to do all the issues. If they get the kind of passion that we have, it will lead them to become more nonviolent and to become deeper spiritually so they can handle the consequences that will surely come.

We also tell them not to be afraid. If they really have a connection with their faith—their Allah or their Yahweh or their God or their belief in God's creation—then they'll have the strength to do what has to be done in direct action.

Sure, they can do political and judicial action, but direct action is the only way any system has ever been changed. It's the only way Creation will be saved, it's the only way God's people will be saved, it's the only way the resister his or herself will be saved.

Carol: Wouldn't it be wonderful to think that the whole planet is going to change like these young people do? But I think we have to realize that we'll always be a remnant.

Ardeth: Well, we need to remember that just before the invasion of Iraq, the greatest number of people in the history of the whole Western world was out in the street. Saying "No!" There *is* a conversion going on in people's lives, and technology is helping in that. Injurious as technology is, it's helping. I think more people are looking at nonviolence today, and talking about it, than ever before in my lifetime. It's a key time in history—an opportunity to stop war forever. True, we're still marginated, but I don't know we're as much of a remnant as we were during the war in Vietnam. This is a kairos moment. Yes, a kairos moment.

4

Catholic Worker Communities and Resistance

The Catholic Worker (CW) movement has been resisting the culture of war since its founding in 1933. Founders Dorothy Day and Peter Maurin first envisioned a newspaper giving Christian responses to contemporary social problems. The newspaper advocated a quasi-anarchism called "personalism," based on the Sermon on the Mount of Jesus and suggesting that one should address economic and political ills personally instead of through institutions. So one feeds the hungry, houses the homeless, resists a militaristic state, and divorces from the corporate world and its policies, all at a personal sacrifice.

Soon Day and Maurin and a ready stream of volunteers put the program into practice, first in Manhattan and then throughout the country in urban houses of hospitality and rural farms where communities try even more strenuously to withdraw from corporate and state control. Today more than 190 CW houses exist throughout the world, only loosely affiliated in what Catholic Workers insist is an organism, not an organization. Catholic Worker houses are not shelters but community homes where volunteers called Workers live with those who come to them in need, espousing voluntary poverty and seeking lives consistent with their ideals. Some come for a year or so, but many choose to live their entire lives as Workers, marrying and raising children in community. Not all Catholic Workers are Catholic, and ties to the larger church depend on the proclivities of individual communities, but all Catholic Workers strive to make a world where "it's easier to be good," as Maurin espoused.[1]

Neutral during the Spanish Civil War (to the consternation of much of the US Catholic Church), pacifist during World War II (to the consternation of almost everyone), arrested for protesting the air raid drills during the fifties, a leader in Vietnam resistance, and encouraging of resisters until the day she died, Dorothy Day saw that resistance was necessary against "this filthy rotten system."[2] When she went to jail in 1957 for resisting the Civil Defense drills, she wrote, "We know what we are in for, the risk we run in openly setting ourselves against this most powerful country in the world. It is a tiny Christian gesture, the gesture of a David against a Goliath in an infinitesimal way."[3]

Many—but not all—Catholic Workers follow her lead in resisting war and its dangerous underpinnings. Some write strong articles in their own newsletters or participate in weekly vigils and schedule films and speakers that promote peace. Others, as did Day, participate in actions with resulting jail time, and some, as we have seen, do Plowshares actions and spend years in prison.

In this chapter, Catholic Workers talk about their resistance lives, particularly as it affects their families and communities. They describe their religious motivations, their trials, their sometimes harrowing jail experiences, and how they manage resistance in marriage and resistance in community. In doing so, they help us to redefine what resistance means and to see that when one person goes to jail, the entire community "does time."

Robert Ellsberg describes two very different jail experiences as a young Worker. He reflects on protest as personally empowering and potentially effective politically, but cautions against it being seen as invariably heroic. Three couples who have chosen the CW as their life work discuss resistance as married Workers. Father Tom Lumpkin of Day House in Detroit and Paul Gallagher of St. Jude's in Champaign, Illinois, show how their Catholic faith undergirds the decision to risk arrest. Brian Terrell and Judith Williams discuss long resistance lives. Sixteen Catholic Workers or former Catholic Workers conclude the chapter in a roundtable on resistance.

In 1969 a young Robert Ellsberg helped his father, Daniel, copy the seven thousand pages of a top secret Pentagon-sponsored history of the Vietnam War, a study that highlighted a pattern of government lies and deceptions. These "Pentagon Papers," published in the *New York Times* and eventually by Beacon Press, did much to finally galvanize the larger American public against the war. Daniel Ellsberg was arrested and charged under the Espionage Act, although the charges were eventually dismissed on the grounds of gross government misconduct. Today Dan Ellsberg still writes and works for peace, as does his son.

Robert came to the Catholic Worker in 1975 and stayed for five years, serving as editor of the *Catholic Worker* from 1976 to 1978. Then he returned to Harvard and spent time in Central America before becoming editor in chief and publisher of Orbis Books, where he regularly publishes books on peace and social justice. He recently edited the diaries and letters of his mentor Dorothy Day, and they were published by Marquette University Press.

Robert Ellsberg

"I went to the Catholic Worker because it seemed to me a place
where the spirit of Gandhi was most alive. It also seemed to me

Christianity on the front lines—the barricades. The Gospel in action."

I don't feel the same kind of call to complete consistency and purity as I did when I was twenty. Call it compromise or getting older or whatever. But I recognize some parts of myself still in that twenty-year-old. I have an affection and a certain respect for that person, but I also see that I wasn't nearly as pure then as I thought I was.

I went to the Catholic Worker with a lot of idealism and a . . . a kind of yearning for moral purity. And out of a sense of too much compromise in my life, too much tendency to intellectualize. I had a tremendous need to *do* something. I was a student of Gandhi and a very committed pacifist. Raised as an Episcopalian, but I had become fairly distant, uh . . . disillusioned with my church background. I guess I still thought of myself as Christian, but in some way the church was not good enough for me.

Ro: You said "not good enough."

Robert: That's the way I thought back then. I didn't feel challenged. I felt called to make a supreme sacrifice, and I didn't feel that the church challenged me to do that. I felt more that my community was the peace movement. I went to the Catholic Worker because it seemed to me a place where the spirit of Gandhi was most alive. It also seemed to me Christianity on the front lines—the barricades. The Gospel in action. I'd grown up with a family very affected by the whole culture of the antiwar movement

Ro: Did the fact that you were Dan Ellsberg's son make a difference?

Robert: I think it had a lot to do with the motivation that brought me to the Worker. I developed from him this urge to test myself, to see if I could give everything, sort of go to the limit. I found ways [to do that] at the Catholic Worker, ways that were probably easier for me than they would've been for somebody else—courting arrest, going to jail, fasting in jail, noncooperating.

The sort of thing that appeared very heroic to some people was really much easier for me than to stick with the personal, uncongenial, difficult work of caring for people in the Catholic Worker house. I came from a privileged background and had, you know, this need to get my hands dirty. My pacifism at the time was such that I felt that nonviolence had to be a complete way of life and not just a political tactic.

[Robert's first arrest was in front of the Indian consulate, demonstrating for democracy in India. Then he got involved with the War Resisters League, "with people who were sort of professional protesters," and once was arrested twice in the same day for "trying to shut down the New York Stock Exchange."]

Robert: It was just part of the culture I was in. Not any big deal at all. Then there were a couple of weeks [in 1977]—thirteen days, I guess—when I was one of 1,400 people arrested at Seabrook in New Hampshire. The Clamshell Alliance, the famous big mass arrest [against the nuclear power industry in New England], where we were held in National Guard armories all around the state. That protest became a prototype for a lot of big civil disobedience actions. Someday those lessons and skills will have to be remembered and relearned.

Rather than just have a big mass of people show up to be doing civil disobedience, which could be scary and dangerous, everybody was organized into small affinity groups of a dozen to fifteen people. So no one was there as an isolated individual; you were all part of a group that had been, I guess, sort of certified for having gone through some minimal nonviolence training—at least to talk about what the issues were, what to expect, how to comport yourself. And to provide a support group.

I was part of an affinity group made up of young activists from War Resisters League and the Catholic Worker. There was a fair amount of local support for the protest, because [nuclear power] was going to have a lot of negative environmental impact on the industries there, including the fishing industry.

There was this rabid governor of New Hampshire at the time, Meldrim Thomson. Very close connections to the nuclear industry. Very anti-Communist, with the "live free or die" mentality you see in New Hampshire. He played just totally into our hands. I guess they thought the safest thing was to let us onto the property. Get everybody there together and then remove us. Or something.

It was a Woodstock atmosphere with music and juggling and building latrines and sharing food. People like Howard Zinn and elders like that. College kids and grandmothers and people of all different ages. We were going to stay there indefinitely. But, you know, after sitting around for a day and using these outdoor latrines and eating granola, it began to dawn on us. "How long can we keep this up?"

One approach the authorities could have taken might have been to just wait us out until people mostly left, and then arrest the leftovers. (Obviously some would stay until the bitter end.) But they decided to arrest us all! On the second day they came with bullhorns and announced, "You are all in violation of the law and you have to leave."

Then all these buses began to arrive, and we thought, "Wow! This is it!" I was one of the first handfuls arrested.

We were all arrested pretty much with our affinity groups intact, which turned out to be kind of amazing. Taken to a gym and the first few people were fingerprinted and given tickets and let go. Then Meldrim Thomson showed up and said, "No bail!" The stakes suddenly got much heavier and *everyone* was incarcerated.

That meant using most of the National Guard armories in the state. People were driven all over the place. I went to a gym in an armory in Somersworth. Guarded by these young National Guards, without weapons. Of course we all had memories of Kent State and there *was* a certain scary kind of resonance.

Using the affinity groups, we immediately organized our discipline and decision-making and decided what we'd cooperate with and what not. I remember that they wanted to impose some minimal decorum by separating the men and women. There was a big protest about that, and people were refusing to move, but they eventually got us moved by dragging people around and setting up a rope barrier.

A lot of people were vegetarians and refused to eat the food, so there was much protest about that, and sometimes it was boring but mostly it was a fun experience. We were making more impact than we could possibly have had by sitting around in a parking lot. Thompson couldn't go back at this point. He was just stuck there and people were mad at how much it was costing the state of New Hampshire.

Eventually, after thirteen days, they brought us to a courthouse and kind of flushed us through. A few people went to trial but most of the charges were just quietly dropped. The year after that there was some sort of legal protest, and it was pretty much the end of both the movement and of the nuclear power industry. At that point, it was becoming clear that it wasn't wise, even on economic grounds.

Rocky Flats was a very different thing altogether.[4] I was arrested there with just a dozen people or so. There'd been an ongoing . . . I don't recall the whole history, but there was this idea of maintaining a continuous presence, blocking the railroad tracks. My father had gotten involved with them very early on. He had the idea that if you could get enough people to really interfere with the operations of Rocky Flats, then you'd actually be shutting down the nuclear assembly line. So he put a huge amount of personal energy into that and asked me to join him. Said it was very Gandhian.

I flew out to Denver with Brian Terrell, a friend of mine from the Catholic Worker. We took a bus out to Boulder and hooked up with my father and went out to join this protest on the tracks. A desolate landscape. It was late spring—May— but very windy and cold with snow on the ground. I don't think we were there very long when some police came along in jeeps and put plastic handcuffs on us and took us to the town of Golden in Jefferson County. We were arraigned right away.

I was sort of a protégé of Chuck Matthei back in those days.[5] From him, I had very disciplined and firm ideas about not surrendering my freedom and showing that I didn't stop being a protester when I was arrested, that it was important to continue to bear witness to the same principles of civil disobedience that had brought me there. They brought me into this room and told me to undress, and they were inspecting me, lifting my arms and opening my mouth. Then they told me to "bend over and spread [my] cheeks."

And I said, "No. I'm not going to do that."

They said, "What do you mean? You have to."

And I said, "No, I don't have to do it. I don't have any power over you, but there are some things I'm just not going to do." Now when I think of the dangers of smuggling weapons into jail and that sort of thing, it's not *just* calculated to humiliate people, and a lot of horrible stuff does go on in jails and everybody's safety, I suppose, is concerned. But at the time, it just seemed demeaning, and I wasn't going to voluntarily do it.

Then this big guard came in. I'm standing there naked and thinking, "This could be kind of painful." For a while, they continued to try to persuade me. Then finally they just tossed in a uniform and said, "Put this on." And they closed the door, and that was it. Suddenly I hear this voice from a toilet in a nearby booth: "I hope you got some dope stuck up there, baby."

Well, they segregated me from the rest of my group because of this little uprising, and the rest of the protesters were sent to this cushy little farm somewhere, where they had a relatively nice time. But they kept me locked down in this county jail.

I decided I was going to fast while I was there. First, they put me in a regular cell, really crowded, with maybe a dozen prisoners and an open toilet in the back. Sleeping on mats on the floor. Everybody smoked, mostly hand-rolled cigarettes, and it was really hard to breathe. And the noise was exhausting. No light to speak of, so it was hard to read, but I didn't have any books anyway or anything to write with. Just dull and depressing. They'd bring in food and I wouldn't touch it.

After a few days, things changed for me. I began to develop this terrible pain, an awful aching in my groin area. I mentioned it to a guard and eventually this male nurse came. He was really one of the most unpleasant people I met at the jail. When he found out I'd been fasting, they put me in solitary. Solitary was a very small, old little cell with a steel door they would close and I'd be in complete darkness.

Ro: You were in darkness?

Robert: Not for long periods of time, but from time to time that would happen. Usually the outer door was open, so there was light from the hallway, and I could reach out to a sink and get water. You could sort of hear music—Muzak—coming out of the walls, and hear people walking by, but it was away from the other prisoners. There was no toilet, just a hole in the floor. A mat and a blanket.

Without the smoke and the noise and the light, though, solitary was actually more restful. And by this time, they'd allowed me to have some visitors who brought me a Bible and a couple of novels and a notepad, and I could write letters and things.

One time, they said, "Ellsberg, come out! Your dentist is here to see you."

I thought, "What dentist?"

So I go to the visiting room, and it's one of the guys I'd been arrested with. He'd been released, and he said, "Okay, Robert, open your mouth and let me check your teeth." He really *was* a dentist!

I was still fasting, and I just seemed to be able to turn off my appetite. The pain went away, which just proved to the nurse that I was malingering or something. Every day, they'd walk me down to the bathrooms. (It's funny, you can fast for days and days, but you still have to move your bowels.) They'd weigh me and take notes and then walk me back. I certainly felt weak, but I wasn't exercising or doing anything, so it really wasn't that hard.

But finally one night I had my mini–dark night of the soul. I tried to reach out of the bars to get some water from the sink and suddenly there I was, lying on the floor. I came to with this aching pain and disorientation and really felt nauseous and . . . just awful. So then I got kind of scared and I called out for help. A kindly guard helped me get down to the bathroom. He said, "Would you like some vitamins or something?" At that point I really would have taken *anything*, not because I was hungry but because I was scared. Feeling frightened, like I might die.

So I said, "Sure, I'll take vitamins." I was sitting in the bathroom, just kind of collecting myself. The blood came back to my head and the pain sort of went away, and after half an hour or so, I felt okay and felt kind of embarrassed about making all this fuss. Then he came back and said he couldn't give me anything without the nurse's permission.

So then it seemed to me I was being tested and I told him I was okay, and after that, I was, actually. I continued to fast but I wasn't scared anymore, and a few days later, they chained me up with some other men and we went to court. I was really weak and I was worried about not being able to make it.

One of the guards, a nice one, said, "Are you going to make it?"

"Sure."

And he said, "Well, you've done a good job."

Then we walked outside, the first time in sixteen days. The fresh air and good light was just exhilarating! Then we were in court, and all the protesters had pled no contest, so we had a right to make a statement. I had prepared this long statement the night before. I have to say, I was very eloquent. [*Smiles wryly.*] When I finished, the whole courtroom cheered. My dad was there and I remember he was crying. The judge didn't say a thing. And so that was it. The next thing we knew, we were outside again, in the brisk Colorado air.

It felt like a resurrection! Being in jail had been such a total removal from the recognizable world. You didn't see the outside or know if it was day or night. There was no color, no natural light, no fresh air, no plants or grass. No furniture. No windows. No pictures on the wall. No women. No anything.

Ro: When you got out, did you start to eat carefully?

Robert: Of course you feel like you want an all-you-can-eat buffet or something. Someone gave me a little cottage cheese, and I took one spoonful and of course felt totally stuffed. I remember one of the guards in the courthouse saying to me, "I hear you've been fasting. I go on a fast every year, to clean out my system. I feel great afterwards." Which was exactly how I felt. It makes you feel very clearheaded and invulnerable, somehow. Like Daniel in the lion's den. Like they couldn't harm me, couldn't touch my core.

Ro: And also that you'd survived your own dark period.

Robert: Certainly that was good, also, not because I'm such a strong, brave guy or anything, but I knew experientially that I'm not really alone here, that there's a higher power watching over me. When I was in jail for a week in Hartford later on [for protesting the launch of a Trident submarine], that was a much scarier thing. In Colorado, I seemed to have this kind of protected status of being a political prisoner, and I felt the respect of most of the guards. When I was arrested in Hartford with Chuck Matthei and others, everybody else was sent home but we were sent to jail because we didn't cooperate. There you had the feeling that you were in a scary place.

They were coming to get us, one by one, and asking us if we would . . . you know, we'd have to take a shower, or be deloused or something like that, and then put on jail clothes. We were refusing to do that, so they dragged us out, using these pressure holds. You could say we were choosing to endure that because we could have just walked normally, but we chose not to do that. They had obviously very sophisticated methods for inflicting pain—ways of holding you so that your whole body weight was on your wrists or your thumbs. I remember they were dragging me with my hands underneath me, so my whole body was falling on my wrists. It was excruciatingly painful. And you know you're totally in their power and you're all alone.

Anyway, they dragged me, really roughly—doing these kinds of holds—into this shower, and turned on this ice-cold water. They had rough scrub brushes, like toilet brushes, and they scraped me all over, then poured some chemical on me and rinsed it off and then dragged me naked into a cell and dumped me there. The whole thing maybe took five minutes but it was scary. That was the only experience I had of . . . Again, they were doing that to make me cooperate, not to single me out for punishment or because they were sadistic.

I was there for about a week, and I fasted there, too, and then they dragged us to a bus and took us to court. I wouldn't get off the bus, so a judge came on the bus and did whatever he does and let us go. But each of these experiences was very different. At Rocky Flats I felt this kind of power and exaltation, where at this Hartford time, I could see how scary and anonymous you can feel.

Ro: How forgotten a prisoner really is.

Robert: Exactly. Even though it was only a few days, I got a sense of what it's like to be in a jail where your life is in danger and there's real brutality.

But as my life gets longer, these experiences become a smaller part of the whole picture. I'm reluctant to overdramatize it or make it seem especially heroic. I remember one of the guards in Colorado asking how my employer lets me do that kind of thing. At the time, I thought I'd never work anyplace where I couldn't go to jail for my conscience. But in fact, that represented a time when I had incredible freedom.

I believe very much in the power of civil disobedience. But looking back on it, perhaps I was a little bit too self-righteous about that kind of thing and had a tendency to think things like, "If you're really committed, you'll go to jail." Now, there are circumstances in which that's totally true, and there are circumstances in which that can also represent incredible luxury. That's not to say that there aren't people who have done this courageously—left their families dangling while they went to prison for years.

I am also maybe not so inclined to glorify those choices uncritically. As someone who personally has a keen sense of how much responsibility goes into having a family, it would be a shame to use that as an excuse or a cop-out for not doing the right thing. But being kind of a professional jail-goer, as I was over a couple of years, that's . . . I could do that because I didn't have to worry about anybody else.

My father has been arrested . . . it must be hundreds of times, but he probably hasn't spent as much time in jail as I have, because he'd have commitments or something, so he'd [sign out on personal recognizance]. Now, he faced considerably more risk—150 years in prison for the Pentagon Papers—but your everyday modern civil disobedience doesn't necessarily entail that much risk.

The first time, that first crossing the line, like when I was arrested at the Indian consulate, when you're suddenly into a kind of outlaw category . . . it's . . . it's extremely liberating. It opens up all these possibilities of what you can do.

Then there are those people who are repeat offenders who get these outlandish sentences of six months or even a year, just for a peaceful protest. I really admire that, because it is also possible for civil disobedience to become just symbolic; I can't believe it shows all this commitment if what you're expecting is something like a parking ticket.

Sometimes these very heavily orchestrated demonstrations where people cross a certain line and are simply arrested and then released . . . That doesn't mean it's not worth doing, but again, it tempers any impulse to be heroic, because, in fact, the investment of time—the sacrifice—is nothing compared to the people who doggedly attend city council meetings or lobby or go door to door to change their neighbors' minds about something. Or publish a letter in the *Times* that might make them unpopular with their neighbors. Things like that require real commitment, real time and sacrifice. And to stress so much just being arrested or going to jail for a day or so . . .

Robert Ellsberg, publisher of Orbis Books, 2005.
(Photo courtesy of Rosalie Riegle.)

On the other hand—there are always so many "on-the-other-hands"—I'm glad I had those experiences. I learned both how to get in touch with my own inner strength, and I also learned about my limitations. To have even a few days where you feel that sort of moral clarity about something . . . and then the words you speak from that situation have a power and impact that they don't have if you're just sitting here in your office talking about peace.

I really felt that was the message we were conveying at Rocky Flats. Not that we were going to magically stop the arms race and not that we were right just because we were willing to get arrested, but that we were willing to put the full weight of our conscience behind our words. And that it would compel people to listen more to what we were saying and perhaps do more themselves. Maybe it did or maybe it didn't, but eventually, you know, the Rocky Flats actions did attract more people to think of taking their own risks.

I think that's a lot of the impact of the Plowshares people. They make us all ask questions about the appropriate response. Rocky Flats was just a small part of the whole wave of antinuclear and disarmament activities. It had a symbolic intensity: the idea of sitting on railroad tracks that carried triggers for nuclear bombs into this factory. In my remarks to the court, I compared it to Dachau, where the trains with their cargo were going in and out and the people around don't even think about what's going on [inside].

So we can't literally stop this whole thing, but we can say with our bodies that you can't do it without arresting us, without removing us physically. And when it comes to the point when not just handfuls of people are willing to make that statement, but thousands or tens of thousands of people, it can change history. And eventually Rocky Flats did close.

Lenore Yarger and Steve Woolford are married Catholic Workers. They lived at the Rock Island CW with the late Chuck Trapkus before moving to North Carolina and founding their own community—Silk Hope. Steve describes his life in a county jail in the South, Lenore the life in the community while he's away.

Steve Woolford and Lenore Yarger

"We went into this [prison experience] expecting our relationship to be on hold for six months, and that wasn't at all the way it was."

Steve: I think being a Catholic Worker is, in itself, a form of resistance. It's doing something very different than what's expected of good people in a capitalist culture, so it undermines a lot of what that culture says you're supposed to be doing. But if you mean breaking laws and confronting the powers in a way that makes them deal with you, that started when we moved to the Catholic Worker in Rock Island in 1994. Living with other people who'd been arrested many times took some of the mystery away, and I didn't have to invent it entirely on my own. We had clear examples and an awful lot of support and encouragement, especially from Chuck Trapkus.

Ro: Is it too hard to talk about him and his influence on you?

Steve: Oh, no! I talk about it a lot, maybe too much. Chuck was probably the most influential person in Lenore's and my lives. He made what previously had seemed sane seem crazy and vice versa, both in discussions and in the way he lived his life. He said we needed to fill up the prisons, so the system could no longer just brush us aside. He talked about all the jailbirds in the early church, and showed us that it's similar to what people are doing in the resistance movement today—confronting the powers and having to suffer the consequences.

One thing that made Chuck such an influence is that everyone knew he'd always do the right thing. He was an extremely moral person. So when someone like Chuck went to jail, people knew it wasn't for any kind of personal gain. He had just this tremendous integrity.

Lenore's arrests have had the same impact. We joke that when people in my hometown hear about me getting arrested, they think, "I always knew he'd wind up in jail." When Lenore gets arrested, people know it's for a good reason.

We moved out here in 1997, and we shopped around a good bit because we wanted to be close to an urban center, so we could do hospitality and resistance as well as the rural scene. We do two weekly vigils in [nearby] Chapel Hill, one with a lot of foot traffic where we have good conversations, and one in a higher–vehicle traffic area. Some of the best conversations were right after September 11th. Some people would hotly argue and tell us we were crazy and traitors; others were really passionate about their Christianity and supported the war, but were still willing to talk about it with someone who was raising a challenge based on religious conviction. One woman insisted that because Jesus got angry, therefore he would bomb people, things like that.

Ro: Now, you were in jail for a protest when the latest Iraq war started, weren't you?

Steve: Right. Bill Frankel-Streit and Steve Baggarly and I were part of a big ALC [Atlantic Life Community] demonstration at a Faith and Resistance Retreat. Seventy or eighty people came to the Pentagon on the Feast of Holy Innocents. The three of us spread blood at the entrance, to show people what the building was all about. This was the first time people had protested with blood after the 9/11 plane had hit the building, and we'd talked about whether it was appropriate, given that American lives had been lost right there, but decided it was, given the mission of the Pentagon.

   This time we won the maximum sentence. Six months, and I served it in two different places. I'd been arrested and convicted in DC before, and this time I was even before the same judge, but there was no record of my first conviction. (I don't think their record keeping is very good, actually.)

   When I go to court, I pretty much do it the way Chuck did. Just explain why I did it and show them I don't have any remorse about it. (There's lots of things I've done in my life that I'm not proud of, but I'm sure not ashamed of these resistance actions.) I don't even know how concerned I am with making a case that legally I should have been doing what I was doing. The Christian anarchist in me says that whether or not I'm obeying some international law, the law of conscience is what I follow.

   This time, though, we didn't get to say much at all. The judge was angry and in no way did she want to make it seem as though the actions of the Pentagon were being judged. This Theresa Buchanan is a Catholic and a . . . finger-wagging lecturer. (I think there's two Catholic Churches, the one she belongs to and mine.) It may be a part of her is scared to listen to us because she might have to change something in her own life. So she's offended when I say, "I am a Catholic and this is what Catholics should do."

   She's particularly offended by our use of blood. You know, prosecutors often say we could have donated the blood instead of "wasting it," and fortunately, I can pull out my Red Cross [donor] card. In many ways blood is really is the truest symbol. In a biblical sense and also literally. That's what these invasions are, that's what the violence means to people.

Ro: What was it like to be in jail when the Iraq bombing started?

Steve: In one sense there was at least some peace of mind that I'd done something strong to object. This war hit me a lot more personally than the others because Lenore had just been to Iraq and brought back stories of all the people she met. She went with September 11 Families for Peaceful Tomorrows and some other Catholic Workers. In her talks about the trip, she'd show slides and tell stories, so I felt so much more connected. "What happened to the shoeshine boy outside the hotel? To the people she visited?"

There had been so much protest against the war, from so many countries, that up until the minute the missiles went into the air, I tried to be hopeful that something would stop it. Then when it started, it was the final punch in the stomach. We didn't stop it and now we *couldn't* stop it.

The men in the jail . . . The jail I was in holds a lot of federal prisoners, and federal prisoners in general hate the government and identify more with oppressed people anywhere than they do with privileged Americans. Still, I was kind of surprised that only two people seemed to support the war. Both conservative Christians; one was a white guy, one was African American. The other prisoners seemed to be just automatically opposed.

"It's just more killing. They kill our people in the streets here, they kill people over there." Some of them even listened to BBC News with me. Actually I was surprised I could even get it in jail. One guy said, "They don't show anything like that on the other news—dead bodies and people being carried to hospitals."

People thought we were weird, though—Steve [Baggarly] and I were in together—and I heard rumors that some people thought we must be cops because we didn't look like guys who had committed a crime. Most people, though, were just plain puzzled, and a few said they were impressed. Others thought I didn't know what I was doing and wanted me to promise not to do anything again, because they were afraid of what a long prison term would do to me.

Some people were genuinely helpful, with good advice, and gifts, even, and then there were people who gave worthless advice. (I guess they just needed to be giving advice on something.) In general, I was impressed at how much prisoners looked after each other.

Ro: Did any Catholic chaplains come in?

Steve: A priest would bring in the Eucharist each week, and in jail, it took on a greater meaning for me than it often does at a regular Sunday Mass. Steve and I also would go to these horrible church services that another pastor gave. I guess he meant well, but the attitude was that we were all sinners and needed to repent. But we'd go because it gave us a chance to be together. We'd been separated after the first week or so, right around the time a journalist called and wanted to do a story on us.

I had a pretty easy time, actually, for a couple reasons: Playing sports helped. And most importantly because I had examples from people who'd done this kind of thing before. Like Bill Frankel-Streit told me about this guy who got his wedding ring stolen, so I knew to leave my wedding ring at home.

Plus, near here, there's a place called the Human Kindness Foundation, that does prison ministry and teaches spiritual exercises to prisoners. Their attitude is that you can treat jail like your life is on hold or you can think of it as a chance to do spiritual work that the world doesn't give you time to do. I had read one of their books, *We're All Doin' Time*, before going in and it helped me with my attitude.

I tried to meditate every day, and in fact, structured my whole day. I did exercises at certain times and set myself little goals. I was also intentional about having times when I'd read and times when I'd write letters. The libraries both in the jail and in the prison were pretty good, and I had more time to read that I'd had in years. I mean, there are days now where if I read a paragraph before I fall asleep, that's a good day. Boredom was never the problem. It was much more not being able to cram everything in.

Lenore: Once I was talking to Steve on the phone and I asked him to write some-thing for the paper. And he says, "I'm *busy*! You don't realize this, but I'm very busy!" [*Laughter.*]

Steve: I was! I had all these opportunities—to read, to practice art, improve my Spanish, to play soccer. All these opportunities. That made it completely different than seeing it as a huge interruption. One thing, though: I couldn't talk to anyone in there about what it was like for me. The last thing they would want to hear is, "It's not as bad as you think it is."

Lenore: Looking back on it, the visits sound as if they were awful. They were short, they were by phone through a glass, and I had to drive three or four hours to get there. But at the time, it just did *so* much good! Just to see him and know that he was okay. He'd always be in really good spirits, so that helped, too.

Steve: I didn't fake it, either. From what you see in the movies, I felt I was in a kiddie jail. I wasn't getting a lot to eat, but I wasn't worried. Even when there were things to gripe about, I didn't feel I should just unload on her.

Ro: Lenore, what was it like in the house with Steve gone?

Lenore: Again, when you look back on it, you wonder how we ever got through. Community was great. Dan [Schwankl] was here, and then a wonderful woman,

Allison [Beloin], came for the summer. Anna [Dioguardi] moved in then, too, so we had a lot of good energy plus good visits from other folks. But Steve is my best friend and I just missed him terribly. Plus there was just a lot of work.

The hardest part was doing the [GI Rights] Hotline all by myself.[6] One of the reasons we went with the Hotline was that we wanted a job that could continue if one or the other of us were in jail. The calls were at their peak because the war was breaking out, but I kept up the forty hours. To be in touch with soldiers who were getting screwed and being sent to their deaths—that seemed concrete. We started in January of 2001 and after 9/11, we started getting about three times as many calls, but we already knew what to tell them or where to look for the information the soldiers needed.

I also continued to give talks about my trip to Iraq, which sometimes required travel. The whole thing was exhausting and looking back on it, I don't know how I did it, but in some ways it was good because you feel like you're doing something instead of just being paralyzed by the war. There was so little I could do to help the people I'd met in Iraq, other than to continue the protest.

Steve: Lenore really had the hardest part. She had tons of extra responsibility, and she took on a huge bulk of the work that I wasn't doing. Plus I'm getting support letters every day. I don't think community members get enough credit for all they do when someone's in jail. People ask me to speak about my jail experience but they don't ask others in the community to talk about all they've done.

In a lot of ways, I was so spoiled! Even though prison was the most I've ever had my life controlled by other people, mine wasn't at all the kind of experience an everyday prisoner gets. I definitely had the kid glove treatment. Now, there are people who have trying experiences in prison, especially with longer sentences. But for someone like me getting six months, I felt sort of like—you know, on the Monopoly board you have "Go to Jail" and "Just Visiting." I felt I was just visiting.

Guards seem to have a sense of moral superiority. "I'm here guarding you and you're the screw-up." When people like us come in, it pulls the rug out from under them. They may not agree with what we're doing, but at least they can't use this moral superiority thing. Whatever power they get from feeling that is taken away when people don't feel sorry about what they did and can look them in the eye and say they're not upset about it.

Ro: Yes, I see. Lenore, how is having baby Geneva making a difference in your Catholic Worker life?

Lenore: Well, we wanted one of us to serve time before we had a child, to know what it was like. That was a good decision, because we really learned how to care for each other as a couple through that time. Hopefully that will serve us well in the future because this house is committed to doing the kind of resistance that will

Lenore Yarger, Steve Woolford, and baby Geneva, 2005.
(Photo courtesy of Rosalie Riegle.)

result in jail time. You know, though, I still feel like a very new parent. We're only four months into it, but I can say that it feels hard for me to even *imagine* being away from Geneva.

Steve: I think before either of us would risk more than a few weeks in jail, we'd want to do a lot of talking about what that would mean to her. And to the parent who stays home. I don't know how single parents do it, because we have teamwork and I'm *still* tired! I know people do it, but it must be really hard, in addition to the missing her, and missing out on "firsts," and so forth. And her missing us.

Ro: Was how you felt leaving each other as a couple different than how it felt as community?

Lenore: Oh, yes! We went into this expecting that our relationship would be on hold for six months, and that wasn't at all the way it was. Instead, we grew closer as a couple. We wrote to each other almost every day and after he was transferred to Butner, every Thursday afternoon and into the evening we were together. It's rare that we get to spend that kind of time together now, where we can focus completely on each other.

Steve: Our conversations were . . . uh, so much more deliberate. Not, "Have you seen my blue socks?" And the time feels so precious that you're careful to focus on what's important. In some ways it was like being on retreat or a marriage encounter. Or the way monastic life seems to focus people's thoughts. Some of the ways you live while you're in prison makes you realize what's important and what are just frivolous details.

Lenore: After I became pregnant, a friend asked me if I felt that had happened too soon after Steve got out of prison, because of the adjustment. Well, I didn't feel I needed time to recover from him being in prison. It was just wonderful to have him home again.

Steve: Prison made us ready to have a baby sooner than we'd thought, I think, because we really grew a lot during that time. Maybe for the right couples, prison is what they need. [*Both laugh.*]

Lenore: That's not to say it wasn't very, very hard, and I was very glad when it was over. Oh, one more thing: Steve's experiences were transformative for relationships outside of our immediate family. For instance, my grandparents visited him when he was at Butner, and that was a huge step for them. They'd never even *heard* of people doing this sort of thing, much less understanding it. For them, people who go to jail are criminals, you know, not their grandson-in-law. I was very touched by their visit. And people at our church . . . One couple has a son-in-law who fought in Iraq and yet they wrote to Steve and asked about him every Sunday. A lot of bridge-building. It's not something people can ignore very easily, so people stepped up and offered wonderful support.

Steve: I've heard that some people compare what we're doing to what the soldiers are doing by leaving their families and going to Iraq, but I think the sacrifices and the suffering that comes from doing the kind of resistance I did are just *so* insignificant. When you compare it to what's happening to people all over the world, the victims on the receiving end of this violence as well as the sacrifices of the ones perpetrating it, there's just no comparison.

Lenore: Carol [Gilbert] and Ardeth [Platte] have pointed out that Geneva is our connection to all the children of this world who live in war and suffering, I don't want to live a life where everything is just to create Geneva's perfect world. It's to create a perfect world for *all* children. And that's the challenge, I think, of being parents—to allow your child to be your connection to the rest of the children in the world.

Claire and Scott Schaeffer-Duffy have been doing resistance together since before they opened Saints Francis and Thérèse CW in Worcester, Massachusetts. Their four children are all now teenagers or beyond. In 2008 they received the Isaac Hecker Award from the Paulist Center in Boston, an award once bestowed on CW founder Dorothy Day. I interviewed them separately, and Scott's reflections are after Claire's.

Claire and Scott Schaeffer-Duffy

*"Whoever is away—whether it's me or Scott—that person
will ask, 'How's it going at home?' That's the most important
conversation to be had when we've got fifteen minutes on a long-
distance phone call."*

Claire: If you're defining resistance as going to jail, I was in jail with the first baby—I mean, when I was pregnant with him—and I also had an experience of risking arrest and going to court when I was pregnant with Patrick, the third child, but I didn't get a jail sentence for that. Since then I haven't risked arrest. So I'm not . . . I call myself a bit of a cop-out activist. Lately I'm trying to put more energy into the writing and so . . . But the Catholic Worker has certainly been happening since '87 in this house.

Ro: Well, some people do their time in jail, and some people do their time at the kitchen sink. Somebody has to be here, running the house and holding down the family, so I think you *have* been doing resistance the whole time.

Claire: Yeah. But I kind of bristle at "resistance at the kitchen sink." I'm not sure I think of myself that way. In fairness to the [other] people in the community . . . I mean, when Scott was in jail for three months back in 2003, there was a lovely couple living here, so the dishes were shared. I don't want to give the impression that it's this single mom and nobody else is helping. It's very . . . uh, high-paced when Scott is gone, but even when he was in jail, I was still writing, so it's not quite a woman staying home with the cooking and the dishes.

I don't know if I expressed that clearly. There's much more day-to-day maintaining of the house when he's gone—writing letters, paying bills, all those things—but I probably should be doing more of that when he's here, so it's always a little uneven, you know. I do feel the weight lift when he comes back, but even when he's gone, there's still time to read and write.

The other piece of it is that Scott covers for me when I'm gone, and I've done quite a few trips on my own, without the kids. Afghanistan and then India in 2004 and Haiti in 2005. I've been to Bosnia three times, the first time when our youngest was just weaned. I attended a women's peace conference, and it was more than a gift, it was a miracle! (And it was really *was* a gift! The person said, "Here's a check so you can go.")

It was *such* a eye-opening experience! I'd been so . . . uh, so focused on the babies that it was really an awakening. That's when I got into looking more at the international scene, which has been in my blood anyway. (My father was working for the US Information Service, and I spent twelve of my eighteen years of childhood overseas. In Burma, India, England, and Japan.) I've been back to the same place in Bosnia twice, to look more deeply at the lives of the women there.

I want to write about . . . it's a bizarre phrase, but sort of the "domestic experiences" of war, angles that I don't think are ever examined—how it affects births and familial relationships, aging family members, friendships, all the separations caused by the dislocation of war. Perhaps a husband disappears, and the marriage was already struggling, so there are all the questions of fidelity and betrayal. And also feeling solidarity with someone that you previously felt uncertain about or even betrayed by. Suddenly you can't resolve the contradictions.

Also the whole complexity of everything, like how to do extremely basic things, such as washing and acquiring food. The women that I talked to in Bosnia, for example, were in a camp with no food, so they'd walk seven kilometers to forage in their destroyed houses, going through their own stores to try to find something to eat.

One of the husbands that I interviewed watched his wife leave every day, and he was terrified that she'd get raped. It was at a very chaotic point in the war, and bands of local men were taking advantage of the situation [by aligning themselves with] paramilitaries. There were "professional" soldiers, members of the Yugoslavian army, and there were also paramilitaries. Some of these groups attracted local toughs who took advantage of a chaotic situation to steal, exact revenge for old quarrels, and yes . . . to rape. A typical pattern of ethnic cleansing during the Bosnian war was that the soldiers waged initial assault and the paramilitaries then descended for "mop up." So the agony of your wife bringing you food, but wondering if she would come back to you intact . . .

See, they separated the men and the women, and they gave the women a certain degree of freedom, but he couldn't go with her. That's another thing that intrigues me: the realm of movement that is permitted in war to women. This is all a side track, but I keep thinking about all these things.

Ro: I don't think it's a side track. It goes back to a definition of resistance. Isn't your travel also a way to do the "acting no" that Jim Wallis talks about? It seems to me these learning-and-then-communicating trips are "acting no." You're bringing these stories to us and risking [yourself] to do so.

Claire: Hmmm. [*Nods.*] I liked interviewing the Bosnian women. I could usually get them to talk to me, and I think it's because I was a woman. One woman told me about being taken to a village and seeing sheets hanging out the window. She was thinking, "How can they be doing laundry now, in the middle of a war?" And then she realized they were white sheets signifying surrender. An ordinary artifact of life suddenly becomes this symbol of what's happening to you.

As a result of these trips, I think of war much more in the immediate sense. And, for me, in terms of resistance, the trips have solidified a perspective that I already had—a long-held distrust of the state. I'm sure this was cultivated as a political science major at the University of Virginia and then nurtured by the analysis of the Catholic Worker. After you've been in conflict zones, you realize there are very few good governments. So the trips have confirmed my . . . um, my distrust of nationalism itself.

Nationalism is really a wretched concept and so counter to the betterment of human development. Most people have been taught to have this allegiance to the state, you know, and they kind of confuse local love with superimposed national icons. Imagine our hospital here in Worcester and people trying to work there without water and electricity. If you break it down, people will see this, but then they'll still sometimes justify why cities have to be bombed.

I'm rambling here, but my suspicion of the state has not waned, even though my activism is, uh, not so high. I'll probably have Homeland Security at my door tomorrow for saying this, but I have no allegiance to the nation state, and I think that you can't. You just can't.

A lot of people I would describe as traditional Catholics support the house. People raised on the Baltimore catechism understand the hospitality and the charity. When you come back from a place like Sudan or Iraq or Bosnia and give a slide show, they have great compassion. Great compassion. But they can't see their part in it. I think that's something the Church—or we—can do better on communicating. "What would be a lifestyle that more closely reflects sharing with the poor? How can we stop using the oil?"

Ro: Yes! Let's talk about children and resistance. As your children are growing and becoming politically aware, what is their attitude toward your resistance?

Claire: Well, they don't know anything else. The older ones . . . certainly, they feel the absence of their father because I tend to be more cranky than usual when he's away. But baseline crankiness is pretty high on my side, anyway.

The last time when he was in jail for three months, Scott wrote a book for them. He'd send chapters, and we put it all together like in a book, and we wrote a review of it and all this stuff, so that was wonderful. The older ones, though, have expressed a certain difficulty describing their parents' world and they feel a bit self-conscious about it. When people ask them what their dad does, they say, "Catholic Worker," but then they've had people say, "Oh, your father does that arrest thing."

Usually the question I get from people is whether I worry about his safety when he's in jail. People just assume that I'm chewing my nails with worry and in reality, I don't. First of all, I'm a very introspective person, and what I lose sleep over is *my* flaws and foibles and the choices I make. Plus when he's gone, it's so busy that there's just no time to . . . and it strikes me as pointless worrying. Now, thank God, nothing has happened. I would worry if he were sick in jail, or if I heard that he was mistreated, or if I didn't hear from him. But so far we've been very lucky, and he's very conscientious about communicating so that lessens any anxiety.

I think in marriage, as with any deep friendship, you want to support the person, to urge them to be who they're called to be and support that in a nonresentful way. Some women from my mother's generation found themselves supporting out of a sense of imposed role, and they resented that. Now, I don't want to misrepresent us here. Resentment does come up, and we've worked at that.

When we were younger, Scott'd come home and be talking all about what he'd been through, and . . . it took years to sort of figure out how to do this. So now, whoever is away will ask, "How's it going at home?" That's the most important conversation to be had when we've got fifteen minutes on a long-distance phone call. Being home is much more trying than wherever the other person is.

There's another side of this, though: The person away finds it very hard to be in such a completely different world than the family is. When you come home, it doesn't matter if you almost got shot at in some alleyway in the West Bank, you still have to do the laundry. The little kids want you to listen to what *they've* been doing. But we're getting better at this transition.

Ro: How do you make decisions about when to travel, when to risk arrest?

Claire: It's nutty because there's very little of the processing that's "supposed" to go on. But it's always been that way with us. For Sudan, for example, on Monday, he said, "I think I'm going to Sudan," and by Wednesday he was pulling together a peace team. Now, he didn't leave for another six weeks, but there was none of this saying we should pray about this, read scripture, and all the things that more sane human beings would do. Maybe. Once it's on the calendar, it has precedence. We're never both going to be away while the children are here with us, but Scott yearns for the day when we can both go together.

Ro: Claire, I first interviewed you here back in 1989, and I'm wondering how your life as a Catholic Worker has changed in those twenty years.

Claire: Well, you know, Rosalie, the big thing I have to fight within myself is a narrowing of my heart in hospitality. As if somehow I've reached some entitlement, that because I've been doing this so long, I'm entitled to limit what I give, both regarding the guests and in resistance.

Certainly the hospitality that we offered before the children came was much more open and wilder and generous than what we do now. But I think that to share the house is just so important. It's so, so important. I have to say that it gets *harder* for me as I get older.

And the same with the wars. The most terrifying thing is that you can hear so many war stories that you're no longer moved. You've heard it again and again, and you can almost predict it on some level. And to separate each person and each story and each . . . each *being* and say, "This is momentous, and it's their life, and I can't treat it merely as a pattern." That's hard, too, as I get older, but it's so, so necessary.

Claire and Scott Schaeffer-Duffy, 2005. (Photo courtesy of Rosalie Riegle.)

Scott: For me, community is the answer. And my wife. I admire Ammon Hennacy's "one-man revolution," but I've eschewed it from the beginning because I fear it would not only weaken the movement, but be bad for me spiritually.[7] So when I act or when I go to a war zone, I try as much as possible to go with others. And in court, even though I may have more legal expertise, everybody bears the weight and everyone asks questions. To the extent that any action is a cult of personality, it's weak, in my opinion.

My wife, Claire . . . we have to act in concert. She's a perfect partner for me, in the sense that she's supportive but not an iota more than necessary. She'll stand up to me when I'm out of line. Very much so. See, I think a good marriage pushes you to be your own best self. And we have that kind of relationship. If I'm intellectually or morally weak on some points, Claire's going to say so. It's one thing to have someone that you love, it's another thing to have someone whom you also respect. And I certainly respect her. We have . . . she's a writer and I write, too, but I'm more of a public speaker. So our differences are interesting and enjoyable and we're not always tripping over each other.

Ro: Now, you do actions with jail time and you also do the international travel with the Catholic Worker Peace Team. Are there any conflicts between the two?

Scott: Well, we both try as much as possible to respond to the Holy Spirit and to be open to doing what God wants us to do. Seeing things in the paper and feeling a tug of conscience and coming up with a creative idea, heads together with other people. Sometimes people call us, or opportunities come up, so I . . . It might look like I'm driving the train but, uh . . . maybe God's laying the track or something.

Discerning what God's will is, is tricky stuff. Ego can get involved, and you can do the wrong thing. You have to ask for God's mercy and go to confession and ask for grace. Evaluate all the time. But remember: I've done nowhere near as much civil disobedience or time in war zones as some people. I've got down to maybe once or twice a year in a conflict zone and maybe once a year in a civil disobedience situation.

I've gone several times to Israel-Palestine, where the presence of an American can actually save lives. The way we do it is with these ad hoc groups, which we call Catholic Worker Peace Teams. We work like an affinity group and ride the infrastructure of other groups on the ground: the Solidarity movement, the Center for Rapprochement between Peoples, Rabbis for Human Rights, groups like that.

A Catholic Worker Peace Team goes into a place with a threefold mission: to gather and bring back information, to do some meaningful relief and some meaningful nonviolence, and to act somehow to promote peace. You go in short term and can get a lot done and be fairly productive and bring back photos and do several dozen slide shows at the colleges. There's risk, of course—there's risk in all this stuff—but we're also trying to be responsible parents and responsible to our local community and also to continue for the long haul, to be around doing this peace work until our natural or unnatural deaths.

That brings me to one thing I want to talk about that seems to be missing in our lives today, whether it's peace work or baking bread or climbing a mountain, as I'm going to do with the children tomorrow. And it's that we need to unify our lives, to see our lives as all of a whole. We've got to get rid of these dichotomies: that time with our family is "time off." Or that dancing is somehow "time away." You know, suffering and ecstatic joy and love and ministry—they all fit together, and they give depth and meaning to each other. So when I see somebody concentrating on just one thing or one person, then I sense that their lives are coming apart.

Saint Paul talks about praying unceasingly. How can you do that and live a life? Well, you do everything in your life under the broad umbrella of your vocation. That it's the will of God for you. It might be the will of God for me to laugh uproariously at a movie. Seeing it all as a whole just stretches it and puts you in a broader space.

Time also vanishes with this unity. Whether there's another war, and then another war—you don't get so frantic. You've still got the same responsibilities: to be joyful, to be loving, to be hopeful, to be compassionate, to be humble—all these things remain the same. At any given moment, even when you've failed at something, you start up again. The next things you do—whether it's saying hello to a stranger or buying your airline ticket to Haiti—can actualize the kingdom of God. It can! So you can retain your sense of humor. I think you can have that balance in other professions, too.

You know, people say our life is so hard. But it's not. I tell them, "I'm the happiest person I know. My life is easy." Jesus wasn't kidding when he said His yoke is easy, His burden is light. It's absolutely true. I've never found life easier than since I entered the Catholic Worker and started to think of my life as a whole.

Steve Baggarly and his wife, Kim Williams, decided before they married that they'd be a Catholic Worker family. After a grounding at the Los Angeles CW, in 1989 they started their own house in Norfolk, Virginia, home of the world's largest naval base. Like their mother community, the Norfolk house has a soup line, provides live-in hospitality, and always, always, resists war. Unlike the leaders in the Los Angeles house, however, Kim and Steve have two children.

Steve received a thirteen-month sentence for the Prince of Peace Plow-shares action in 1997 and served part of it in Maine with the other resisters and part in West Virginia. Later, a Pentagon blood-pouring action with the Atlantic Life Community sent him to a privatized county jail in Virginia. The experiences were different for each incarceration. I interviewed Steve and Kim separately, each speaking with me while the spouse dealt with children and hospitality issues.

Steve Baggarly and Kim Williams

"Kim had the harder part, though, staying home. It's a retreat time for us in jail, more of a meditative experience. In Maine, it was sometimes even a party experience."

Steve: Albert Camus said in the aftermath of World War II that "Christians must speak out and utter their condemnation in such a way that never a doubt, never a single doubt, can arise in the heart of even the simplest person."

That quote was an inspiration for me at the Pentagon action in 2003. Breaking the laws that allow for the warmaking is the strongest nonviolent statement we can make. But we do other nonviolent actions, too. Vigils against the death penalty. Vigils at the Norfolk Naval Base here. Vigils at the Seymour Johnson AFB in North Carolina, and the Yorktown Naval Weapons Station, which used to store nuclear warheads for Tomahawk cruise missiles. This kind of resistance had been part of our work here from the beginning.

In 2002, I think it was, Bill [Frankel-Streit] and I got on top of a B-52 at an air show at Langley Air Force Base in Hampton. Unfurled a banner that said "Weapons of Mass Destruction, Nothing to Celebrate." Because these air shows are incredible! Just a glorification of military hardware. The most sophisticated machinery in the world, all for mass destruction.

We also feel ourselves very much a part of the Atlantic Life Community. In 2003, Bill Frankel-Streit and Steve Woolford and I did an action in DC with the group. Poured blood on the columns at the Pentagon on the Feast of the Holy Innocents. This was the first major action there since 9/11, so even though they've been having these Pentagon actions for thirty years, we didn't know what to expect. But it went great!

The new entrance to the Pentagon is right up the escalators from the subway, and there are two escalators, so the main body of protesters went one way and kind of created a diversion, and the three of us went the other way and easily got near the columns and were able to throw the blood.

The arresting guards there are the Pentagon security people. You know, not military but rent-a-cops. They treated us fine, just wrote us up and let us go. They take you along this big hallway, then you're arrested and on the wall are pictures of what they do. Now, half of what they do is arrest protesters, so there are these big, beautiful pictures of our friends, and processions with crosses, and blood on the building. A museum of protest at the Pentagon!

We went to Alexandria Federal Court before Judge Buchanan. She'd sent Bill Frankel-Streit to jail several times, so we were expecting to get whacked. And she whacked us. I mean, even Steve [Woolford] got the max, and basically it was his first offense. So we all went for six months, right from court to jail.

Ro: How do you feel about the repetitious nature of these Pentagon actions?

Steve: I think the Pentagon is probably the best site [to protest]. Its tentacles are everywhere. The people who have been doing this consistently for so long, I think are just . . . [*long sigh*] . . . It strikes me as being one of the most important things Americans could be doing.

The only things I've spent long times in prison are for "altering of property" charges—this one at the Pentagon and then up in Maine for the Prince of Peace Plowshares in '97. I got a year for that. We went to Bath Iron Works on Ash Wednesday and hammered and poured blood on the USS *The Sullivans*, which is a guided missile destroyer with Tomahawk cruise missiles that can be armed with nuclear warheads.

The rest of the group were stopped right away, but it was the middle of the night and Steve and I got to do what we wanted to do—to begin the conversion of the weapons into plowshares. We got into the pilot house and hammered and poured blood there and also on the helicopter launching pad and on one of the missile hatches.

The next morning, the judge let us go, saying that Phil Berrigan was the "conscience of a generation." (He was pretty sure we'd come back for trial, so he didn't see having to spend the state's money to keep us in up there 'til then.) So we all went back home, but then the feds took it over from the state. We knew they'd come looking for us, so we made it easy for them. Came back to the scene of the

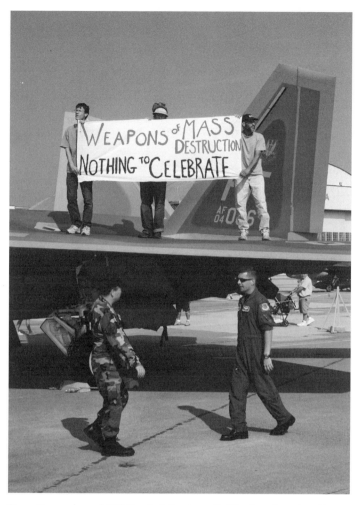

Steve Baggarly and Bill Frankel-Streit on B-52 wing, Langley Air Force Base, 2002. (Photo courtesy of Scott Langley.)

crime—the ongoing crime, which is the building of the ships. We held a vigil at Bath Iron Works, and the feds arrested us there, all together.

We were in the Cumberland County Jail for the nine months before the trial in May. Then sentencing was in October, and the month after that, we were shipped out to federal places. I did my last few months in a new jail in Morgantown, West Virginia.

Two totally different experiences! Maine was like being in a seminary. All the guys in our group were together. Scripture study every night. We met as community every morning and processed things. You know, "How are you feeling? How's it going?" It . . . it was extraordinary. I was Phil's cell mate and I wouldn't have traded that for anything.

It was also great preparation for going to jail after last year's action. In that one, Steve Woolford and I were [in] the same cell block for only a couple of weeks 'cause as soon as the head honchos figured out we were codefendants, they split us up. In Maine, we had our own community so I didn't have to confront my own demons and my own shortcomings or how I relate to people.

It's interesting. When people from other countries learn that I've been to jail, they really resonate with it. To think that people in America, this "land of freedom," are willing to give up that freedom on behalf of the victims of their American culture. See, going to jail is one way of saying that this system only exists because we support it. It's not a given like air or water, it's something that we've created and it only perpetuates itself through our support. By risking arrest and going to jail, we remove ourselves from that support.

I think Kim had the harder part, though, staying home. It's a retreat time for us in jail, more of a meditative experience. In Maine, it was sometimes even a party experience. All kinds of local people visited, and Kim drove up several times, too. Sometimes they'd let in fifteen, sixteen, seventeen people at a time. Certainly having Phil as part of the group was a big draw.

Ro: Bad days?

Steve: Ah . . . I guess my most vivid recollections are of last year's six months. The roughest were the fights. I was there for being against killing, against violence. And I'd do a Bible study every day, talking about justice for the poor and nonviolence as being the key to the Gospels. So what do you do when there are fights? Sometimes I'd get between people who were fighting. This is really not done very often because people usually just kind of gather around and watch people who are fighting.

Ro: What about the guards?

Steve: They look at us on these monitors and when they see a fight—in this regional jail, anyway—they rush to break it up and take people away to solitary and make big lists of who not to put together. So they keep rearranging where people live to try to minimize the violence. It's a pretty inadequate system and also pretty nerve-wracking.

Ro: So you'd walk into the middle of the men who were fighting?

Steve: Yeah.

Ro: When's the best time to do the intervening?

Steve: Well, it's something we've done pretty regularly on our soup lines, both here and in LA, so it was nothing new for me, but I think probably it's easier if you know the people involved. Maybe that's part of trying to be wise as serpents, to get to know people in the cell block. Then you can try to urge people to resolve [conflicts] in a different way.

When people know you're in jail because you practiced nonviolence, you can establish some of those things. Building relationships with people and knowing their stories is really key, but fights always shake the whole cell block up, put it on edge.

Ro: If you'd intervene, would you get the support of the other bystanders?

Steve: The last time I did. I got between two guys who had already thrown a couple of punches. I knew both of them and got in between them and tried to talk them down. Then one of the guys who was watching said, "All right, cut it out." And that's what actually led to their stopping.

Actually, one of the two guys who was fighting started coming by my cell block regularly after that, and we'd talk. Phil would say that listening to people is the most important thing to do when you're in. . . . Actually, it's a luxury to have the time to listen to people, to listen for God's voice in God's people. We hardly have time to do that at home, with the kids and the soup line and the house.

Kim: When Steve's in jail, sometimes there are good things, but sometimes it's very hard. Like the 2003 trial in DC when I couldn't go because the baby woke up the night before with a 103 degree fever, just screaming with an ear infection. Steve got six months, and he went right into prison that day, so the boys didn't even get to say goodbye. He ended up in this regional, privatized jail a two-hour drive from here. The visiting conditions there were dreadful, with just a half hour a week and you have to use a phone and be behind glass in this big room. The voices sound real soft and tinny and when you have that in a room full of people, they start yelling, so it gets really loud.

Letters were better and sometimes he'd call, but the system was geared to cut you off after five minutes, and each call was something like $6.00. Of course the boys would always want to talk to him, too, so I didn't get much time.

This privatized county jail is a nasty place. People are basically warehoused in a huge dorm. They don't get outside, they never see sunlight. For exercise, Steve'd walk up and down the stairs. We're pretty much a vegetarian family, but in jail Steve decided he'd eat whatever they gave him, and not spend any money on junk food from the canteen. When he came out, he'd lost twenty pounds and he looked so . . . so pale and so thin. So that was a rather difficult six months for both of us.

When Steve did a year for the Plowshares witness up in Maine, the visiting conditions were much more humane, plus I only had Daniel, and he was five, so much more mobile. Also, we had community here at that time, so I could get away and we went up every other month or so. The visits lasted longer and we could come three nights a week. In fact, I have a real sense of joy about that time. And up there, I guess because it's Maine and not Norfolk, a lot of people thought the action had been a good idea, and Daniel and I received lots of hospitality and friendship. Once Steve said, "You know, if this wasn't jail and if you were here all the time, I'd be having a really great time!"

I'd had a hard time driving all the way up there with a five-year-old, and was a little strung out, I guess, and I said, "Well, kiss my foot." When I'm stressed out, I can be very not fun to be with.

Ro: Were you ever able to just be with Steve alone and not have it all party time?

Kim: Yes, we did. And it was a contact visit, so it was easier all around. Steve could hold Daniel, and it was just a much more humane jail than the last one in Virginia or in Morgantown, West Virginia, where he finished his Plowshares sentence. That was an eight-hour trip from here. Not as long as driving to Maine, but . . .

When he's [in jail] a lot of the stuff here falls on me. Like putting out a guest. I've done it before, but I'd be a little resentful at having to do that. We had some people with major addiction problems coming through the house when Steve was in Maine, but, as you know, that's just part of the Catholic Worker life.

I wouldn't call the house much when I was gone but I'd be just a mother hen when I *did* call, especially if I heard something [from the other community members] like, "We're having a little rat problem, but we're trying to sweep it out with a broom." I'm up in New England thinking, "I don't want to go home."

One thing I've been told is that I don't ask for help very well, so I guess it would have been better if I could have named what I needed and not made people guess. I would say, though, that community has been our lifesaver. It's hard in this culture to do something that's so oddball and so extreme. You need somebody to keep reminding you about why we're doing this. Community helps you know that you're not alone and that people care.

The first time, people I knew from the parish or the children's school acted like it was embarrassing or something. Or maybe they were afraid to talk about it, or didn't know what to say to me. I would just get so despairing. I *know* people don't agree with our stance on nuclear weapons, but their attitude the first time was really depressing. But at the beginning of the Iraq War, there were a lot of people vigiling on a regular basis. (I mean, a lot of people for this area.) And people supported me and understood.

Ro: What's it like when Steve gets out?

Kim: Well, in this most recent incarceration, he got out in September, after Daniel had already started school and there wasn't really any time to take off together as a family. And we had one crisis after another, like a huge hurricane, with two big trees down and no electricity for five days. So he immediately had to get in the swing of things and that's probably not the healthiest thing. Plus there was a lot of nuisance sickness in the house that winter, so it was kind of a rough coming home. Took like a year before we got back into our routine.

We had kind of a rough coming back from Maine, too. He was supposed to be on probation in Norfolk, but they put all kinds of barriers in his way. First they called me in for an interview. Wanted disclosure of our income, and I told them how we live and gave them a general idea of who our guests are. So they decided the guests could be felons and told Steve that he couldn't live at this address because there might be felons in the house. Now, this probation officer was young and trying to act tough. I'm sure she knew that if any of our guests were felons, that has absolutely nothing to do with Steve's political action.

Next they wanted us to give them the names of all of our donors. And we told them, "No way, José." I think they were just trying to make up problems because they wanted to make it difficult for him to come back here and be a peace activist in the home of the world's largest naval base. Three Plowshares actions had happened here since 1988, and they don't want to see any more.

Finally they said he couldn't come home without risking immediate arrest. So we made a little trip. Went up to Massachusetts where Steve's parents live, and then to Maine because that's where he thought he could be on probation. He stayed there for ten weeks, living with friends, and I came back here, so we had this ten weeks of limbo. Finally they worked it out [so] that he was able to come back home but still be on probation in Maine, but the whole thing was a real hassle.

Ro: Is there anything you think the partners of people going to prison need to be sure to talk about before the action happens?

Kim: Hmm. Well, I think they definitely both have to be on the same page in their values and seeing it as a good thing to do. The right thing, and the right time, too. But you know, the right time may never exist. For instance, our older son was angry the first time, and most of the anger was directed at me, probably because he didn't know any other way to express the pain of his father being away. He was only five at the time, but it really did mark him.

Now Daniel's thirteen, and he has quite an analysis of our world, one that's definitely in keeping with ours. When Steve was away the last time, he was a fifth grader and he was totally in agreement and *so* against the war in Iraq. I don't think he was happy that his dad was in jail, but he says it's the price you pay to have these beliefs.

Now he's going through a stage where he calls himself an anarchist, so that gives us a whole new level we can talk about as parents and teenager. He doesn't share our faith-based way of looking at things. Who knows if it's going to be that way forever? He's a pretty intelligent and thoughtful young man, and it may *be* that way forever, and . . . you know, I just hope he finds some hope in the Church. He very much agrees with us on nonviolence. I don't think he sees yet that it implies

Daniel Baggarly with his family, June 2010.
(Photo courtesy of Virginia Williams.)

actively taking part, maybe even in initiating situations. I feel serving time in jail is the strongest way we can teach our boys how much we're against war and how much we would never want them to engage in war or support war.

It's interesting. There was a time when I didn't even want to *think* about my own children doing civil disobedience. I'd say it was okay for us but not for them. But now I'm at a place where it just might be a reality I'll have to accept. That if they're going to be people of conscience, they're going to have to do this, too. I don't think they're going to get actual encouragement from me, but . . .

Ro: Do you ever think about risking arrest yourself? Leaving Steve to do the child care and take care of the house?

Kim: You know, a word I can't say anymore is "never." So many times I've said, "I'll never do that; it's too hard." Then I end up doing it. I know I find hope in the courtrooms; that's where I find that my faith *lives*. So it's a definite possibility.

I *do* have all these worries, though. I hope it's not a cop-out, but I do feel that maybe I'm the one better suited for the incredible multitasking that has to happen when one partner is in prison. And I'm not even well suited for it, either!

In our relationship, I'm the more practical person and Steve is definitely the philosopher, the ideals person. But I don't want to be sexist and say that the mother role is so valuable. My boys have an incredible relationship with their father. So maybe it's really my own fear. Although sometimes when things get wild around here, I think, "Gee! Prison would be a *break*!" Who knows? If I went to prison I might get really centered and calm.

I can remember once—I think it was in 1995—I poured blood on the sidewalk near the Pentagon. (This was before Steve did.) I had walking pneumonia at that time, and I watched Daniel's little face as he was driving away with Steve. I remember thinking, "I can't do this again."

I didn't go to jail for that action but got a year of unsupervised probation. Then I *did* do it again because I was so torn apart by the thought of the Iraqi mothers and their children. I poured blood or oil on the sidewalk and didn't get any jail time then, either. (I haven't made it to the wall yet, which they *really* don't like, just the sidewalk.) Bill Frankel-Streit was in this little group, and he got four months and no one else got anything. But you never can predict. I thought I might go to jail for that action, and was just praying for the grace to be able to accept it. So you never know. You never know.

Brian Terrell spent the late '70s at the New York CW community, then moved to the house in Davenport, Iowa with his wife, Betsy Keenan. In 1986, they purchased five acres of farmland in a lonely section of southern Iowa, where the surrounding farms were either abandoned or owned by corporate agribusiness. There they have carved out a good life—raising two children, providing farm hospitality, weaving rugs, leading in local politics, growing most of their own food, making cheese and beer, and going to jail for resisting war.

Brian Terrell

> *"More than any other thing I've done, being in jail has given me the perspective of the person who is less privileged than I am."*

I've spent the same amount of time in jails as I've spent in college—about a year. Not one straight year, like college, but a few months here, a few days there. It's interesting: I'll go for months without thinking of my year in college but not a day goes by where my jail living doesn't come to mind, not a day that I don't find something useful in that experience. For one thing, you learn how little you really need, learn you can do your laundry in a tiny sink, for instance.

I remember once spending five days in the DC City Jail. Now that's a fantastic, strange place. Bigger than most state prison systems. I went in with Larry Morlan, who had blond hair and blue eyes, and we threw them. See, they fill out the booking forms ahead of time, fill them out for black people with black hair and black eyes and dark complexions. They didn't have any blank forms, so they had to white-out and photocopy some in order to even book us. A real reality check as to who DC sees as the criminals! Every time I hear of some white government guy doing something despicable, I think of that and realize that the DC jail doesn't even have the paperwork to receive the *real* criminals.

In our time there, the question was always the same: not "Are you a protester?"

but "What were you protesting?" Because the only way in Washington that a white man can give up the privilege of being a white male is by actually confronting the system head-on. The prisoners knew that was the only explanation for a white person being there. More than any other thing I've done, being in jail has given me the perspective of the person who is less privileged than I am.

Ro: Can you remember the first time you went to jail?

Brian: Sure. It was a couple weeks in 1978, for blocking the railroad tracks carrying plutonium into the nuclear weapons factory at Rocky Flats in Colorado. We had filled the county jail there, so they moved us up to Georgetown. This poor rural county in the mountains makes money by building a big jail that has room for the city and federal spillover.

The prisoners were mostly protesters—Daniel Ellsberg, several professors, a bunch of students, a Vietnam War veteran. There wasn't any work to do, like at a prison, but we were able to make our own schedule. We had school, and were very disciplined with exercise and lectures. That first experience was very helpful for me, because except for the initial moments, there wasn't any terror or fear.

Other good things: we were together and we knew who everybody was. We had support from the outside. Dorothy wrote about us in her column and people in the environmental movement knew we were there. Rocky Flats was a horrendous scene. You know, plutonium being put into fifty-five-gallon barrels and buried without anybody even keeping track of where it was. Horrible things like that. A couple years later, the FBI came in and sealed the place off.

Ro: Have you ever been in jail or prison where you felt like a loner, where you didn't feel supported?

Brian: [*Long pause.*] I've *felt* that way, but I don't think it was ever actually true. One time I was arrested in Rock Island, Illinois, and was in federal court with about a dozen people. We had blocked a new tank that was being brought to the Moose Club in Davenport, "to be toasted at a cocktail party," as the paper said. Going to bring jobs into the neighborhood somehow, so they were getting all the business people together to toast this new boost to the economy. We blocked the path of the tank.

Well, the judge kind of had a fit. At twenty-six, I was the oldest one arrested. Even though the charges were crossing at other than a crosswalk and disobeying a police officer directing traffic—two misdemeanors with thirty-day maximum sentences—the judge felt fit to sentence me to six months in prison, I guess because I'd done these sorts of things before. Totally unexpected! Betsy was pregnant with Elijah, our first child. We hadn't thought anyone would go to jail for these minor traffic charges.

As the marshal's car was taking me away, I saw all my friends and family outside the courthouse, and I knew they were talking about where to go for lunch. Now I don't blame them or anything, but I really felt torn from the community, and for a while, I was feeling very, very alone. Feeling like I'd done something really stupid and had made a terrible mistake. I got out after two months, but I've done sentences of three months and four months when whatever friendships I've made face-to-face in the prison were pretty much all I had. They'd always put me in Southern Illinois—Marion, Illinois—which is so far away that I didn't get a lot of visits, so I had to make connections.

Ro: How did you interact with the other prisoners?

Brian: I've had a lot of different experiences—some good, some bad. Never personally felt threatened or endangered, but I've been with some people who were real assholes and if I'd any choice I wouldn't associate with them. Anywhere you go you'll find people you're drawn to and other people that you do your best to avoid. In that way, prison's just like any other place—except that you're stuck.

People have compared coming into a jail with being the new kid in school, and that was an experience I had a lot when I was a gawky kid. But eventually you find friends and you play cards with them and take walks together.

Ro: Have you ever kept up with anyone, any of the people that you were walking with, being with, in jail?

Brian: Umm . . . never for more than a few months. I've had better intentions, but I'm a bad correspondent, period. I think of all the people in jails that I've really loved and really felt close to, and then let go. I remember one time I messed up in particular, and I feel bad about it. I thought we were friends so when I left, I sent him money for his commissary account, and I never heard back from him again. What I did was stupid and patronizing and I see that now. If I had developed a new relationship after I was out, which makes us unequal at the get-go, and then nurtured that as best I could, I could've said, "Well, we're friends and I share with my friends." But I messed that one up.

Ro: When you're incarcerated, can you find "the consolations of your religion"? Practice your Benedictine spirituality?[8]

Brian: It's different in different places. In some county jails, you're lucky to have a King James Bible, and the noise is constant. One thing that was very, very helpful to me once in Marion was . . . We're in these little divided cubicles and in the cubicle next to me was a Muslim man named Michael, who was born in Jerusalem and was in prison on some immigration charge. Michael was very devout, and he'd chant the Koran, just over the wall from me. So I would time saying Vespers with that. I really felt a sense of solidarity, that he and I were praying together, but there weren't any Christians that I felt that with.

I remember one Advent Sunday. We had a Communion service, with a deacon, and he said in his homily, "I know you feel bad being away from your family during the Christmas season, but let's face it. If you were home, you wouldn't be doing your family much good anyway." I didn't go again.

But there were two spiritual communities there that accepted me and I them—the Jewish services and the Native American Church. Neither of these communities assume that someone's in jail because they're bad—their history won't let them assume that—and I found that very affirming. And neither community had a chaplain that was BOP [Bureau of Prisons]; they had people who were contracted to come in from faith communities on the outside. So they weren't imbued with the BOP culture. They got paid by the bureau, but that was all.

Chaplains who work directly for it have to qualify on the shooting range. And their social connections are with the employees. The two full-time chaplains at Marion would go into the mess hall with us, but they'd take their tray into the employees' dining room.

Another thing about religion in prison—there's a term, "Jailhouse Christian." It looks good to go to church when you're in prison, particularly back when there was parole. But when somebody would leave, I'd often find the cross they'd worn every day just tossed in the garbage. They're going out where there's booze and broads! Baptized? They're won't take that with them! They were just "Jailhouse Christians," because of the incentives.

Well, I guess I was a "Jailhouse Jew"! But I find Christianity in prison to be really horrific. I just don't want be a part of a church that seems to be supporting all this, so I found my spiritual community in other places.

Ro: Are there any tensions when you go away to jail or prison?

Brian: The kids grew up with the possibility of my going. Betsy and I . . . we were arrested together before we even had a conversation. Now, I'm not saying it's without tension, but . . . I really feel for couples and families who have to struggle with that. I have had to postpone actions because it wasn't a good time to go to jail. And when I've done things to risk prison, I always talk it over with my family. What they say, I hope I've taken into consideration. But I've never had the pain of feeling I have to decide between my conscience and my family, and that's been a great grace.

Ro: In prison, what's your relationship with the institution?

Brian: Mostly, I just try not to be noticed. I've always been a pretty obedient prisoner. Doing things, you know, that I feel silly and complicit about, like standing by

Brian Terrell, Ankeny, Iowa, 2007.
(Photo courtesy of Michael Gillespie.)

your bunk for the evening count, just staying there until they tell you that you can move. I'd really rather just lay on my bunk and thumb my nose at these people. But I don't. See, what motivates me to be an obedient prisoner is very venal: I don't want to be locked into the hole. When you're in the hole, either you can't have visitors at all or can only see them for twenty minutes through a piece of glass, on a telephone. If my family comes, they drive eight hours to get to Marion and if I've been good, I can sit with them for hours. Also, if you don't follow the rules, you only get like one phone call a week, but if you follow the rules, you have a lot of phone access. So I'm pretty obedient, and I'm lucky that I've never been put into a position of moral complicity, where I'd feel I had to disobey.

Ro: Are you afraid of violence in the prison?

Brian: I *have* seen some violent things happen in jail, but it's not really so different than other places. Sure, things happen. I've never actually seen rape, but I've seen young men being abused sexually because they feel like they have to pander to larger, older inmates in order to be protected. People are scared to begin with and they give in to their fear.

Because of the crowding, there's always a tension. In a place like Marion, you eat in a dining room constructed for a third of the number of people who use it. One person bumps another, and there's a moment where either person could apologize. Nobody's going to be considered less than a man by apologizing. But at least one guy has to do it, or there's a fight. When the fight happens, it's when neither one does.

The myth is that you have to stand your ground, even if it's an accident, and that and the fear . . . I remember once in Sangamon County Jail in Springfield,

Illinois. I was put in the cell block, and the prisoners were playing Spades. We're having a nice time, getting to know each other, and in comes this very young kid. He's shaking, and he gets up against the wall, and he says, "I want everyone here to know that I know karate." Of course, all the guys just roll their eyes. Fortunately his mother posted his bond and got him out within a few hours. But he would have gotten into a fight for sure, because he went in thinking that it was dangerous and that people were out to get him. I see this as an analogy for the whole world. You see it as a dangerous place, and damn it, it's gonna be!

Paul Gallagher does not share Brian's experiences of incarceration. We talked in June 2004, only hours before Paul and I went to trial for crossing an imaginary line in front of Offutt Air Force Base near Omaha. Offutt is the command post for the entire US nuclear arsenal. With me and four other resisters, Paul knelt down, said the Lord's Prayer, repeated it when asked to leave, and was arrested. Usually first-timers at Offutt receive simply a ban-and-bar letter saying they can't enter the base of year. This time the feds decided to prosecute and we were facing six months in prison. I took the coward's way out and pleaded "no contest," but Paul decided to plead not guilty and take it to trial. It was his first one.

Paul Gallagher

"Part of disarming is clearing yourself so God comes through."

Ro: Paul, how do you feel, knowing that you might be in jail this afternoon?

Paul: Well, I've been praying and reading and dealing with that fear, but as I've progressed in resistance, I've gotten to the point where jail isn't so much a fear anymore. Not that the fear isn't there, but I'm feeling that it's somehow going to be all right.

Ro: Can you talk about this progression?

Paul: Sure. I'm part of the Catholic Worker in Champaign, Illinois. I started by crossing the line at the School of the Americas in Columbus, Georgia. When I became aware of the threat nuclear weapons pose and the effects they have on the poor—people I live and work with—I decided I needed to do more. In late December of 1999, I went to the retreat and millennium protest at the Nevada Test Site, along with about three hundred others. That New Year's Eve protest signaled a giant step for me. I'd been trying to discern the value of civil disobedience, and I was struggling, because it was completely contrary to how I'd formerly responded to social ills, especially with my law degree.

The afternoon prior to the [midnight] line crossing, I just felt empty and kind of irritable and couldn't see any reason for engaging in a civil disobedience trespass. I had with me a book by Father John Dear, where he describes going down to Central America for the anniversary of the assassination of the six Jesuits and their housekeeper and her daughter. He tells about experiencing a transforming moment when he learned that the anniversary was really a celebration, really about the Resurrection.

Protest is about the Resurrection, too! About the promise of God beyond what you can see, beyond what you can rationally understand. John Dear's reaction inspired a similar reaction in me. And from that moment forward, I just knew that the protest in Nevada was right.

There were all sorts of biblical images out in that Nevada desert. Those nuclear weapons are just gobs of metals, fashioned by human beings. They represent idols, but more deeply, I think they represent our own fears. Fears that keep us from engaging the world in a way that can bring about substantive change. And thinking about all of this confronts you with your fear of your own death and fear of God and how all these fears operate in our lives.

For me, now, it's all about the Resurrection, about God's promises and also about a surrendering of yourself, and placing that trust in God's hands. A dying to self, in the recognition that you very well *could* die.

See, I've . . . I've been thinking about a Plowshares and what one risks in a Plowshares action *is* death, especially when you're in what they call a "shoot to kill" zone near the nuclear weapons. I've been thinking and learning about this for eight years. Reading people like Martin Luther King and Mahatma Gandhi and learning about the civil rights movement and other social movements that have included civil disobedience. I've gone through low-risk actions, not even risking a real arrest but simply being bused off of a place, like at the School of Americas. And now at Offutt, it's risking jail. I feel now that I have some perspective and can see how God can lead you in these unexpected ways.

Now, I sure don't want to go to jail. But I know the absolute power of the legal system. How culture defines what's right and wrong. We folks who crossed the line and knelt down and said the Lord's Prayer . . . we're not the ones engaging in criminal conduct. It's the state, with the support and the protection of the court system. I'm coming into court to hold the system guilty, the system which protects these weapons. I'm there to tell the truth, and I'm free to do that, even if doing so sends me to jail. So I've decided to plead not guilty, so I can accuse the state of wrongdoing.

An attorney suggested that perhaps I could be acquitted on a technicality. But I'm at the place where I know it will be all right. Whether I'm declared guilty or innocent, I'll follow God and just try to be as faithful as possible. This is actually a

Paul Gallagher, 2004. (Photo courtesy of Rosalie Riegle.)

mini-experience of a resurrection. Everything else—technicalities and so on—just falls away.

It's a here and now thing, and you take it as it comes. I just have to trust that this is the way that I'm being led. It's an exercise in faithfulness. If I were to do a Plowshares, the possibilities range from being shot in the kill zone to acquittal. And our protest at Offutt carried possibilities from no arrest to a six-month sentence. It boils down to the catchphrase, "Expect the worst, hope for the best, but be prepared."

Ro: What are you going to say in court today?

Paul: Oh, boy! I've thought about it a lot and finally decided not to write anything down. Whatever comes out will come out. Maybe I'll go blank! [*Laughs nervously*.] But I'm keying into Jesus's saying that following Him means that you're going to experience the same things that He experienced. You're going to be brought in front of kings and princes and judges and asked to explain yourself. He tells us not to worry, that the Holy Spirit will provide the words. I keep coming back to Martin Luther King and his saying that it's no longer a choice between violence or nonviolence, it's a choice between nonviolence or nonexistence.

In a way, resistance is an extension of Catholic Worker personalism. A Catholic Worker sees a hungry person and invites them in and you eat together instead of sending them to a food pantry or a shelter. You listen to them and take responsibility for their hunger.

It's the same way with resistance. You take personal responsibility for US policies in terms of their structural inequalities. An act of civil disobedience is one way, among many, of taking personal responsibility for the fact that our country possesses weapons of mass terror. In spite of the protection that our law enforcement agencies give to the whole system, you're still free to expose it, to speak truth about it, and to try to stop it, creatively and nonviolently.

In the act of doing that, there's a freedom. See, it's a dual process. Not only am I seeking disarmament in others, but as I seek it, I'm also finding that it happens inside myself. So even if what we did at Offutt doesn't close down that base, there *is* an effectiveness. There *is* a disarming going on—in me.

Part of that disarming is clearing yourself so God can come through. Rabbi Abraham Heschel talks about God as seeking us, instead of the how we usually conceive it as us seeking God.[9] Then there are the prophets, like St. John the Baptist, who tell us to, repent, change, turn, transform. "Make straight the way of the Lord." Make room for God to be present. We say that "wherever love is, God is." And this is another way to love. By being disarmed, by surrendering ourselves in this way, and letting go and trusting in God, we're making room for God to be present.

Judith Williams is a mainstay at the Catholic Worker in Waukesha, Wisconsin, where she practices hospitality, shares her music, participates in a weekly peace vigil, and does jail ministry. She has had many peace arrests over the years, both here and in Honduras.

Judith Williams

"I'm in this typical cell, six by ten. Bare light bulb. And my panicky self thinks, 'What if the light bulb goes out? And do I have enough air?' Typical paranoid stuff."

I have to tell you that my biggest fear was of being raped in prison. Because the guards always have ultimate control. And I'm ashamed to say that I was especially afraid of being raped by an African American.

My first time in prison was around 1986, in Niantic Women's Prison in Connecticut. I was working with the Atlantic Life Community and had crossed the line and prayed at the launching of a nuclear submarine in Groton, Connecticut. We were put into solitary confinement because we refused to have an internal examination to rule out venereal disease.

One day, when I was sitting in my solitary cell, an African American guard came in. He looked around rather furtively and then shut the door behind him. And I thought, "Here it is! My worst nightmare." Then he sat on the bed, and leaned toward me. I'm just holding myself very stiffly. Then very softly, he said, "I want you to know that my wife and I are very proud of what you did."

Oh, these prison experiences have changed me so much over the years! You see, I have claustrophobia, and I'm also afraid of the dark. Hangovers from childhood. I remember an arrest in Washington, from an action on the White House lawn. It was in . . . uh, in 1991, part of a Faith and Resistance Retreat. A group of us decided to go over the White House fence and spread bloody baby dolls on the lawn. Another contingent climbed a tree and hung a banner that said "Slaughter of the Innocents—1591–1991." Relating our foreign policy back to the early, early days.

We didn't have a whole lot of time to act before an officer came up and put my hands behind my back and cuffed me. But as I've noticed in other arrests, he was shaking. Again, there's such humanity. The teaching that goes through all the major religions about the prayer for enemies—for opponents—is so very important to our work, because if we harbor any anger or animosity for the ones who arrest us, it complicates the whole situation. So I felt a human sympathy for him, that he was frightened. Worried, maybe, that I would be carrying a gun.

The thing that gave them the most trouble was the bloodied baby dolls. They were afraid of AIDS, so they had to get gloves to round up these bloodied dolls. (I think nowadays officers often wear gloves when they're arresting.) They also had trouble getting everybody down from the trees, but finally we were taken to the central cell block of the DC jail. Secret Service came and interviewed each one of us because we'd breached White House security. At the time Bush Sr. was the president and they asked how I felt about him. With the schooling we'd had in the love of enemies and so on, I said, "I have no animosity toward him personally." After that, they booked us and let us go but we had to fly back to serve our sentences, which were a few days in jail.

Ro: What's it like in the DC jail?

Judith: Well, it was very surrealistic. First you're in a holding cell and they put you in orange uniforms. You're in this limbo which is prison and what you think and feel has no importance. We were there for hours and hours—I think until two o'clock in the morning, and finally we go with the guards, one by one, up an escalator into the south cell block.

An electronic door opens, I walk into the cell, and the door slams. So I'm in this typical cell, six by ten. Bare light bulb. And my panicky self thinks, "What if the light bulb goes out? And do I have enough air?" You know, the typical paranoid stuff because of my childhood fears.

Then I turn around and on the wall of the cell someone had painted in really big letters: "Don't worry, baby. God loves you." Wasn't that wonderful? So I started just saying, "Don't worry, baby. God loves you. Don't worry, baby. God loves you."

Over and over. At a certain point, it *did* begin to address my little-girl fears, and I was okay. But every time I'm in a cell, there's always that time of dealing with those childhood issues.

Now, because I've been doing prison ministry in Waukesha [since the early 1990s] and going in and out of the jail twice a week, I've developed more comfort with the doors and the locks. Twice a week, in and out. And multiple doors; we go into what's called the sally port, show our IDs, and then go through another set of doors, get on the elevator, and . . . at some point the elevator starts—we know not from where. Up in the corner, a camera is whirring away. Then we get off and go through another series of doors and yet another, always locked behind us, until we're in the inner sanctum. But we're in there for the people, and we know and love these men that we come to see, and they love us. Behind all those locked doors there's a little community.

Ro: Do they know that you have served time?

Judith: Yeah, I'm pretty open about that, and when it's relevant I'll talk about it. Sometimes they're shocked, but I just say I'm a peace activist and relate it to something like Paul being in prison as they are. So I think there's a certain validity there that builds a level of trust.

You know, I wonder about my life. They say that God is leading you on a certain path, and as I look back, God may be leading all of us into the prisons to experience in the flesh and bone the horror inside, so we can help to change it.[10]

Did you know I was arrested in Honduras? In 1988. Eighteen of us went down in an action called "Liberty for Captive States." Before we left we'd done what's called a *campo pagado*, put paid ads in newspapers across Central America about what we were doing and why we disagreed with our government. It listed all our names and occupations. We fanned out across Central America and blockaded US embassies and did our action at Palmerola Air Force Base, now Soto Cano. At that base, there were one hundred officers from Honduras and one hundred officers from the United States. (Today the situation is still the same.)

We took a bus to the base, and we really didn't know how we'd be able to get from the bus stop at Palmerola over to the base. But isn't it amazing how the Spirit works? The bus blew a tire just as we were passing by the base entrance, and everybody had to get out, so there we were, all set for our action.

I was going to play Uncle Sam in a street theater, and I had pants rolled up underneath my skirt. Uncle Sam was capturing Nicaragua with black paper chains. Somebody else had the black paper chains, and another person in a sombrero played a campesino. We thought the [role play] would keep the officers from being tempted to shoot us because we'd be so ridiculous. Well, we sure were, because the Uncle Sam pants came down when I got off the bus and were dangling there underneath my skirt. [*Giggles.*] Of course, we were arrested pretty quickly as soon as we went up to the gate. As we were being driven to prison in Tegucigalpa, the officer next to me had a Colt rifle. I thought if I were shot, it would be with a rifle from my own country.

They put us in one large scuzzy cell. But you just can't imagine the glory and the comfort of being together. And we made friends with the jailers, who were lovely people. One of them was named Rudolfo and some of us could talk to him in Spanish. He told us he blamed God for his grandparents' death. Now all along, we'd been singing songs together with the guards, some in Spanish and some in English and some in a combination of both languages. One day we were singing, "Gloria, gloria allelujia, en el nombre del Señor." [*Judith sang this to the tune of "Glory, Glory, Hallelujah."*] Rudolfo knew this song, so he was singing along with us, on the other side of the bars.

Then Art [Laffin] got Rudolfo talking—this is pure Artie Laffin—and Rudolfo started crying, and Artie continued talking to him in his inimitable way.[11] The next day Rudolfo came back, and he said very softly through the bars, "I'm going back to church. I'm going back to God." I was wearing a rosary around my neck, and I took it off and put it around Rudolfo's neck, reaching through the bars. And I still think of him, that he may still have that rosary, and that because we were there, he came back to God.

Sometimes I wonder, did we go through this whole thing—eighteen of us flying down there, going through all this rigmarole to look like tourists and do these actions and risk our lives and all of this stuff—was it for Rudolfo? Was that actually what it was all about?

Ro: What finally happened? How did you get out of that Honduran jail?

Judith: We called the US embassy, but they made things worse for us rather than better. Finally, after three days, we were taken to the airport in Tegucigalpa and put aboard a jet. But there was some lag time there, while we were sitting in the waiting room, so we decided to have a little talent show. The guards got the biggest kick out of it! One of the young women did a rendition of "Honey Bun" from *South Pacific*, and they just loved that. And then as we were getting on this jumbo jet, one of the men threw a Frisbee back to the guards, and they caught it, which was a lovely symbol of our connection.

My latest arrest was at the Pentagon in the spring of 2005. I'd come to DC to attend the spring lobbying session to close the School of the Americas.[12] Artie Laffin came into the preliminary meeting and asked for volunteers to risk arrest at the Pentagon the next day. There's a certain sense, Rosalie, of connectedness, not only that God may be leading us along a certain series of events, but also that there are certain people who come into our life, and when those people ask for something, we can consider it a religious sign. Artie is one of those people for me.

So I said I would, even though I hadn't planned to be arrested. Because I've got a life to lead and responsibilities and jail ministry and . . . But I guess you'd call it a

Judith Williams, 2005.
(Photo courtesy of Rosalie Riegle.)

higher calling, especially when it comes from somebody like Artie, who has lived it so clearly and so long, and I love him. When I heard him ask, I thought, "This is for me; I'm supposed to do this." So that's the point in which you step out in faith.

My decision was as weightless as a ray of light and an open door saying, "Come this way." If it weren't for my faith, I wouldn't be doing any of this. I wouldn't have the blessings; I wouldn't have the difficulties; I wouldn't have the discomforts. But I do this because of my Lord. I feel that my Shepherd speaks the language of all the people, and I felt the touch of the Shepherd's crook on my neck, saying, "This is the way you're supposed to move."

So I did. Three of us got together: Betsy Lamb from Jonah House, and Christine Lavallee from the Catholic Worker in Worcester, Massachusetts, and I. We decided, because we were people of faith, that we would kneel and pray in front of the entrance to the Pentagon and block the entrance to the employees. We took the subway to the Pentagon the next morning, and as I knelt down, I may have leaned into an officer. I don't think I did, but I might have. Well, he kneed me in the back, a real karate move. Fortunately he got my butt, which is well endowed, but I slid forward and skinned my knee rather badly.

At that moment I realized I had an option. I could go "police brutality" or I could go Gandhi. I decided on Gandhi's way. So I said to him, "I don't know if you realize this, but you've skinned my knee."

"You fell against me. You skinned your own damn knee."

So that was the starting point. That was "go." But as we were walked to the bus, I found out his name—Officer Behe—and got him to talk about himself. We found out we both had three cats, so we talked about them, of course.

The ice was beginning to melt. He was beginning to see me as a person. When we went into the interrogation room, the officer in charge asked, "Where's Art Laffin? He owes me a cup of coffee." We saw that Art had built community here. We were fingerprinted and gave our stories and they took a picture of my bloody knee and leg. (Apparently when anybody's injured they have to do that.) They asked me what happened and I realized it was an official statement, so I was going to follow through on the Gandhian thing and I said, "Oh, you know, when I was twelve years old I skinned my knees and this is the same thing. I'll probably have one of those thick scabs again."

A little while later, Officer Behe went to the medicine cabinet to find a bandage for me. He had gone from "You skinned your own damn knee" to fixing me up. Then we got to talking and he said, very seriously, that he thought it'd be better if we'd lobby instead of getting arrested and having to come back for trial and all of that.

I said, "Oh, we *will* lobby this afternoon." And I told him, "We come from a position of Gandhi, through Martin Luther King to us, which is that unmerited suffering is redemptive."

Well, his eyes grew wide, and I could tell he was really thinking about that. You know, the people who arrest us are very human, and we try to build community with them. When we got out, they drove us to our subway in squad cars to save us the thirty-minute walk.

Ro: Reaching hearts, one by one. Did you have to go back for a trial?

Judith: Yes, in April. And they dismissed the charges! They said they have five thousand arrests at the Pentagon every year. (Now, we never hear that, do we?) "We can't send all that paperwork out to everyone, so they've got to come here to get the cases dismissed."

Again, that's part of the commitment. I mean, stepping out as a fool for Christ. Nothing seems to really hurt you. You're carried by a wind, like a bird. The trip back was forty-eight hours and twenty-four of those hours were on buses, and I was fine. (I do a lot of yoga, so my body adjusted very quickly to the bus.) You're just carried on a lot of levels.

I could in no way do any of this without my faith. I pray in the morning, and then in the evening I do what's called passage meditation, a Hindu form of meditation where you memorize scriptures and quotations from various religions around the world. The founder, Eknath Easwaran, was a friend of Gandhi, and he believed that if you memorize these passages, they become a part of your subconscious and you begin to live them.

One of the phrases I've memorized is from Meister Eckhart: "She becomes one with God in every thought." I've always prayed, but that kind of meditation has really bumped everything up and now I see more coincidences, more serendipity, much more . . . a quicker chain of events that I feel is divine in my life. I think these things are always happening all around us, but maybe we haven't developed the antennae to understand them, to perceive "the divine milieu" as Teilhard de Chardin calls it. I try to feel that in everything I do, especially in the jails. Especially in the jails.

I'm carried in my relationships with my parents, too. If I don't pray before I go to see them, things go unutterably badly. You see, they . . . their political views are very, very different from mine. (My mother wears Barbara Bush pearls and they read all the Bush biographies.) You know, the phrase in Jeremiah, "Before I formed you in the womb, I knew you." Well, before God found me in the womb, I told Him, I wanted to be a peacemaker. Then God said, "Have I got the parents for you!"

Father Tom Lumpkin, cofounder of Day House Catholic Worker in Detroit, was very active in peacemaking during the '80s. I recorded his thoughts at a Michigan Faith and Resistance Retreat in August 1986.[13]

Father Tom Lumpkin

"If we look at things historically, any social change movement in our country—from women's voting to civil rights to forming the country itself—has been accomplished through a combination of some legal actions and some civil disobedience actions."

Ro: Tom, why do some people hear the call to peacemaking and not others?

Tom: I don't know. Perhaps it's the mystery of vocation. Why, for instance, in the wide arena of peacemaking do some people feel a calling to civil disobedience and others a calling to work in legal ways? Probably every person can give rational reasons, but I think it often comes down to the mystery of calling.

Ro: But how do you know if it's God calling to you or if it's your own ego?

Tom: Well, you probably never know for sure, but there are some general kind of "rules" for discerning. First of all, some way an idea comes into your mind that this or that might be a possible thing. You pray about it, certainly. Talk to other people about it, people you respect as having a certain amount of holy wisdom, if you will. And then if it's possible, you even try it out, tentatively. I think those would be kind of common steps that anybody would try to see if a particular feeling or call they're hearing is indeed the will of God.

Also, I think there's something to say, generally speaking, that God's call in some way corresponds to the particular gifts that you've been given. Like, I don't feel I'm a very good organizer. And one of the things that attracts me about civil disobedience, you know, is that I can kind of do my own thing. I mean, I'd get boggled by trying to work in a congressional race, or something like that—to try to enlist people to help and so on. So some of it is a question of particular gifts and talents.

I also know there are other priests who just have no desire to do the work I'm doing. And I'd *much* rather do this than be in a parish. So, in some way, I think that's a confirmation of a call. It shouldn't be something that you feel makes you a martyr. Particularly if something is hard to do, there should be some sort of an appetite for it.

Ro: I've read that the mainline churches are becoming the peace churches. What's your take on that?

Tom: Well, as far as the Catholics go, by the sixties with the growth of the US as a nuclear power, there was a sense by many concerned Catholics that if they weren't total pacifists in the Catholic Worker sense, they were at least nuclear pacifists.

I think that's ultimately why these Faith and Resistance Retreats started, to say to people that civil disobedience is an appropriate response for believers, for Christians. Now, the religious leaders in Oscoda [home of Wurtsmith Air Force Base, which housed nuclear weapons] recently published a letter publicly decrying this retreat. I think it was signed by all the pastors in Oscoda except the Catholic priest. Basically, it says that civil disobedience is *not* appropriate for Christians, that they're "to follow the king."

They echoed a wide feeling, I think. The Faith and Resistance Retreats are an attempt by some of us who *do* see it as appropriate, to try to communicate that. I don't think that any of the people who are resisting have ever said that it's the only response, but we're saying that it is *one* response, and a necessary one for some of us.

If we look at things historically, any social change movement in our country—from women's voting to civil rights to forming the country itself—has been accomplished through a combination of some legal actions and some civil disobedience actions. We need people working on the legal ways, too, you know, need people writing to Congress and stuff like that. But, no significant social change has ever taken place without some element of civil disobedience.

But you know? It's more than just pragmatism about changing policies. For us it goes deeper. There's a sense among the Faith and Resistance Christians that the Gospel shows us what to do and how to do it.

Michele Naar-Obed is married to Greg Boertje-Obed and they live in the Duluth Catholic Worker community. They're committed resisters as well as committed parents to their daughter, Rachel, sharing parenting and resistance work equally. With that in mind, Michele spends part of each year in the Kurdish north of Iraq as a member of Christian Peacemaker Teams

(CPT). Both of them are them frequently jailed, both for Plowshares actions and for other acts of "divine obedience." The troubles she faced as a mother in prison form the heart of this narrative.

Michele Naar-Obed

> *"I'd like to be another link in the fence so that these dreams, these visions, these ideals don't get lost—that somebody from this generation puts them into human practice and leaves them for the generation following."*

My first time: They were deploying soldiers from the Armory in Baltimore, and we were pouring blood, oil, and sand down the side of the building. To make the statement that blood would not be shed in the desert for oil. We were arrested and when we were arraigned, we learned that the maximum sentence for our charges was three years in prison. Max Obuszewski, who had a lot of experience in this, looked at me and said, "Don't faint!"

We had some months before we actually went to trial, and I realized I had to be prepared for whatever was going to happen, so I began to read and to talk and study. I learned about US policies and also about the great tradition of peacemakers in this country, particularly from Howard Zinn's book.[14] In the end, nothing came of that arrest for me, but I got a lot of education.

My first jail experience was five days for demonstrating against the christening of one of the Trident submarines up in Connecticut. It was short, so that made it doable, but it was a really, really hard time because I wasn't prepared for it. And I realized then that if I was going to do anything like this again, I needed to have a much deeper grounding in faith.

Ro: What was hard about that first sentence?

Michele: Well, I'd read about Corbett Bishop, a World War II resister who did total noncooperation, to the point where he wouldn't even use the bathroom.[15] He wouldn't move from his bunk, he wouldn't eat, he wouldn't do anything, and in the end, they had to literally drag him out of the jail. I was very inspired by that and wanted to do something very much like it. I'd use the bathroom, but I wasn't going to eat or sign any of the forms or cooperate with the medical exam or anything else.

So they put me in solitary, which was in the psychiatric unit. Nothing to read and nothing to write with, so I was left with just my own thoughts. After a few days, I began to . . . the thrill and admiration dwindled, and I began to question what I was doing and why. And I found I had no answers deep inside myself.

I kept the noncooperation up until I was released, but now I'm not nearly as ex-tremist. I look at what I can do for the long haul, because I'd like my life to be about this for as long as I live. And now with Greg and our daughter, Rachel, I don't want to give up all my privileges, like being able to visit with them and call them so we can stay connected as a family. See, when you noncooperate, you lose everything, every "privilege."

I've learned, too, that every kind of resistance requires a lot of stamina, a lot of searching, and a lot of faith, even if it's not extreme like Corbett Bishop's. My hardest times in jail are when I start asking questions. Not what can I gain for my-self, but what good does it do? Is it even making a statement? Sometimes I feel a uselessness, that maybe it isn't the best way to spend my time, so I had to come to terms with . . . with those uncertainties and questions.

Ro: Would those questionings come to you mostly when you're in jail?

Michele: Oh, they come sometimes when I'm not in jail, too. But you know what gets me out of that? It's hearing about or reading about other people who have done this kind of work throughout their entire life. I think of Phil Berrigan giving his whole life to this work, right to the time he died. And that brings me out of the questioning, because I know the impact he's made on this earth. I'd like to be another link in the fence so that these dreams, these visions, these ideals don't get lost—that somebody from this generation puts them into human practice and leaves them for the generation following.

And think of the impact Phil has had on the spiritual level! You know, saints are very important to Catholics. There's a line in the Mass about a "communion of saints" and I think about them and about contemporary saints, too, the ones who haven't been canonized—Phil and many, many others. There's also the idea of redemptive suffering. Part of what we do is an offering. We offer our own lives so that other lives may not have to be taken. And if you're in a lethal force zone, there really is a possibility that you can be killed.

I think, though, that this last trip to Iraq [as a member of CPT] was probably the closest I've felt to potentially losing my life. People going into the war zone stand in solidarity with the people who are being victimized by the war, and the CPT people who have been there since 2002 have been truly risking their lives. The fear is still there. Iraq is not where I want to die, but I had to kind of say, "If I do die here, then it's God's will."

Ro: Michele, unlike a lot of mothers in the movement, you seem as "out there" in resistance as Greg is, both in big actions and in going to war zones.

Michele: I think a lot of that has to do with Greg. He's a very special person, truly he is. I've gone away for longer periods of time than he has since Rachel was born, both to prison and to Iraq. At the time of the second Plowshares action in 1995, women were angling for combat status as soldiers. They were leaving their children behind to go to the battlegrounds. I felt there had to be a sacrifice for peace comparable to what they were doing for war.

We were living at Jonah House, and I was pregnant when we were planning this action. We realized that Rachel would be ten months old when it happened, and we agreed that if she was thriving and was okay physically without my being there, I'd be the one to go.

She was a very healthy baby and was really thriving. We did a lot of preparation. Even though I still nursed, we had to make sure she'd take a bottle from other people, and I turned her over more and more to Greg. And to Liz [McAlister]. It was very, very difficult. Extremely difficult, because I was there, but I wasn't there. Greg was incredibly wonderful and took on the role of being the primary parent, with a lot of support from the whole Jonah House community. (The community at that time consisted of Phil and Liz, Ardeth, Carol, and Kristen [Betts].)

I did the action when Rachel was ten months old and went to prison for a year when she had just turned two. Then I had this whole difficulty of not being able to go back to Jonah House. I had asked to have my probation transferred up to Baltimore from Norfolk, where I was sentenced, so I would have supervised release up there. Baltimore probation refused to take supervision, so I couldn't go home without it being an automatic violation.

It really comes down to how the judge will treat you for violating. My judge released me to Norfolk, and Greg and Rachel and I found a temporary spot there, in an attic apartment. Rachel was really kind of torn from her community, from Carol and Ardeth and Liz and her home and her Head Start and the kittens and everything. But I'll never forget her . . . She was just over three and when she saw the little attic apartment, she said, "Oh, Mom, this is so cozy!"

It wasn't cozy to me, though! After being in prison for so long, I'd expected to go home and to connect with people who'd been through similar experiences and to regroup and heal from all of it, especially the effects of being away from Rachel and Greg. I was just in a total emotional tailspin. But Rachel and I were able to connect right away, and I think part of that had to do with the fact that the people in the [Jonah House] community had kept my presence very much alive for her while I was in prison.

We stayed in Norfolk for six months and then came to Duluth for ten months, so I had a good stretch of time where I was out [of prison] and with family. I felt connected and grounded again and ready to deal with possible consequences, and we decided to go back to Baltimore because I thought the issues should be challenged. The probation officer here [in Duluth] was a pretty decent guy and he really tried to work with the Baltimore probation department. He'd say to me, "Those people are crazy! Why do you even want to go to Baltimore? Stay here! We like you!"

Instead I went home to Jonah House. Within a month, they came for me. Ardeth and Rachel were out in the garden. Rachel saw a cop with his gun out coming down the driveway. Ardeth told the guy, "You don't need that gun. Put that gun away." Which he did, but I was handcuffed right away. Carol asked if they'd take the handcuffs off so I could give Rachel a hug goodbye, and he said no.

Ro: And Rachel was four?

Michele: [*Voice briefly weak.*] She was four. I'd been picked up with a special notice from the judge that I was not to be released on bond and that I was to be brought to Norfolk under custody. But the magistrate in Baltimore let me take myself there, and Greg, Rachel, and I drove down that night. I went to the Norfolk courthouse the next morning.

[The judge] was willing to have me released but under very, very strong conditions, including $50,000 cash, on the spot, and all these requirements, and I decided it wasn't worth it, so I stayed in jail for a month until the hearing and was sentenced then to another twelve months but with no further conditions after that, no paper or probation or anything.

They sent me to Alderson instead of to Florida where I'd served my other year and had worked in Horticulture. At Alderson we happened to have a warden who wanted the compound to be full of flowers, and I got to work in Horticulture again. I made a friend there, Elizabeth, and we'd scope out places to put new flower beds. She knew how and when to plant and all that stuff, and we were able to design and install a huge floral display in front of the visitor's building. It was gorgeous! We'd spend our evenings in the greenhouse, transplanting all these little plants from seedlings to their next step. We sure did work, but the time just flew and doing this garden kept us both going. I also took a eucharistic ministry class and was certified as a eucharistic minister.

When it was finally, finally over and I came home to Baltimore, I didn't . . . We didn't deal with it in a very healthy way. We didn't take the time to come together as a community and talk about the things that had happened while I was gone, and the expectations that people had, and maybe the expectations they had when I first returned.

First, there was the transition of me coming back into Rachel's life and the communication wasn't too good. People had really grown to love Rachel. I mean they took responsibility and made major decisions that I wasn't there to make. And with my blessings. I trusted them to make these decisions, but when I came out, it was really difficult to make the transfer from them making those decisions to me and Greg making them, especially when our decisions were different from the ones they would've made. Then Greg had a jail sentence to serve shortly after I got home, and that was hard, too.

Anyhow, it was difficult and we . . . we didn't take the time to talk about it in a healthy way. Our relationships just deteriorated to a point where it was, uh . . .

Michele Naar-Obed and Mike Walli with defaced sign, 2005.
(Photo by Bob King/*Duluth News Tribune*.)

really heading towards being irreparable. It seemed that our presence—Greg, Rachel, and I, but my presence in particular—just made things worse.

So the most nonviolent thing at that point was to leave, because in staying we were doing more harm to each other and to Rachel, who was caught in the middle. It was . . . it was one of the most painful decisions I've ever had to make. So Greg, Rachel, and I moved to the Duluth Catholic Worker in June of 2002, two years after I was released from Alderson.

You can't help but come out of prison kind of changed. In prison you have to guard yourself from being chewed up because that's what the system is designed to do. And so you're really working on every possible inner resource, to keep yourself from being chewed up like everyone else. When you do a Plowshares action, you come into it with time to prepare and time to build up your internal resources. And external resources, too, so you have a lot of things going for you. But still, I don't know that you can come out not feeling battered by the whole thing.

I think Phil had a way of sloughing all that off, and he expected everyone else to slough it off, too. You don't whine about your prison experiences, you just get right back on the horse again and go do another one! He's a very stubborn, stoic German kind, you know, and that's how he dealt with it. I guess there are times I probably felt expected to live up to those expectations, to jump right back into things.

When I got out of Florida from the original sentence, I just wanted to go home and be around people that I loved and people who loved me and to be healed. So to go through that extra time of being not allowed home and then another twelve months in prison, it was just . . . it was like being smacked down onto the ground.

Ro: Michele, lately you've been spending more of your time in Iraq rather than in prison, haven't you?

Michele: Yes, but I go to Iraq as an act of resistance, too. I try to do actions here in Duluth that won't get in the way of my going there again.

You know, before I moved to Jonah House, I qualified as a pathologist's assistant. A few months ago, I saw an ad for one and wondered what it would be like to go back to work as that. But more people are inclined to do that work than resistance work. If we were in a better place in our world, I would probably be doing pathology, but the times are what they are and I don't feel I can.

I think for families, particularly, there's a real crossroads. A lot of people think that if you take the responsibility of having a family, doing resistance as we do is irresponsible. Maybe there's some truth to this, but there's another truth that says our families are just as important as all the families around the world and that we have an obligation to defend *those* families, too.

So which way do you go? Being responsible for the world's children as well as for your own takes a lot of sacrifice. Also, you have to be a part of a community that will support that idea. It's not easy to find other people who are willing to help raise your child as well as their own.

Community is very, very difficult. And communication is of the utmost, sometimes painful communication. I think that's partly where we failed at Jonah House, when we left. The blessing is that communities go beyond the one that you're living in. Like the Catholic Worker. In many ways we're one big family. Even though each house is autonomous, as a whole we're very much connected with each other.

So we left a community, but there was another community to come to. We had to be willing to go through the risk of connecting someplace else and then maybe having the same type of thing happen—a breakdown in relationships. So anyone who chooses resistance and community is going to risk [that break].

Ro: Well, living in a nuclear family is a risk, too. But we don't live in a society that supports the model of community you describe. So how do you deal with that?

Michele: Well, you know, when we were planning an action, Phil would remind us that we can't plan absolutely everything. He'd say, "You've got to leave some room for the Spirit to work." And I think it's the same with community. We're in a good community, but I think the resistance would go on here whether we were here or not.

For me, coming out here has given me an opportunity to come into my own, as if I felt like kind of an apprentice, maybe, at Jonah House. Under the wings of Liz and Phil. It's like leaving home as a teenager. Here we don't have the guidance and we've got to take more responsibility all the way around, but this is *us*, not because we're protégés.

The final segment of this chapter is constructed as a roundtable, modeled after the freewheeling discussions called "clarification of thought" that have been a staple of Catholic Worker life since they were suggested by cofounder Peter Maurin. Roundtables often tackle difficult issues and try to reach new insights through rational conversation.

In this roundtable, I've woven together material from interviews collected from 1986 to 1991 and 2004 to 2008.[16] This weaving necessarily has a fictional component as the narrators weren't actually in conversation together. I contend that they could have been, however, perhaps at a national CW gathering such as the one held in Las Vegas in October 2011. Try to picture them "sitting around talking," to use a familiar phrase from the final page of cofounder Day's autobiography, *The Long Loneliness.*[17] Most of my questions and comments are taken from the interviews; a few are interpolated as connectors. Heard in the roundtable, in order of appearance, are Jane Sammon of Maryhouse in New York; Brian Terrell and Betsy Keenan of Strangers and Guests CW in Iowa; Sue Frankel-Streit, formerly of Dorothy Day house in DC, now of Little Flower CW in Virginia; Willa Bickham of Viva House in Baltimore; Steve Soucy of Chicago; Char Madigan of St. Joseph House in Minneapolis (now Hope Community); Tina Sipula of Clare House in Illinois; Jerry Berrigan of Peace House in Kalamazoo, Michigan; Ciaron O'Reilly of the London Catholic Worker; Thom Clark of the Community Media Workshop in Chicago; Paul Magno of Washington, DC; Mary West of Day House in Detroit, now living in Washington, DC; Pat Coy of the St. Louis CW (now a tenured professor at Kent State); and Tom Cornell of Peter Maurin farm in New York. In this fictionalized compilation, I've quoted from one narrator who is deceased, Mary Aileen Schmiel, formerly of Chicago.

Roundtable on Resistance

Jane Sammon: There has to be a certain *posture* of nonviolence, it seems to me. To really learn to listen to another's point of view and respect what another is saying. I know I don't do that half the time. It's a conversion of heart, but that doesn't mean you get a little membership card that says you're now truly nonviolent. It's a lifelong process. Also, we would try to put ourselves in the place of those who have to use their bodies as commodities. And that can sober one into realizing how people can get caught up in work they can't bear doing, how work they do just for a paycheck becomes so . . . does any of this make sense to you?

Brian Terrell: Have you read Hannah Arendt's *Eichmann in Jerusalem: The Banality of Evil*? Eichmann wasn't an anti-Semite at all; he was just doing his job. Most of the people involved in "the final solution" weren't anti-Semites, just bureaucrats or draftees.

In the here and now, I've hardly ever met anybody guarding a missile who really believes in his job. Usually they don't even know what they're guarding. "Hell, man, I'm just doin' my job!" We don't have to worry about bad, evil people. We have to worry about people obeying orders. Even though people might feel squeamish, they do it anyway. For the most part, the people in the US military know their bread is buttered by the government. They're being exploited, but they're given a little piece of the action, just enough so they'll identify with the system.

Brian's wife, Betsy Keenan: Well, some of that may be denial.

Brian: Yeah. But you don't hear the young men guarding the missile silos in Missouri say, "I'm here keeping my country free. This thing is defending us." They know that's just media hype.

Sue Frankel-Streit: I don't know how you talk to them, though. How can people in Congress transform their hearts when they have to accept PAC money? Change sure isn't coming from the top. We do a lot of protesting, but they don't see it and we don't have a lot of concrete answers. Maybe we have answers about the way to live our own lives, but somehow things have to change at another level and that's not happening. So how can we reach the people who can change things?

Mary Aileen Schmeil: The hardest part is learning how to talk to people who don't agree with us and who don't even see the problem. I think the dialogue is essential, though, because it's in the Gospel dynamics that we can't just go off and become a separatist pacifist movement. It's important that we acknowledge the society we live in, and find the language to express that ours is a legitimate stance. In words people can understand.

Willa Bickham: Well, as part of our role as Catholic Workers in Baltimore, we try to make things pretty clear by making the connections between the military budget and the poor. For instance, Johns Hopkins gets more money from military research than any other university in the country. (We call it Military U.) It's also the largest employer in the city, and the center of power. People on the board of trustees of Hopkins sit on the boards for the gas and electric companies and the banks and the newspapers. So we're up against the power, fighting Hopkins.

When we did civil disobedience at their labs, we'd often go up on the rooftop, so we're seen pretty clearly. We'd bring our ladder to get up on the roof, and then take the ladder out on a truck. After the arrest, they'd take you down in a cherry picker, one at a time with your police officer.

Steve Soucy: Yeah, but does that [kind of protest] help people understand? My first real live demonstration was when I was visiting the LA Catholic Worker. We went to a Witness for Peace protest out at the Federal Building near UCLA.[18] Kind of a mob scene. We were given the signs and told how to behave when we marched. It felt real weird and uncomfortable, partly because I didn't really see what good it was doing. The big picture I could see—you have to do something. But there wasn't any opportunity for dialogue or understanding, or even for folks to see what we were saying, other than the leaflets. There was no opportunity for them to understand us in a personal way.

Char Madigan: I had a real stage of outrage at one time, and tried to make other people behave in a way I thought was right for them. The outrage led me to oppose dominating systems, but I finally saw my attitude was similar to one country trying to make other countries behave. At Honeywell, for instance, they were the bad guys, and I the good guy. That mentality has to go in order to have world peace, and we don't have models—not a lot of them anyway—of how to make that work. It's been a real growing experience for me to learn the *practice* of nonviolence. And to make the connections, when I'm talking in the churches, between the poor women we serve and the corporate greed of the companies who build the weapons that take so much of our tax money.

Tina Sipula: Hospitality comes first. If your cornerstone is getting arrested and wearing that red badge of courage, I think you ought to get out. "If you haven't been to jail, I really can't talk to you." I feel it everywhere, even in the Worker. I can only speak for me, but I don't judge people who do *not* do it and people who *do* it. I can only think of what they're thinking in terms of Jesus, and I know they're also thinking in those terms. How else could anybody go in and hammer a nose cone and take eighteen years in prison? God! *Think* about that! To know that they're going to get eighteen years.[19] I've spent many, many, many hours thinking about this. And I could do it someday. Today's not my day.

Ro: How will you know?

Tina: I don't know. I don't know.

Char: On my bad days, I think none of it makes any difference. So why do I keep doing it? I . . . I celebrate Christmas even though Christ doesn't come. Or Easter, even though a lot of the Resurrection I don't see. So I guess I do it as a spirituality and as a prayer. You know, Gandhi said about [Jan] Smuts, the leader in South Africa: "He won't stop fighting because he has no more strength to fight, he'll stop fighting because he has no more *heart* to fight." Not to win out over them, but to win them over.

Ro: I've heard talk about being empowered by protest. Can someone speak to that?

Jerry Berrigan: I think resistance begins to bear fruit when others are troubled by it and kind of reevaluate their own lives, and say, "What more can I do?" When I poured blood at the Pentagon during my senior year in college, I wanted to affirm what Dad was about to do [with another Plowshares] and put myself at some risk, as well.

Another benefit, though, is in preparing your court statement. I felt I had a responsibility to the court to be clear. For me, writing is difficult, but if I put the time in, it's rewarding, and I can learn what I want to say.

Besides [learning] all the background, you learn about yourself and what you believe, so that makes you strong, I guess. I think it's like exercise. We can endure more and do more than we can imagine. Nelson Mandela has this wonderful quote about our greatest fear being not that we're worthless, but that we're powerful and beautiful beyond our imaginations.[20] We're afraid of the responsibility that comes with that. We're responsible for the choices we make and we're not powerless to do things differently.

Ciaron O'Reilly: Choices! We'd have a dynamic antiwar movement if 1 percent of the people who marched against [the latest Iraq] war chose to go to prison resisting it. And weren't isolated in their moral superiority but were in a dynamic relationship with the other 99 percent of people who had marched, who didn't sit at home resigned or cynical or feeling guilty. The more solidarity there is, the more resistance there is.

Thom Clark: All of us can be involved in speaking truth to power. That doesn't mean we have to put ourselves at risk the way we did in our Evanston [draft board] action [back in the Vietnam era]. I tend to be a little less judgmental about where someone is coming from than I once was. Like Tina, I find myself less tolerant of folks who still have their Trotsky-like line in the sand.

Ro: I think we think of the Plowshares people when we think of long-term witnesses who haven't done much to really get rid of the weapons. But there are so few people moving into the space for civil disobedience between a high-risk action and a legal rally. Lots of folks I talk to about CD will say, "Well, if a hundred people would get arrested, I'd get arrested." In other words, they'd get arrested as long as there's no real risk of big prison time. So how do you move . . .

Thom: My sense is that we're a little too comfortable now to be able to see how at risk we are, what the true impacts of our lifestyle represent. I'm not trying to be judgmental here; I'm just making an observation about why there's not more civil disobedience. In our relative affluence, we're a bit more insulated, I think. That said, I think people are sometimes hard on themselves because they can't possibly consider doing a Plowshares thing. But that doesn't mean they can't circulate a Plowshares court statement. In this Internet age, it can reach a far broader alliance than Plowshares support groups can do on their own.

Paul Magno: Resistance is really an ongoing workshop. Something of a contemplative experience. I think we do resistance for its own value, not for its impact on the workers [at the Pentagon] or its impact on the public, but just for what it does for me—the resister.

Ro: So one does resistance for one's own soul?

Paul: Yeah, I think so. Franciscan pilgrims don't go to Assisi to encounter people or to make a public statement. They go for their own spiritual growth, because they need that experience. One does resistance to restate your place in the world, and your purpose in the world.

Ro: Do you feel drawn to what people call "systemic change"?

Paul: Well, I see that it's very, very important.

Ro: I'm talking about you . . .

Paul: It really needs to happen.

Ro: You, personally.

Paul: [*Pause.*] Let me put it this way. I get apprehensive that I'd get too far removed from my basically healthy outlook on life if I were to . . . for instance, take a job in a think tank or a lobbying organization that works on making that something called "systemic change." I try to integrate my approach to politics and my approach to faith and lifestyle by assuming that my faith and lifestyle component is invariable and unquestionable. What I do politically can vary as long as it's reconcilable. I guess I'm sort of biased toward making politics secondary, or at least contingent.

The people who invest themselves in social change organizations always say that the best inspiration they get is from the people who actually *do* it. People who [collect money] for hunger relief are inspired because Mother Teresa goes from person to person in Calcutta. I'd rather be *doing* it. And learning to do it better and more creatively. Because I think that will be my best contribution to political change. That's not just true for the service work, but also for the resistance work. I'll never say "never," though; I've got another fifty years in front of me, God willing. Who knows where life will go in all that time?[21]

Mary West: It seems to me we need to think about sources of power. In the Old Testament, the people of Israel are always being tempted to idolatry—the idols of war and the idols of fertility and everything that their culture had to offer. It isn't any different in our time. We have idols of eroticism and idols of war in a proportion unimaginable to people in the Old Testament. The seductive power of that kind of idolatry is almost irresistible and the prevailing culture has, by and large, bought into it.

Yet there seems to be kind of a remnant, a ragtag group of people, who find their power in the transcendent, very personal God. They kind of stand against the prevailing culture and witness that power. I don't think they're ever fooled into thinking that the power is theirs personally. I don't think that's what protesting means, although it's often misinterpreted that way and [the resisters] are seen as being self-righteous and know-it-all. I think a true witness of protest says that we're powerless, basically, but that we have found the source of power in a God who loves and gives and is a God of justice and mercy.

We saw it work at Wurtsmith [Air Force Base in Oscoda, Michigan]. There was a movement of the Spirit. Now I'm not one who easily speaks in charismatic terms, and yet, my deepest experiences of the spirit of God came through liturgies at Wurtsmith. Easter Sunday morning, the first time we went up there to Oscoda, was striking in that respect. We stood literally in the shadows of these bombers, and we were surrounded with machine guns, and we said a Eucharist. It was clear to all of us that the power was in these simple elements of bread and wine, not in nuclear arms. When you confront that, when you take your . . . your little prayer in the face of what is symbolic of the powers of war, it's a transcendent experience, almost a mystical experience. On the surface, you know, you're frightened and cold, and tired, and yet there's a real spiritual sense of the ultimate power of the Resurrection.

Tapping into that power makes you unafraid, or at least tells you that fear and anger aren't the last thing—aren't the ultimate thing. None of us have denied that we're scared when we go out there. We're scared about nuclear weapons, and we're scared about the tensions among the [nations of the world], and yet there's something about that kind of resurrection experience where you understand the power of life over death. That the life of God really has conquered fear and death in an ultimate way.

Ro: Maybe the resistance, or the protest, is a way to get rid of our own fear. For example, one year I went to the Pentagon all by myself, as part of Jonah House's "Year of Election." I felt really vulnerable. Mrs. Middle Class, in my T-shirt with little strawberries on it. I'd never been in the Pentagon—this was back in the days when you could get inside—and God, it *is* scary! But part of the reason I did it . . . uh, this may sound a little trite, but for me it was meeting the beast. After I went there, I wasn't as afraid anymore. Maybe the people who beat on the silos in a Plowshares action, or do any other kind of protest or resistance, are doing it so they won't be so afraid. Like me.

Pat Coy: Martin Luther King used to talk about creating moments of tension. To consciously and pragmatically create a moment of tension where the truth could be spoken. Where falsehood would be stripped away because you would see more clearly the forces of evil and the forces of truth.

Ro: Some people see these tension-building but nonviolent acts as provocative and therefore against the spirit of pacifism. How do you answer people who say that?

Pat: Well, first we have to realize that all human relationships—people to people, people to institutions, institutions to institutions—all three of those levels have inherently within them a certain degree of tension. Even in chosen relationships—in friendship, in marriage, in community life, it's always present.

Now, nonviolent actions create these moments of tension. King would create these moments of tension merely by his presence in support of a particular group like the garbage workers in Memphis or the open housing people in the northern cities. I don't think this is provocative in the sense that it provokes violence. It's provocative in the sense that it provokes the necessary condition, the possibility for people to deal with tension creatively. It creates the possibility for us to honestly look within ourselves to find our own violence. And also to name the violence that's always present in our relationships, even our relationships with institutions. It's usually destructive if it's covered up, just like it is in our personal relations.

Ro: In other words, pacifism does not just mean smoothing over tensions?

Pat: Quite to the contrary. Pacifism has almost nothing to do with passivity, which is what it is often confused with. It has to do with courage, and it has to do with honesty. Honesty to the moment. It doesn't have to do with sitting back and not becoming involved but rather with the opposite—putting forth the truth and trying to be honest with ourselves in that process.

Ro: Tom Cornell, you're seen as kind of a great-uncle of the Catholic Worker movement. What avuncular advice do you give folks who are thinking of creating these moments of tension through civil disobedience?

Tom Cornell: Well, I tell them to beware of four things: beware of romanticism, beware of sentimentality, beware of adventurism, and beware of sectarianism, either religious or political. We certainly want to affect a larger society and by defining ourselves as too very alternative, we break the link with that larger society and we are not understandable. If we do that, people don't see us as representative of the community that they're a part of. So you have to be aware of that.

It doesn't mean that an alternative community like the Catholic Worker isn't the thing to do. I live in one, but I can't give up on the larger society, as rotten as it is in many ways. That said, it's a delusion to think that we're really separated because we're all part of the system, no matter how alternative we live. But you have that tension Richard Niebuhr wrote about it in *Christ and Culture*. Is it Christ *in* the culture, is it Christ *of* the culture, or is it both of these?

Ro: What about the people who say they do it to be faithful to Christ, and not to effect a political change?

Tom: You know, I still struggle with Thomas Merton's letter to Jim [Forest]: "Do it not with any view to achieving results." Then today, I read in the Holy Office the prayer to the Holy Spirit to make our work effective. So part of the equation has to be the possible effects of whatever actions we undertake. But then there are times when you just have to do what you have to do and say what you have to say. Because it's true. That's all. And you do it.

5

Resister Communities

Syracuse, New York, and Hartford, Connecticut

Some cities are blessed with cohesive resister communities. These groups can plan large local actions together, host out-of-towners who come to attend actions or trials or to stand trial themselves, and most importantly, support each other in psychological, spiritual, physical, and sometimes even economic ways. Such communities are also conduits for education and information—about actions, trials, and the process of doing time, both inside and outside of prison. They're even places for the glue of gossip about who's doing what and where. I was able to visit three such communities while collecting narratives for this book—Ithaca, New York, animated by the Ithaca Catholic Worker, Cornell University, and a vibrant progressive milieu; Syracuse, New York; and Hartford, Connecticut. Voices from Syracuse and Hartford appear in this chapter.[1]

Since 1936, the Syracuse Peace Council (SPC) has worked faithfully against war. Rae Kramer told me proudly that it's "the oldest locally based continuously running peace and justice organization in the country." Many in the group focus on the campaign to close the School of the Americas (SOA; now called WHINSEC, or Western Hemisphere Institute for Security Cooperation). This campaign, called SOA Watch (SOAW), was founded by then–Maryknoll priest Father Roy Bourgeois in 1990.[2] As a missionary in Bolivia, he had learned from the poor how US foreign policy favored the rich in countries throughout the Southern Hemisphere and how our country trained foreign soldiers and police officers in techniques used to torture and kill their own people.

This training takes place at the SOA in Fort Benning, located in Columbus, Georgia. Over sixty-one thousand foreign military have learned counterinsurgency, sniper training, psychological warfare, interrogation techniques, and other "dirty war" applications at the base. Graduates of the school have been linked consistently to human rights violations and to the suppression of popular movements throughout Central and South America.

SOAW's coordinated campaign to close the school includes education, lobbying Congress, persuading nations not to send their soldiers and police officers to the United States for training, a large nonviolent vigil at Fort Benning every

November, where the death caused by the SOA are commemorated, and direct action, both at that vigil and at other times and places throughout the year.

This chapter tells the story of five very different members of the Peace Council and the varied ways they approach peace and justice work, both through SOAW and in other campaigns. What doesn't come through in my questions, but should have, is how closely the members of the Peace Council support each other in their endeavors. With a paid staff and a storefront, it's a busy place, with three focus areas: the US global agenda and militarism, Neighbors of the Onondaga Nation (NOON), and a monthly newsletter published at *www.peacecouncil. net* that provides information and analysis on local, state, national, and international issues.

The group plans frequent actions, especially against the Reaper drones that fly from nearby Hancock Field. They vigil together with Peace Action four times a week and raise the money for their staff and activities through a large craft fair and peace festival every December. Below are five stories of SPC members: Ed Kinane, Ann Tiffany, Andy Mager, Rae Kramer, and Kathleen Rumpf.[3]

Ed Kinane has worked to build a nonviolent world for most of his life. He's taught math and biology in a one-room Quaker school in rural Kenya and anthropology in a community college near Seattle. He's also worked as a peacekeeper with Peace Brigades International in Sri Lanka and other countries, and he's been imprisoned for a creative action protesting the SOA. With his partner, Ann Tiffany, he's extremely active on the council.

Ed Kinane

> *"Both going to a war zone and going to jail are investments of your body."*

Ro: Ed, you were in Iraq with Kathy Kelly and Voices for Creative Nonviolence during the "Shock and Awe" bombing of Baghdad in 2003. Why did you risk being killed by your fellow Americans?

Ed: Well, if you're going to be an antiwar activist, I think you should know something about war, so that was part of it. I also felt there should be alternative media voices covering the invasion—alternative to the embedded journalists, who would have a skewed and inadequate vision. But part of it . . . you mention risk, and part of it may also be my own personal need or desire to take risks.

I was there from early February until mid-April, and then I returned from August until mid-November of that year, to see what the occupation was like and to be with the Iraqis. It felt gratifying to be part of a team of such high-caliber,

Banner on Al Fanar Hotel, February, 2003. (Photo courtesy of Thorne Anderson.)

seasoned activists. Their calm under fire was contagious, even though we were under no peer pressure to stay for the invasion. The attitude was more like, "Isn't it a privilege to be here in solidarity with the Iraq people at this time?" To be with people our country's power structure was trying to kill.

One moment that struck me was greeting the marines as they came in. When else has an invading army met its fellow countrymen and women who were making a statement for peace? We were in the Hotel Al Fanar, across the street from the Palestine Hotel, which housed the international press. The marines surrounded the Palestine Hotel with tanks and machine gun nests, protecting it in a very intimidating way, and that meant they were doing the same to us, because we were so near.

We hung a mural and photos of Iraqis on the wall outside the hotel. Then when the marines came in, we unraveled a long banner that said "Courage for peace, not for war." Some marines yelled from their tanks, "Are you Red Sox fans?" A very humanizing moment, actually, which one of them initiated. In turn, we shared our water with them.

One of the lessons I took from that encounter is the importance of making those connections. It's Gandhi in action. The marines are mixed bags, and . . . are not we all mixed bags?

I wasn't ready to speak to them, at that juncture, because I had too much anger about the invasion, so I just stood near the tanks and let my T-shirt speak for me: "War is not the answer." But some of our people engaged the soldiers right away and got talking about issues, and I *was* able to talk to them later. A couple of team members from South Korea brought with them this huge vinyl banner, and they unrolled it in the street amongst the tanks and it led to conversations.

When I got home, I was asked to give the Syracuse Peace Council annual birthday keynote talk. It was maybe the best-attended talk ever, with about three hundred people. Very welcoming—heady, in fact—because people here were very supportive and eager to listen. I got virtually no flak, and that's generally the case as I speak around the country.

Ro: How do you tie your presence in Iraq to your going to jail?

Ed: Going to a war zone and going to jail are both investments of your body. Personally I don't feel much apprehension about either. I can't even say going to jail or prison is a risk, because, being more or less a full-time peace and justice activist, my style of life makes it not very disruptive to go to jail. For instance, I've deliberately never had children, for a range of reasons. I guess I have neither the wherewithal, the resourcefulness, or the energy to raise kids and do activism and enter some of the extreme living situations I've been drawn to.

I also lead a very low-income, low-consumption, low-spending sort of lifestyle, and I live collectively, so I'm just not very "monetized." So although I owe thousands of dollars to the feds for fines and so forth, they know I'm uncollectible, so they leave me alone.

Ro: What do you do about taxes?

Ed: I haven't earned above taxable wage since '87. I stay under . . . *well* under! So the IRS has pretty much left me alone, too.

The war zones: I've worked in a number of war zones. Zimbabwe way back in the eighties, Guatemala, El Salvador, Haiti, Sri Lanka, Iraq. I've traveled in others. In contrast, our lives in the West don't have much risk in them if you're bourgeois and privileged, as I am, being a white male.

I think risk-taking keeps us on our toes, helps us to build resistance muscles, I guess you could say. It keeps you in practice so that it's easier to resist, so that the resistance becomes more second nature.

Now, did I consciously think about that when I was in Africa? I was pretty politicized, but probably wasn't thinking in those terms. And later, with Peace Brigades International, for example, it really seemed like I was playing a modest role in the historical process—that my presence in accompanying a threatened human rights worker really made a difference. I mean, you give them some safety, but more importantly, you help them do their work. Their work is important, and your being there helps them to be part of the resistance for a longer period of time. I mean, maybe the death squads will eventually catch up with them, but in the meantime they've had time to do more work.

Ro: About going to jail, do you remember your first arrest?

Altered Fort Benning sign,
September 1997.
(Photo courtesy of Sister
Jackie Doepker, OSF.)

Ed: First political arrest? New York City in 1970. All together, I guess I've been arrested between thirty and forty times. Maybe half those times, I've been behind
bars, but sometimes just overnight. My longest sentence was a year at Allenwood
in 1998, for an action at SOA. They charged us with a felony because they claimed
we did over $1000 worth of property damage. That was a trumped-up charge
'cause the damage was minuscule. We just stenciled "SOA=Torture" on their sign.
Used red paint mixed with our own blood.

Ro: How did you feel when you knew you couldn't be doing any activism for that
year?

Ed: Oh! I *was* doing activism in prison. Very much so! I strongly believe in prison
witness. To have people going to prison for principle has a wonderful ripple effect
on other activists and potential activists. That played out concretely in the SOA
Watch issue, where, in our wake, many other people risked arrest and many went
to prison. Not *just* because of us, but that early action provided the momentum for
other people to take a risk.

Ro: When you're in prison, how do you spend your time?

Ed: Reading, primarily. A lot of movement activists do very good works in prison,
counseling people and advocating for them. Maybe I don't have those skills or that
orientation. I take it as a sabbatical and an opportunity to catch up on my reading so I have more background for writing, although I'm more of an editor than a
writer, I would say. My partner, Ann, sent me the books—I'd preselected them—
and others would send mail and books, too.

I did very soft time in Allenwood. I always called it "work" in parentheses,
because I could read all day. I was the clerk of the tool room for the landscape

department. Had my own office, and all I had to do was check out the tools in the morning and check them in the afternoon, and sweep the floor once a week. Some of the other prisoners of conscience had much harder times than I had.

Ro: Ed, what's the wellspring for your activism?

Ed: I'd say conscience is my motivation. I came out of Roman Catholicism, but I haven't identified as a Catholic since puberty. In fact, I was hostile to the Church until maybe the mid-eighties when I became aware of liberation theology. I saw that it had inspired a lot of really good people to do good work, and I've worked with people of faith a great deal since then.

Ro: How do you decide where to concentrate?

Ed: Well, things come up and they just seem right. It just flows, somehow. Daily life is all about discernment, after all. Deciding what to do and when. For me, the complicating factor is really Ann and our household. I live with Ann, my partner of twenty years, and Aggie, our housemate. We've been together in this house for over twelve years. Sometimes it hasn't felt fair for me to be absent, and I haven't done it, and other times, it's seemed right. And my housemates have flowed with it very well.

Ro: What do you say to young men who want to be activists but also want to "have a life," I guess?

Ed: Well, I guess I wouldn't put that way. Activism is very *much* a life. It can be a vivid life, a rich life, an engaging life, with a lot of social and spiritual gratification, if you want to use those terms. You feel you're living meaningfully and richly. And if part of your life involves a partner, well, what better way to find a partner than to be engaged in something that's already meaningful to you and to meet your partner in that realm? Then plan your lives so you can be away—in other countries and in jail—because I think we have to fill the jails.

One piece of advice that I try to slip into talks to students is "Stay out of debt!" That's the way this system traps people. Also, try to keep your consumption low and not get addicted to consuming. People feel so trapped by the debt. And they are! But with low consumption, you'll have so much more freedom. Much more!

By the way, I haven't repaid my student loans. I paid for my education through jobs, through scholarships and fellowships, and also with borrowed money. I repaid my undergraduate loans before I went to graduate school, and then I was teaching anthropology and getting a regular paycheck and paying my loans. But when my contract wasn't renewed, I simply stopped paying. That was in 1975.

For years they couldn't find me, because I led such a peripatetic existence, but they found me in my prison year and have kept track ever since. I guess they could go after Social Security, but it'll probably be below the threshold they can tap into. My rationale in not paying is that I don't want to divert the resources that I use to sustain myself and my activism, and I *certainly* don't want to contribute to the government!

They frequently phone me and I simply say, "I don't want to talk to you. Goodbye." They can't garnish anything because I don't have a wage. I don't have property. A bicycle and my laptop and half-interest in a canoe are really the only pieces of property I have. So there you have it. Real freedom, I'd say.

Ann Tiffany is Ed's partner. She has a strong interest in South American issues and protests regularly with SOAW. As a community health nurse, Ann had to report her arrests and convictions when renewing her license. Threatened with a letter saying she was guilty of "unprofessional conduct," she took her case to the Board of Regents of New York, and won.

Ann Tiffany

> *"Going before the regents was more difficult than going to court for SOA, because it was my professionalism that was on the line. Challenging authority—particularly as a nurse from the 1950s when the doctors were, uh . . . 'divine.'"*

I've been working with Latin American issues for a long time and have traveled to Colombia six times. In the eighties, we harbored [undocumented] aliens from Guatemala and Honduras in the Sanctuary movement. It was illegal, but I never suffered any consequences. I remember when Miguel d'Escoto, the foreign minister of Nicaragua, spoke to us here. He made it very clear that while he loved to have us come to Central America, "the real work is in the US, where your foreign policy has affected our lives. That's what has to change."

I knew I needed to respond in courage to this and to the people I met south of the border, to put my body where my words were and join the prisoners of conscience by protesting at SOA. It wasn't a hard decision. As a retired grandmother of ten, I finally had a chance to say, "Hey, this is who I am!"

I hope I'm a role model, but it's been more difficult after 9/11. Very hard for my son who was a marine, hard for him to understand, to get beyond the emotionality. But we have a good relationship, and they all let their mother do what she does. But could I have done it alone? Doing it in community with the good folks from Syracuse made it much easier.

I first became involved in SOAW in 1994, when I fasted for three and a half weeks on the steps of the Capitol in DC. It was an easy fast, because we drank fruit juice. In a water-only fast, you have to be more careful in terms of electrolytes, but juice will take care of all your needs. After the third day, I didn't even feel hungry, and it was a liberating experience, because I didn't have to think about cooking and meals. Of course, it's easier to fast when you're not going about your daily work routine.

The next year I went down to Fort Benning and got a ban-and-bar letter, so when I went on the base again in 1997, along with twenty-six other "repeat offenders," we were arrested. The MPs and the federal authorities were very nice to us that time, but this isn't true now. Since 9/11, things have changed significantly, but in '97 they even served us dinner.

We were tried for trespass and sentenced to six months in prison and a $3,000 fine. By an old-timer judge, who had, in fact, sentenced Martin Luther King Jr. We were prepared for the maximum and we got it.

Four of us self-reported together to Danbury, Connecticut. I'd been a community mental health nurse for twenty-two years, so my time there was a continuation of my professional work because so many of the women were like the women I'd worked with. Being able to retire at age fifty-five opened the way for me to do these things. On the other hand, I wish I'd had the prison experience during my working years, because I learned so much about what my patients went through. A lot of them had been in mental health situations similar to a prison camp. Also, the dynamics of a mother having to leave her children and the powerlessness you have when you're not able to go home. That would have helped me as a community nurse.

Ro: Did you have any trouble keeping your nursing license?

Ann: Yes, I did. Twice. When you renew your license in New York State, you have to write if you've been arrested and found guilty. Each time I did that, I was accused of "unprofessional conduct." That's automatic here, even for misdemeanors. Initially they wanted to fine me $500 and put a letter in my file saying "unprofessional conduct." I didn't like that. I'm very professional and proud of my career as a nurse. Had wonderful evaluations.

I also thought it would be good to sensitize the Board of Regents, so I wrote them a pretty forthright letter. Then some lawyers said, "Ann, you've really got to challenge them on this." And I did. Ended up going before the Board of Regents. I had a wonderful lawyer, pro bono, and eventually they gave me an administrative letter that didn't even mention the word "unprofessional."

Ro: Oh, that's wonderful! Will this help other nurses who do civil disobedience?

Ann: I don't think so. It's all individual, and you have to do it every time you renew. The second time, they really got upset. Because I wasn't accepting their definition of reality, I guess. By that time, I was retired, but I still had my license and I just felt very strongly that my action was not unprofessional but was, in fact, *very* professional. This time, a criminal lawyer from Long Island took on the case.

Going before the regents was more difficult than going to court for SOA, because it was my professionalism that was on the line. Challenging authority—particularly as a nurse from the 1950s when the doctors were, uh . . . "divine." But I had wonderful witnesses, and it was a great experience in the end. I kept my license, I was not fined, I was not called "unprofessional." The best part was that one of the three judges voted to exonerate me and said he was proud of me.

I'm guessing that anyone who's licensed by the State of New York and wants to keep their license without a letter in their files would have to go through this. If you're found guilty of any misdemeanor, it's "unprofessional behavior."

On the whole, it's not very threatening, though. It became threatening because I fought it. They told me, "You could lose your license by fighting this." But I didn't. I won. It depends on which state you live in, I guess; I've known lawyers and doctors and social workers who've been arrested and not been questioned. I certainly think it's worth looking into, and I don't see it as a threat to your license.

For me, I'm sure I'll keep on being arrested. It's made a difference in every part of my life—my personal life, my relationship life, and my life as a woman. The more often you confront authority, the more often you speak your truth, the more empowering it is.

Andy Mager became an activist at Brown University in 1980 when he refused to comply with the newly instituted draft registration. When he moved to Syracuse, a group called Upstate Resistance helped him organize his trial and use it for education about the issues. He was one of the few young men imprisoned for refusing to register under this law. Because the Solomon Amendment denies any sort of college aid to all who don't register, most now comply, and the self-interest organizing tool that fueled the Vietnam War protests is lost to the peace movement. Today, Andy continues in resistance work with the Peace Council; his focus is NOON, a grassroots organization that supports the sovereignty of the government of the Onondaga Nation and works to reclaim traditional lands.

Andy Mager

> *"I see resistance to war as a way to stop war, and that's not going to happen by a handful of radical pacifists taking individual stands, but through their inspiring other people to think about their responsibility as well."*

How did I get into this? There wasn't a directly religious basis, but I am Jewish, although I grew up feeling Judaism was hypocritical. (I think much other religion is, too.) So Judaism isn't a direct motivation, although, certainly, there's an ethical-spiritual basis. Sometimes I speculate: I have an older brother who was quite abusive towards me, so one piece of me wonders if my nonviolent resistance wasn't a way of responding to that.

President Carter called for a revival of draft registration when I was a freshman at Brown University. That was in January of 1980, and there was a big upsurge in activism, unlike now, unfortunately. The draft was seen as a real infringement on the rights of young people and a significant step towards increased warmaking. The idea needed congressional approval, so I very quickly dove into organizing and became very active in opposing the legislation.

Then at some point I realized that I wouldn't obey it if it were passed. That seemed to just come naturally. I'm not . . . I think some other folks grew up with a greater sense of obedience to the law than I did. At a fairly young age, it became clear to me that laws were made by people with power to protect their own interests and didn't necessarily represent the common good, so it wasn't a terrifying step for me to break the law.

I didn't register but I didn't speak out publicly at first. After my first interview—which wasn't published, by the way—I continued to be active in a variety of issues related to world peace. I dropped out of college, and the following summer I went to a national conference of the War Resisters League on the West Coast and there I met six or seven other nonregistrants of my generation, as well as people who'd been in prison for refusing to fight in Vietnam, Korea, and World War II. Then I really felt part of a community of people who were nonviolent resisters and who were committed to the same radical pacifist vision of the world that I had. That contact propelled me into deciding that I needed to be public in a more ongoing way.

The following December, I moved to Syracuse and joined a group called Upstate Resistance. It was a perfect match, because they were a small but very vocal group, without an active resister at that time. So it was a great coming together, and I was speaking out and writing fairly regularly about my decision not to register.

For me, there were a couple of pieces that were critical. One was being open and honest about what I was doing. I'd fight tooth and nail that the word "draft evader" was not a relevant word, at least for people like me. I was resisting, not evading, and being very open and clear about what I was doing and why.

The other piece of it is being true to my ethical beliefs but also seeing resistance to war as a way to stop war. That's not going to happen with a handful of radical pacifists taking individual stands, but through inspiring *other* people to think about their responsibility as well. So that was always my hope. I'm also a war tax resister, and in that I don't feel as compelled to tell the government everything that I'm doing, but I do feel compelled to be honest with my fellow people.

After the feds began prosecuting people for not registering, it became clear that a major goal was to intimidate people. So I wrote to them, primarily to say that tactic was not going to work, and there were [several letters] back and forth before my case was moved to the local US attorney's office.

The arraignment for failing to register came in late August, and the week after I was arraigned, I was sentenced to forty days in jail for a civil disobedience action at Griffiss Air Force Base. So that gave me a bit of a trial run. I did five weeks of that sentence, and for some reason, for the last three weeks they sent me down to Lewisburg Federal Prison Camp, so I even had the experience of a minimum security federal prison, which is where I expected to end up for resisting the draft. That was actually very helpful in that I felt, "Okay, this isn't fun, but I can do it." So I realized before the draft trial that I didn't need to compromise my principles because I was scared of the consequences.

By the time of the draft trial, I was well networked with other draft resisters and supporters around the country, and we were very focused on how to both try to convince a jury that I wasn't guilty—that they should instead find the law guilty—and also to use [the trial] as a public education and organizing tool. We worked very hard to organize support demonstrations at all of the court hearings.

The trial was in early January of 1985. I represented myself, both because I wanted it to be in my own words and because I didn't want the trial to be about legalistic arguments but about moral and ethical issues. I ended up deciding not even to have a lawyer sitting with me at the defense table as counsel. (I did have a lawyer friend in the courtroom so I could ask for a recess and talk to her if I was confused about anything. And I got help with some briefs from other lawyers. I think they might have been connected with CCCO [Central Committee for Conscientious Objectors].)

My parents would have preferred that I be defended by an attorney, but overall, they were extremely supportive of my actions. My mom even organized a support demonstration in the town where I grew up, and as far as anyone can recall, it was the only demonstration that ever happened in Oyster Bay, Long Island.

Candlelight vigil for Andy Mager trial, January 1985.
(Paul Pearce/Syracuse Peace Council.)

We did good organizing work for the trial, so there were a couple of hundred people there for a vigil in freezing, freezing cold. There was a demonstration at the courthouse the morning the trial started, and then that evening we led a candle-light march through downtown Syracuse to a recently finished Korean-Vietnam Veterans' memorial. Part of the message, obviously, was that honoring veterans meant putting an end to war. One of the TV stations picked it up and went to some right-wing veterans and asked them what they thought of the "peace activists and draft resisters going to 'your' memorial." That generated a sort of unfortunate controversy. I think having antiwar vets as part of whatever you do is really helpful, and we *did* try to do that, but one veteran who was supposed to speak didn't show up.

In court, I basically argued international law and the necessity defense. The most likely legal argument to have had success was one of selective prosecution, arguing that I had been singled out because of exercising my free speech rights, and that such a prosecution violated those rights.

The judge in my case was the same judge as the Griffiss Plowshares, Howard Munson. He allowed me to say most anything I wanted from the stand but told the jury to disregard most of it. They were out for less than an hour before finding me guilty, and he gave me a very sophisticated sentence—three years in prison with thirty months of that suspended. In essence, I was sentenced to six months in prison with a possible thirty months hanging over my head if I were to do anything that the probation department didn't like during the long probation. Trying to stop me from organizing, obviously.

I stayed in the Syracuse City Jail for about ten days and then went to Lewisburg. When I was first brought to the cell block in Syracuse, the evening news was

Andy Mager with Barb
Kobritz and her cake, 1985.
(Paul Pearce/Syracuse Peace
Council.)

on and my sentencing was the first story. One of the people on my cell block said to me a day or so later, "You know, my dad thinks they should take people like you out behind the barn and shoot 'em."

Until she went to prison for an SOAW protest in 2002, Rae Kramer mostly practiced what she calls "checkbook activism," including work with Peace Council fundraisers. The mother of two teenage sons when she went to prison, she used the same combination of humor and intelligence in Danbury as when she's the "raffle lady" at the Craft and Peace Fair.

Rae Kramer

"I've come to feel that at least for me, the point of the prison
witness is to be a presence for the women there, to show them
that there's another way to look at the world."

Intrinsically, I guess I've always had trouble with someone telling me what to do. So that made prison, uh . . . different, I guess I'll say. But not the sacrifice people try to make it out to be.

Some of the people on the Peace Council had been involved with SOAW almost from the beginning, like Kathleen [Rumpf] and Ed Kinane and Ann Tiffany. I started going with them to Fort Benning and crossed a number of times with no penalty. They'd do this make-believe stuff—put you on the bus, drive you somewhere, gave you this nonsense piece of paper that tells you not to come back again. Totally meaningless. Then it changed. The second time I crossed was November of 2001. They'd put up this post-9/11 fence, and we knew things would be more acute.

Ro: What did your family think of your moving to this stage?

Rae: Um . . . [*Pause*.] I think they were intrigued. And proud afterwards. I *did* talk to them at some length about the factors that led me to say, "Yes, this is an okay time." At that point in my life, I didn't feel that I was making a great sacrifice. I wasn't working anymore and the kids were old enough.

The significant thing was that the boys came to the trial, as did my husband and my sister. Both my kids are good cooks, and they got taken in by the Ithaca Catholic Worker folks and totally absorbed in providing hospitality and cooking. Although we were put in a small courtroom on purpose, to limit the number of spectators, folks doing the support work had done a fabulous organizing job, so when my group of five was testifying, my family was able to be there. In fact, I think that whole week was a turning point for both of the boys. Seeing the lived values

School of the Americas die-in at the base gates, 2005. (Photo courtesy of Rosalie Riegle.)

of the "beloved community" in action. (We have our own set of lefty clichés, you know.) They were intrinsically part of it, and that was significant.

Ro: Can you describe your action?

Rae: We went around the fence. There were a number of us dressed in black shrouds with our faces painted white. We carried mock coffins. I very purposely chose a child-sized coffin, and we made a kind of tableau, lying there for about two and a half hours, even after the other people in the group had crossed. Erik Johnson stayed with me even though his people had already crossed. He's a minister and he said he stayed "because no one should die alone." Even though the whole thing was pretend, his saying that made it so absolutely real.

Finally I crossed with Mike Pasquale from here, carrying the coffins around the fence. It was a little bit tricky, a little bit stony and wet. We went maybe fifty yards in, and the soldiers were there, and that was it.

Ro: You weren't scared?

Rae: No, not then. Not then. The weather was beautiful, and there was lots of energy. I'd made the decision, so the action itself was almost the frosting on the cake.

Ro: Your mental crossing had already happened.

Rae: Yes, exactly. I felt proud of myself, but I didn't feel it was heroic or a sacrifice. Not like the people in Colombia who really *are* heroes, who risk their lives just going to a meeting.

Ro: Now, you went to Danbury, didn't you? What was it like for you?

Rae: For me—and this is part of my embarrassment when we talk about going to prison—I . . . I missed my family, without a doubt. I missed other things that I do every day. Having a cup of tea. Smoking a joint. All that stopped, of course. Cold turkey. The tea in prison was dreadful, I didn't do the crossword puzzle. I certainly wasn't smoking dope. I'm a reader, a voracious reader, and I hardly read at all. But this is the thing: I was able to do without all of that easily, and I had *no* sense of suffering.

I also stopped drinking Coca-Cola. I'd been a big Coca-Cola addict, and my younger son called me on it, because of the union organizers who were assassinated in Colombia. "Put your money where your mouth is, Mom, and stop drinking that stuff!" And I did!

So, for me, prison was probably six months of the healthiest time in my life. I lost weight, I didn't smoke very many cigarettes, I was getting more exercise. I actually had to struggle not to be prideful. Because the reason I was there was so important and so just. I was not a pawn of the system. I wasn't a victim and I didn't feel like one.

My sense of energy . . . I mean, I was *energized*! I never stopped for a second. I picked up litter, including cigarette butts, and I had credibility there, because I was a smoker. I started a recycling program for cans and bottles. I did a lot of good in prison. Sure, I caused a little bit of trouble, but not as much as I could have. See, I purposely avoided being sent to segregation because I thought I could do more good staying with the women. But people have to do their own personal journey on that.

I've come to feel that at least for me, the point of the prison witness is to be a presence for the women there, to show them that there's another way to look at the world. You don't have to be a victim, you don't have to be a sucker. I got along fine with the women, and I think the fact that I was from New York City helped. (Most of the women there were from the city, or from another urban area, and I didn't sound like an upstater.)

What they had the hardest time with was the nonviolence stuff. I had conversations with people about this every single day. Someone would ask me, "What if someone badmouths my kid?" And we'd talk about what you could do to not retaliate. They'd invoke all this crap about respect, which I think is code language for an excuse to be violent. "She disrespects me." Those magic words are supposed to make it okay to strike out. But I'd preach nonviolence all the time.

I ended up being the dessert lady in the cafeteria, and I was able to kind of change the atmosphere there. Before I got that job, though, I washed pots and pans for a while. And that's really a job for a younger, more fit person than I was. I ultimately got out of it because I had carpal tunnel that was acting up pretty bad, but I washed pots and pans for about a month, and I think the fact that I was an older lady who did that, without bellyaching, gave me good credibility.

The dessert table became my performance area. I'd sing out, "Hello, ladies! Welcome! We have lots of choices today." It was kind of funny, because the choices were usually lousy pudding or lousy Jell-O or wonderful cookies. But my singing out kind of changed it for them and people began to say they looked forward to coming to meals.

Then I started a mini–art gallery at the dessert area. The only stuff that people saw, the only "art," was the cardboardy stuff you get at Woolworth's. Like at Halloween there'd be the pumpkins and witches and at Christmas a Santa Claus.

A little bit of digression: Many of the women did extraordinary crochet work. I mean, museum-quality, I'm not exaggerating. But they had great fears of showing it in any public way and wouldn't let me display it at the dessert table because much of their crocheting was against the rules. You had to request permission to do crochet and it could only be one color and it couldn't be bigger than a certain size and you had to send it home, and so on. All justified on the grounds that people aren't allowed to do any business while they were in prison. Now business happens all the time. But these petty rules intimidated people enough to not share their work, even with me guarding it.

The rules at Danbury were total bullshit and the arbitrariness was sometimes hard. Ann [Tiffany] had warned me, "The only thing you have to know is to pay attention to the rules. The difficult thing is that they change the rules without letting you know."

Ro: Like Kafka.

Rae: Exactly! The Bureau of Prisons has certain policies that must be carried out across all the minimum security places, but how you operationalize those can vary. People at Danbury were like big fish in a tiny pond, exercising authority and making rules for no reason other than wanting to feel like big shots.

So I had to get permission to use this tiny space above the dessert table to put up a little bit of art. My plan was to use the Syracuse Cultural Workers peace calendar, because some of the pictures were just wonderful. So I asked this so-called counselor guy, and he looked at me as if I were a trained monkey. "You mean people like you have an appreciation for art?" Those weren't the exact words, but that was so clearly the message. And then, when he came to understand my educational background, he said, "But you don't really think *they're* going to appreciate it?" *They!* That's the kind of things he'd say. But I kissed his ass a little bit and got permission.

I used the peace calendar and got some other pictures from home. There was one about black women at church, all wearing fancy hats. And I remember one black woman started to cry. (I'm getting teary just thinking about it.) Just the opportunity for her to see that and to talk to me about what those hats meant.

So that was one thing I did. Another thing was . . . There would be food choices every day, but the women couldn't see the menu board to even know what they were. So I was able to get the sign-making job and put the choices where they could be seen. Another source of irritation gone. I used the bottom of the board for little messages—things like a notice of International Women's Day. Taking chances to poke a little bit.

When the build-up to the war was really accelerating, I was getting stuff from home—peace newsletters and all kinds of stuff—including some posters. I cut out a small one and glued it to the back of the book I was reading, and I'd carry the book around with the sign facing out. Lean the book on the dessert counter while I was working. I think stuff like that was meaningful to the women. It showed them a way to be other than subservient.

Another time, I was allowed to help the bakers. We were making chocolate chip cookies, and there was a lot of extra dough, so I made a huge chocolate chip cookie that said "peace." It was the beginning of Ramadan, and I suggested to that we give the cookie to the women who were breaking their fast at sundown. And it was great! I mean the gesture was nothing, but it was so symbolic of white and black women connecting, affirming their rights to celebrate.

Here's a story, which is part of my feeling of embarrassment when people say I made a sacrifice. At Christmas, they make a big deal about decorating and such. As if you would forget you were in prison or something. One things they did was to arrange it so you could make a videotape to send home to your kids. They brought in this fake backdrop that showed a mantelpiece and a tree and a snow-covered window. You would sit in front of it and say, "Hi, kids, this is Mom. I love you and I'm really fine." That was what you were supposed to do, anyway.

Well, I decided to use my videotape to tell another story. I said to them, "You know, I'm Jewish, and I don't really want to be in front of this Christmas tree." More "Jewish manipulation" to talk about. [*Laughs.*] I suggested that I could just sit in front of this blank wall, with a window and skinny Venetian blinds. Beige bland like any office in the world.

The women did their hair and got all dressed up, as much as they could, in their ironed uniforms and makeup. The standard joke my husband tells . . . He said I was the only person who looked better-dressed in prison than out. I was neater in prison than I am in general, that's for sure.

But I wanted my tape to be real. So I wear my kitchen smock and white shirt and pants—it was kind of classy looking, you know, with the white shirt collar sticking out of the smock. I walk in with a bag of my soda cans, for the recycling. The woman doing the taping is definitely taken aback, but I explain to her that I was involved in this recycling thing, and she got into it, and said she'd focus on the cans, and then pan the camera back up to my face. Fine.

I start talking and it takes her about a minute and a half to realize that I'm not following their sort of script. I started by saying, "Hi and I love you very much." Soppy stuff, but authentic. Then I said, "If I look a little tired, it's because I was up at 4:00 doing my laundry. See, we have only one working washing machine for 230 women." (I had made notes. I had pages and pages of notes.) Anyway, I indicted Danbury, on tape.

Ro: And she continued filming?

Rae: Well, after three minutes, she leaves. I learned subsequently that she called the warden, but she didn't stop the tape. After we finished, I left it with them to mail, like everyone else did. Except my family didn't get mine.

So I'm thinking that they've destroyed the tape. If they're smart, they'd say it got screwed up in the mail. "So sorry! We'll give you your money back." Anyway, now it's January, and I'm talking to this official, and he hands me the tape and said the warden had confiscated it.

"You were supposed to say, 'Hi, kids, this is Mom and I'm fine. Say hi to Grandpa for me.' But we've decided you can have it back." So I got it! I wasn't enough of a dope to try to mail it after that, but it . . . I won't tell you how, but it *did* get smuggled out.

I definitely pushed the boundaries, but I don't think I was ever in any real danger, even though I had some serious raised-voice conversations with the resident bastard in the place. In his memory, there were several of these older white women resisters, and he lumped us all together. A lot of them are nuns. That's one of the nicest things about the SOA Watch stuff—all the great troublemaking nuns I've been hanging out with. People used to ask me why I'm not a nun, and I tell them I have a problem with obedience. But with this group of nuns, you wouldn't think of using the word "obedience."

He . . . [*lowers her voice and speaks slowly here, mocking him*] treated . . . all . . . of . . . us . . . as if we were a little mentally deficient. Around Election Day, he hangs all this political stuff on the glass wall of his office, fronting the corridor. But of course I couldn't put anything up and when I asked him why, I got this bullshit answer. Then he says to me, "And you can't vote!" So I said to him, in a totally childish voice. "Well, as you well know, I am a misdemeanant, not a felon, and in fact I *can* vote! Not only can I vote, but I've already sent my absentee ballot in." So it was definitely "Nyah nyah nyah!" Childish, I must admit.

He commented to me, a day or so before I was leaving, that he missed the old days when the prisoners at Danbury were men, not women, because they were more interesting. Desperados and international financiers. Women were boring to him; he liked the challenge of psychotics and he missed telling stories about all the mafiosos he knew. You could see then, in a nutshell, the symbiosis of the officers and the prisoners. I mean, the clichés are totally true. A guy that works in prison for twenty years, who the hell's "the prisoner"?

Kathleen Rumpf has been working in both jail ministry and prison reform ever since her first long prison term for a Plowshares action in the eighties. (See Chapter 2.) For years she concentrated on local reform in Syracuse. Then a stay in the Carswell Federal Medical Center in Texas for her part in an SOA protest galvanized her to take on the federal system, particularly its treatment of women prisoners who are sick. Since our 2005 interview, she has camped out twice at the gates of Carswell, once in sweltering August heat.[4]

"Camp Diane," her last stakeout in front of the prison, was named after Diane Nelson, a forty-eight-year-old terminally ill cancer patient. Nelson's plea for compassionate release was denied by the Bureau of Prisons despite letters from the federal judge who sentenced her, the attorneys who prosecuted her, and the senator from her home state of Nebraska. Finally the judge changed her sentence to "time served," so Diane could die at home. A small victory for one terminally ill prisoner, but Kathleen works ultimately for systemic change.

So she has protested and fasted and prayed and lobbied Congress, calling for an investigation and reform at Carswell. Attorneys and judges and celebrities such as Molly Ivins and Kathleen's friend Martin Sheen have joined with her, and many think the prison will be forced to change eventually, just as the Syracuse jail did after Kathleen's long campaign there. Because she just doesn't give up. In 1988, when I first met her, Kathleen was funny and upbeat and hopeful. Here we hear a different voice.

Kathleen Rumpf

"Death means nothing in prison. When you die, they shackle you before they put you in a body bag. You stay shackled for twenty-four hours at the funeral home, in case you're faking it. These are Bureau of Prisons rules."

It took years to expose and stop the torture in the Syracuse jail. The jailers were stretching out prisoners and shackling them, naked, to the bars. Jailers and inmates called this "The Jesus Christ."

I was told by the judges, over and over again: "Miss Rumpf, you don't need to be arrested [to get reforms]. There's a system in place." So at first I used the system. I knocked on every door in the city and in the county—the mayor, the congressmen, you name it. I was everywhere, and nothing happened.

"What am I going to do now?" Then I remembered the tiger cages in Vietnam. So a friend and I built a cage, about the same size as the jail cells, and we moved it in front of the jail, with a sign that said "Low-income housing" and "The jail is no solution." (At that point, I had learned that they were using HUD monies to build prisons and jails.)

The police looked at me like I was crazy. I turned to them and said, "There goes the neighborhood" and got into my cage. I stayed there almost ten days. Ate only bread and water. (Not many people knew that, but it was kind of symbolic for me, you know.) I'd go into the police station to use the bathroom. [That cage] was one of the most profound experiences I've ever had, out of many profound experiences, I guess. You can never have enough, you know. [*Chuckles wryly.*]

I handed out a flyer and basically I was gathering evidence, because this cage became a focal point for people to come and tell their stories of what was going on inside. "This one was hung up, that one was hung up."

A newspaper reporter asked the sheriff: "Are you hanging prisoners on the bars?"

The sheriff said, "No! She's crazy." But I gathered more and more evidence, and when I got out of the cage, I called Physicians for Human Rights and also *60 Minutes*. Physicians for Human Rights went on the show, which *60 Minutes* called "Cellblock 3A and the Jesus Christ." They called the Syracuse jail conditions its first case of documented torture in the US. (In their [show], they called it "cruel and unusual," but the physician who actually investigated the case went on record as calling it torture.) But the day after the *60 Minutes* piece aired, there was no huge outcry. The sheriff said they were going to continue the shackling, even after they'd been found out. Unbelievable!

Then I worked with a civil rights attorney here in Syracuse—worked out of his office for two years through Jail Ministry—and finally, finally, finally got an injunction to stop it. When I spoke about the torture at the jail, I'd say, "This is not just about the jail, it's about our community and *us* as a community. It comes from the community into the jail."

People didn't want to care. "Why shouldn't people be shackled? So what?" You know, the criminals are this or that. So there was a lot of educating to do. When the injunction finally forced the shackling to stop, the mindset of the community still hadn't changed. And within weeks, the jail had their first wrongful death case. Then there was another one. Then a third.

Everyone was a story. The third one was a woman who lived right around the corner from Jail Ministry. She was a crack addict and a prostitute, and we'd bailed her from jail many times. Mother of three. The children had been taken from her, and she was trying to clean up her life and was living in a drug-free apartment complex. She really was trying, making an effort, but she ended up in the jail.

One morning a prisoner called me about 6:30. "They just killed another one." She'd had an ectopic pregnancy and was begging for help all night in the jail, and they just gave her laxatives; finally they took her to the hospital but they released her from their custody because they didn't want to pay the hospital bill.

I sat at her bedside for twenty-six hours. Singing "Be not afraid," even though

Kathleen Rumpf at "Camp Diane," Carswell, Texas, 2006.
(Photo courtesy of Vishal Malhotra.)

she was brain-dead. Finally they began pulling off all her life support, to let her die. Suddenly a phone call comes into the hospital, and it's Ben Vereen, the actor from *Roots*. She was his sister! You really don't know, do you?

So when I was arrested at Fort Benning in 1998 [for an SOA protest] and was going to do a year, I had seen it all—the wrongful deaths, the torture, the cruel and unusual . . . I mean, everything. But I was not prepared for what I saw when I went in that time. When I was sentenced—to a year in prison and two years probation and a $3,200 fine—I asked Judge Elliott if I could go to prison like the poor did, right from court.

First, for close to forty days, I was held in the Columbus, Georgia, jail, in the dungeon, a literal dungeon. They didn't keep me with the rest of the population; instead, I was down there across from the drunk tank. There was a big solid iron door and one tiny window, and the rest was steel and filth. Twice a day, they'd open this iron door and kick my food in on a metal tray. That was my only contact with anyone.

For those forty days I had no toothbrush, no hot water. Nighttimes were the worst because they'd bring in the drunks. Oftentimes, they were young military men out on the town, getting drunk and getting in trouble. In the morning the MPs would come pick them up and take them back to Fort Benning, but all night long these guys would bellow and yell and scream.

One night this fellow banged and banged on the iron door 'til his hands were raw. But it was what he was screaming that really affected me. He kept saying, "You can't do this. This is America!" And I'm thinking, "Yeah! This *is* America."

Finally I started being transported through the South, going from little jail to little jail. For *four* months I was in transport! When you're en route, nobody knows where you are, and you're just completely in limbo. I'd be dumped here for ten days, there for thirty days, someplace else for two days. When we'd be moved, the marshals would come for us early, early in the morning. They'd strip us naked to make sure we had no contraband. I mean, you couldn't have anything, not even a Bible, because in a Bible you can sneak phone numbers and addresses on slips of paper between the pages. I had long hair, and sometimes I'd try to make a tie with the plastic forks and spoons they gave us to eat with and use it to keep my hair out of my eyes, but they wouldn't let me keep that, either.

When we'd go by plane, we'd stand shackled on a tarmac and see the sun come up, with the mist rising off the ground. Maybe two or three hundred prisoners, all being transported on Con Air. Surreal. And you're so dirty and exhausted that you . . . you just get into a zone, this numb place where you're not really existing, you're just going through motions.

Finally I ended up at Danbury, Connecticut, which is now a women's prison but used to be for men. (Dan Berrigan said they used to call it "Bury Dan.") I was inside the walls, not at the camp, and that's where I started seeing a difference in the prison system from when I was in Alderson in the eighties.

At Danbury, I was in with some very sick women. If you're on meds, you have to stand outside for your meds several times a day, depending on what [regime of medicine] you're on. And you have to climb a two-story metal fire escape to get to the medical unit. Sometimes in pouring rain, sometimes with ice and snow.

Now, the federal prison system is supposed to be compliant with the Americans with Disabilities Act—ADA. This stairway was compliant with ADA? Now, there *was* an inside door with a stairway to the unit, but inmates weren't allowed to use it. Anyway, one afternoon a woman in my unit was having chest pains and we walked her over to the medical unit and up those stairs. They told her to go back to the unit and rest. Well, that night she stroked out really bad and finally got to the hospital.

Now, I've got a knee replacement, and I just couldn't do the fire escape in the ice and snow. So they sent me to Texas, which is now the only place where a woman in the Bureau of Prisons with medical issues can go. The night they came to transport me, we stopped at the hospital to get this woman who'd had the stroke. They said they didn't expect her to live through the flight, but they still had her in shackles and chains, even on the stretcher and even though the medic said she was a vegetable. Of course, I was handcuffed and chained, too. I'm right next to her in these small quarters on a Lear jet, and I'm holding onto her and praying and I notice that she's trying to get her handcuffs off. So I knew she wasn't brain dead.

So we get to Texas, to Carswell Air Force Base. The prison is on the base, in an old military hospital. At first they'd let me sit and watch in the nights with this woman who was so sick, but then they transferred me to the dorm for regular prisoners. See, Carswell has both, and the typical prisoners do the work in the prison. The woman did not die—unfortunately, in some ways. She was a fighter, but she was under their control, and paralyzed, so totally helpless. She loved to smoke, so we'd try to sneak her cigarettes or get her outside. But she was held captive in the medical unit, even though she wasn't a threat to anybody. It hurt them, it hurt me, it hurt her.

Carswell was a different animal from the prisons we were used to. This animal—the prison-industrial complex—swallows up resources and swallows up opportunities and swallows up hope. After I got out of Carswell, I was lobbying Congress, and the head of the Bureau of Prisons was there, testifying under oath. He testified that they *know* three out of four women in prison don't belong there.

That's part of the difference between before and now. Now they don't even care whether you're innocent or not. There's no pretext. It's just about money, about women doing prison industry, fueling this massive *thing* which is the domestic equivalent to our military-industrial complex.

Ro: Wasn't it in Carswell where you met Martin Sheen?

Kathleen: No, long before. He came to the Griffiss Plowshares trial, and then he visited us at Alderson, and I've maintained a friendship with him ever since. When I was at Carswell, I wrote to him and he came to visit me. Came on Mother's Day, which was just a gift. By that time, I had a local support group on the issues—Lon Burnam, a Texas state representative, and a lawyer, and someone from the diocese—and we were able to arrange a little bit of a group visit, so Martin got to be with the community of people who were trying to support me.

Because it was Mother's Day, the visiting room was absolutely packed. And of course the inmates are the mothers and grandmothers, and they're in wheelchairs and so forth. I remember Savannah, a tiny little woman from Alabama. When Savannah came into my dorm, she was seventy-eight years old and she was shackled and strip-searched, just like everybody else. Savannah was arrested for refusing to testify against her grandchildren. (It involved drugs.) So Savannah and sixteen other grandmothers were in this visiting room.

Ro: How did the women react, when they saw Martin Sheen?

Kathleen: Well, the guards kept trying to keep people away. Martin just tried to be a typical visitor, you know, his usual low-key self. At one point, a small child ran up to him and asked for change for the vending machine. Martin just reached in his pocket, as natural as could be, and pulls out some change.

Well, the guard comes running over: "You can't do that!" Once he was called to the front desk and he said, "You know, if I've done anything, it was not my intention. But please, if I *have* done anything wrong, don't retaliate against Kathleen Rumpf."

This guard doing the reinforcing looks at him like she was horrified, and said, "We'd never do that!"

Well, he looked right at her, straight on, and said, "That's not what I heard." I was . . . I was afraid, at the moment, but Martin really stood up to them.

My sentence was one year, two years probation, and a $3,200 fine. So I did my year, day for day, and toward the last month or so, they wanted to know when I was going to pay my fine.

Now, they knew that in my presentence investigation I was declared indigent. I was on disability, I had health issues, and had nothing to my name. But they start dickering right from the beginning. You're supposed to pay back so much every month from your paychecks and [any money people send you]. The way it's set up, the prison system gets a kickback from the federal court system for every dollar they collect toward the fines. But they made a mistake and hadn't set up anything for me on this big fine.

So it's almost time for me to be released, and they ask me what I'm going to do about my fine. I said, "Well, you ain't got nothing coming." That was the big laugh there because that's what we'd hear whenever we needed anything like an aspirin or a stamp or a bar of soap: "You ain't got nothing coming."

I was standing up to them, and I thought I was home free. My lawyer said not to worry, they couldn't make me stay in. Well! When the day of my release came, they wouldn't let me out!

Word had come from Washington. They were going to hold me for my whole probation—two more *years*! Which they apparently *could* do after all, because I didn't pay the fine. Now, the fine was $3,200, and it would have cost the taxpayers close to $100,000 to keep me in prison for two more years.

My lawyer wanted me to fight this injustice, and it might have gone all the way to the Supreme Court, but by that time the two years would've been up. But I got out after three days. The Syracuse peace community helped, and then Martin paid it. When I got out, he and two friends from Syracuse had been waiting for hours for me, out in the hot sun. He . . . he's helped me in *so* many ways over the years.

That time I was really scared, and I felt he was actually saving my life. With what I had seen, I was scared I'd die in that prison. I had personal experiences in this place I had never seen anywhere else. I think they doctored the records more than they doctored the women. If you got a lump in your breast, you were told it was a pulled muscle because if they didn't diagnose you, they didn't have to treat you. They'd delay surgery and treatment, and I saw several woman die from these delays.

I saw women stroking out. They'd be on a certain medication before prison but once you're inside, they give generic drugs. Which are fine if they work, but blood pressure medicine is so incredibly tricky, and it's hard to find the one that works for you. Friends of mine in Carswell were walking around with stroke-level blood pressures. One time, a woman collapsed in the dining room. Other women rushed to help her and were ordered out of the way, but then they didn't even try to do CPR on her. Just let her go, right there in the dining room.

The system was so bad that some of the guards themselves would try to advocate with the health staff for the women, but they'd be turned away, too. "Oh, they're just faking it."

I saw good people working in the prison system. Some of the guards really cared about the women, and we had good relationships. But when a woman died, they wouldn't allow us to call anyone. If they heard us talk about deaths, we'd be sent to the hole. Sometimes our case managers—or "case manglers," as I called them—knew about all this malpractice, but they'd keep their mouth shut, too.

I had seen cruelty and meanness before in other prisons, but never before such deliberate indifference. And of course, I'd try to get this out, and when my visitors were lawyers and people who could publicize this stuff, the guards started escalating my strip searches. Stripping me in very odd ways and removing me to abandoned areas. Very, very scary.

I need special orthopedic inserts in my shoes, and I wore them into prison. When I got to Carswell, they took them away from me, and said they'd prescribe them for me "if I needed them." So I saw their doctors and they wrote scripts for me to have shoes. But for almost my entire stay, I was given transport shoes with holes in them and absolutely no arch support, like Chinese slippers. My feet got to the point where I couldn't walk well at all from the lack of support. I'd see their doctors and they would prescribe things, and then the medical review committee would write "Not medically necessary" on their requests. Over and over.

A blind woman came in. She was young and traumatized and we'd have to lead her around. She asked the prison for a blind cane, and they wrote back, "Not medically indicated." They told her she was faking it. Finally, thank God, a judge ordered her out of prison.

This prison was all about sensory deprivation. You wore uniforms. You made your bed military style. You had one small locker for everything you owned. You couldn't have a picture of Jesus or your mother or anyone. Now, the place was shiny, and the floors were very clean because the women did all the cleaning. But totally sterile. I fell for it at first, too, because it looked just like a movie set. Six computers in the library. Imagine! I found later the computers were never hooked up.

Then there was the mail room. The staff would go through the magazines and rip out all the pages with perfumed strips in them, so you didn't get to smell the perfume. They took the time for that when all sorts of other stuff wasn't getting done, like [processing] women's requests for visitors.

It's part of the new regime. To make money, not spend it. Before Carswell existed, Lexington, Kentucky, had the prison hospital. When they were getting ready to move the hospital, the GAO [General Accounting Office] recommended against moving these hospital prisons to military bases or to Texas. (I have a copy of that recommendation.) But they went against the recommendation, I think because they *want* to limit access. There's also more isolation there in Texas, and it's easier to hide stuff, and they have the most conservative courts in the country.

I *did* try to start a project there, because women were coming in from other prisons who were *so* sick, and they had no information on wellness or on what was really facing them—death and dying. So I wanted to start a library project. A few people had sent me books, and the women were just grabbing them. So I wrote a proposal but it was refused. I also had Hospice send a letter saying I was trained in hospice work and asking if I could be part of their so-called hospice program. Didn't get that, either. For some women who are dying, there's such a thing as compassionate release, but it's all political and it's almost impossible to get and the process takes so long that you're usually dead before you get it.

I had a lot of problems coming out of prison this time. Post-traumatic stress, I guess. Waking up in the middle of the night hearing the women banging on my door, begging me to help them. I guess because I felt awful for leaving them.

Ro: Because you let somebody pay your fine?

Kathleen: No, not just that, but because I was basing my decision to leave the prison on fear. I have lived my life—tried to live my life—in faith and hope, in community and in standing with those who were less fortunate. But for the first time, and still, I am fearful for my life and my health in that prison. I knew I wasn't totally powerless, but I *felt* totally powerless, and in the end, I *was* powerless.

Death means nothing in prison. When you die, they shackle you before they put you in a body bag. You stay shackled for twenty-four hours at the funeral home, in case you're faking it. These are Bureau of Prisons rules. Autopsies? Forget about it!

Another thing: a lot of the women doing time now are from other countries. After they finish their time, immigration picks them up on their release date, drives them to the airport, and gets them out of the country. The taxpayers are footing all of this, and it's madness. Sixty-billion-dollars-a-year madness.

Ro: Did you do anything in Carswell to sort of mitigate the madness, anything like the singing and the peace cranes that you did in Syracuse after the Griffiss Plowshares action?

Kathleen: Well, it's always the women, you know, and the relationships. But I'd not expected to land in such a wasp nest of issues. I was buying the limit in stamps every week, which was two or three books. I'd write and write and write and write, and try to tell everybody I could. There was very little levity this time, but lots of kindness. I mean, I was so . . . [*stutters and falters*] I was just . . . It was so unbelievable, what I was seeing. [*Long pause.*]

Ro: Would you risk going into prison again, with this new system and your worsening medical problems?

Kathleen: You know, I'm still working through this, remembering that the decision I made was based on fear. Real fear. I've got some very real mental health issues as well as the physical ones, and I struggle with this because so much of my heart and soul and my gifts—my vocation—has been going into the jails and doing what I do.

If I go in again, I'll go in with the knowledge that, yes, I could die. I'll have to come to peace with that before I go. Because whether it happens or not, that's where I'd have to be in my head. Right now, I'm saying no more felonious activities. Because your vulnerability skyrockets, if illness gets to be an issue. The best way to do time is to not need anything. Because once you need something and have to ask for it, they've got you.

The group in Hartford is different than the Syracuse peace community. Here, an amazing Catholic Worker house and an extended family form the community I interviewed, a group that touches many in Hartford's beleaguered East Side, particularly with an after-school program and summer camp. The founders of the Catholic Worker house—Brian Kavanagh and Jackie and Chris Allen-Doucot and their children—are surrounded by a warm extended community of family and friends. Chris, the father, regularly travels to war zones and speaks throughout the state about what he learns, thus providing an international edge to their resistance lifestyle of simple living and withdrawing from many corporate institutions. Jackie, the mother, no longer spends time in long prison terms as she did before her marriage. I was privileged to interview four of the Hartford Catholic Workers as well as Jackie's indomitable mother, Mickey, and one of Jackie's sisters, Teri.

Mickey Allen's first arrest was when she was sixty-five. When I interviewed her, she was eighty-six and still going strong. Her daughter Jackie sat with us as we talked and sometimes interjected details.

Genevieve (Mickey) Allen

"It's the unknown that's so frightening. Once you've been through something, though, it's not near as bad as you think it's going to be."

This year we did Stations of the Cross again, at the submarine base in Groton. The officers know me. Most of them are young boys, and they call me Grandma. They're mostly good guys. Apologetic and very gentle.

Ro: Now, you were an army nurse during World War II?

Mickey: World War I . . . oops, II! I feel like World War I. The things I saw in the war made me antiwar. I used to tell the kids the war stories and I wrote a book about all of it—*Chip on My Shoulder*. See, my head nurse told me that I walked around with a chip on my shoulder. I objected to all the old obedience stuff we learned in nursing school.

Ro: You have had nine children, didn't you?

Mickey: Yes. Eight girls and one boy. (We called him "the prince.") Twenty-four grandchildren. I really had to wait to speak out for peace. Couldn't do anything while my husband was alive, because he was very . . . he was a lieutenant colonel and . . . I'd go to Pax Christi meetings and things like that, but I didn't risk arrest until my youngest child was in college.

Ro: Now, did your daughters get you into it, or did you get them into it?

Mickey: Oh, I think I've learned more from them than they learned from me.

Jackie: No, Mom! You got arrested before I ever did.

Mickey: That first time, I was scared to death. Scared to *death!* It was a Good Friday. I'd mentioned it to a leader of Pax Christi and he said, "Oh, no! We don't *do* that."
   I figured, "Who's the 'we'? Why should I let him decide for me what I'm going to do?" Since that first time, it's been every Good Friday for twenty years, twenty-five years. And then every time there was a launching of a submarine, and then . . . well, Hiroshima Day and all those things. I had a son and a brother and three nephews that were policemen and all this malarkey, you know, so at first I wasn't into breaking laws. But I just knew I was doing the right thing.

Ro: Do you make a statement when you go to court?

Mickey Allen with soldiers, Groton,
Connecticut, 1998. (Photo courtesy
of Jackie Allen-Doucot.)

Mickey: Yeah. I don't do well, because I can't say what I want to say without crying.
I'm up there with all these smart people, and I always feel like an old wimp!

Ro: I don't think the crying is bad!

Mickey: Ooooooooooh, I do!

Jackie: Other people cry when they hear it.

Mickey: But, ooooooooooh, it's awful! To get up in front of people and talk—I hate
it! I was scared, scared of the arrest and of the trial and of going to jail. It's the unknown that's so frightening. Once you've been through something, though, it's not
near as bad as you think it's going to be.

I'd never get any jail time because they didn't know what to do with me. Age
and all, I guess. One day I overheard somebody say that I wanted to get arrested
but not do the jail time. I figured, "Well, it's not much use saying you're going to 'risk
arrest' if you're really *not* risking arrest." So finally what I did was refuse to sign the
"promise to appear."

Then they threw me into jail for five days. I think I was about seventy-five. They
were going to keep me until I signed and I finally had to, because my eyes were all
swollen up from the delousing soap, and I couldn't see. I went to my doctor when I
got home and he gave me a cortisone shot and said I was an idiot.

Jail—it was amazing! Like I say, they don't know what to do with me on account of my age, so they put me . . . uh, where do they put the ones that disturb everybody? In isolation. Anyway, I was way back in a supply room. When I went back into the day room the next morning, this big black woman put her arm around me and said, "They put you there to protect you from us bad guys." Well, those "bad guys" treated me better than the cops did!

Oh, here's a funny story! Once two women had a fight and they threw one of the women in the room next to me, way in the back. I gave her a magazine, stuff like that. Then a little later, they threw the other woman in the cell next to her, and I heard the first woman say to the one she'd been fighting with: "Hey, Millie! If you need anything, ask that old lady, because she don't know from shit!" [*Loud laughter.*]

The women were very, very good to me. When I was admitted, I was with a bunch of prostitutes, and they were all happy because the cops had taken the names of the johns. I remember one guard, too. After one of my kids visited, she said to me, "I couldn't help overhear what you said to your daughter. I agree with you and the only difference between the two of us is that you took a stand and I've never taken a stand in my life." That alone made my whole arrest worthwhile.

But my friends kept calling me crazy. Now, we had played cards every week for twenty years, and I tried to tell them why I did it. I told them that maybe it was because I saw things in the war that they never saw. Then one of them started saying real nasty things. That I thought my kids were better than their kids and so on. Now, I *do* believe my kids are better than their kids, but I never said it, you know? We never had any trouble with the kids. Never. And I knew their kids were in trouble a lot, but you'd be an ass to compare them, to say that.

"And you're so holy." I used to go to Mass every day, but I didn't think that made me holy, you know? Then she said, "I don't see why I should have to pay to feed you in prison when you get arrested on a whim." That "whim" just got to me.

Here I'd been in the church for hours on Holy Thursday, praying for guidance, staying late, late after the services. I had been thinking and praying about it a lot. *It was no whim!* What hurt me the most was that not one of those supposed friends defended me against this woman.

Some of my family . . . they didn't do well with the arrests, either. Like my son. He went in the navy after high school, and submarines are close to his heart. When he got out, he became a policeman. He didn't talk to me for two years. No Mother's Day, no Christmas, no cards, no visits. He's good, now, thank God, but we still don't talk about it. He said once, "I'll bet Daddy's spinning around in his grave."

I told him, "Well, now Daddy's dead, and he knows I'm right." But he wouldn't have understood when he was alive.

You know it's never too late! I'm still nervous every time, but I'm so sure I'm right. Once me and Chris, my son-in-law, chained the front doors shut on the Federal Building so nobody could get in. That was a federal offense, and they're not as nice as the New London cops.

Jackie: I remember that trial. By the end, the charge was reduced to creating a public disturbance, and [the judge] just gave her time served. He said from the bench, "Sometimes the public should be disturbed."

Teri Allen is another one of Mickey's daughters. She's married with small children and, as she reminded me, she has the luxury of bowing out when conditions in her life don't give her the opportunity to respond. "People in war-torn countries don't have that. The women in Iraq with their babies, they're in the same spot every single day, always dealing with the reality of war and being scared."

Teri Allen

> *"People are being swallowed up by the government's propaganda,*
> *especially with those obscene recruiting billboards. So we try to*
> *counteract that, to correct some of the lies."*

How can we be really mindful of the reality that we create in the world? Some people become so despairing that they let go, but I think we have to keep some passion alive, have to work together to keep holding the light of what it means to be human.

Maybe the protest art does that to some extent. We so often meet each other in our heads with political analysis, but art can give us a visceral experience. It drops a lot of people back into what it is to be most human, drops them into their bodies. Because you react to art with your body.

I remember during the first Gulf War, when a group of us made this giant mourning mother puppet. We didn't have any money to buy materials but Jackie had learned how to do this stuff up [at] Bread and Puppet.[5] We didn't have enough clay to do it right, but we got bags of rice and covered them with mud and brown paper and finally, it worked! We had this mourning mother face about ten feet tall, and her mouth was kind of open and just *so* intense. We dressed her in black cloth and made hands and took her out on the streets, with a person in a death specter costume walking in front of her. Death was carrying a dead baby, which was a doll wrapped up in bloody rags. It just hit you in the gut. We could actually hear people gasp!

Now we're in another war and people are being swallowed up by the government's propaganda, especially with those obscene recruiting billboards. So we try to counteract that, to correct some of the lies. We call ourselves "HAFTA," which stands for "Hartford Artists For Truthful Advertising." We started about twenty years ago. If there's a really offensive billboard, we sneak out at night and change it. We

Rally against UN Sanctions, New York City, 1999.
(Photo courtesy of Jackie Allen-Doucot.)

use either spray paint or buckets of paint, depending on how big the billboard is, and add other messages, message that kind of clarify what's really being said.

I remember one sign had a marine saying something about becoming a man, and we added, "Like raping, killing, murdering." Then one had all these military planes, and it says, "Take the Expressway to Your Career." We changed it to "Take the Expressway to Murder." On that one, somebody spelled it wrong, though, and we had to go back and fix it. But this is something I can do, even with my young kids—put forward my little piece of truth.

Ro: Right. How old are your children?

Teri: Five and seven. And Dan, my little guy, has asthma. Now, I'm an American mom, and I've got electricity and I carry around a little breathing machine and the medicine for my son. When he gets an attack, I put the medicine in his mask and I hold him on my lap and put his mask on and immediately his breathing is better. It's magic! Right away he's back to playing.

Once when that happened, my dear Palestinian friend, George S. Richmani, was here with me. (George does amazing work with nonviolent response in Palestine.)[6] He told me about his friend in Palestine who also has a kid with asthma but can't go out of the wall to get help. So he just sits with his kid and prays and rocks him when his breathing gets really bad. After hearing that, I remember that little Palestinian boy every time I hold my Dan and give him his first-world medicine. That little boy . . . [*chokes briefly*] he deserves it, too.

Ro: Teri, how can you keep that emotion from turning into anger?

Teri: Sometimes I *do* get angry, and I think that's okay, too. The other day I was driving down Flatbush Avenue in Hartford. Having a good day, not stressed or anything. I was in a really poor neighborhood, and suddenly I saw a Hummer driving up the street. Well! You wouldn't believe what I did! I got up and hung out the window and just screamed: "F— you! People are dying in Iraq and you're driving that monster thing!" Then suddenly I heard myself and it was like, "Holy God! Where did *that* come from?"

Anger is okay, but when we become our anger . . . At that moment, I wasn't experiencing my anger and moving from it; instead, I *became* my anger. I was actually hanging out of my car and screaming.

How can we feel stuff and not become it? I wonder. Maybe it's by having our discipline, so that we're able to separate our observer self from who we are. I don't know. What I said to that Hummer was quite a shock and where it came from is still a mystery. I went home that night and got my little journal book out and was drawing it, you know, and saying to myself, "Let's just hang out with this." [*Voice drops to a whisper.*] Maybe . . . maybe we *should* feel rage when things are not okay.

Brian Kavanagh lives in the Hartford Catholic Worker with Jackie and Chris and their children. Now in his sixties, he helps to support the house with his art.

Brian Kavanagh

> *"I hate hearing from these maniacs who are running things that 'the American people' agree with them, making it sound like all of us. It isn't!"*

For many years, I'd been going to the Good Friday Stations of the Cross down in Groton. They usually culminated with some folks risking arrest for praying and refusing to leave when asked, usually in front of the gates of the Trident nuclear submarines. Finally one year, when I was in my late forties, that little voice inside of me said, "It's time to ratchet it up." (This was before I joined with Jackie and Chris at the Worker house.) I didn't tell anyone, not even any family. I went to the planning potluck the night before, but as these things go—and I can understand it a little bit better now—it was people just sitting around talking, and I didn't really learn anything.

The next day, the weather was terrible! We started at Electric Boat, where the subs are made, and then it was a long, long walk in sleet and freezing rain to the sub base. I was soaked to the skin. I knelt in a puddle of freezing water and then I was arrested and put in the wagon. I just felt shell-shocked. Someone offered me a piece of his sandwich—he was just completely relaxed, you know—and I was thinking, "Who can eat at a time like this?"

When I was put in a holding cell at the police station, I finally realized that for the first time in my life I was someplace where I couldn't leave of my own volition. People said "Happy Birthday" to me because I had "come of age," being arrested the first time. Everybody was in kind of a celebratory mood, except for me. The processing dragged on and on and by the time I got out, everybody else had gone and my car was clear on the other side of Groton. When I finally got home, I took a long, hot shower. But the next day I was euphoric, because I had done something and survived it.

Nobody told me what to expect after the arrest, so I went right down and got a postal money order and paid the fine the ticket said I had. Later I find out that they usually just kick out first offenses, so I could've saved the $60. Also, I didn't know that there's kind of an unwritten code that you never pay the fine. But I'd taken a step and I'd move on from there.

I remember calling my family. "Ma, I got arrested. I just want you to know." Dead silence on that end. Then I could hear, "Brian, Brian got arrested" going through the house like a tidal wave. And my older brother said, "Well, we could see this coming." I guess he thought because of the "riffraff" Pax Christi folks I was hanging around with. [*Chuckles.*]

Now, the second time . . . I get uneasy when people say, "Well, I've been arrested four hundred times." I think there's a danger in that, looking at it as the world does, as quantity. I mean, Jesus only got arrested once, you know? Some wonderful activists have never gotten arrested. But there have been times when my motivation wasn't as pure as it should have been, and maybe I was doing it the second time because I thought it was expected of me. Like peer pressure or something.

Ro: How do you tell whether it's peer pressure or real?

Brian: Well, I try to tell people that they'll . . . that an inner voice will say, "Damn the consequences. I feel moved to do this." I think it's got to come from the heart, not the head. My second arrest was kind of from the head and I wasn't comfortable with it.

That was also the first time I went to court, but in court I wasn't really speaking from the heart, which is the powerful testimony. I didn't know then that God'll give you the words, and I was just saying what I thought people wanted me to say. So live and learn. As you get older, you realize that if it's coming from God, God will provide.

As I got along in this, I knew that if I continued on this track, sooner or later I'd be looking at serious jail time. So when I got to the Catholic Worker, I can remember almost having a panic attack about prison, laying in bed one night. But I also was remembering that the devil gets to you through your fears.

So what were my options? Do I go just so far in resisting injustice and violence and back off when the risk of prison appears imminent? Or do I put my trust in God and throw caution to the wind and come across those stormy seas? Like my friend says, "Every day you're called to step out of the boat like Peter." So I just hoped to do the right thing when it presented itself.

Ro: And did it, in fact, present itself?

Brian: It did. Many years later there was a concerted effort here against the sanctions in Iraq, demonstrations the first Friday of every month at Senator Joe Lieberman's office. To go there, try to meet with him and then do a sit-in in his office. Of course, he was never around. Jackie did the first one, I think, and then her mother, Mickey, did one. At the third one there were five of us. We said we weren't leaving. We read a paper about a child dying from the sanctions every two minutes and rang a bell every two minutes, to remind them that another child had died.

The bell ringing got to them, I think, and they finally reached the end of their tether. We got a criminal trespass in the first degree or something. It was a Class A misdemeanor, just under a felony. Four of us asked for a jury trial, and it lasted the better part of a week. We were able to use the necessity defense, but the judge ruled that, given Lieberman's record, there was no reason to think that what we did *would* change his mind.

And of course as people of faith, our comeback to that is that God moves people in various ways. Lieberman is a devout Jew, so there really was a hope. But when you're speaking in court from a theological and not from a secular point of view, eyes kind of glaze over.

So we were found guilty and did thirty days. It could have been a year. Jail was noisy and boring, and for the first couple of days, there wasn't even anything to read, so you go a little stir crazy. I tell people, "It takes some wear and tear out of you, but it's like a door to another place in this country."

The inmates were very attentive and very astute about the injustice of war. They called me "Pops." Now, I may be older, but I'm not dead yet! If I can do thirty days then I can probably do sixty days, you know? So that's one less thing the powers can hold over my head. It's like fasting, and I've done a couple of long ones, like at the UN, just before 9/11. I know without a doubt, both in prison and on that long fast, that if God's hand wasn't in it, there's no way I could've done it. I don't have that strength or courage by myself. I also don't know if I could get arrested on my own without other folks. There's a power in the group.

My last arrest was with a group at the Sudanese embassy. I'd never been to the DC central lockup, and it's quite the place. The water had been turned off because there was lead in the pipes, so everybody was dehydrated, and it was a very, very unpleasant twenty-six hours with just a little Kool-Aid twice a day.

Oh, here's a quirky thing about one of my arrests: now they're doing video arraignments, to make it easy on the court or something. This was up in New Hampshire, after an arrest at Lockheed Martin. You walk into a dark room with three TV monitors. Pitch black and you're talking to a TV monitor, not a human being, but you can see a judge and a stenographer on another screen. There's also a third monitor so you're also looking back at yourself. I felt like a deer in the headlights.

Ro: Geez! What do you say when people say getting arrested doesn't make any difference?

Brian: Well, we get that a lot. From the inmates, from guards, from friends. "Nobody listens, nobody cares." And it's hard to argue against that except to say you're doing it for your own integrity. It's very, very important to at least say what's wrong, in a nonviolent and loving way. There's got to be people who do that. I hate hearing from these maniacs who are running things that "the American people" agree with them, making it sound like all of us. It isn't! I might not stop torture, but I can stand out there with my little sign saying that torture is wrong under any circumstances. Don't do it in my name. Don't put me in that group of "American people." I stand with the tortured, not the torturers.

And if more people did it, you know . . we know there are people who feel the same way but they don't do anything because they don't think it will make a difference. Well, maybe it would if more people came out.

Ro: Why don't they?

Brian: I think a lot of people are concerned, but they're prioritizing. It's getting harder to just get through a day and to help your kids get a decent education and keep them out of the army and stuff like that. We're very lucky here at the Catholic Worker in that with our kind of lifestyle, we can earmark certain times to risk arrest. A lot of people can't do that. Other people put their energies into something that more directly affects them, like [not paying] taxes. It would be nice if we had millions on the street, but I don't really look anymore at the numbers. Before the Iraq War there were huge marches all over and it didn't stop the war.

I believe if change is going to come, it is going to come from faith-based people. I know a lot of people come from a secular bent, but I just don't know how they can keep up with the battle without . . . We do what we're compelled to do, what we're inspired to do, and we have this assurance and this hope—fool's hope, maybe—that something of our little paltry arrests are going to make a difference.

I think it was Thomas Jefferson who said there should be a revolution in every generation. I believe in the "r" word—revolution. Not insurrection, but noncooperation. "We're not sending our kids to your wars and we aren't paying for them, either." When enough people do that, you'll see the change. And it *has* happened, particularly in the old Soviet Union.

I don't think it's necessary for everybody to get arrested. God calls people to different things. Be careful of ego and worrying about what people will think. Saying, "No, I can't," can be a very mature thing, but I do think there's a *value* in getting arrested. Reading about it isn't the same as actually doing it, to see what the court system and our jails are like. Even spending twenty-four hours in a lockup changes you. I know when I'm walking down the street and see one of those [paddy] wagons go by and know those guys or women are sitting in there—hot, scared, and chained together—I know how it feels.

Jackie Allen-Doucot and her husband, Chris, are the parents of two children, Micah and Ammon. They live with Brian at the Hartford Catholic Worker, a purple house set in a section of the city where many fear to go. Jackie was only twenty when she participated in the 1983 Griffiss Plowshares. In her interview, she talked about both early actions and more recent resistance.

Jackie Allen-Doucot

"You know the saying, don't you? 'If I can't dance, it's not my revolution.' I think the fun and the silliness may tie in to maybe the basis of my resistance. It comes, I think, out of my refusal to live in fear."

It started when I was arrested with a lot of people for an antinuclear protest on International Peace Day. About fifty of us noncooperated and stayed in jail, at the Niantic Women's Prison. That's when I met Kathleen Rumpf. About a week later, someone called and asked me to a retreat and invited me to reflect on a citation in Isaiah.

I said, "Sure, I'll come." Then I said to my mother, "Let me see your Bible." And when I read what Isaiah quote it was, "Oh, my God! What have I done?"

But it was a pretty amazing process. Four women: Liz McAlister, Kathleen [Rumpf], Clare Grady, and myself, and then Vern Rossman, Karl Smith, and Dean Hammer. Seven of us altogether. I was twenty years old.

We did Bible study and also community-building because we wanted to make sure we really knew each other well before doing it. People talked to us who'd been doing resistance stuff for a long time. Later, they'd be called our "unindicted, unnamed coconspirators." We also studied the weapon system that we were looking [to disarm] so we could talk about it to people on the jury. We also spent a lot of time scoping out the base and looking for a safe place to go in because we didn't want to be seen as a threatening presence for people who worked there.

We did it early in the morning on Thanksgiving weekend. It was surreal! We went [into Griffiss] through a golf course and had every expectation of being stopped before we even got near the hangars where the B-52s were being retrofitted for nuclear cruise missiles. But we got there and were in the hangar for a couple of hours. Actually had to call someone, to tell them we were there.

Ro: This has happened in other Plowshares, hasn't it?

Jackie: Well, we always say that these weapons have no security for us and they also can't be secured. For instance, there have been, I think, four or five Plowshares actions at Electric Boat shipyard, and it's supposed to be one of the most secure places in the world.

Ro: How did the Griffiss folks treat you when they finally came?

Jackie: Oh, they were pretty angry! We sat on the bus for hours and hours, waiting for the FBI to come, and we weren't supposed to talk to each other. I stayed in Syracuse after we were released and did support because I'd already quit my job at the nursery school. I felt that was important to do, to kind of let go of that part of my life.

We wanted to be *pro se* for the trial, to represent ourselves, but because the charge [of sabotage] was so serious, we also had these amazing women lawyers who had worked on Attica cases.[7] They were really good at helping us learn how to help ourselves. So there was a lot of reading, a lot of writing of legal memorandums and discovery motion stuff. It was a whole new world.

Ro: Now, at first you were looking at eighteen years or some phenomenal sentence, weren't you? When did you really think about that possibility?

Jackie: I think just right before the action. You know, one of the things some of the older people told young people to be mindful of—people like me and Clare—is that you have to think that if you're sentenced to fifteen years, you might be saying no to having children. Those were some heavy realities.

Ro: It's just really hard to imagine. When you were on the base, were you afraid that people would come at you with guns?

Jackie: I had that fear beforehand. But I do a lot of dream work with my spiritual director, and have since I was in high school. Just before the action, I dreamed about being in a park and we were all singing and playing and having a great time. That seemed to be a sign that things were going to be okay.

Actually, when we went in to do it, that was the spirit. Running through the golf course, there was a real freedom and release from the fear and anxiety. I think that happened because we'd spent a whole year working through everything.

We were sentenced to two years. Even though it was less than we might have got, two years seemed like this incredible . . . I mean, I didn't even stay in *college* for two years!

After a couple of weeks in the county jail, we had this horrendous FBI marshal–escorted trip through the mountains to get to Alderson, West Virginia. The ride was horrific! We left early in the morning. All handcuffed—chained or shackled around our ankles—with a waist shackle and hands cuffed to our waists. You're in this van with plastic seats, sliding around all the corners, and the guys drove like complete maniacs.

At bathroom breaks, a woman guard would watch you pee. It's not easy to take your pants down when your hands are cuffed together, you know. Liz, I think, had the hardest time with privacy issues because of her convent background. I don't think she peed for the whole twelve-hour drive.

Clare and I were handcuffed to each other, so at McDonald's we had to eat in unison. (That was kind of funny, actually.) We were all exhausted by the time we got there, but Alderson was in a very beautiful setting, so our anxiety went down a few notches. There were some fences and barbed wire, but because it was minimum security, it really wasn't the prison picture I'd had in my head.

And I really, really loved the women! There were definitely hard parts, but there was a lot of joy, too. That time in Alderson felt like my college—the place where I learned the most and the place what made me the person I am today. The first month is probably the hardest because you really don't know anyone and you're still settling in. For instance, I remember making pancakes one day. This woman came in—her name was Pork Chop—and she was giving us a hard time. Just really verbally abusive.

Finally I said, "You want your pancake? Here!"

And I just took the plate and put a big scoop of raw batter on it and gave it to her. Well, she threw it back at me and started coming over the counter! The guy in charge of the dining room was a really good guy, and he kind of grabbed her and said, "Oh, come on, you two! You're both wiseasses."

I went to her right away after I got out of the kitchen and said I was sorry, and she was fine with it, but I definitely learned not to have such a big mouth.

Later I took a job as a steamfitter. We kept the radiators working and so forth, and I was able to convince myself that my work made the prisoners more comfortable. The boss was this awesome, awesome man! I'll never, ever forget him. He actually came to my room and cried the day I left. Told me to go home and have children and stop all this radical stuff. His name was Roy Zimmerman, and he was just this real mountain man and he loved his crew. Got us a real Christmas tree at Christmas, did all kinds of stuff he wasn't supposed to do. Treated everybody in a real fatherly, respectful way and never judged anyone. And that's pretty rare in that environment.

The other crews used to call Roy "Ali Baba" and we were his "thieves" with these five- or six-foot toolboxes that took two people to carry. When we worked in a dining hall, we'd bring the toolboxes in empty and fill 'em up with food and stuff, so we always had food in our shop. Sometimes we didn't go to lunch because we had so much food. We were ba–aad!

Ro: Pipefitting sounds like kind of a neat skill to have.

Jackie: Well, not around here. I was a Grade One steamfitter, but any work around here would be at Millstone Nuclear Power or Electric Boat! And who's going to do that, you know?

Actually I learned a lot at Alderson and got really healthy, too. Was able to run five miles every day, and to take a vegetarian cooking class. We did lots of fun things, too, like parties when people had birthdays.

When we first got to Alderson, though, the staff was paranoid about us and thought we were going to be organizing and demonstrating in the prison. I remember one day . . . it was a really beautiful day, and we were outside with this whole group of people and we showed them a silly tag game where you're coupled with another person. It's really funny, and pretty soon there were like forty people, all running around in different directions.

Well, the guards freaked out! Pulled up in these cars and they were watching us very carefully. Finally, it dawned on them that it was just this goofing-around game and they didn't know what to do with themselves, with all the cars out there. Just so silly!

I only served eighteen months of my two-year sentence, 'cause they still had "good time" then. Leaving was bittersweet because I knew I'd never see a lot of those people again. Of course I was really joyful about coming back to my family and having my freedom again and not having to urinate in a cup and that kind of thing.

Ro: But you did another Plowshares, didn't you?

Jackie: Yes, the Thames River Plowshares in 1989. I got only sixty days for that. Anne Montgomery and I spent most of that up in Danbury. I met [my husband] Chris after that, when I was doing support for the Anzus Plowshares.

Ro: So it was a movement wedding. Can we fast-forward to the present, now, where you're living in a Catholic Worker house with your husband and two children and Brian Kavanagh? What's your resistance like now?

Jackie: Well, because of the children, I don't do high-risk actions anymore. I think also my feeling about Plowshares actions has changed. Since September 11th . . . uh . . . I still feel very called to prophetic witness and resistance and direct action, but my focus has changed to other things. I still greatly respect people who do Plowshares, and I've always tried to be of support to people who make the choice, but after the Thames River Plowshares, I really had this longing to build up community and put down roots, instead of coming together and doing an action and then splitting. So doing a Catholic Worker feels right.

Ro: How did 9/11 change things for Plowshares actions?

Jackie: I think that if we did our actions now, we'd probably be shot right in the head. In the Thames River action, we went to the Naval Underwater Systems Center. Some of us were in canoes and some of us swam. We came right up on the submarine, and I was able to hammer on it. I think today if they saw me floating on the side of that submarine, they'd shoot me. So the fear level, the intensity, the focus . . . I think the risk is probably 500 percent greater now, and I don't feel I could put someone in the situation of shooting me like that.

Back then . . . When it was over and the FBI came, I was just very joyful that everything had worked out, that we were all safe, and it had gone so well. We'd been meeting and swimming and training and practicing and praying together for a really long time. Some people thought we'd never be able to do it because so many Plowshares had happened there, but we really wanted to target the Trident, and it was important for me to be on my home ground.

I remember that morning when we got ready to go. We had our hammers tied around our necks on strings, because we'd be swimming, and I remember someone put music on and Kathy Boylan and Elmer Maas began waltzing around, and then everyone started dancing and it was just this very joyful, wonderful thing.

But when we finally got arrested, the navy people were horrible to us. Because, once again, they were caught with their pants down, and they looked terrible! We were in the water on the side of the sub, and had gotten very hypothermic and exhausted because we kind of swam upstream. They were literally hosing Kathy and I with power hoses.

The coast guard came fast, though, and when they saw what the navy people were doing, they were furious! They quickly took control of us and brought us to the coast guard station to wait for the FBI. They were wonderful—gave us coffee and doughnuts and blankets. Laughed and told us how much they loved us for humiliating the navy. Because the navy calls them "puddle-jumpers." It was just very nice. Until the FBI came, anyway.

Wow! What memories I have. But another Plowshares . . . There are conflicts between a Plowshares and community. I've seen a lot of communities and marriages and relationships hurt by a long-term witness, and I know our Hartford Catholic Worker couldn't sustain someone leaving to do a Plowshares action. It would mean closing one of the houses and stopping other parts of our ministry, and that's just not where we are right now. We've all done things with jail time, but the focus and intensity is different than a Plowshares. And it still gets a little crazy around here with different court dates and all.

Ro: Can you talk about the yearly Good Friday action?

Jackie: Sure. Brian [Kavanagh] and I made this cross and we always take it to lead the outside Stations of the Cross. We found the Dan Berrigan quote about the swarm of witnesses, so Brian uses a wood-burning tool and adds the names of resisters who have died. My mother keeps saying, "Save space for me."[8]

Good Friday Protest, Groton, Connecticut, 2000.
(Photo courtesy of Jackie Allen-Doucot.)

Anyway, we do different kinds of things now, some serious, like Good Friday, and some not so. One of my favorite actions was in 2004. The Democratic National Committee was meeting at this big bourgeois fundraising dinner at the conference center, so we went down there and had a mock pro-war rally. We got all dressed up and wore wigs and I had a fur boa and really high heels. Just outrageous outfits! We had the best time making signs like "Soccer Moms for Cluster Bombs."

When we got down there, the police had a pen set up for us so we were screaming, "Yes! The freedom of speech pen." When Hummers would drive by we'd yell, "Go! Eight miles a gallon." Everything was very fun and funny.

I got interviewed on TV for that and I stayed in character. This beautiful blonde reporter seriously thought . . . like I was saying, "You know, we need to be honest. The Democrats and the Republicans, there's really no difference, so let's call them Republicrats and then we'd only need half the campaign money." She thought I was totally serious, and just kept asking me questions.

I said, "Really, we all have the same agenda. It's all about the military and the weapons, and screw the poor. Nobody cares about them anymore anyway." She just didn't get it. And they had it on television! Every channel. That's the best time I've had at a demonstration in years!

We've had a lot of fun at other demonstrations, too. I remember being with all these women in a holding cell on Lafayette Street here in Hartford, for the original Gulf War. We played this game with little pieces of toilet paper on our head with things written on them. You had to guess what was on your own head. It was ridiculous! We've had other good times in holding cells. Singing and . . . lots of good times.

We had a great action at the sub base right before Christmas one year. They were launching a fast attack [sub] or something. So we had a whole "Grinch Stole Christmas" with alternate words to the songs.

You know the saying, don't you? "If I can't dance, it's not my revolution." I think the fun and the silliness may tie in to the basis of my resistance. It comes, I think, out of my refusal to live in fear. Some people might be afraid to get arrested because they're afraid of jail, and our country has all these weapons because we're afraid of the terrorists. The culture is so enmeshed in fear and the media and the government are so into fearmongering that I . . . I try to be constantly mindful that fear is useless.

We need to encourage each other not to be afraid and to help our kids to not be afraid. We've been operating with this model for a while so we take a leap of faith, and then we're kind of rewarded in that because after a while you get stronger. It's not that you can't be afraid, because everybody . . . I mean, we're all afraid sometimes. It's just that you can't let your fear debilitate you and keep you from doing what we really need to do.

Micah Allen-Doucot is one of Jackie and Chris's two children. He attends a magnet school with a global studies emphasis, and in 2005 journeyed to Darfur with his father, delivering food and supplies to a refugee camp. The journal he kept of the trip was published in the *Hartford Courant*. Micah was twelve when we talked. We started the interview with his impressions of the trip to Sudan.

Micah Allen-Doucot

"When I grow up, I want to live in a Catholic Worker."

I said to myself, "Dad's here, so nothing's going to happen." But oh, God! I got so sick to my stomach from the food! The being homesick was the hardest part, though, even though I knew Dad was just absolutely taking care of me. All the time. And the trip gave us a neat chance to bond. That was a big thing—all this time we had together. I really learned a lot about him, like how skilled he was at interacting with the people and speaking their language. He was great! So it was a good experience for us in our relationship.

Ro: What's your dominant memory about the trip?

Micah: The children. They were just so nice! Very polite and helpful. They'd come up to you and shake your hand and say "Hi." (That was like the only word they could say in English.) We gave away soccer balls and when we ran out, we went to town and got a lot more. And the last time we came to the camp, we saw them playing, out in the field. So that was good. You think of what you've got here and realize they have nothing. The things you take for granted over here would go a long way for them.

Ro: But you don't have much, as a Catholic Worker kid. Do you ever regret being one?

Micah: I wouldn't say regret. Sometimes it gets hard. When you see things other people have and you go [*spoken in a sighing, self-mocking voice*], "Oh, I'm in voluntary poverty, I can't have that." But I would never regret it. I like what I do and what the community does.

Ro: What's important to you in living the Catholic Worker life?

Micah: Helping people. People that we know, if they need help, you can't turn them down. You have to do what you can, and that's really important to me. Seeing what we have and what others don't and knowing that you can do something gives you the power to do it.

Ro: Do you have friends in the neighborhood?

Micah: Lots. We do the after-school program and I know these people. I help out there. Do the dishes and put also play with the little kids.

Ro: Do you ever have to ask anyone to leave?

Micah: Sometimes, but somebody else does it, not me. In general, if they're acting up, I'll try to talk to them. Some people argue, but now we have this warning system and they say, "I've got a warning, so I'd better clean up my act." That's made it a lot easier.

Ro: How do you feel when your dad or mom get arrested?

Micah: When I was little I used to hate it. I remember crying at the demonstrations. My big brother, Ammon. would take me to the cops and say, "You're taking the wrong person." But, um . . . I know it's the right thing now.

Jackie: Ammon tends to be the fresher, more outspoken, contrary one of the two of them. At one point I said to him, "You are ten years old and you cannot be so disobedient." And he said, "Oh, Mom, relax. In a few years, maybe it will be *civil* disobedience."

Chris Allen-Doucot grew up in a working-class family and graduated from
Holy Cross in Worcester. His interview enlarges our understanding of the
scope of nonviolent resistance.

Chris Allen-Doucot

*"You know, if we believe in resurrection, if we believe that this
world is not the only world, what the heck are we afraid of?"*

I was a student at Holy Cross. Nominally Catholic. I'd go to Mass, listen to the radical
message of the Gospel, take the Eucharist, but couldn't see how it was reflected in
my life. Then I learned about the Catholic Worker and about Dan and Phil Berrigan.
I remember I called Dan Berrigan and interviewed him for a paper I was writing. I
prefaced one of my questions by asking him, "If you were a contemporary of Jesus
. . ." and he interrupted me and said, "Well, I am! Aren't you?"

That was a kairos moment! It really changed my world perspective. That Jesus
wasn't simply a historical figure two thousand years ago, that He's alive and present
in the world today, living among us, particularly disguised as those who are poor
and persecuted and marginalized. When I left Holy Cross, I knew if I didn't continue
on this path in some manner, I would have had to reevaluate my identity. So I went
right into a Catholic Worker in Worcester and then in 1993, I started this house.

Ro: Chris, you told me yesterday that I didn't need to talk to you because you hadn't
done much jail time. And that bothered me, because I don't want this project
to give the idea that the real nonviolent resisters are the ones with heavy jail

Hartford Catholic Worker Community, 1995.
(India Blue/*Hartford Advocate*.)

sentences. I don't think that's the way resistance works and I'm betting you don't, either.

Chris: No, of course not. But part of the reason time I haven't done much jail time is that I've been lucky. I've been arrested up to three times a year for the last twenty years, and I've only done a couple of weekends in jail. I've done three blood pourings and gotten off. And not because I used technicalities or copped pleas.

At one of the blood pourings, down at Electric Boat, I was charged with disorderly conduct and at the trial, the judge didn't think I was disorderly, so I was acquitted! One time was on the White House driveway and nothing really happened, and another time was after one of the bombings in Iraq, in '98 or '99. I threw my blood on the white marble pillars of our federal building. And again, nothing. We had a trial but no consequences. I argued about the motivation and about the symbolism, and I guess it was persuasive.

Ro: Now you do a lot of public speaking and you seem to have good relationships with the press.

Chris: Yes, we have one heck of a relationship. I think too often we allow our contempt for the inadequacies of the press to get in the way of our effectively using it. They're megaphones, so let's use them as such. I have no less contempt for them than the next pacifist, but I don't wear that on my sleeve.

We learned pretty quickly that the most effective way to get press is to develop personal relationships. Not press releases, you know, but to be able to . . . I think the small talk is essential, because that opens some of them to be human beings, not just reporters. Several television stations and different reporters and editors have given us their cards. Folks on the networks, too. That's Catholic Worker personalism, to my mind. You know, the reporter may work for a corrupt organization, but he or she is still a person, so you try to communicate on that level.

Another thing—the reporters do the stories about the charitable work of the house and that gets us invitations to speak at churches and colleges, both around here and farther away. We're even invited to places like Kiwanis Clubs.

People support our work in the neighborhood and that gives us legitimacy to also speak about the justice work and about war. In fact, it'd be dishonest for us not to do so. Speaking about how we treat the symptoms gives us the platform to speak about root causes and about the militarism and the violence and our responses to it.

Part of our moral authority at the Catholic Worker—if we have any—stems from the fact that we live here in this neighborhood where we do our work. And when I travel, I don't live in the "green zones." So I'm not secluded from the people in the street either here or abroad.

Scott Schaeffer-Duffy at the Catholic Worker in Worcester put together the first Catholic Worker trip [to Darfur] in December of 2004, and I went. Then in April

[2005], my son Micah and I went. We went to a camp that's not officially recognized by the government of Sudan, and since it's not officially recognized, they don't give permits to the aid agencies to bring in relief or to organize the camp. This camp—Camp Dreig—has fourteen thousand people. And there are *dozens* of camps like this!

Actually, we went to do civil disobedience, went with the idea that we'd rent a truck and bring food into the camp and see if the government was stupid enough to stop us. For a week we brought in food, several tons of peanuts and sorghum and dates and onions and carrots and rice and sugar and dried tomatoes. Even some beef.

At the end, a photojournalist who was with us was arrested, and their miscalculation of arresting a white American brought the attention of the international media and several members of Congress and the State Department, and generated a lot of interest about what was happening over there. And that's what we wanted.

Gene Sharp, the political scientist from Harvard University who does all the stuff on nonviolence, has this term he calls "moral jiu-jitsu," where you allow the force of the opponent's immorality to fall on itself.[9] Like the lunch counter demonstrators. They sat at a lunch counter and exposed the violence in the system by [allowing the white supremacists] to beat the crap out of them.

Well, we brought food to this camp in Darfur and they stopped us from doing that, and that stopping exposed the brutality of the system. It really encapsulated the racism perfectly. One white journalist gets arrested and suddenly there's all sorts of media and commercial attention. Four hundred thousand black Africans are killed and everybody ignores it. It's like the genocide in Rwanda. Roméo Dallaire was a Canadian general who worked with the UN forces there. In his memoirs, he talks about a Pentagon official who actually said one of the reasons the US didn't get involved was that they deemed one American life to be of equal value to 85,000 Rwandan lives.

Ro: Would you say that your trips to Iraq and to Sudan are your forms of resistance?

Chris: Well, it's certainly part of it. If pacifism is understood to be passive-ism, then, really, we're just cowards. I was only there for two weeks. We need to build longer terms for peacemakers in conflict zones, like the Christian Peacemaker teams.

There's historical precedent. The fellow Bacha Khan who was a contemporary of Gandhi: He was a Pathan, lived in what is today the border between Pakistan and Afghanistan. (At the time it was part of British-ruled India.) He organized a nonviolent army of a hundred thousand men. The Pathan people, the Pashtun people, are known for their bravery and their vengeance, but he disciplined that into a nonviolent effort to resist the British occupation. We need to figure out a way to do that today.

Just a simple international presence can act as a deterrent. The African Union has about two thousand troops in Darfur right now. They're not allowed to inter-vene, but just their presence has acted as a deterrent. If we could get internationals in all the different villages and camps, that perhaps we could begin the process of repatriating people to their villages to grow their crops in peace and security.

If President Clinton—perhaps as an act of atonement for doing nothing about Rwanda—took his entourage to Darfur and plunked himself down there, that would be an incredible nonviolent deterrent. Would it be simply symbolic? No! It would be an effectual intervention.

Ro: How do you get money for your trips to Sudan and Iraq?

Chris: Either from money I get from the speaking engagements about them, or from direct appeals to people who want to support it. Interestingly enough, the trips earn money for *all* our work because more people get on our mailing list after hearing me speak. For the trips I took to Iraq, I was leading delegations for Voices in the Wilderness.[10] Part of the delegates' expenses were to pay my way because I made all the arrangements. I've taken a fair amount of activists, but I've also led delegations with journalists and labor leaders. I was able to get the *Hartford Courant* to send both a photojournalist and a journalist on one of the trips, and they ran a weeklong series of stories with photographs.

Ro: How did you learn how handle the logistics?

Chris: With the Iraq stuff, Kathy Kelly showed me the ropes. With Darfur, Scott Schaeffer-Duffy initiated it and we learned how to do it. Frankly, a lot of it is Provi-dence. You know, to get to Darfur, to leave Khartoum, you need special permits or an invitation from the Catholic Church. When we got to Sudan, Scott had done some decent advance work and things just fell into place. I don't think you can underestimate the role of the Holy Spirit in all of this.

One of my favorite stories about Jesus is about Jairus coming to save his daughter. Jesus keeps putting him off, but He finally goes there and she's dead. Jesus sees the girl, and he comes back out and he tells Jairus: "Fear is useless. What is needed is trust. The girl is just sleeping." You know, if we believe in resurrection, if we believe that this world is not the only world, what the heck are we afraid of?

Ro: Okay, but when you're driving a truck down an unknown road in Darfur, how can you help being physically afraid?

Chris: I would say nervous more than afraid. Certainly, there are things I'm afraid of. (Ask my kids about my fears of clowns and bridges.) But we need to learn to be unafraid. Not to be stupid, but to be unafraid. You know, you get butterflies, you get nervous. But then there are the instances that you can't prepare for and you find yourself unafraid and you just trust in the Providence of God.

Here's a story: A few years back, there was a man in this neighborhood named Mark. (Subsequently he's been murdered.) Schizophrenic and a heroin addict and he drove us crazy. He came by the house all the time, and we'd help him with this and that.

One morning I was in our furniture pantry, and he came down there. His veins were bulging and his eyes were bulging and he was all sweaty: "Chris, please help me! He's going to kill me, gonna kill me, gonna kill me."

And I'm going, "Nobody's going to kill you."

Then this kid comes running in. "Get out of the way, I'm going to kill him!" Mark had stiffed him on a drug deal or something and the kid was high on what's called "wet pot," dipped in embalming fluid.

I told the kid, "This is holy ground. You're not going kill anybody here. Go cool off."

He says, "God's never done shit for me. Get out of my way." Mark is screaming, so I turned my back on the kid—which was a mistake—and told Mark to get behind this pile of mattresses. When I turned around, the kid took out a gun and pistol-whipped me. Eventually he took off out one door and Mark went out the other. I think if I had been afraid, he probably would have shot both of us. If you're going to be afraid, what can you possibly do?

If you want to see the effects of the war, come to the cities. Most of the abandoned buildings and vacant lots in this neighborhood are still from the riots of 1968. And the inadequate level of social spending is a result of the gross amount of money that we spend on war preparation and warmaking.

Connecticut and the US as a whole has an infant mortality rate of seven deaths per a thousand live births. For Hartford, it's seventeen! That's higher than some third-world nations. In Connecticut, the wealthiest state, per capita, in the entire nation, the median income for a family of four in this neighborhood is $6,900. That's obscene! There are people in this neighborhood who don't have electricity or heat in the winter. So I repeat, if you want to see war, come to the city.

That's not saying that it's an awful, dangerous place. It's not. It's a beautiful, wonderful place. It's a very caring place. There's too much fear of our cities, fear that's fostered and fed by our mass media. A lot of the fear comes from not knowing. We meet many people who want to volunteer here, but are terrified at coming to the neighborhood. All they hear from the mass media is the shootings and the drug dealing.

It's not like that stuff's happening right now as we're talking. Now the birds are singing and the flowers are blooming and the kids are in school across the street. But folks take the tidbits of horror they see in the news and extrapolate them to fill up the day and the week in this neighborhood, so that, in their mind, the city is nothing but an uninterrupted series of shootings and violence. So of course they're terrified.

It's similar to the trip to Darfur. People were real upset, at first, that I was taking Micah. Now, if you've never been there and all you know are the horrible things . . .

if you don't have the other experiences, then you have nothing to fill in the gaps between the horror experiences. You don't know the context. So a lot of fear is based on unknowingness or ignorance. (Ignorance is the more accurate word, but it too often is a value-weighted word, so I call it unknowingness.)

We *can* know. It's not beyond our means. Particularly in this world of the Internet. And we can go places. We can leave our communities and see what's happening for ourselves and make relationships with people that aren't exactly like us. I think a lot of the residual racism in our society is simply a result of our separation. We live in a segregated society.

It's particularly apparent living here. We're the only white people for miles. When we take the neighborhood kids out of the neighborhood to get a video, they'll say to us, "Where do all the white people come from?" They live in an overwhelmingly white state, but they don't leave the neighborhood, and white people, by and large, don't come here unless they're cops or teachers or coming to buy drugs.

So the people here don't really have much contact with white America. And white America doesn't have much contact with black America. Prejudice comes because we take what limited, stereotypical knowledge we have of the other and extrapolate to fill in a picture that ends up being a racist caricature. That can only be countered with actual relationships.

Look at America today. Who do we fear in this society? Black men! Black men are feared in this society, and so they're more or less hated. And more or less they're killed. They have lower life expectancies, they're more often the victim of violent crimes, they're more often killed by the police, they're more often imprisoned. We fear them, we hate them, we kill them. We need to overcome that. And now we have to overcome our new fear, fear of Moslem men.

6

Resister Families

Resister families are as diverse as all families are, underneath, and the narrators in this chapter show this diversity as they speak candidly from the depths of their relationships. One thing they have in common with most of the people whose stories you've heard is that their resistance decisions are faith-based. They are "people of the book," those who read and ponder what Christians call the Old and New Testament and Jews call the Torah, especially those passages calling believers to be active peacemakers. The parents in this chapter speak of this faith and of the intellectual discernment that undergirds decisions to resist, the commitments and compromises such decisions often entail, and both the excitement and the changes when one partner is incarcerated for resisting. As they describe their experiences with arrests, trials, and prisons, they recall how having young children made resistance decisions both harder and more compelling.

The chapter begins with five memories of the campaign to stop the deployment of Trident nuclear submarines from the Bangor Naval Base in Washington State. Kim and Bill Wahl, a professional couple from Seattle, were some of the first folks active with the Ground Zero Center for Nonviolent Action, which continues the campaign to this day. Now called Naval Base Kitsap, the base houses more than two thousand nuclear warheads, about 25 percent of the US arsenal. (Other nuclear submarines are based or homeported in Connecticut, Virginia, Georgia, California, and Hawaii.) Jim and Shelley Douglass were leaders in the campaign. They speak particularly about the White Train, which carried nuclear components to the base, and about the Agape Communities, which traced the train's progress across the country. Pastor and mother Anne S. Hall describes her time in a tiny county jail after she protested the entry of nuclear submarines into Kings Bay, Georgia.

A Midwestern resister family—Barb Kass, Mike Miles, and their daughter Ollie—talk about the seeming inequalities of life with a vocal activist father, a hardworking breadwinner mother, and a teenager upset with it all.

Frances Crowe, a Quaker mother, has grown grandchildren and is now a widow who provides a model of wisdom to the justice community in Northampton, Massachusetts. Hattie Nestel, a Jewish mother who began living alone after her sons grew up, stays in shape for peace walks by mowing a large lawn with a push mower. Joni McCoy, a Catholic mother, became a resister when her children were in their teens, while Harry Murray and Tom Karlin had young children during the resister periods they describe.

Kim and Bill Wahl became active with Ground Zero shortly after it was founded in 1977. In 1982, Kim participated in the widely publicized Peace Blockade, where tiny boats challenged the arrival of the first nuclear submarine. Her husband, Bill, played the support role at first but later became an active resister. Bill and Kim were the nucleus of several faith and resistance communities, studying and praying together and leafleting in downtown Seattle every week for years. Twenty-five years later, they share both the tension and excitement surrounding their earlier work and the complexity of their current feelings.[1]

Kim and Bill Wahl

*"We were so caught up and so determined on saving the world
from this nuclear scourge. And we didn't."*

Kim: I had kind of a sense of justice as I was growing up, I guess. I remember going to Washington, DC, on a senior trip and discovering that all the bathrooms were [segregated]. We made it a point to use the colored bathroom and caused quite a stir. That's the first thing I remember doing that was outside the Catholic good girl mode I was taught at Trinity High in Lake Forest, Illinois. Then I went into nursing and married Bill, and we went into the military and had three children, and I was a good army wife for ten years. After that, we moved to the Northwest and Bill started his medical practice. I worked some in his office but was mostly an at-home mom, always there when [our children] got home from school.

We had a number of Jesuit friends and we'd have marvelous discussions and one day I picked up a copy of Robert Lifton's *Death in Life*. About what we did to Hiroshima with the first atomic bomb. And oh! It just ripped me apart. I went through a . . . tremendous grieving process—for myself, for my country, for our lack of compassion. That we didn't atone for what we did. That book destroyed my assumptions about my country, about us as citizens but especially about the government, which continues to get all excited about other nations having nuclear weapons, but forgets that we're the only ones who ever used one.

I remember when our youngest daughter was . . . I think she was about nine. She kind of started me off, in a lot of ways. She ran into our bedroom very early one morning: "I had a bomb dream."

I said, "Oh, honey! What happened?

She said, "Well, I was sitting on Barbie's lap, and . . . and her lap melted." [*Voice quavers at the memory*.] Barb's her older sister. Just the image of that . . . It stayed with me. And probably moved me from reading books to real action.

So now it's 1978. My kids were teenagers and President Reagan was threatening Russia. We started going to conferences given by PSR [Physicians for Social Responsibility] and in 1981 we did our first vigil. Held signs at the Boeing cruise missile plant. I remember we got ugly comments from the workers. But we began doing more and more.

Bill: PSR began a huge campaign, showing people the health effects of nuclear war. I joined and Kim joined with me, and I became a lecturer for PSR during those years. I had to get my facts straight, so I did a lot of study about nuclear weapons.

Kim: Then I went to an archdiocese event, called by Archbishop Raymond Hunthausen and hosted by the Ground Zero group. It changed my life, just absolutely changed my life! It lasted all day, and all these people talked about how we had to resist the nuclear submarines which were coming to Bangor. And I hadn't even known Bangor was there! Literally. It's so close but so hidden, even though it's enormous.

A bit later I started going to the Wednesday night meetings out at Ground Zero. Which was just an enormous kind of a trip to make. Alone, at night, in the dark. Jim [Douglass] started using me to connect with people in Seattle, although we were still living in the suburbs at the time, in Bellevue.

I began to seriously consider being in the blockade. The penalties for violating a national security zone, which we were planning to do, were ten years and a $100,000 to $150,000 fine. [Afterwards] I said to one of the sisters in the blockade, a sister of St. Joseph of Peace: "Well, now, why didn't we think about going to jail for ten years?"

And she said, "Because we thought we'd die in the water." [*Laughs somewhat nervously*.]

Bill played the devil's advocate. I wouldn't say he didn't want me to do it, but he wanted to be sure that I knew what I was doing.

Bill: Which she did not know. [*Laughter*.] I couldn't believe she did it! She was just terrified of the water. I shouldn't be saying this, but . . .

Kim: I am *not* terrified of water. I just don't like open, deep water.

Bill: Well, *I* was terrified of the water.

Kim: We had to rent wet suits and [the salesperson] said, "When will you bring this back?" I said I wasn't exactly sure and told him what we were going to do. When I returned it, he said, "Forget the bill."

Planning the blockade was a huge process—weekend retreats and meetings and meetings and meetings and meetings. And prayer. Most of the people in Bellevue disagreed with what I was doing. We'd already created a stir collecting signatures and trying to get our friends to be involved, and to do something like this was just far . . . just way far out. We were also tax resisting, which was probably our first real civil disobedience. We'd resist half of our tax liability, which was sort of the war budget, and continued that until our income was so low we didn't have to pay.

Then it was the blockade: August 12, 1982. We stayed in a camp, as near as we could get to Oak Bay, and practiced for weeks. Fifty of us were planning to be arrested for going into the deep water and blockading the submarine—the *Ohio*—as it came up into Oak Bay. Originally, the sub was supposed to enter the Hood Canal, which is very narrow, but they moved it out into more open water, into Oak Bay, which made it even more dangerous.

Internationals joined us—from Canada, Germany, all over—along with quite a few locals, including [people from] California. A boat called the Pacific Peacemaker sailed all the way across from Australia. Greenpeace helped us with water safety issues, and they were horrified at how inadequate our Zodiac rubber boats were.

I was in a Zodiac, which we called "Plowshares." With John Nelson, a Lutheran minister from Minnesota, and his mother, Ruth Nelson. (She'd been Mother of the Year in 1972.) Also, there was Gracie Baranski from Portland and Charlie Meconis from Seattle.[2] We'd been out on the water for days, waiting for this event. The Guard was practicing with their water hoses, and we were practicing with our lifelines. (The boats would be connected to each other with rope.) A very, very intense time.

We had watchers who traced where the submarine was somehow, so we had a pretty good idea that it was coming. But still, for the last week, we had to be out there all the time, so we wouldn't miss it. We'd hear the radio traffic clatter increasing every day. They'd called in every coast guard unit on the West Coast, and as I said, it was really, really intense.

Archbishop Hunthausen and lots of other people were in "witness boats" and had been on the water, but on the day of the blockade, the authorities closed Oak Canal. Made it a "safety zone" and that meant nobody could be on the water, even the people living on the banks.

Finally we learned that the sub was coming down. "Get to your boats." We struggled into our wet suits and went to the boats. This was it. But they tried to preemptively arrest us before we even got out there. John and Charlie were navigating so well, though, and they just turned the boat away and headed straight for the submarine. Three coast guard boats took out after us, one on the front and one on either side. We were literally chasing the sub, and we actually got quite close. One other boat got closer than we did and was able to circle the submarine. We saw it, so we know that really happened.

Then the coast guard was going to hose us. Ruth Nelson, the one who'd been Mother of the Year, says to this kid with the hose, "Not in my America, young

Trident Blockade boats, August 1982.
(Photo courtesy of Loren Arnett.)

man!" They looked at each other—this young kid and this seventy-two-year-old woman—and he didn't do it. But they hosed the rest of the people into the water and left them out in Oak Bay. Those were the ones who were in little one-person boats which couldn't be boarded for an arrest. But ours was bigger so they could get on, and they boarded us and we were arrested.

They took us first to a coast guard boat and then they put us on a big, ocean-going coast guard vessel, which actually had a brig. The FBI and federal marshals and the navy and the coast guard were all waiting for us on that big ship. They'd also built two huge chain-link fence encampments at Bangor Sub base, with numerous sani-cans and so on, so you could see they were prepared to arrest a lot more. In the end, they only arrested fourteen of us and only charged eight.

Bill: I'd been her support person at home during all of this, but I was there when she went out to meet the sub. That blockade got more publicity than we'd ever imagined. Daily on the television. They showed the Trident, they showed the *Pacific Peacemaker*, and the Australian sailboat, and the encampment. It was on TV every day and on the radio and in the newspapers. I learned that sometimes when you do something outrageous, it gets a lot of publicity which can't be gotten any other way.

Kim: A week later, they dropped the charges. Didn't want the publicity. With the internationals there, it had been in all of the world's press, and they knew it would be a huge trial. We had enormous good legal support, and they knew that we'd be able to reach the people, and they didn't want that.

Missile Motor Train action, April 1986.
(Photo courtesy of Bill Wahl.)

Somehow, though, that didn't seem the biggest part of it. The biggest part was being there and stopping the submarine. Being out on that water and saying no. But it's still right here, among us, in spite of it all. [*Pause.*] In spite of it all.

We never did another waterborne blockade. We found out about the White Train and then began tracking and meeting the trains and trying to stop them.

Ro: Did you sit on the train tracks?

Kim: Oh, yes. The first White Train that I acted on was March of 1983.[3] The really dangerous train was in July of 1984; then there was a night train in the fall which we didn't advertise. It was just a smallish group, and a lot of church people were on the tracks. The police would move us off so the train could get through.

Then one day some people went further down and were right in front of the train and [the police] just grabbed them and threw them off because the train didn't stop. Then later there were meetings with the railroad, and they'd stop the train so that people could actually stay on the tracks. It has been argued that this agreement was colluding with the authorities.

It could be . . . There were safety issues—huge safety issues—because a lot of people would come to these demonstrations [from outside]. We'd try to train them in advance, even do trainings in the city here, explaining that the train would be moving, and it can't stop when it's got momentum. In that July train, some people ran out in front of it, and the train didn't stop and it was extremely dangerous. We never had an injury, but with that train, it was a miracle no one was killed.

Bill: Kim and I had an agreement that we wouldn't be on the tracks at the same time, so one of us would always be available. We moved here to Seattle in the summer of 1984 and this house became the nucleus of the Seattle resistance actions.

Bill Wahl with arresting officer, December 1987.
(Photo courtesy of Jeffrey Wahl.)

I quit the practice of medicine that January and took a job teaching half-time to medical assistants. I didn't have papers to correct or anything, so it was the perfect job.

That year, I had an inspiration! It was now my turn to do resistance. After training, nineteen of us went onto the tracks, in February of 1985. We were arrested by the Kitsap County Police and then put on trial there in June. The jury seemed to understand what we were about and acquitted us, one of the first acquittals in a resistance action in the country. After the trial, a visiting professor said, "This acquittal has reverberations all the way to Washington, DC, where they're studying the problem right now, tonight."

[After the White Train campaign broke the silence, the government responded first by changing the routes of the train and then by threatening to make tracking the train a felony. Finally, they gave it up and began shipping the deadly weapons by truck. Bill was arrested several times after that and once was put on a year's probation instead of serving a six-month sentence in federal prison.]

Bill: My one jail time: I went in with a feeling of resignation; you know, I took my licks. I saw it as a time to reflect, and I actually got through all the 150 psalms, studying them, which was one of my goals. I also read a lot of *National Geographics.* I found the time in there, as I had arranged it, to be very profitable.

Kim: We had one big White Train trial. Eighteen people in federal court, with experts and so on. Four were charged with conspiracy, and I remember having to do a deposition on how we trained people. That's the only time we were charged with actual conspiracy, but after the depositions, they dropped the charge.

Jim and Shelley Douglass
with Kim Wahl, 1987.
(Photo courtesy of
Jeffrey Wahl.)

Then the Department of Defense painted the White Train, so it was harder to spot, and finally they decided to bring in the rest of the warheads and the other weapon components by truck. By that time, they mostly had what they needed for the nuclear subs, anyway. Now everything comes and goes by truck through the ammunition gate.

There was a truck watch from Wisconsin and other places, but it's so much easier to track a train because they can't move the track. They'd try to hide the train on sidings, like on Indian reservations, but the people in those little towns across America were very persistent. God love 'em, they were wonderful. We had an extra phone in our home that we called the hotline, and of course Jim Douglass had one, too. *Everybody* did phone work when a train was moving.

Ro: Now, you formed a resistance community in Seattle, didn't you?

Kim: That came out of the first White Train. The little communities along the tracks were called Agape Communities and we became the Seattle Agape Community. By 1987, we had formed Puget Sound Agape and took equal responsibility with Ground Zero to plan what was happening at Bangor.

We decided we needed to really address the railroad, and the Burlington Northern headquarters was right in downtown Seattle. Seattle Agape Community began a leafleting campaign there, and for five and a half years we wrote a new leaflet *every* week and distributed it downtown. Even today, people who worked in those buildings will tell me that they'd discuss the leaflets all week, and wait for the next one. So they were learning, learning. We'd sometimes pass out over two thousand leaflets a week.

Ground Zero leafleted at the Bremerton shipyard and also at the base, and after the Burlington Northern stopped the White Train, we joined them out there. The base was getting missile components from other trains, though—the explosives, the rocket propellants, and the missile motors—and we'd have actions against them, but weren't arrested much after the acquittal Bill told you about.

I don't know how many times I went to trial, and I don't know how many times I went to jail but most of them were only short stints. I'd get like a year and serve five days or something. My longest was twenty-five days, for protesting the murders of the Jesuits in El Salvador. So after all of the things I'd done, my longest jail time was for walking with a cross on Boeing's sidewalk. Actually, that was my best experience because I got to know the women more and became very attached to them.

I was in the King County Jail, and there was absolutely nothing to do. I remember I finally got a pencil and paper from the chaplain, but you had to yell for the guard to sharpen your pencil, and I was too scared to do it. [This other prisoner] grabbed my pencil. "I can't believe you dare do those things that got you in here, and you're scared to even ask the guard to sharpen your pencil! You're a wimp!" But she got it sharpened.

Ro: Did some of the old good-girl stuff kick in when you were on trial?

Kim: No, I don't think I ever felt cowed by the judges. People would tell me that the judges occasionally deferred to me, because I was a suburban doctor's wife, so I tried to watch out for that and always be respectful, but also pretty clear. Usually I had some specific task to accomplish. We did a lot of preparation, and we'd do *voir dire* and the whole thing. (Finally we started just taking the first six jurors.)

Ro: I'm sensing that going to jail wasn't the important part for you.

Kim: I think that's definitely true. I saw it as an integral piece, though. Jim [Douglass] wrote an article, "Civil Disobedience As Prayer." It *is* a prayer. It gives you an opportunity to . . . You know, I could have paid a fine on the Boeing [protest] and not served the extra twenty-five days. My grandson Jason wailed, "Pay the fine, Grandma! Pay the fine!" But to me, it wasn't something to try to get out of.

It was all of a piece. Every single piece—the preparation, the trainings, the decision of which trains to meet and act on, the arrest and trial and going to jail—it was all a part of the process for us. As opposed to a lot of the people who just came to *do* the action and didn't have the option of the preparation. Writing the leaflets every week and proofing them and . . . And living in community. So it was all of a piece, there was no question about it. So no, prison was not a goal but just a part of the process.

You tried to be as faithful as you could. It wasn't always easy. People had many reasons why going to jail wasn't a good thing or why it wouldn't work. And in the trainings, we wanted them to feel free to say it wasn't their time to be arrested.

Ro: Bill, do you miss the action, the intense activity around these campaigns?

Bill: Well, it had an up and a down. I always looked forward to the time when it would stop, because I was not enthused about it. I liked the people, and it was good to get together with them, but the leafleting and the standing in line in all types of weather and so on . . . it was a penance for me.

Ro: Dorothy Day used to say the suffering redeemed the action.

Bill: Well, I'm not sure I suffered enough. Somebody said once that if a group stays together for ten years, you're really lucky.[4] Place and people are very important in holding a group together.

Ro: Kim, what did your kids think of all of it?

Kim: The children all helped us and supported us and helped set up for the PSR meetings. But when I got close to the blockade, Kate seemed to be more upset than the others.

I said, "Well, Kate, I just have to do this."

And she said, "You don't have to do this, Mother. You *want* to do it!"

So I've always had to sort of live with that, you know. I still went ahead and did it. We were so caught up and so determined on saving the world from this nuclear scourge. And we didn't.

[*Long pause.*] In a sense, the children of the community—including our first grandchild, Jason Ledingham—were the heart and soul of our work as we sat through interminable meetings, folded thousands of leaflets, and walked and vigiled. They were the reason we were there.

Our son, Jeff, became the photographer for the actions, and Barb was wonderful and a huge help, but I'm sure they all felt some loss of our attention. Barb was pregnant with Jason during the preparation for the blockade, and she told me later that she was disappointed that I wasn't as involved with the pregnancy as I would've been if I hadn't been so totally immersed.

I remember our twenty-fifth wedding anniversary. Ground Zero was doing a "Families in Resistance" thing, and so we went out there with the kids, and they talked about what it has been like for them. It was very interesting. Very, very interesting. We heard stuff they'd never told us before.

Kate told about being in Bellevue High when a missile motor [train] came in. I was present at the action but not arrested. They just left me on the tracks that time, much to my dismay. In a civics class, a teacher was talking about this: "Does anybody know anything about these people?" And Kate slunk down into her chair. "It was my *mo*-ther." The students and the teacher sincerely wanted to know, though, so she became okay with it, but I didn't hear about that until years later, in that "Families in Resistance" program. It was more difficult for the children than we realized at the time, but we were so caught up and so determined.

Ro: How do you feel about not stopping the nuclear subs from coming?

Kim: [*Slowly.*] Well, when I'm feeling my best, I say we made an impact. That people . . . *our* lives were changed. Two or three weeks ago, we had the twentieth reunion of Ahimsa, which was my affinity group at that time. There was a richness of experience and bonding with literally hundreds of people that I never, ever would have had. The people who have come through this house—Daniel Ellsberg, Richard Falk, if you want the big names—and then all of the little people, and all of the Catholic Workers, and all of the visitors. One woman from Chicago came out and left me a crystal that hangs in the living room window. She said I was a light to her teaching.

People changed. Of course some didn't, but . . . workers left Bangor, left the shipyard, left Boeing. Because our campaign merged into a Boeing campaign and we became Galilee Circle. Inspired by Ched Myers's insight into Mark, and more scripturally based.

I still do things with Ground Zero. But since the nineties, we've had a lot of caretakings and a number of family and community deaths, and I've had some health issues with rheumatoid arthritis. I'm not sorry for a minute of it. I regret, deeply regret that . . . [*long pause*] that we didn't impact the violence.

Now I know we're not willing—I'm not willing—to give this up, to give up my comfort. I know that now, at the deepest level. At some level, I could have lost everything. [*Pause.*] But when I didn't, I didn't keep up. Because I didn't know what to do next.

For thirteen years, I knew what I was supposed to be doing. I don't know now. Maybe . . . maybe it's because I'm not open to it now. I'm comfortable now. Of course I feel uncomfortable about a lot of things, but it's easier not living in community, it's easier not going to meetings, and it's *a lot* easier not going through trials and jail. I can't even imagine going to jail now.

Catholic Workers Jim and Shelley Douglass, now of Mary's House in Birmingham, Alabama, are longtime nonviolent resisters known especially for their leadership in the campaigns Bill and Kim described. Jim's theological writings on peace remain important to the faith-based peace movement.[5]

Jim and Shelley Douglass

> *"We experienced profoundly . . . the capacity of 'ordinary' people*
> *of faith to respond with nonviolent action to the nuclear threat.*
> *. . . Their response . . . broke open the silence and invisibility of*
> *this train to hell."*

The White Train at Naval Submarine Base Bangor, 1983.
(Photo courtesy of Marya Barr.)

Jim: If anything looked like the evil we were trying to resist, it was the White Train. A heavily armored all-white train with turrets on the top, with the guns of the guards sometimes poking out through the flaps. An image straight out of hell. And it had been going for two decades before any of this happened! People would spot it once in a while but it was always denied.

We ourselves didn't see it the first few months after we moved to live by the tracks. Then one day a call came from a reporter who had seen it north of Seattle. I walked outside and looked up the tracks and there it was! I had a camera, fortunately, and I took a picture of each of the cars as it passed, so we had a gallery of these scary pictures. Right away we phoned a friend in the peace movement who was a railroad buff, and he identified the most likely routes and the contingencies and possibilities.

We traced it back and learned that it came from the Pantex plant down in Amarillo, Texas. So then we made hundreds of phone calls, and people formed the Agape Community along the tracks, and the network began. A wonderful woman named Hedy Sawadsky moved to Amarillo and became the watcher for when they'd leave Pantex. Then all of us along the tracks monitored the trains, and it became a national campaign involving from 250 to 300 towns and communities across the country.

Ro: How did you get all the people for these communities?

Jim: We'd had a retreat at Ground Zero, before the White Train became [known] to us, and we invited people along the tracks of the missile propellant trains, which we *had* seen and had tracked back to the Hercules plant in Utah. (Some of that route was in common with the White Train.) We decided we didn't want a stop-the-train community, but a community of love, so it became the Agape Community. Community of love. We took it from Martin Luther King Jr.

[On March 18, 1983, another train left Amarillo and before it arrived at the submarine base, vigils were held in thirty-five different towns and cities along its tracks, some on alternate routes after the White Train was rerouted to avoid known protests. *Sojourners Magazine* featured the White Train in its February 1984 issue with articles describing the campaign by Douglass and others, a map of the known train routes, a strong call to resistance by editor Jim Wallis, and "A Call to Agape" by Archbishop Raymond Hunthausen (of Seattle) and Bishop Leroy Matthiesen (of Amarillo). Archbishop Hunthausen had earlier urged tax resistance to his flock and Bishop Matthiesen urged his to stop working for Pantex.

Jim Douglass wrote in the *Sojourners* article:

> We were on the phone continuously during the ninety-four hours of the train's journey: monitoring the train, updating vigilers up the line, sharing information with media, and meeting [by phone] a series of people in the heartland of the United States whom I have never seen and will never forget. We experienced profoundly during those four days the capacity of "ordinary" people of faith to respond with nonviolent action to the nuclear threat. . . . Their response . . . broke open the silence and invisibility of this train to hell.[6]

The train was constantly rerouted, skirting around Colorado after Bill Sulzman and Marshall Gourley were arrested in Denver. The government, "alarmed at the direction the case was taking," dropped the charges after Sulzman won a subpoena ordering the Burlington Northern Railroad to release documents describing the dangers in the White Train.[7]]

Jim: As a result of the White Train, the Agape Community mushroomed all across the United States, connected by the tracks. It was a kind of miracle, really, because the tracks were carrying nuclear weapons, but they also became a connecting rod and a hopeful link for all the members of the Agape Community. Truly, as the song says, a train was "running through our lives."

There's a Train
by Jim Strathdee

There's a train that's runnin' thru the town,
We have to stop this train.
Spreading fear where e'er it's found,
We have to stop this train.

It carries a cargo of nuclear death
For a world that's gone insane.
We come together by these tracks,
God help us stop the train.

The train is runnin' thru our lives,
How can we stop this train?
First see the hatred in our eyes
Lord, help us stop the train.

Care for the ones who disagree,
Be not so quick to blame.
Only love and humility will ever stop the train.

We pray for the workers in the Pantex plant
To help us stop this train.
We pray for the guards in the turret cars
To help us stop this train.

We pray for the children of the earth
When the missiles take their aim.
Because all life is sacred,
God help us stop the train.

Come peaceful people throughout the land
And help us stop the train.
Come railroad workers, give us your hand
And help us stop the train.

Scientists, generals, and government folks,
See what we all have to gain.
We'll form a new community
And finally stop the train.

There's a train that's runnin' thru the town,
We have to stop the train.
Spreading fear where e'er it's bound,
We have to stop this train.

It carries a cargo of nuclear death
For a world that's gone insane.

> We come together by these tracks,
> God help us stop the train.[8]

Ro: Jim, did people sit on the tracks and get arrested when the White Train came?

Jim: Yes. And that's when they stopped the train. It was getting harder and harder for them to run it with the visibility the campaign gave it.

Ro: How do you see the jail experiences as fitting into all of that? Did a lot of people go to jail for the White Train actions?

Shelley: A lot of people went to jail for the Trident campaign and a lot of people went for the White Train as part of it. All along the tracks, not just where it ended.

Jim: Our idea was always of a Gandhian campaign, never primarily civil disobedience. We never had a primary focus on civil disobedience.

Shelley: Civil disobedience would grow out of living in Kitsap County and leafleting the base. We leafleted the base every week, without fail, for twelve years, and they're still leafleting the base. We were trying to communicate, you know, organizing meetings in homes and doing everything we could think of. Civil disobedience was part of it, but it wasn't like we went there to do civil disobedience.

Jim: Leafleting was primary, not civil disobedience. We always felt that has to have a context, and the context has to be agape or Gandhi's vision of *satyagraha*, truth-force. In a sense all life is a Gandhian campaign or a Gospel story. (You can use different ways of saying it.) The idea is not to do leafleting or civil disobedience or anything else, it's just to keep following the truth as deeply as you can. And if you keep doing that more and more deeply, they kind of converge, I believe, at the Cross.

Shelley: It was also a program in building relationships and making the connections between funding the arms race and the lack of funding in the communities where the train went through—all poor communities and usually people of color.

Jim: So it was much bigger than stopping trains.

Shelley: Before the White Train campaign, we weren't sitting on the tracks, we were climbing a fence. And there was a whole sequence of arrests for handing out leaflets because wherever you stood, you were on somebody's property, and they'd arrest you and put you in jail because they didn't want leafleting.

What I served my time for was trespass, basically. Going into the Trident base, either over the fence or through the gate or down the tracks, and getting arrested for trespassing. That's a federal offense on the base so there's a six-month maximum. The longest sentence I got, though, was three months, from Thanksgiving through Christmas and New Year's. I got out right before our youngest son's birthday. Jim was still in for another month after that.

Ro: What was it like to be in jail over Christmas?

Shelley: Well, we missed the kids, of course, but once you make up your mind to be in jail, it's okay. Remember the saying: if you don't want to do the time, then don't do the crime! On the women's side of the jail—boy, this is a long time ago—on the women's side of the jail, there were probably five or six of us who were in at the same time, and the kids drew a Christmas tree on brown paper, and sent it to us, and we stuck it on the wall with toothpaste. The jail folks made each other odd little presents.

This was when we still lived in Canada so the kids were at home with the rest of the community, with all the people who supported what we did. They felt sorry for the kids, so they took them to the Ice Capades and gave them more presents than they'd ever gotten before. For years afterwards, they'd say, "Remember the good old days when Mom and Dad were both in jail?"

Jim: When I was in jail [that time] I was fasting, so the authorities put me in a public health hospital, with a full-time guard in my room. I fasted for thirty days. It began when I was making my sentencing statement. I said I was going to speak both as a Canadian and as an American, because I was a dual citizen. (We had come down from Canada to do the action.) I spoke first as an American and then the magistrate said, "I don't want to hear anything from you as a Canadian." I continued to speak and he threw me out of the courtroom. So I just stopped cooperating.

Actually, it was not a very good way to do things. I hadn't prepared to fast or anything, but I was sort of fed up with what was happening. I noncooperated in other ways, too. Didn't leave my cell or anything.

Oh, here's an interesting thing! One day, about fifteen days into the fast, I was ordered to leave my cell. When I refused to cooperate, they put me in a wheelchair. Then a bunch of guards, at least five or six of them, started running me through the jail and out the door and onto the sidewalk. No coat or anything.

"What on earth was happening?" Nobody was explaining a thing! Was this a disappearance act? Then they put me in a car and drove me through the streets of Seattle. And still nobody said anything. It was just these three big guards. They wheeled me into the courthouse and into a judge's chamber.

I said, "May I ask what is going on?"

"You have a visit from Archbishop Hunthausen." They wouldn't allow him to my cell, so they took me to the courthouse to see him. The archbishop was just being a good pastor. He was concerned, you know.

Shelley: And this was before we really knew him. He was probably also wondering about us a little bit, at that point, but later on you two developed a relationship. At the time, there were all sorts of rumors floating around that you were being beaten or abused, so he was making sure you were okay.

Jim: Actually, the guards were doing a very nice thing, to take me to the courtroom to see him, but I had *no* idea what was going on when they wheeled me out of that jail! So, maybe difficult jail experiences, but I haven't had any really *bad* jail experiences.

Ro: What was the most difficult?

Jim: Well, the Los Angeles County Jail, where I've been several times, is extremely violent, just by the nature of the system. They use it as a way station for federal prisoners, and I'd go there on my way to a prison camp out in the desert, to Boron or Lompoc. The Los Angeles County Jail is terribly understaffed—or was in those years and probably is today. It's a city within a city, with literally tens of thousands of people. Very overcrowded, and we were sleeping on floors, so they have very strict rules as to how you conduct yourself. You walk to meals with your hands at your sides, one by one, with so much space between you, and guards stand by with big clubs. While I was there, people were being killed [in the prison], so there was a lot of tension.

Ro: Shelley, were you ever in the LA Women's Jail?

Shelley: No. I was in King County Jail and Tacoma Jail and then that little jail, uh . . . Buckley. Way out in the country, where I was the only woman in the jail, so I was in the holding cell for two months. You have to do something when you're on your own for sixty days, basically in solitary, so I worked on translating St. John's Gospel into Greek. I was a candidate for the ministry in the United Church of Canada. So that I could still be a theology student—a theologue—while I was in the States, they commissioned me officially as a missionary to the US. To work on the Trident campaign.

Jim: And their mission ship came down and welcomed the first Trident sub with a huge banner proclaiming resistance to nuclear weapons. It anchored offshore from the Trident base, and the church people came ashore and visited Ground Zero. So it was a big support.

Ro: What was it like living right next to the base?

Jim: Well, for a while we were concerned about Tom going to school in the community. The other children were gone by then.

Shelley: But it turned out to be a really good experience. We always had sympathetic teachers. Tom grew up with kids whose parents worked in some form for the navy, if not on the base itself. Some of his friends could come and play at our house and with others, Tom could go to their house, but they couldn't come to ours. When we went to a soccer game, it was all navy people. But his senior class chose "Imagine" as their class song and sang it for their parents. All in all, it was a good experience.

Jim: By that time, because of what our leaflets said, they knew we weren't against *them*, that it was a systemic question. They had questions about what they were working on, too. It wasn't like most of them were enthusiastic about nuclear weapons.

Shelley: Not all of them, anyway.

Ro: What made you decide to leave Ground Zero for Alabama?

Shelley: At the time, a new base for Tridents was opening up in Kings Bay, Georgia, so the trains were going to start coming this way, both the weapons trains and the missile motor trains. People invited us to come here to Birmingham, so we came. But I don't think a weapons train came through after we moved here, did it?

Jim: Well, the White Train never again . . . We moved to Birmingham, and that was the end of the White Train going anywhere. The Department of Energy stopped it.

Shelley: And we know they stopped it because of the protests, because we got the minutes of their meetings through the Freedom of Information Act.

Jim: It had been a symbol of the whole systematic evil of weapons that could destroy the world. The White Train brought it home.

Anne Hall is the mother of two grown sons and was pastoring at University Lutheran Church in Seattle when we met. Years ago, a church conference called "Community of the Spirit" introduced her to Ground Zero, and she and her psychiatrist husband, David, continue to be active in the community. At her first arrest, for sitting on the tracks as the White Train brought

Trident components into the base, she realized that "if everyone who was opposed to those weapons would sit on those tracks, there's no way the missiles could be put together."

Anne S. Hall

"They asked me to say grace for supper that first night [in the Georgia jail], and you know? I couldn't think of a thing at the time that I was thankful for. Well! We were in that Georgia jail for six days, and by the time we left, there was everything to be thankful for."

I've kind of lost track, but I think I've been arrested twenty times and been in jail four or five times. Let's see. . . . The Georgia action was in 1989 when the first Trident was coming into the Kings Bay base. They had scheduled it on Martin Luther King's birthday and the folks at the Metanoia Community invited people from Ground Zero to come and join in a big protest.

We did a training in a little church in St. Mary's. *So* perfect to do it in a church like that on Martin Luther King's birthday. A Native American man was with us and he was on parole and not supposed to go near any naval base, and the federal marshals came and arrested him.[9] In the church! As he was walking out, we all began to sing.

The next day, the sheriff of this little town apologized to us, saying that if he'd known what the marshals were going to do, he wouldn't have let them do it. And he read to us the passage from the Book of Acts in which Gamaliel says to the Sanhedrin: "Don't worry about trying to stop the apostles from trying to do what they're doing, because if what they're doing is wrong, they'll fail. And if what they're doing is right, no one is going to be able to stop them."

Now, they only have three police in this little town of St. Mary's—the sheriff and two deputies—so we had this idea that some people would try to walk in the main gate of the base, and while the three police were busy with them, others of us would climb up on this brick wall and hang a big banner that said "All life is sacred."

The next day we went down to Florida. The Trident sub was going to pass by the beach on the very north edge of Florida, and then come into the base, which is on the very south edge of Georgia. People had been invited to come and see the boat come in, so all these families were there for a big celebration, with their beer and their lawn chairs and their children.

We came dressed in black and carrying coffins, and we processed down the beach and then back up, and then when the Trident came in, we tolled a bell twenty-four times, one for each of the nuclear missiles it carried. A real loud gong. Then we all symbolically fell down dead on the beach. As that death machine came in, and our bell was tolling, there wasn't another sound on that beach. The people got it. [*Pause.*] Yes, they got it.

Then our cars processed to the base—there were several hundred cars—and the sheriff actually led the procession. When we got there, we saw *hundreds* of Georgia State Patrol guarding the gate, and they wouldn't let us anywhere near! And here we were with our little coffins and this ladder to go up the brick wall, hidden under one of the coffins. So we rallied on the road outside and were trying to read the words of Dr. Martin Luther King, and this helicopter begins circling over the people. Making so much noise that we couldn't hear ourselves.

Martina Linnehan, who was one of the leaders, said, "All right. We'll just sit down until this helicopter goes away." So everyone just sat on the road, two hundred people right at the gate to the base. Then there were these negotiations and finally they agreed to take away the helicopter so we could have the rally.

Right after the rally, the people who were risking arrest started trying to go into the base, trying to go between the policemen's legs. They wouldn't let us through. Then the three of us—the ones who were supposed to climb the ladder and hang the banner—started to walk up to the fence.

Right away the state patrol came running after us. Somebody grabbed me from behind and threw me down into this ground cover, and was kneeling on my back. I'm thinking, "This is Martin Luther King's birthday and this is Georgia, and they're going to beat me up." (I was wearing a picture of King around my neck.) So I just went limp, and I sort of accepted that whatever was going to happen was going to happen.

They pulled me up, and I felt this hand around my throat and a lot of pressure on my glands. People started yelling. "They're strangling her! They're strangling her!" Later, my picture was on the front of the *Jacksonville Herald* and the Atlanta paper [and other papers]. I learned that the officer was doing what he called a "come-along hold." It's designed to make you walk by pressing up on your glands. If you walk, it takes the pressure off, but if you just let your weight hang, it hurts a hell of a lot. Holding my other arm, though, was a large African American patrolman and he was trying very gently to hold me up while the other one had his hands pressing into my glands.

Now, a police tactic to get nonviolent protesters to become violent is to pick on a small woman. Then other protesters, men in particular, will try to rescue her. But luckily we had talked about that in the training, and I was really impressed that the other demonstrators held the discipline and didn't run over.

When I was getting in the car, the nice patrolmen broke my plastic handcuffs because they were so tight. But the other guy was so angry that he turned up this country-western music station as loud as he could, so it was blaring at us. (Just the other day I just heard that loud music is one of the torture techniques in Guantanamo.)

Eight of us were arrested, but one man hadn't planned to be. See, we were

Pastor Anne S. Hall in stranglehold, Kings Bay, Georgia, January 1989. (Jody Kestler/*Florida Times-Union*.)

carrying crosses, and we'd handed our crosses to other people so they wouldn't be seen as weapons. He didn't hand his over and because he was carrying a cross, they swept him up. That's what happens when you carry the cross!

So we were booked into the Camden County Jail. I was really in a lot of pain from being thrown down. Finally, around nine o'clock, they got us into the cell and gave us peanut butter sandwiches and iced tea for supper. We were with a group of almost all African American women prisoners, very poor.

They asked me to say grace for supper that first night, and you know? I couldn't think of a thing at the time that I was thankful for. Well! We were in that Georgia jail for six days, and by the time we left, there was *everything* to be thankful for. We had an incredible experience of solidarity with those women. They were the poorest of the poor, the absolute bottom of the scale. Oppressed because they were women, oppressed because they were black, oppressed because they were poor.

And the television . . . We were there on Inauguration Day in 1989, and the inaugural ball came on this little broken black-and-white TV where you couldn't change the channel. Everyone was wearing tuxedos and ball gowns, and it just hit me that none of those people in Washing even knew or cared that we existed.

But our experience with those women was amazing! We just filled that jail with music! This was [the] Bible Belt, and all those women had been in church choirs, so they taught us gospel songs and we taught them peace songs.

We were able to point out some inequities in the prison system, too. The press was always calling me, because they wanted . . . someone had just died in a Georgia jail from being strangled, so there was a big controversy about whether or not [the officer] was strangling me.

Ro: Did they let you talk to reporters?

Anne: Yes. The calls came into the cell block. The phone didn't really ring, though, so every time you went by the phone, you'd pick it up, just to see if there was someone calling in. My attorney, Ken Kagan, would let it ring for fifteen minutes or so, until somebody would walk by and get it. (Ken was a volunteer from Seattle and has defended me numerous times.)

We had this enormous support community. Every night they held a candle-light vigil around the jail. We refused bail, which was only $200, because it wasn't fair that we could be released and these other women, who had been there for months, waiting for their trials to come up—some of them not even charged with anything—they couldn't be released.

We started a juice-only fast, and then we took up all these inequities between the ways the men and women were treated in this jail. The men got to go out and work, and the women didn't. The men had a very well-appointed exercise yard, and the women just had an empty one, no equipment at all. So one day the sheriff called for Martina and me to talk with him. We're wearing our little orange jail suits, and we walk out of our bare cells into this plush office with carpeting and all this mahogany furniture.

The sheriff said, "So I understand you have some complaints about the jail."

And I said, "Well, first of all, I want you to know that your guards have treated us very well." And they had.

"Just a minute. I want to put this on speakerphone to a reporter." So he did and then he said again, "Do you have complaints about the jail?"

So we got all this out and the reporter heard it all. The sheriff just kept saying, "I'd better talk to my chief deputy about that."

Then after he hung up, the sheriff says, "You know, you aren't the only people here who are opposed to the Trident. Don't they cost 1.6 billion dollars per sub? That money could go a long, long way to solving the drug problem in this country. And if this base is targeted, it's my children who are going to die."

But the whole thing was really straight out of the civil rights era. The prosecutor said, "We had a nice, quiet little county here until you folks stirred up all this trouble. We actually just arrested you for your own safety, for your own good, because, you know, people were really angry with you." He even called us terrorists. (My seventeen-year-old son loved that. He came home one day, and I was cleaning the bathroom and he says, "Mom, don't you know terrorists don't clean bathrooms?")

So anyway, Martina went to trial and was sentenced to six months. By the time she got out, she had absolutely revolutionized the whole jail for the women. She got exercise equipment. She got books. She got jobs for the women, working in the library.

Ro: Neat! What did they do with you?

Anne: Well, the prosecutor finally struck a bargain. "If you don't come back to Georgia and do it again, we'll forget it. But if you do, we'll prosecute this one as well as the next one."

[Anne's other jail terms have been brief, as well. She says she has "found God in these experiences." She concluded her interview with, "I'm probably called to do it, and I don't want to go. I tell fun stories about it, but I've never been in for more than six days. The idea of six months or a year . . . I would dread it. Jail is just a horrible place to be."]

Since 1987, people in northern Wisconsin have used Anathoth Community Farm as a base for protests on issues ranging from Indian rights to wars in the Middle East. Barb Kass and Mike Miles founded Anathoth and raised their children there. The community continues, with other couples and single people coming and going throughout the years and Barb and Mike staying firm. When they're not protesting, they work on the land, growing much of their own food and building solar-powered water heaters and straw-bale houses.[10]

Mike met Barb in 1973 at Iowa State. They married in 1978, when they were both seminary students. A class called The Biblical View of Oppression "trained them out" of their first goal of youth ministry with suburban kids. While they come from an evangelical rather than a Catholic tradition, they were right at home in a two-year stint at Jonah House. Then they moved to Wisconsin and eventually established Anathoth Farm, with its motto of nonviolence, community, and sustainability. They count themselves part of the Catholic Worker family and often attend the yearly Midwest CW retreats.

Barb Kass

*"Crossing the line is important. But there's a luxury in being able
to do that, and it's the people at home who make it possible."*

There's always the wind beneath the sail. Sometimes I think those who supply that wind get forgotten because we're not out there and visible. We have two in college now, and our income is low enough that we . . . it's a big financial burden, but what I'm really talking about is that daily keeping-everything-moving sort of thing. Mike has been project-oriented for a long time, so since we moved to the farm, pretty much, I've been the main worker. That means I rarely make the choice to "do the time" in prison because I simply can't take time off.

Ro: What do you do as the main wage-earner?

Barb: First, I worked at the battered women's shelter in Luck—the Welcome Home Shelter—and then for ten years I worked with a Polk County mentoring program, similar to Big Brothers and Big Sisters. For the last three years I've coordinated adult community education at our school.

I also volunteer a lot because we had kids in school. Do costuming for school plays and cook dinners for fund-raisers. Lots of visibility at school events. People *do* look at you and try to figure out what resistance means. So, if you have relationships with them, they can't write you off quite as quickly. And that's been . . . That is work. That is work.

Always being the one to . . . to raise your hand at the Boy Scout meeting when they have the World War vets come to talk about the glory of being in the foxholes. I'm sitting there, trying to figure out how not to offend the vets, because that was not my intent, but how to bring some truth into that situation for the little boys who had little glittery eyes?

So you raise your hand and ask how we can have a world where these little boys won't have to risk being killed in war? As soon as you see the roll of the eyeballs, you've lost them. And you don't want to embarrass your kids. So you go gradually. "Can you reflect on this for the boys?" These vets didn't really answer my question at all, but that time, at least it was asked.

Crossing the line is important. But there's a luxury in being able to do that, and it's the people at home who make it possible. The few times that I was in jail when the kids were little it was like, "Hey, this is living! I get to sleep, and read! I'm not cooking and I'm having adult conversations with other women." This jail business could be a young mother's dream.

But it *is* hard. It's difficult for the kids, too. I don't mean to glorify jail. There's nothing restorative about it, you know? But it's something everybody should do, if only to experience firsthand the feeling of powerlessness.

I remember once when Mike was in jail and I was pregnant with Philip. Emma's a year and a half and Ollie must have been four. I'm really frustrated with all the work at home, and in the county jail, Mike's playing backgammon and getting twenty letters a day from all the supporters. I'm thinking, "There's $50 in the bank. I'm not working, and the house is cold. And no one asks *me* if I need anything!"

And do I have time to get a decent letter out to Mike? So you feel guilty but yet, in public you gotta have a brave face. Of *course* it's the right thing to do, and of course this is how we work for social change. But you have that schizoid . . . So that's when you really need community, someone to tell the truth about how you feel. Sometimes even your close friends, those who aren't quite on the same page, will say, "Well, you do the crime, you do the time." And that's so noncomforting. What you need is to have someone listen and say, "You know what? Sometimes it doesn't all make sense."

Then I'd be able to say, "Sometimes I don't know if the cost's worth it—on the kids and on relationships." There are very few safe places to say that. That's why we're so blessed to have the community at Anathoth now.

Mike is always going to be busy, always going to have projects. Now our kids are out of the house, and I have summers off, so who knows? I may be more free to do actions now.

But the kids . . . I remember my "one minute of fame," when I was on *ABC Nightly News* talking about the GWEN towers. It was the "Your Money—Your Choice" segment, with Peter Jennings. The acronym stands for "Ground Wave Emergency Network." It's a series of towers that can survive a nuclear blast and will continue to carry communications to those who have survived. There is no other purpose than post–nuclear war communication. Absolutely no one, except maybe the power elite, would be any safer with an expanded GWEN tower network. Well! They were starting to build the tower before the funding was authorized and ABC found out and came out. And, in fact the funding wasn't approved because of the ABC report and the pressure we helped to generate across the country and a lot of other factors. It's a long story but what I want to talk about was Ollie's reaction to the newscast.

Before I left for the protest, Ollie's like, "Don't do anything dumb, Mom." I said, "I'm not! I'm just going to hold the banner." Well, after the bit on television, Ollie wouldn't go to school for two days. "Nobody else's parents ever . . ." As I'd heard before.

Actually, our life is pretty normal, though. The bulk of it is raising our kids, washing our dishes, doing laundry, going to the job, plowing out the driveway. But somehow we must speak volumes to the community, somehow people must think we're too intense, because socially we don't get invited out very often. I don't know. Maybe it's just intimidating, or people don't want to deal with a life that tries to really reflect values. These people are good people, though, and I have nothing but respect for them. I think at times, we have . . . we have pushed people. What you hope is that people will realize that we're not out of our minds and decide to do something themselves.

Sometimes it works. Like having the ten buses go from northern Wisconsin to Washington in January 2003 to try to stop the Iraq War from happening. That was amazing, truly amazing!

And that's where Mike himself gets amazing! He really goes full tilt at a project. At Christmastime we were thinking it would be nice to get one bus to Washington. (We usually just take a van, so one bus is forty people more than we've ever taken.) Then it was two buses. Then five. Then it's seven buses. It was crazy! And then just hoping the money will come through. But it does. It does, right to the penny. Dorothy economics, you know?[11]

Actually, we're the ones who are converted by anyone who takes a bigger risk [than they formerly had], because then we have to examine our own lives and see what more we can do the next time. "How can I push myself just a little bit more?" It's like a runner who's trying to beat her own speed, rather than the one who's trying to win the race.

Hearing stories of arrest shocks you out of your comfort level. And hearing stories of the wind behind the arrest doesn't shock people. But it makes the ground a little more fertile, so that when something more public happens, it's in the context of a relationship and understood as an ongoing thing. Maybe the learning from this conversation is that both parts work, but one doesn't work without the other.

Ro: Yes. You cannot have trees without the ground. But it seems that even today, it's often the women who are relational, who provide the ground. What would you say to women who were contemplating having a resistance marriage and a resistance family? What would you tell them?

Barb: That it's certainly difficult. I mean, the statistic of relationships in the resistance community is . . . is not all good. That's true with any kind of high-stress work. One thing . . . I've *liked* my bread-money work, even though a few meager benefits would have helped.

Earlier, we were developing the farm and there seemed to be more balance. But I remember Ollie writing in her second-grade autobiography, "My mom's a social worker and my dad doesn't work." God! He works all the time! Works like a maniac.

But when he's gone . . . the basic survival chores in the house take more time than they would if we lived otherwise. Like I have to crank up the fire when I come home from a long day, and it's too cold in the house to really relax.

Ro: So maybe the "stay-at-home" life of a resistance couple should be as simple to handle as possible. Maybe not quite so much "living off the grid."

Barb: Yeah. Sometimes you have to emend your expectations of the simple life. Also, you have to realize that you can't fill the void of the absent parent. The kids are always going to rebel against the parent staying home. "Why did you let him do that?" Resistance is adult work and kids can't make adult decisions, so you have to be there for them when they don't understand. You have to be the wind beneath their wing, too.

Barb and Mike's daughter Ollie was twenty-four when we talked about her childhood.

Ollie Miles

"Now they just think, 'Oh, that's what Ollie's dad does.' But I
remember earlier on, I just . . . I was very embarrassed. It was
really hard, actually."

I remember when I was in fourth grade and my dad went to jail over the beginning of the Gulf War. I was *so* embarrassed, because it was all over the papers. I just hated them, then. Hated my dad, hated my mom, hated everything about it. "Don't do this to me!" They were very accommodating, though—let me stay home from school and everything.

Ro: When you got to high school, did it stop bothering you?

Ollie: Um . . . Not at first. I'm the oldest, so I was the first one to be put through all of it. I felt different than all my friends. But when I got into high school, I finally realized that the people who would tease me didn't know what they were talking about anyway. So I just brushed it off and then it stopped. Now they just think, "Oh, that's what Ollie's dad does." But I remember earlier on, I just . . . I was very embarrassed. It was really hard, actually.

There was a [big change] when I went to Iraq with my dad. I was seventeen and a senior in high school. After I came back, I didn't care what people thought. Now, living away from my parents, I rarely bring up [what they do], unless I can tell it's something my friends would be interested in.

I wouldn't be as aware of things without [my parents]. My dad's very good at saying his views, you know. My mom always says, "Don't let your dad dictate what you think." And so I don't let it, but if something comes up on the news that I don't know about, I call him and he'll explain it all, and then I usually agree and can explain it to other people. So that's pretty useful.

Ro: Are you sorry you didn't have a "normal" childhood?

Ollie: Um . . . I used to be. Like, I remember thinking it would be nice if we had some money. But even if we didn't, we did *so* much more than any of my friends. I've been everywhere in the United States, and in foreign countries and done all this stuff that I now value way more than having basketball shoes or whatever I wanted at the time.

If there were things that we really, really wanted, though, they always made it happen. And they gave us the *best* life! Very rich in experience. All of us are very adaptable because of how we were raised and all the different people coming through and us visiting people and sleeping on floors and driving around in funny cars. We can just roll [with] any situation.

Now when I think back on my thirteen-year-old self, I realize that if it's not one thing you're embarrassed about by your parents, it's something else. So it really wasn't a big deal. *Now* I can see that, but when I was thirteen, it felt like a *huge* deal.

Now I'm really thankful for growing up with so many different people and always having a community around. There was always someone to watch out for us. Going in and out of people's houses and eating together. Any night of the week could be a party. "Let's play volleyball and have a bonfire."

I definitely formed opinions, good and bad, on people coming through, though. With all these dietary . . . like vegan, blabbety blah. I'd see my mom slave all day, making all this food for like thirty people. Then someone comes in and says they can't eat this, this, and this, and expect her to accommodate them. That made me . . . I really learned what kind of adult I wanted to be, I guess.

Now I wish I could go back and say to myself, "Don't waste all that energy worrying about what other people think of you, or wishing for something different!" Because now I really appreciate everything that I had.

Mike Miles

"Do serious stuff but don't take yourself too seriously."

In 1979, the Army Association Arms Bazaar came to Chicago. It's like a Tupperware party for weapons. Everything was really hot in Central America at that time, and we protested [at the bazaar] and actually had some suburban high school kids come down with us. After that, the people we were accountable to said that our gifts lay in different areas. So we sold everything we had, moved into our car, and decided that we had to take the naive edge off our developing understanding of nonviolence.

After some searching, we came to Jonah House, and there's been no looking back. The first time I got seriously arrested was Holy Week of 1981. Euro-missiles were moving into Germany and England—cruise missiles and Pershing IIs. We went through the tour at the White House, and then threw our blood up on the pillars after we came out. We spread tax forms on the driveway and poured blood all over them, too, and had banners and flyers. Then all the blood pourers knelt on the driveway and joined hands and we were singing and the police came running. But when they saw it was us, they slowed down. "Oh, it's just you guys."

We got two charges: good old failure to quit and depredation of government property. They gave us six months in the DC jail. We were some of the only white guys there, and the other prisoners liked our action. Their only question was, "Why didn't you run away before you were caught?"

Okay, so we had three years at Jonah House—two years, actually, at the house, and then one year living nearby but still working with them on the paint crew and everything.[12] Then we got pregnant with Emma and moved back to the Midwest

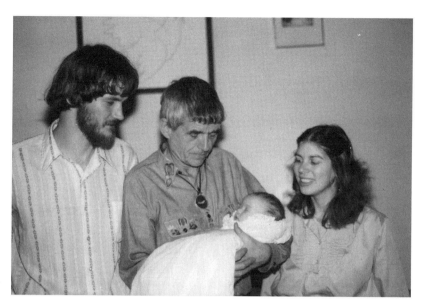

Mike Miles, Father Dan Berrigan, Ollie Miles, and Barb Kass at Ollie's baptism, Jonah House, 1981. (Photo courtesy of Mike Miles.)

when Ollie was two and Emma was nothing. We were homeless. (Actually, we did some house-sitting and house-painting for my parents, who were getting ready to move to Arizona.) During those days we were looking for where we were going to land out in Wisconsin. And we found it through the Honeywell Project.[13]

Right after we moved out here, they had the biggest arrests ever, about 577 people. We jumped in on that, and they prosecuted everybody. Trial group after trial group tied up the courts forever. Almost all jury trials, all trespass charges. They had a claim-of-right statute at Honeywell, so if you could argue that you had a right to be there . . . Some people were acquitted and some were convicted. Most people were getting probation and community service and fines. (Some paid and some didn't.) A few people did two to five days, here and there. If you got the right combination of a jury that had something going for it and a judge who would allow the arguments, you had a chance. It's kind of like what we've been doing lately at Alliant Tech.[14]

In April of 1986, we had found some land we wanted for a farm so we went out and walked it to bring on labor. And Phil was born that day. (We named him after Phil Berrigan.) That helped us to decide, "This is it!" We put together a letter saying, "We want to do a Catholic Worker farm with resistance and sustainable farming and hospitality for people fleeing war-torn areas." Mailed out maybe two hundred letters in September of 1986, asking people to consider sending us a hundred dollars. "If we get enough money we'll do this; if we don't we'll send it back." Well . . . in six weeks we had over $20,000 in pledges and cash, so we did it. It was all kind of amazing.

Ro: Yes! Now, Mike! You were active against Project ELF, weren't you?[15]

Mike: Sure was! At first, you could walk right up to the gates. We'd sit in front of the gates and dig holes and plant trees and get arrested. Later we made a ladder that would go over the fence and crunch the razor wire down, but we usually just got fines, although sometimes a couple weeks in jail. Doing extended time in Ashland County Jail—it's all rural. (You can always tell who the minorities are in a community because that's who's in jail. So DC was all black people and in northern rural Wisconsin it's all Indians.)

But so different! At Thanksgiving the deputies slid in extra holiday food from inmates' families, so we got these big hatboxes full of Thanksgiving dinners. Some of the food came from the altar guild of the Catholic church. At that time, we were still living at Hunky Dory Farm.[16] Barb's got two kids, and she's heating the house with a wood furnace, and Ladon Sheets and I are in jail and having the time of our lives. Barb's home trying to keep the kids warm and we're having backgammon tournaments. It just wasn't fair.

The early stages of the protests were small potatoes, climbing over and praying. Then Barb [Katt] and John [LaForge] moved to the farm and we started ganging up on ELF more. That's when Tom Hastings cut the first [ELF] pole, over in Michigan, and then Jeff Leys cut a pole here in Wisconsin.

After that, the actions were several times a year. Then in the late 1980s, the Women's International League for Peace and Freedom [WILPF] decided they were going to do four nationwide actions for Mother's Day and that ELF would be one of them. That's when we got into our pattern of closing the place down four times a year. One action was the Web of Life, with miles and miles and miles of yarn weaving it all shut. One winter we stacked mountains of snow in front of the gate.

We had extended encampments for Hiroshima and Nagasaki commemorations, where we'd spend a week up there in tents, doing all kinds of different creative actions. One that tickles me was when . . . It was Mother's Day. All these warrants were going out, because people weren't paying fines and so part of the action was a fundraiser with all these little plastic animal masks. The theme of it was, "Got a warrant? Get a mask." People were running around wearing these animal masks, and it was just one of the funniest things ever.

I wasn't going to get arrested, so I didn't wear a mask. But then, before the action started, one of the officers waded into the crowd and snagged me. He didn't want me to get another arrest because I had too many charges. (With those guys up there, it was all first name, how are your kids and all that.)

Our daughter Ollie was mad. "You could have worn a mask and you didn't! When I grow up, I'm going to be a lawyer and prosecute people like you!"

Ro: Now the government has finally decided to shut ELF down. Any connection between that decision and the protests?

Mike: We'll never know for certain, and I don't know if there *is* any way to know. When the Soviet Union collapsed, all reason for ELF went out the window, because it really was only around for initiating preemptive nuclear war with the Soviet Union. For years and years, it was this Cold War relic and our protests would [highlight this]. Then [Wisconsin] Senator [Russell] Feingold introduced a bill to cut ELF funding, so we were in on that, too, doing both the actions and this legal stuff. When they finally closed it, the press release said that "the mission and the technology had changed," which was what we'd been saying for decades.

I know that we contributed to the closing. There were hundreds and hundreds of arrests and years and years and years of jail time all together. It had to be a burden for the feds to just keep going through this thing again and again. And we got kind of tired of it, too, 'cause most of the trials were all the same.

Here at Alliant Tech it's more interesting because we have "claim of right" and some judges are willing to entertain international law as a basis for that. "Claim of right" is the legal term for the right to be on someone else's property, even if it's posted, if you believe they're doing something illegal with their property. It is a form of competing harms—doing something even if it is illegal to prevent a greater harm.

Ro: What advice do you have for people contemplating a life of resistance?

Mike: Well, first of all, community! You just get filled up with grace if you hang around the right people. But also, importantly, maintain a sense of humor. When we first got started, Barb and I were in our mid-twenties. Nuclear Armageddon is on the horizon. At the time, I was appalled at some of the levity that came in along with all of the seriousness, but now I'm relentless on the other side. We *need* the levity! Well, I guess I have to keep a balance there, too, and people like me who've been doing this for a long time need to be reminded of how hard it was and how upset we were when we first got into it.

Do serious stuff but don't take yourself too seriously. And have a sense of history—how long it's been going on. I remember we used to think we were doing something new. Then you find out that people have been doing this forever.

Ro: How do you deal with ego when you've been doing it so long?

Mike: Barb and I were just talking about that yesterday because the most recent thing I did was running for Congress on the Green Party ticket. I actually ended up doing really well and had a ball doing it. And that's all about promoting yourself, you know? So I have to look at who I am and who Barb is. She's the one who's made us not look weird in Polk County, because of the work she's done, and the volunteering at school. (I coached there, and that helped, too.) So people no longer think we're all weirdos at Anathoth Farm.

Barb does all that community building, but she feels invisible. When we have the college kids at Anathoth for spring break week, they want to hear about Iraq and nuclear weapons, not about being a good loving neighbor and remembering everyone's birthday, all those things Barb's so good at. Also, there's . . . call it ego, call it personality, call it whatever, they're the traits that make me *me*.

For someone with an ego like mine, I have to learn when to hang back. Inviting people who are new, giving them opportunities, and . . . the [Wheels of Justice] bus has been really good for that, you know.[17] There you've got all these really great young people who have been to Iraq and to Palestine. They aren't the big-time speakers, they aren't the movement heavies, but we put them on the bus and send them to schools and say, "Okay, so here you go."

Ro: Mike, why do you keep on keepin' on?

Mike: For me, it's a matter of my understanding of both faith and effectiveness. "We're not called to be effective, we're called to be faithful," everyone says. That's all good and well, but I want to be effective, too, because I don't want the world to blow up.

Some of what I do are experiments in being effective, such as knowing the difference between a campaign and witness. ELF turned into a campaign where we actually were effective. And then our work with Native Americans on treaty rights, with nonviolence as the tactic . . . in those we were effective, because we were on the landings [with the Indians] and we made it more calm. (Both the newspapers and the police attributed that to us.) So I'm not ready to go with just being faithful, even though that's my bottom line.

Frances Crowe was eighty-six when we talked. After we met, I wrote in my notes, "Every community needs a Frances Crowe." Raised Roman Catholic, she has found a home in the Society of Friends because it "fits her drives for justice" and she can live out the peace testimony. She has been an active resister since the end of World War II. A sign on the front door of her Northampton, Massachusetts, home asks, "Does our lifestyle demand war?"

Frances Crowe

> *"Going to Washington [to protest] lifts our spirits, but that's*
> *all it does, and we should be honest about it. It'd be a stronger*
> *message if we'd all stay home and not shop."*

My grandchildren's generation will be forced to change. They're so into the dominant shopping culture. When I try to talk to them about peak oil and to think about it for planning their futures, they don't want to hear. "That's too unpleasant to think about. Don't talk to us about not having enough."

I say, "Just wait! Just wait!"

My children? They're supportive [of my peace work], but not active. You know, they have a different . . . They're all typical young people, extremely busy with their lives and family.

For many years I was the Western Massachusetts Area Office of the American Friends Service Committee, working out of a Peace Center in the basement of my home, which I started in 1968. Now it's the Northampton Committee to Stop The War in Iraq, with a very specific focus.

But I have a lot of concerns and am very active with a group that's dealing with peak oil. Oil and war are all mixed up, you know, and if we could get off oil, we wouldn't have to be at war. So I walk every place in Northampton, and I'm seriously trying to downsize and use as little oil as possible.

I'm also really interested in making my yard productive for fruits and vege-tables. Last week I planted a new apple tree and some blueberry bushes and went out and collected rock dust. I'm trying to rebuild the environment for the long, long haul, especially the soil. I bought a dehydrator to dry summer greens, so I don't have to buy vegetables from far away. I'm a vegetarian and a vegan, and this winter I'll be able to eat locally for all my fruits and vegetables, as well as grains, beans, nuts, and local tofu. I think it's a matter of survival. What's at stake is whether or not we're going to make it as a human species. And I think more people realize that every day.

It's all just so connected. And the military . . . After my husband died, I literally . . . I found myself on tax day of 2002 just unable to write that check. All I could think about was, "How can I continue to be a 'good German?'" So I sent the return in with a handwritten letter about why I wasn't paying and sent copies of that letter to my congresspersons.

I've been very open about it, filing every year and just not paying. I do an hon-est filing, but they consider it "frivolous" because I include the letter, and they fine me. (They call it "frivolous" if you include any paper.) I said there's nothing frivolous about it, that I don't pay because of deeply held religious beliefs. I redirect the amount of money I don't pay to public education, US peace and justice groups, and international peacekeeping.

Now every month, they take part of what I owe them out of my Social Security, but, by law, they can only take 15 percent a month. I don't have to go to court or anything, just do paperwork. I do my banking in Canada and put everything in trust for my children so they can't get it. I also write about how to do this and encourage other people to stop paying. (The IRS says that's against the law, too.) All of this is very "do-able" for retirees, especially, and not very hard, really, just a lot of paperwork.

During the Vietnam War, I started what I call feminist draft counseling. We had groups three times a week, and everybody who had questions came, whether they were in the military or not. As we talked, I would give the information about the law. They came back week after week. We role-played and I showed films. (It was before videos, you know. And before Xerox machines, so we had to cut stencils.) What I was doing was legal, but the newspapers said it wasn't and wouldn't take my ads about it.

I had to figure out how to reach people. In those years students hitchhiked; we didn't have a five-college bus.[18] So I stenciled and mimeographed a big pile of literature, including maps to my house, and one Monday morning I started out, after our kids left for school, and drove between Northampton and Amherst, picking up students.

I'd fill up the car with kids and then I'd say, "What are you going to do about the war?" As they talked about maybe cutting off an index finger or going to Canada or Sweden, I'd drive slow and talk fast and hand out the stenciled literature. By the next day, I had a room full of young people.

After that, we were off because they spread the word. As a result, nobody who came here ever went into the army. They didn't do dishonest things to fake their physicals. We tried to get them to really face it and to address the draft boards about their conscience. And it worked! We worked with them on the draft board questions and the references and walked them through every step. And they became empowered, you know, and then stayed and helped the others. They still come back, and bring their own kids now!

Ro: Now, why did you call it feminist counseling?

Frances: Well, every draft counseling center I visited in those years was run by men and they were always trying to help them fail their physicals or to resist in ways that weren't productive. We wanted to really help them make good and long-lasting decisions, and I felt it was more of a woman's approach.

And they grew in the process. I always felt that if they failed their physicals maybe later they wouldn't be able to get insurance or health insurance. Clearance for jobs they might want overseas, things like that.

Ro: After the Vietnam War was over, how did your activism play out?

Frances: Well, it became nuclear power and nuclear weapons. Then, you know, I think we began to see that it was more than individual weapon systems and that we had to build a community of resistance, looking more seriously at nonviolence as a way of life. Now I think we've kind of reached a point where we're beginning to look at constructive engagement, like the Gandhian movement.

The biggest barrier we have is that most people are in extreme denial. Amy Goodman does more than anyone I know of to break through that. The only thing that will really make a difference is mass action. Strikes. Massive boycotts. No one

Frances Crowe protesting
in the snow, 2009.
(Photo courtesy of
Ellen Davidson.)

buys anything, and we just shut down. That's what Phil Berrigan would say—dear,
wonderful Phil. I think we're moving closer to that vision. Going to Washington [to
protest] is one tiny thing. It lifts our spirits, but that's all it does and we should be
honest about it. It'd be a stronger message if we'd all stay home and not shop.

Speaking of Amy Goodman, in the middle '90s, I came to realize that the greatest obstacle to organizing was the lack of alternative media in our area. I went to
WFCR, our local national public radio station, and tried to get them to carry Amy's
Democracy Now! Their reply was that it was "not their type of programming." So I
organized petition drives and later on an alternative pledge campaign. I also tried
all the area college radio stations and all the AM stations, but none were willing to
carry the program.

About that time I learned that someone was climbing up to the top of our
highest mountain with a battery transmitter on his back, throwing the antenna up
in a tree, putting in the disk for the *Democracy Now!* broadcast of that day and il-
legally broadcasting the program. It was wonderful! Went all over the valley! But as
fall approached the park would be closed, so I started to look for someone in a tall
building in the town, who would let the fellow up to the roof to broadcast. No one
was interested so I did it myself. I put up a pole in my backyard with an antenna on
it, upgraded the transmitter, and we were on the air! Now a lot of people around
here are addicted to *Democracy Now!*

Then we did the alternative pledge campaign and raised $40,000 in one week
which would be donated to the NPR when they agreed to broadcast *Democracy
Now! Then* they were willing to talk with us. They agreed to help the University of
Massachusetts stream the program through their satellite. It took us over the year
to get WMUA [the University of Massachusetts station] to carry the program but
now they love it.

Some of the original supporters of *Democracy Now!* got a license for a low-powered radio station, so now we have WOXJ, a wonderful community station that is changing the thinking of many people.

This act of civil disobedience was of the best type because the community really benefits from it. I was willing to take on the full consequences of this action as I feel the airways belong to the people.

Prison is not an easy place or a safe place. It's very hard. But there's also a wonderful sense of community. [In the spring of 2004] I was arrested in New York City. We blockaded the recruiting station at Times Square and eighteen of us were arrested. The women were all together in one tiny cell.

We chose to stay together and it was a rich, rich six hours. The women were mostly Catholic Workers from the East Coast. We started by each one telling what aches them the most. It was beautiful. Then we went around again and talked about what we were doing about it, what we were working on in our community. Then the last one was where we find our joy and hope. And that was just great! When they told us after about six hours that we were going to be released, we felt we'd been really privileged to have that sharing together in a way that we wouldn't have out in the world.

Ro: At eighty-six, are you going to continue to be arrested?

Frances: Well, if I'm called to. I have no plans to go to a retirement home. I'm going to work as long as I can, and then I'll put my body in front of the biggest weapon I can find and let the state deal with me.

Hattie Nestel raised her children in Brattleboro, Vermont, but lived in Athol, Massachusetts, when we talked in 2007. She's been a peace resister for years, travelling to protests and frequently going on long peace walks. She once walked eight hundred miles from the Oak Ridge National Weapons Laboratory in Tennessee to the UN building in Manhattan.

Hattie Nestel

"I told [my younger son], 'Gad, you cannot be a killer. You cannot be a killer.'"

Phil Berrigan was my mentor and my guide. I met him in 1982 when I started going down to DC. Ever since then, I've been doing actions at the White House and the Pentagon and then locally in Brattleboro, Vermont, where I used to live. My children were still young, then, and I took them to the retreats, took them to the actions.

I remember one time I was in DC with the little one, who was nine years old,

I guess. People had thrown blood on the pillars of the Pentagon, and the security came out with big fire hoses to wash it away. He stood there all by himself and chanted, "You cannot wash the blood away, you cannot wash the blood away!" Somehow he had this clarity and determination within him.

Actually I remember the first time I was arrested. It was a Yom Kippur Trident launching out in Connecticut. A woman came with me from the Church of the Brethren in Brattleboro and she became his guardian angel. Because he . . . he was bereft when my older son and I went under the barricade and got arrested and left him. "I want you to get arrested but not yet. I'm not old enough."

Gad's job that day was to blow the shofar. He took it totally to heart. They put us in the fire station, and my little one stood outside and never stopped blowing that shofar until I came out. That was his job and that's what he did. That woman, Betty, she was just an angel to us. I remember being so naive when they put us in the fire station. I saw some donuts behind the counter and I thought they were for us.

Ro: Were you afraid when you went under the barricade?

Hattie: No, I was not. Being Jewish, I was very upset about it being Yom Kippur and that was my focus. But I didn't expect a six-foot-six dude to land on me with the force that he did. I was pretty naive then, but since then, I've had other intense times where I've been dragged away and all that kind of stuff.

Ro: Do you go limp when you're arrested?

Hattie: Yes, pretty much.

Ro: And you're not afraid of being hurt?

Hattie: No. In fact one time, we were arrested at the Pentagon with Phil. I was with my seventeen-year-old son, and he was the first one arrested. After that, they formed a cordon to keep us out, and the only way in was to like dive between their legs. You know, you had to really be alert to any opening. Finally this huge black guy said to me, "I heard that young man say to you, 'Bye, Mom!' Do you want to be with your son?"

I said I did, so he said, "Okay, come with me." And he arrested me. He was in tears, actually. Very moved by this mother-son thing.

Ro: Have your children stayed activists?

Hattie: The older son is very politically astute. He was a draft resister, a nonregistrant, but they never arrested him for that. He's still fairly active and was actually arrested at the recruitment center in Brattleboro a few years ago.

Ro: What did he do about college after he didn't register?

Hattie: Well, you know the Solomon bill says you can't get financial aid if you don't register. His father had a lot of money and was willing to send him, but he felt it wasn't fair to people who didn't have money, so he didn't go to college. He's very bright, though.

The youngest one is much more middle-of-the-road, but he understands exactly what I'm doing and why and supports me. I'm worried about him now because he just entered Yale business school, but I think he'll do some good things. For example, he just came back from Peru and Guatemala, down there helping the indigenous people.

But I've got a story to tell you. It's really a story of faith and I think it's very important. I was doing all these Trident actions, and one time I remember I had three charges: violating probation; going limp, which amounts to resisting arrest; and the trespass. I went in front of this brutal judge. You know, really brutal. And sure enough, he gave me forty-five days.

It was in December and my youngest son was a freshman at Annapolis. See, he has a father who was in the military, and he'd seduced him into thinking that Annapolis was "a golden key to his future." Those were the words. My son was trying to please his father, and was a very confused young person, and so he went, and of course, I was bereft.

So here I am in jail. He came out for holiday break and came down to visit me with my older son who was also very unnerved by this whole thing. I was fasting and I was gray and I had come into the building shackled and chained and all this stuff. And I stunk. . . . I reeked of cigarettes because everybody in this dorm of fifty-six people was allowed to smoke. My younger son said to me, he said, "I'm going to talk to the warden because you don't belong in jail."

So he did and the warden, who was a woman, said, "Well, all your mom has to do is sign that she won't do it again and she won't have to serve the remaining two weeks of her sentence." He came back and told me and I said, "I can't do that. I will not sign my soul away." And of course, he cried and cried and cried because there he was, basically in jail at Annapolis and here he is home for vacation and *I'm* in jail!

So they left. But before they went I said, "I want you to do one thing for me. I want you to write a letter to the newspaper." And they did. They wrote a letter to the *Brattleboro Reformer* and said, "Our mother is an angel of mercy and she shouldn't be in jail."

He stayed in Annapolis for two years, and here I am doing all my peace work, and with every breath, I'm praying for this child. Every single breath of my existence. I wrote to him every single day—three- and four- and five-, six-page letters. I'd decorate the envelopes with peace signs and stickers, so everybody could see them. Paint them, color them, whatever I could think of to connect with my son.

Now, up until two years, they can leave the Naval Academy without penalty. As the two years approaches, they were seducing him. "We need people like you in the

Nancy Smith and
Hattie Nestel beginning
a peace walk, 2010.
(Photo courtesy of
Hattie Nestel.)

navy. You're going to change the navy, you're remarkable." Because he *is* a wonderful person.

I told him I'd never leave him alone, never. "But it's not okay. It's not okay." At the end we'd have these two- and three-hour conversations, and I thought, "I'm never getting out of bed again. I can't live with this!" And . . . when it came time for him to sign to continue, he couldn't sign. He didn't sign. Now, he's never said this, but I believe he learned from me that you cannot sign your soul away.

It had to be so, so painful for him. His father is having all these navy buddies write to him about how proud of him they are. And his friends, you know—his cohorts—that's a big thing they develop in the services. He didn't want to let his buddies down, but he didn't sign.

I'd be furious with moms who would say, "Well, it's his decision." Baloney! Baloney, baloney! Your son is your child and your son doesn't know. In Judaism, if you save one soul, your life has not been lived in vain. And that soul had to be my son's.

I love a Buddhist practice, but I'm Jewish. And I go on peace walks with a Buddhist prayer drum. My first one was in 1985, walking from Tokyo to Hiroshima. And I've done India and Gandhi, Central America, and things like that. The last one was eight hundred miles. It took seven weeks, walking twenty miles a day, and I beat the drum and prayed Nam Myoho Renge Kyo all the way. We went from Oak Ridge, Tennessee, to the United Nations, in time for the conference on the Nuclear Non-Proliferation Treaty. Oak Ridge is where they process the uranium for all the nuclear weapons.

I train for every walk, partly by mowing this big lawn out back, mowing with a little push mower. I also do aerobics at the Y and work on a machine that really builds my legs up. Then during the walk, when I'm having a knee problem, I'll use a Japanese mugwort treatment.

I have a whole scrapbook of these walks. It's just so powerful and people are so moved to see us out there. That's what we need—for people's hearts to be moved. It's like when my son's heart was moved because he saw me in jail.

I was with a group the other day, and they were talking about doing a sit-in. "Well, you need a thousand people." I said, "No, you don't need a thousand people. You can have two people, or three. It doesn't really matter." In fact, I've done walks with just one nun, with just the two of us walking, and it's wonderful. Very powerful.

You can move people's hearts, and you do that by moving your own heart. By saying, "I'm willing to do this because nuclear proliferation has got to end. Somebody's got to be on the streets and telling people about it." You're motivated, so however tired you are, however wet and cold you are, whatever lousy food you have, you keep on going.

Some people can't take it . . . the discomfort. I'll drink coffee sometimes when I'm home but if I'm on a walk, I will never, ever drink a cup of coffee . . . never. You know, I'm there to focus on this walk and not on my own comfort. Even in jail, fasting helps you keep your focus.

Ro: What advice would you give a middle-class woman who's called to do this?

Hattie: Well, I think you have to embrace whatever spirituality or tradition you have. You get your strength from that. Also, you have to be with the right people. Another thing: read about people who've spent time in jail. People like Gandhi and Phil Berrigan and Sam Day. Read about Hans and Sophie Scholl. Read Abraham Heschel and Dietrich Bonhoeffer.

What I really need is a group to be faith-based to the point of not being concerned with the consequences and the outcome. Then there's a clear focus and I'm comfortable. The Hasidic tales I've read talk about a leap of faith, about not worrying about the consequences, and I've always kept that in mind.

I've probably been arrested about 125 times. (I haven't always gone to jail because often they drop all the charges.) But when you're in jail, you've done all you can do. That's the bottom line, so for the moment, you can be at rest. There's the irony. You're locked up in chains but you feel free. Absolutely free. It's just . . . You're beyond anything that's holding you back.

Ro: Who would care for your children when you were in jail?

Hattie: Oh, different people. [With my younger son,] sometimes his older brother did and sometimes [Juanita and Wally] Nelson took care of him.[19] I remember once his schoolteacher, who he was very fond of, moved into our house and took care of him. Once he told me that he had a dream that God was taking care of him while I was in jail.

My sons, they're amazing. They get it. My younger son said to me years ago—when he was maybe in tenth grade or something—he said, "You know, Mom, when I get married, I'm going to have an apartment in my house for you. I'll make sure you can do all your actions, drive you, and take you to court. And you can go to jail whenever you want."

Joan (Joni) McCoy and her attorney husband, Pat, raised their children in Saginaw, Michigan. She began working for peace when they were teenagers, helping to keep ROTC out of Saginaw Valley State University and working with others through the Home for Peace and Justice to close Wurtsmith Air Force Base. She still coordinates the activities of that group and in 2011 organized a peace walk from Saginaw to the capitol building in Lansing as part of Michigan Moveable Peace 2011.

Joni McCoy

> *"I didn't have street smarts. Oh my God, I didn't have street smarts!"*

I did a little jail time before going to prison. More after, though, like three months in the Bay County jail after being in Lexington Federal Prison. My first jail time was just "summer camp." Only a few days. And such a to-do when we got out! A party and the whole bit. I think back on it now and I have to chuckle because that first jail experience was mostly fun. But it's really good to have that time prior to a longer confinement. It was a learning, and it probably took away a little of the fear.

Ro: Now, you had a supportive husband in Pat, but what about the rest of your family?

Joni: It was real hard for my mother, because she never really understood. I hated that . . . that her "little girl" caused her pain. But she'd write letters every day. Even though she was upset, she was being a mom who loved me, there's no doubt about that. She had to deal with it, though, just like the children did. Because they didn't like it, either.

Prison wasn't as hard on them, though, as my work in Palestine.[20] The danger, you know. "How dare I put myself in that position?" And how it affected them! "A gramma's not supposed to do that!"

"But I'm not your regular gramma," I'd say. That thinking was hard on them, too. When I talk about what I do and why, they just sort of roll their eyes. They love me, there's no doubt about that, but some of the five don't like some of what I do.

But they . . . You know, I gave them my youth! Maybe some of it is because they now have their own children and have gotten into the conservative thinking. The only one who really understands me is the youngest.

Joni McCoy, Saginaw,
Michigan, 2011.
(Photo courtesy of
Janice Coty.)

Ro: How old were they when you first started doing serious peacework?

Joni: I didn't do serious stuff until the Carter administration and draft registration. That's when my feet hit the pavement. For my kids. Three of them were in high school then, and I began to do a lot of on-the-street action, including keeping ROTC out of Saginaw Valley State University. Selfishly, at this point, it was hitting my own children. I didn't do this stuff in the sixties, like I wanted to, because I was in the house with the children. I told myself when I was freed up, I'd do what I need to do.

Ro: What advice would you give to people who face these kinds of pressures from family?

Joni: That's tough. You know, we're all responsible for our own lives. Our children were adults when I went to prison, except for Ryan. It was in the press, so people knew it was happening. Before I left, I met with each one of Ryan's high school teachers. To make sure they knew, but also to feel them out because I didn't want them to take out any anger with me on him. I told them his father would always be around, and they had his work number.

Ro: What made you change from a five-day misdemeanor to big actions?

Joni: Uh . . . a burden of knowing, I guess. The study, the study. Scripture, the newspaper, prayer. Just that ongoing understanding of what this world is like, and what it should be like, and my responsibility to it. We had an ongoing campaign at Wurtsmith, up in the Thumb [of Michigan]. Went up every month and vigiled against the nuclear weapons systems. Wonderful community retreats, too, and we built up a strong community to close that base.

I don't know. I just . . . every month I did another action and another action and another action and they begin to get [us] into court. Hiroshima-Nagasaki day actions were the ones that I mainly did my time for.[21] Jail would sometimes be through the holidays, even, which made it kind of difficult. But that was what I was called to do. I did a lot of discerning, so it wasn't just off the cuff.

When I was sentenced to the three months in federal prison, it had to do with the multiple charges. All misdemeanors, though. Ardeth [Platte] and Carol [Gilbert] and I all went in at the same time but to different places. The Bureau of Prisons is the authority, and even though our judge wanted us to stay together, he had no impact. Sister Carol went to Alderson, and Sister Ardeth went to Fort Worth, and I went to Lexington in Kentucky.

I self-reported. I had really wanted to go the same route that Carol and Ardeth went—they do it like poverty folks do it, you know—and be transported from jail to jail with the marshals. But that really distressed my husband, who's a lawyer and knows what it's like, so I agreed to report, for his sake.

He went with me. His law partner had an airplane, and we went by little plane. I remember flying over Lexington and looking down on the institution. It looks beautiful on the outside, with flowers and all, but the front entrance kind of made me think of Auschwitz. And the silence of our parting, you know, just a kiss and a "goodbye and I love you." It was painful for both of us, so the next time I went in for any length of time, I had a friend drop me off.

Lexington was both a male and a female facility at the time, and the men used to peek at us through this big keyhole between the sections. Really sophomoric! We ate with them and walked with them in the yard, and that was nice. Women would have "walkies."

Ro: What's a walkie?

Joni: In a male-female prison, it's male-female companionship. That's your entertainment, this walking. All you can do is hold hands and walk around this big track or around what they called Central Park, which was this square right in the center of the institution.

I walked every night. Walked whenever I could. And there again you meet different people. I'd sometimes walk with this man I met in church. My husband used to tease me that this man was my walkie because for about ten Christmases after that, I'd get a card from him. I can't even remember what he looked like, but he told me that he had been going to commit suicide, and if it hadn't been for me, he wouldn't be alive.

There were love relationships going on in there, big-time. Sexual relationships, and pregnancies. I heard stories. Some of them had their babies right in their bunk. If you do get pregnant and have a child in prison, the government is mandated to care for that child until age eighteen.

Money runs a whole lot of stuff in prison, just like outside. And you can only have so much money on you, so there was a woman who made a lot of money being a sort of banker and money-changer. People would slip big bills in—in their vagina, I guess, because they didn't do cavity searches there—and she'd change them into smaller bills, for a fee. She'd tie her stash with a string and hide it in a vent or something to escape the shakedowns.

I didn't have street smarts. Oh my God, I didn't have street smarts! I didn't know how the money stuff worked, and I never did learn where the men and women went to have their secret time together.

Some women made money prostituting themselves. Like if you wanted a shower box—something to put your deodorant and stuff in when you went to the shower—the guys in the woodshop made them. One of the women told me you could get a shower box for a blowjob. [*Laughs in embarrassment.*]

Ro: When did you get your work assignments?

Joni: I think it was maybe ten days after I went in. They put you through this regime. You know, they want you to do an education program and other stuff. I refused the education, refused the psychological study. Got away with it until the very end. I was getting ready to go, and they realized I hadn't done the education part, and insisted that I go to some classes, so they could get money from the state of Michigan. The bottom line was money.

I did a fair amount of noncooperating. I was there as a resister, so I resisted the institution. I wouldn't wear the military clothing and I wouldn't work in their higher-paid industry because it was military. So my assignment, finally, was just cleaning the halls and the area around the chapel.

I stayed in the dorm called the "bus stop" for the whole time. Resisted moving because I had a short term, compared to everyone else, and you don't want to tell people who are doing years that I [was only doing] three months.

But oh, the noise! You know, you put a whole bunch of angry people in one room, and . . . the anger level, the violence level, the . . . oh, my God! The stuff that came out of the mouths! I had to work really hard at not using prison language. It was not my language—I mean, I never could say the f-word—but I'll tell you, if I hadn't worked at not saying it, I'd have come out able to use it like any street person, because that's all you heard. It's not that the words are so bad, it's the anger.

Ro: Was the anger at each other, or anger at the institution?

Joni: Anger at their whole life situation, there in the institution. And yes, certainly they got angry at each other. There was one woman in that dorm . . . she was the controller. Used to just scare the dickens out of anybody new. So I took it upon myself, when somebody first came in, to take them under my wing, because they came in frightened like I did. And I was really nice to the controlling one, and towards the end she mellowed big-time. I'd say things like, "Ah, don't worry about Elaine; her bark's worse than her bite. She's really a sweetheart underneath." Well, she became that. She became that.

You know, I wanted to come out of there better than I went in, not worse. So I could see that I had to work on myself big-time, all the time. I worked hard at not making any enemies, either of guards or inmates. I also kept a daily journal while I was there and I'm awfully glad I did.

Oh, here's a fun story: At Christmas you could get a little slip that you send to your family, and they'd send you a specific Christmas box. I sent mine to my mother, and got a box from her. Now, a gal who had the bunk underneath me still had her slip when I left, like on the last day of December. So I said, "Let me take your slip and I'll send you a box."

You know, you want to beat the system. One thing she could have was unopened candy, straight from the manufacturer. So I first bought a bottle of perfume, which is contraband, big-time, because it's alcohol, I guess. I picked out a good brand, and I took it to Fanny Farmer and bought a big box of candy and they put the perfume inside the candy box and shrink-wrapped it and sent it off! And she got it ! I beat the system!

When you go into prison you get a copy of the rules and regulations, and one of them is no organizing, no petitions. But I did some; people would send me petitions that would get through, and I'd have people sign them. Ardeth and Carol and I weren't supposed to communicate with each other, but we did, anyway, and it'd get through.

I mean, it's crazy, it's absolutely crazy, but you learn to get into the flow of it if you're going to survive. You can't just lay in your bunk and cry. Actually, I found the three months I did in jail more difficult than the three in prison. I was trying not to be any different than the other women in the cellblock, to get extra visits or anything like that. But I could get these attorney visits, which were my husband, being an attorney.

Now, the guards didn't want him coming both for family visits and as my attorney when he wasn't official. So he went to court and got the proper papers to say he was. That power—that's what attorneys can do.

I never told these women that he was, because I wanted to be one with them. Well, they started asking me about my attorney. "What's his name" and blah blah blah blah blah. Come to find out, they thought I was having a thing with my attorney, not knowing it was my husband. So I finally told them and told them why, and they said, "Oh, that's all right. We're just glad you're not having an affair."

Tom Karlin came from a large Roman Catholic family and spent time in the Trappists before joining the Jesuit Volunteer Corps and becoming an activist. While he was in the navy, he had worked at the Bangor Naval Base; later he campaigned to prevent it from housing nuclear submarines. Tom's first wife, Ida, passed away in 1994. He and his second wife, Laura, were members of the Tacoma Catholic Worker for years; they now care for aging family members. Because they've always been able to live below taxable income, he's been a lifelong legal tax resister.

Tom Karlin

> *"When I heard about Abu Ghraib, I wasn't surprised, because that goes on in our prisons, too, that kind of violence and those tactics of humiliation."*

Becoming an activist was a long, slow process. Not much happened until I was about thirty-three years old. I was a cradle Catholic, grew up in a farm community. You know, God and country. I was one of fifteen, and we were all encouraged to consider the religious life, which we all did or tried to. And all the boys dutifully went off to the call of war. After my four years in the navy, I joined a Trappist monastery.

After seven years, I came out and became a Jesuit Volunteer and was exposed to activism, and it was a gradual process from then on. It led me, ultimately, to civil disobedience at the Trident submarine base here in Washington. I had worked there while in the navy, so it was rather exciting to be on a different side of the fence.

We did a symbolic garden planting, just a handful of us, back in the early '70s. One of the first actions. We went over the fence and planted a garden and were arrested and given barring letters. We kept going back and the movement kept growing to where there were hundreds of people outside the gates, and over a hundred going over the fences.

Ultimately, many of us were sent to jail. At first we'd get suspended sentences or probation or just the barring letters, but the government was becoming more concerned, I guess, and they brought in a judge from Orange County—Judge Thompson—who was nicknamed "Tommy-gun Thompson" because he was so strict.

Well, Tommy-gun Thompson handed out four- to six-month sentences to twenty-six of us, the ones who had those previous barring letters. And they took us directly from court into jail. Suddenly, I'm gone!

Ro: You didn't know you'd go right to jail?

Tom: Oh, no! When I left home that morning, I figured it would be the same as before—suspended sentences or probation. But I didn't enter the house again for four months! Didn't even say goodbye to Ida, my wife. She was a nurse and had to work that day, and my baby daughter was only about seven months old. We had two more daughters, too, one six and one four.

We hadn't planned for this, you know. But one of our affinity group members, who actually had gone over the fence with us but was a first-timer . . . he and his wife moved their trailer onto the property and helped out. He'd been working with me in my woodworking business, and he took that over while I was gone, along with another friend. I had a whole lot of support.

They took us to King County Jail in Seattle, just before noon. We were on the concrete floor of this huge holding cell until the next morning, when they finally booked us. So we got quite an eyeful of the treatment people received as they were brought in and saw a lot of violence in that first twenty-four hours.

My wife got the toughest sentence, with her work and the three little kids. And there was some anger, you know? She was under pressure from her siblings. I remember a brother-in-law saying, "It's an exercise in futility." With them, it was just, "I told you so." They also didn't approve of even our coming to work [at the Catholic Worker]. What they would call the riffraff. [Chuckles] We had to deal with the anger, because it was primarily my idea to do civil disobedience. She'd done some herself, and we'd agreed that only one of us would risk jail time at any one action. But we hadn't really thought this action would warrant jail time.

It was a couple of days before I even got to talk to her on the phone, and then two weeks later they moved us to California, to federal minimum security prisons. They didn't let us know beforehand, just marched us out and put us on the train without being able to notify anyone.

We didn't know where we were going, we were just gone. My wife was working in a pediatric clinic just a block from the railroad tracks and that was quite a feeling, to go right by her when she didn't even know!

Then we were two weeks in the LA County Jail. Another eye opener! They put us through a disinfecting process. You had to strip out of your clothes, and then they'd shoot you with disinfectant through high-power hoses like fire hoses. They'd just about blow you over.

After they deloused us and gave us prison garb, we nuclear protesters were all put into protective custody. Segregated in the psych wards. We'd ask guards and they wouldn't say why, but maybe it was that they just didn't have room in some of the other holding cells. It wasn't just us; one guy was serving three murder raps. And then a big-time drug dealer. Actually, the psych ward [in LA] was more comfortable than the King County Jail. By that time, too, the shock had worn off and the support had come. The affinity group people were wonderful support to my family and to me, too.

After another two weeks, I ended up at Boron, a small prison out in the Mojave Desert near Barstow. It was fenced in, but a fairly large property, and we were quite free to walk around. I worked in the carpenter shops eventually, but for the first couple of weeks, we were just raking rocks. Fifty people raking these gravelly yards because it was out in the desert, with no lawns. All make-do work.

We had been practicing Gandhi's mantra: "I love you, I bless you, I forgive you." Even in the courtroom to the judge, we were saying that mantra and praying to accept. You see, when we do civil disobedience, we accept the consequences. So I

Tom and Ida Karlin and children, Eatonville, Washington, 1980.
(Photo courtesy of Michael Sage.)

think I personally was prepared enough so I didn't experience anger, although my
wife did, as I said. I'd asked for it, in the sense that I knew that sooner or later, if you
keep resisting, you're going to end up paying jail time.

Midway through my three and a half months at Boron, my wife and the two
oldest kids were able to visit, and I could hold them in my arms. During the two
weeks in King County Jail, we could only speak on phones, through a glass. My
youngest one didn't come to Boron, and I had missed her first birthday.

But wow! When I got out, and I flew home and I'm coming up the ramp, my
wife saw us and set her down—we were about thirty feet apart—and I knelt down,
and my daughter looked at me and then she looked down. [*Pause, remembering.*]
Then she came running, running, running, and jumped on me. Whew! Oh, gosh!
That was my dominant memory of coming home. She hadn't been walking when I

left. Every time I think about it, I get teary. I . . . To be recognized and welcomed by my child. She didn't forget me. She remembered.

So being away from the family . . . that was the hardest. Boron itself wasn't so bad. We developed quite a few friendships. There was a black fellow who was gay and he was being harassed a lot, so I became a good friend to him. We did a lot of sharing and supporting each other.

But time moved slowly. My mind was on my family a lot. We had a pretty neat chaplain, an American Baptist. We were the first nuclear protesters he'd ever known. He was actually able to take us out to a church in Barstow, where we gave a little talk. Afterwards, we played softball with the parishioners. Such a treat!

Ro: Were there ever any times when you were afraid?

Tom: A little bit in the two county jails. Particularly at the LA County Jail, in the huge holding area, packed with people incoming off the streets, mostly blacks and Hispanics. Two male guards and a female guard. There was some kind of scuffle going on in one of the cells, and they pulled one guy out, stripped all his clothes off, and then started kicking him and beating him. Out in the open hallway, so all the rest in the holding cells could see what happens if they didn't behave. To humiliate him, strip every stitch of clothing off, and then to start kicking him! Even the female guard was kicking him in his gut. He finally fell to the floor, and they grabbed him by the back of the head and banged his head into the concrete floor so hard that his forehead split open. Then they threw his clothes at him and shoved him back in the cell. When I heard about Abu Ghraib I wasn't surprised, because that goes on in our prisons, too, that kind of violence and those tactics of humiliation. It's nothing new.

The guards at Boron were a completely different breed, quite friendly, and we could chat with them and explain what we were doing. I even talked to the warden about energy conservation. They were still burning oil and here we were, out in the desert, with all that sunlight. I had been working on energy-efficient home construction, so I talked to him about using thermal energy instead of fossil fuels. That was a good way to enter into talking about resistance, too. I showed how the militarism is linked to our dependence on oil.

You know, I knew I'd be getting out pretty fast, and there was a sense of gratitude and also sadness that we had it so easy, really. So I'd try to practice being in solidarity with people imprisoned for so long in other countries. But even with the mild sentences, it's still punishment. The system tries to prevent you from speaking out.

After that prison experience, I didn't do any resistance where I went to jail. My wife and I both decided that we'd be active in other ways, and we focused on doing tax resistance. I was self-employed and I kept my work hours and income low. We lived very simply and she limited her nursing hours, and we had the right amount of deductions and so forth to keep our incomes below taxable level. So we never paid any federal income tax.

And then we decided to work at Habitat for Humanity and also at L'Arche in Tacoma, which needed quite a bit of construction work. We still did the big protests out at Trident, with Archbishop Hunthausen and others. But we figured no more jail until the kids had been raised.

The most important thing in all of this is to make sure you have a community of support. That's number one. Number two is [to know] that you're not going on your own but are being sent—that a community feels and discerns with you and sends you to represent all of them. If it's just your own will, so to speak, there's too much ego in it.

Harry Murray lived in several Catholic Worker communities before marrying and returning to school for his PhD in sociology. His dissertation was published by Temple University Press as *Do Not Neglect Hospitality: The Catholic Worker and the Homeless* (1990). Now on the faculty of Nazareth College in Rochester, New York, Harry combines a career in teaching, family, and a life of resistance.

Harry Murray

"The county executive called two press conferences to denounce me as someone who was 'misleading our youth.'"

Ro: Harry, how do you balance resistance with your college work? Particularly in the early years when you didn't have tenure.

Harry: Uh . . . I'd say very poorly. Actually, Nazareth gave me tenure while I was a guest of the Federal Bureau of Prisons, so they really had every opportunity to get rid of me. I was incarcerated at the time for protesting the first Gulf War. Sentenced to ninety days and five hundred hours of community service. That was my first arrest that wasn't a yogurt bust.

Ro: What's a "yogurt bust"?

Harry: That's Dan Berrigan's word for an arrest with no sentencing. Yogurt busts "go down easy." About thirty people had climbed into the parking lot at the Seneca Army Depot. Four of us were singled out because we'd been there before and already had ban-and-bar letters. Slow learners, I guess you'd call us.

At the time I was teaching a crime and justice course, which happened to meet

Harry and Marianne Murray and
children, Rochester, NY, 1988.
(Photo courtesy of Elizabeth Murray.)

at the same time as our sentencing hearing, so I invited the class to the courtroom
to hear me get sent up the river for ninety days. (Well, not that far away, just to the
Community Corrections Center run by the Salvation Army here in Rochester.) The
students learned more about the criminal justice system in that hour than they did
all semester from me. It was, I think, a traumatic experience for some of them to see
their professor sentenced to confinement, although some felt that justice had been
done, since, after all, I'd broken the law.

Ro: Now, after some initial reluctance, [your wife] Marianne has been with you in all
of this, hasn't she?

Harry: Oh, yes! One of her great quotes after this long incarceration was, "Next time,
I go to jail and you get the kids."

Ro: Yeah! Now, did your children visit you?

Harry: Yes. In fact, one of them learned to ride his tricycle in the Salvation Army
parking lot. That was the same kid who . . . One year our church was doing a
campaign against war toys during the Christmas season, and we were passing out
anti–war-toy leaflets at the downtown mall. We brought Thomas along, and after
about forty minutes he was getting tired and wanted to go home. We told him we'd
promised to be there for a bit longer.

So he immediately starts screaming at the top of his lungs, "Buy war toys! We
love guns! Buy war toys!" Which was a very effective protest. When he was one,
we had bought a "question authority" T-shirt for him and for better or worse, the
authority he learned to question was ours.

Ro: Couldn't you have delayed your sentence so that you could finish the semester?

Harry: Well, no, but because I was at this Community Corrections Center, I could continue to work. One of the purposes of a place like this is to get prisoners readjusted into community life and to get them working. Many of the federal prisoners were working day jobs and coming back there at night, and I was able to negotiate my hours.

Then we had five hundred hours of community service—picking up sticks from an ice storm at the public golf course. I guess the judge kind of put "ice storm" and "Desert Storm" together. [*Chuckles.*] Ciaron O'Reilly was at our sentencing, and he yells out, "What about Desert Storm clean-up, Your Honor?"

Also, I was the coordinator for the Saturday meal at St. Joseph's House of Hospitality, and when I was sentenced, I petitioned to be released on Saturdays to continue to do the Saturday meal and to have to those hours count as my community service. The folks at the college were really supportive! They sent a petition to the judge complaining that he considered that cleaning up a golf course was community service but feeding the hungry wasn't.

Well, at one point, we were out at the golf course picking up sticks and my probation officer pulls up. (It was the first time he had visited.) Our supervisor at the golf course was pretty sympathetic to us peace resisters. He says, "Shit! It's a good thing we happened to be working when your probation officer came."

But anyway, my probation officer starts screaming at me: "Don't you know that it's utterly inappropriate to send letters to the judge? If you don't like your sentence, you fill out Form 3842 or whatever in triplicate and send it into the Bureau of Prisons."

Then he says, "Well, and I want you to know that this has nothing to do with the letters, but we *are* counting [the soup kitchen] as community service, and we're going to start giving you weekend leaves from now on. But I want you to know that has nothing to do with the letters."

Ro: That support says a lot for Nazareth College, I think.

Harry: There's only been one time when I heard that a trustee was upset with me, and that was with the finger-imaging protest. We were protesting the county's decision to finger-image welfare recipients by placing our inky fingerprints on the waiting room walls of the Department of Social Services. What I heard, and this was secondhand, was that he didn't like that we had damaged *property*! There was somebody on the board who really, really liked property.

Ro: Makes sense for trustees. Did your fingerprints wash off?

Harry: Well, no. We used indelible ink. That became a real issue, and we had a lawyer for that one and plea-bargained it back down to a misdemeanor. All kinds of compromises there, but we had a judge who was very, very sympathetic. The sentence was to pay to have the walls repainted and to write a nonviolence curriculum that could be used in the public schools.

Ro: Oh, that's a beautiful sentence!

Harry: It was! The Department of Social Services was pretty outraged. They wanted us to be sentenced to cleaning their toilets or something. One of the people I was arrested with there was Eric LeCompte, who went on to work with the School of the Americas Watch. Eric was just eighteen at the time, and he's such a charismatic guy. People just love him. As he's sentencing him, Judge Geraci says, "You're an upstanding example of what youth today should be, and I just wish more young people were like you."

Eric's probation officer came the morning of the sentencing to wish him luck, but my probation officer recommended a sentence so harsh that the *prosecutor* even said to the judge, "Your honor, I think that's a bit excessive." I seem to have a way with probation officers. Probably because they're trained to be good judges of character.

Ro: Do you get much publicity for the actions you do?

Harry: Yes, I guess we do. Sometimes . . . like with this latest arrest at President Bush's visit, one channel actually interviewed me before I was even sure that I was going to do anything. I said in the interview that I was a professor at Nazareth, and then about a week ago I did a "Speaking Out" piece [in a newspaper] as a professor of Nazareth, talking about some of the issues. In the fingerprinting arrest, the county executive called two press conferences to denounce me as someone who was "misleading our youth."

Ro: Corrupting young people, like a certain teacher in ancient Greece. And in those plans for corrupting our youth, aren't you faculty advisor for the social justice group?

Harry: Yes. I take them to the [SOA protest] every year. Before they changed the rules and closed the gate, many of us crossed the line together. We'd just get ban-and-bar letters, so we never were prosecuted, but it was a powerful decision for the students and a real bonding experience. It's also a good experience to kind of break down professor-student boundaries, because when you're driving twenty hours with folks and sleeping in the same motel rooms, you can't keep up all the professor images.

I don't ever encourage a student to get arrested. If we're going into a situation where arrest is a possibility, we'll spend time reflecting on nonviolence, thinking about all the issues. I think if somebody chooses to do it, it's really important that they've thought it all out very carefully.

The thing about the social justice group that was so great is that within a very short length of time, the students were planning their own trips, and it didn't matter whether I went along or not. They went down to protest the first inauguration of Mr. Bush without me, for instance.

One time when we went to SOA, two exchange students went with us, one from the Ukraine, and one from Kyrgyzstan. The woman from the Ukraine had been involved in a lot of political activity back in the Ukraine, and that was the year at SOA when the army was blasting out all this military music, trying to drown out people's singing. I remember Zoriana saying: "Wait a minute! This is how they treat protesters in my country. I thought America was different!"

Ro: Yeah. Can we get back to your current arrest, the one about President Bush?

Harry: Well, a couple of weeks ago, President Bush came here to speak about his destruction-of-Social-Security plan at one of the suburban high schools. A group was going to try to be as close as possible to the motorcade. I got there a couple of hours before the scheduled event, with a sign that said "The occupation of Iraq is a sin." Went over to the high school side of the road and was told right away by a Secret Service agent that I was in "a presidential protection zone." He asked me to go across the street to an area behind a snow fence. I talked to him a little bit about my concerns for free speech and the way that protesters were being kept away from the president.

What really struck me was that the day before that, Laura Bush had been in Israel and the protesters there were able to get within earshot of her, whereas here in suburban Rochester, you couldn't get within a football field of Mr. Bush if you had a critical thought in your head. So after the presidential motorcade got there, Sister Grace Miller from the House of Mercy and I moved a little ways into the presidential protection zone. We had the idea of just extending the zone of free speech in America by a couple of feet, which seemed fairly modest.

A couple of police officers told us we had to leave. So I knelt down with my sign and they started to . . . well, they grabbed me from behind and started dragging me. They were also dragging Sister Grace. Later they charged me for resisting arrest, but then still later, they dismissed it.

I feel guilty [about the trials] because Gandhi said you should just plead guilty and ask for the maximum possible penalty, and I haven't done that. In my last arrest before this Bush thing—what we call the Ash Wednesday Thirteen where thirteen of us were arrested just a week before the invasion of Iraq—we just walked into the first door of the Federal building and were stopped before we even got to the metal detectors. We had planned to kneel and pray there.

They charged us with misdemeanor trespass, which was clearly not what we had done. Well, first the judge told the DA to drop the charge to a violation, and even then, she found us not guilty because she ruled that the initial order keeping us from entering the second set of doors to the Federal building was illegal. That just because they knew we were coming in as protesters they weren't allowed to deny us entry.

Ro: How did they know you were protesters?

Harry: Well, we had a lot of ashes on our faces. See, we'd had an Ash Wednesday service right outside the Federal Building. Burnt dollar bills and smeared the ashes on our faces. We were pretty obviously coming in as protesters.

Ro: Any other arrests that stand out?

Harry: Well, the other one I can think of was the first year I was teaching. I was a sabbatical replacement at Union College in Schenectady. This was during the time of Contra aid. A group of us blockaded the street in front of the armory in Albany. Not really a blockade—I was in the street for less time than it takes to get across. Most people pled guilty and were fined a hundred dollars and that was it. I decided to take it to trial and did a necessity defense and the judge—I always liked this one—the judge said, "You argue better than most lawyers I know." [*Chuckles.*] But he still decided I was guilty because the emergency I was trying to prevent wasn't happening in New York State but in Nicaragua. He gave me the choice of a $200 fine or fifteen days, and I told him I couldn't pay the fine, so he sent me off for the fifteen-day sentence.

This really disturbed some of the more conservative professors at Union, I think. In the first place they really couldn't believe that one of their number could be going to jail. They also thought I was a lunatic to spend two weeks in jail rather than pay $200. But the people in jail disagreed. "$200 . . . fifteen days. Yeah, you did the right thing." For them it was a good economic decision; for a professor at Union College, it was utter lunacy. I think that illustrates so well who the jails are designed to hold.

You know, I've seen a lot of kindness among the prisoners. I remember once we were playing Dirty Hearts, playing for push-ups. You had to do however many push-ups the losing number of points was, and most of the guys were in pretty great shape, so they'd be ripping off 102 push-ups and so on. I'm so out of shape that it'd be "One, two, uh . . ." [*breathes heavily and pants*]. So I left the tier owing something like eighty push-ups. One of the guys who was a Black Muslim came over to my cell afterwards. "Hey, man, it's not good to be in the shape that you're in." And he outlined an exercise program that I could do in my cell to kind of try to get into shape. Wasn't that kind?

Ro: And also, he was the teacher there.

Harry: Yes, which was really neat. Oh, another thing about going to jail that time. It was while I was trying to get the job at Nazareth. The search committee had picked me as somebody they wanted to see, but they hadn't called me for the interview yet. So my wife, Marianne, asked me what she should say if they called while I was in jail. I said, "Oh, tell them I'm interested, but I'm 'out in the field' and I'll be back soon."

Ro: They didn't know your record when they hired you?

Harry: No, they didn't ask the question: "Have you ever been arrested?" I think they probably now ask. Now, this is just my theory, but I think being at a small college as opposed to a university probably helps, too. Nazareth doesn't have big CIA or Defense Department contracts, so there's no pressure in that way to control faculty. Now at other small colleges, of course, I might have been less welcome, but there's also maybe more academic freedom in a smaller school.

Combining career and family and trying to do resistance work has been a real . . . it's a real balancing act. I don't do as much resistance as I should. I don't feel I can handle more than one arrest at a time, so to that extent deterrence does kind of work. You have to plan it out, but I'm convinced it's still possible to continue to do civil disobedience, and it's important for people who have careers to take some risks.

I've made a lot of compromises. To be employed. To decide to become a professor. To no longer do tax resistance. [*Long pause.*] You don't know all the compromises. If I were really serious, we'd be doing tax resistance and not just the civil disobedience. This is just a . . . a minimal attempt to maintain some degree of dignity.

7

After the Millennium

The events of September 11, 2001, turned the world upside down. I remember seeing the second plane hit the World Trade Center tower and realizing that much of what I'd worked for since the sixties had now to be redone, that the government's stance was likely to be retaliation and revenge, and that peace workers would once again be reviled and ostracized, as they had been in other times of war.

Depending on the larger community in which one lives, however, criticism of those who work for peace has not been virulent. Instead, a plethora of new groups have come into being to call for nonviolent solutions, groups like the September 11 Families for Peaceful Tomorrows and Military Families Speak Out. These groups proliferated after the invasions of Afghanistan and Iraq and some groups now brag because they were founded before the Iraq War. Some, like the forty-state network called the Project for Justice, the Environment, and Peace (PJEP), stress the connections between justice issues. Others concentrate and specialize.[1]

These groups join with older and more established communities in busy Internet work, and from them come seemingly endless online petitions, documentary films, peace team visits to invaded lands, and local commemorations of one or another of the US invasions. Many groups attempt to rise above seemingly ineffectual party politics and to unite with other justice groups throughout the world in challenging corporate and military interests. However, a casual observer can see a marked decrease in resisters who do nonviolent direct actions, especially compared to the large campaigns of the eighties. Jittery local police, tighter federal and local security, severe retribution by the courts, media neglect, and just plain fear seem to have dampened civil resistance to war, despite the fact that US troops are in more countries than ever.

Yet there are still brave souls who risk prison terms to live out their beliefs in concrete ways and to show that the increased surveillance of peace activists by the FBI and the Homeland Security Act of 2002 can't quash dissent. In this chapter, six contemporary resisters tell their stories, some illustrating the loss of constitutional rights since 9/11 and some describing new methods of nonviolent resistance.

Ana Grady Flores was arrested at an upstate New York marine recruiting center, shortly before the Iraq War started. She was only sixteen. Dan Burns was part of the St. Patrick's Four, an Ithaca Catholic Worker group that protested at the same recruiting office. Becky Johnson focuses on the ongoing campaign to close the School of Americas (SOA), using techniques learned by training with the Ruckus Society. Kathy Kelly, a veteran peace activist from Chicago, describes violent military arrest procedures at SOA protests. Attorney Steve Downs was arrested for wearing a peace T-shirt in an upstate New York shopping mall and now devotes his life to protecting civil liberties. Camilo Mejia, the first Iraq soldier to refuse to return to duty for moral reasons, concludes this collection.

Ana Grady Flores is a third-generation activist: she is the daughter of Ithaca Catholic Worker Mary Anne Grady Flores and the granddaughter of Theresa and John Grady, who were active against the Vietnam War. Ana remembers going to demonstrations as a child—to the Pentagon, to the United Nations, and to the Trident submarines stationed in Connecticut. As she says, "My cousins and I . . . we're the Grady kids. The troublemakers."

Ana Grady Flores

"We can't vote yet, so we have no voice. So [the action] was my way of finding my voice, of saying, 'You're not allowed to do this.'"

I think I began to become an activist on my own after [one of] Phil Berrigan's trials. He and some others had hammered on a B-52 warplane, and I remember watching how the judge just shut them down. Didn't allow them to use the word "Bible," didn't allow them to talk about how their faith intertwined in what they did. I just sat there watching it all and . . . When it was all done, they were found guilty and sent to jail for [a year]. I was feeling so incredibly sad because I was finally able to understand what was going on. Phil was getting older and was sick. He was going back to jail, and he'd already been in jail for maybe a third of his life. I remember deciding then that I was old enough to read and do my own investigation and to understand on my own. So I made a plan for myself. I wasn't going to be like an ordinary teenager.

Then in 2002, when I was sixteen years old and the war in Iraq was about to start, I did my first action. I was arrested at the Marine recruiting center. Before the action, I said, "Ma, you've got to let me do this. I know why I'm doing it, and it's not because you told me anything, it's because of what I believe in." People tried to say it was just because of my family, but it was me going to these meetings. On my own. It was me helping to plan the action, and at the same time, I was organizing kids in my high school. The young people have to be the ones to say no. We can't

Ithaca teen resisters, 2003.
(Photo courtesy of Laura de Flaun.)

vote yet, so we have no voice. So [the action] was my way of finding my voice, of saying, "You're not allowed to do this." Not in my name.

There were thirteen of us at the recruiting center, and four of us were minors—me and my two cousins, Oona and Maria, and a friend of ours, Anna Ritter. We were all sixteen or seventeen and we were with family and good friends. My Aunt Clare [Grady] put red paint on us, and we pinned names and pictures of dead Iraqi children on our clothes and did a die-in in the lobby of the recruiting center. I remember my Uncle Peter [DeMott] saying to people, "We're here to recruit you to the peace movement."

We lay there for about an hour before they arrested us, and we had like two hundred people outside supporting us and singing songs. We read a lot of stuff out loud, a depleted uranium fact sheet and things by Martin Luther King Jr. The officers listened to all of it and when we were done, they arrested us and charged us with third-degree misdemeanors. Before my mom would let me get arrested, she'd made me, uh . . . articulate my reasons. I told her I didn't want my brothers recruited to fight in a war that's built up of lies and deception.

Ro: Were you scared when you were arrested?

Ana: No, I don't think so. Instead I was sad. Because my family has been doing this and now it's my turn—my generation's turn—to shoulder it, to be the ones who protest. Because it's still going on.

It was hard going to court but it was fun, too. I felt like the little lawyer. My cousins and I, we were very close. Basically a little team. We had a lawyer mentoring us and helping us, but we did it all ourselves. We had so many meetings. Writing motions, practicing direct examination. A teacher of mine helped us do a mock trial, so we had a lot of preparation.

The actual trial process was insane. They made it incredibly hard for us. First, they separated us from the adults and dropped the adult charges to a violation—like a parking ticket—but kept our charges as a misdemeanor. Which meant we were facing three months in jail. Then they tried to plea bargain!

We were like, "Wait a second! Why are you doing this to us? We're sixteen, and we're facing three months in jail!" I guess they dropped the adult charges so they wouldn't have to spend money on a jury trial. As juveniles, we couldn't have one, so they took *us* to court because it was cheaper. It's only a town court, and the judge doesn't even have to be a lawyer, so he was basically being led along by the prosecutor.

We had filed a motion asking if we could have people in the courtroom, but they wouldn't allow it. There were about sixty people there for this first trial date and this guy was really worried because he'd have to declare all these people in contempt, so he finally gave us another date. Then we wrote another motion asking for everyone to be in the courtroom, and that time they allowed it.

We did our own direct examination, examining each other and then wonder of wonders! They let an international law expert come and testify—John Schuchardt.[2] The judge listened to him for a really long time, and it was a real lesson for all of us.

I was nervous, really nervous, even though we'd practiced. See, the prosecutor would object to everything, and I was worried that the judge wasn't going to hear what we had to say. At the end, he said he'd give the verdict in two weeks, but it actually took him two and a half months. I think he was really torn on what to do. He finally found us guilty, but he wrote us like a five-page letter saying why.

The prosecutor wanted to make an example out of us kids, to scare everybody else away. And that's what they did. But we had so much . . . We were always on the news. On the radio or in the paper, and on e-mail. We'd get e-mails from people in the military who were trying to opt out. "Thank you so much for doing this." E-mails from all over the world.

If I hadn't had the community and all this that support, I couldn't have done it. The judge finally sentenced us to four consecutive weekends in jail and a $250 fine. But we appealed, and it went to county court and then he finally changed it to time served. He didn't drop the charges down, but he said, "You've served your time in all the time you've spent in court and in preparing for court."

So that was a victory, yet not complete. I mean, they pulled us along for a year and a half. I think about it now, and I can't believe I made it through high school. [*Laughs a little shakily.*] Emotionally it was hard for me. Here I was, trying to define myself. I knew this was something that I needed to do, knew that it was right, and that's what I kept telling myself. Because we had so many people disagreeing with us and saying we were threatening our future, with a juvenile record and all.

We'd tell them it was *for* our future, and the future of our children. It's crazy to think about that, but it's our children that'll be affected. So now I'm very interested in helping other young people learn about conscientious objection. I've gone through a training on how to support people in the military and how they can opt out and stuff like that. Did you know that when you sign up for your driver's license now, they automatically register you for Selective Service? So if you want to be a conscientious objector, you need to know how to start your file.

Ro: What would you say to young people who feel a stirring to resist?

Ana: Well, it's hard to just say educate yourself because it's hard to know where to start. There's always the alternative news on the Internet and Amy Goodman. And going to peace meetings. Tapping into the Catholic Worker.

Ro: How can they fight the prevailing youth culture? "Have fun because tomorrow we die."

Ana: Oh, man! Um . . . I don't know. I think there's a little bit of that in every kid. You're always going to have to have some . . . But I know I had so much fun discovering the law, so it's not that this stuff isn't fun. It's definitely important and you can make it fun.

> [Other Ithaca peace people protested, as well. On St. Patrick's Day in 2003, two days before the bombing of Iraq started, a group called the St. Patrick's Four entered the same recruiting center and poured their own blood on the walls, the floor of the vestibule, and on some cardboard cutouts.]

Peter DeMott: Our hope had been to voice our opposition to this way as dramatically—and yet as nonviolently—as we could. Just to tell anybody and everybody that this war must not happen. We were trying to say "No!" as strongly as we could say it. There had been protests against the war all over the world, in major capitals in Europe and in Australia and here in this country as well. Literally millions of people turned out to voice their opposition, more than at any other time before a war.[3]

The group was immediately arrested, as expected, and the local press concentrated their coverage on some blood that had inadvertently hit a US flag. The first jury trial, for a state felony called "criminal mischief," couldn't muster enough guilty verdicts to convict, resulting in a mistrial. Several months later, the four received federal charges, including conspiracy to impede an officer of the United States, a felony punishable by up to six years in prison and a fine of $250,000.

Between the two trials, I spoke with each of the St. Patrick's Four: Clare Grady; her sister Theresa Grady; the late Peter DeMott, married to Ellen (another Grady sister); and Dan Burns. Their voices, their lives, their personalities are distinct. What they have in common is their Irishness, their Catholicism, their parenthood, and their commitment to Catholic Worker pacifism. Here's Dan's story.

Dan Burns

"The Catholic Workers have something I want and it feels good."

As a young adult, I was working in the film business and that was a whole different thing. Drinking and using drugs. Living a self-centered life and sort of numbed to everything. Even before I started doing resistance, I'd spent time in jail, but it was the kind of being in jail where you think your life is ruined. Once I got sober, I was given life again. And life was powerful stuff. Everything was open for reconsideration, you might say. I knew I should look at things differently and I was willing to do that.

After talking to a lot of people, I realized that everything from my [birth] family that I'd lost, all their Catholic values of helping the underdog and all, I'd lost because I'd been suckered. I'd been lied to. We all have. When I got sober, I felt betrayed. It was like somebody lifted the curtain and I could see under it. Ah, the wizard! There he is. It's all baloney.

See, I'd always fancied myself as somebody who had a little bit of an insight, and when I realized I had no insight whatsoever, I was keenly interested to find it. So that's how I started going to Catholic Worker meetings. I went with Jessica Stewart, who is now my wife and the mother of our two boys, Finian and Francis. She's the one who turned me on to the Catholic Worker and the Atlantic Life Community folks. The Catholic Workers have something I want and it feels good.

Resistance became very appealing to me. You know, my parents told us all the good stories about giving a voice to the person who doesn't have one. You see somebody getting beat up, what do you do? You stop the fight. You don't allow anybody weaker than yourself to be attacked. And you don't pick on anybody weaker than yourself, either. For me as a Catholic, it's a sin if I don't physically put myself in the way of [someone committing] violence.

So that's how Jessica and I want to live our lives. We took a vow of resistance. When I do it, I don't do it alone, I represent both of us. She's done resistance for years, but now that we have the two children, she doesn't risk arrest. She's with me just the same, though.

We always had to go to the Stations of the Cross when I was a kid. Well, the Ithaca Catholic Worker does the Stations of the Cross, but on the street. With this big cross. It begins at the courthouse and then goes over to the soup kitchen Clare Grady helps to manage and then the FBI office and then the newspaper and another one at the police station. Then we go to the Fleet Bank and then up to Cornell, and we have a station at the small nuke up there. Then we hit the Morgan Stanley office and College Town and we end up at the recruiting center for the final station. That's the religion I can get into—showing the sins of our culture.

My first resistance arrest was in New York, just after 9/11 happened. About

The St. Patrick's Four with banner.
(Photo courtesy of Jessica Stewart.)

twenty-five of us did an action across the street from the United Nations building. It was fun and exciting and . . . and emotional and spiritual. When you're in a cell with priests and nuns, you know you're in the right place. There was one old man, and his coat had food stains on it, like somebody you'd see on the subway, you know. But he spoke so eloquently and so spiritually. And you know who it was? Elmer Maas![4] I was just so happy to have spent that time with him before he died.

I also did a weekend in jail because of a die-in in December '02. Then there was the St. Patrick's Four. People ask me if I'd do it again. "Yes, I'd do it twice."

Some months after this interview, the St. Patrick's Four were retried on federal charges in Binghamton, where Dan's father had served as mayor, with the government perhaps choosing that conservative venue in hopes of a stiffer conviction than they might get in Ithaca. Local activists staged protests outside the courthouse each day of the trial and organized a six-day "Citizens' Tribunal on Iraq," featuring prominent peace movement speakers. Assisted by attorneys, the four defended themselves but weren't allowed to mention the Iraq War. They were convicted only of misdemeanor charges and they served four to six months in prison instead of the six years and huge fines a conspiracy conviction would have given them.

Becky Johnson graduated in environmental science from Oberlin College in Ohio. While she was in college, she joined an affinity group that protested at the School of the Americas and had several SOA arrests but no convictions. Finally, in 2003, she was sentenced to six months at Alderson. Here's the way

Becky Johnson described herself at her sentencing: "I am a twenty-three-year-old queer, pacifist, Unitarian Universalist, former SOA Watch staffer who hopes to eventually become a social justice minister. I am proud to be on trial for my small role in shutting this SOA/WHINSEC down for good."

Becky Johnson

"You can do lots of things if you look like you know what you're doing."

I felt so strongly that the School of the Americas was a violent part of our foreign policy, and I didn't want us, as a country, to be involved in it. My first arrest there was in 2000, when I was a junior at Oberlin. Just a regular line crossing, and even though we weren't charged, that was really my awakening to civil disobedience work.

So when we got back to Oberlin, the SOAW affinity group I was part of decided on another action. We went to DC and protested at a meeting of suppliers to the Sikorsky Corporation. The government has spent millions on Black Hawk helicopters made by Sikorsky. Now, these are army transport vehicles, specifically designed for warfare. Of all of the things we could give to Colombia, these are what the government decided to give as "development." The point of all of these suppliers coming to DC was to lobby for *more* Black Hawk helicopters, to add still more to the appropriation bill.

I'd say we do technical direct action. Very highly trained, by the Ruckus Society, which taught us direct action techniques such as climbing and other skills. They teach other things, too, like lobbying techniques and media work and other aspects of direct action. And we've also learned from other protestors at mass demonstrations along the way.

We're inspired by the older generation of activists who have come before us—and we're proud to be working in the same movement—but our culture's a little different and probably more secularized. Although we all have religious and personal reasons for doing this work, they're not all the same and we don't have common symbols, as many of the older generation do. We *do* have common actions and common media outlets, as they've developed over the past few years in the antiglobalization movement.

Our first Oberlin SOA Watch technical action happened in a conference room Sikorsky had rented at the National Guard Memorial Museum, right next to Capitol Hill. On our way in, we'd greeted these two Sikorsky vice presidents and they even showed us where the bathrooms were. (We were dressed up because we didn't want to look out of place, but we were carrying gigantic bags of these long PVC pipes, and they assumed, I think, that we were caterers.)

We used a device called a lockbox, which is basically a long piece of PVC pipe that you can put your hand in up to your elbow. We decorated the outside of the pipe and put a pin down the middle, a piece of metal. And then we put little hand-cuffs around our wrists and handcuffed ourselves to the pin, in the middle of the pipe. We went right away to a pole in the conference room, sat down around it, and started attaching ourselves into the lockboxes. Our spokesperson wasn't chained in, and her job was also to get us water or any help we needed. She also had a chain around her waist so she could lock herself to us, which she did, eventually.

They didn't notice us right away. Then they were sort of confused because only the caterers were in the room, not anybody in charge. We were chanting and sing-ing, and finally one of the vice presidents came in, wearing his Sikorsky badge.

He said, "You know, you're at the wrong place. You're protesting the wrong thing."

"Well, we're here to protest the Sikorsky's suppliers' conference, and I see you work for the Sikorsky Corporation. So I think we *are* in the right place."

"Oh, well, it doesn't start tonight."

And I said, "Then why are you setting up the wet bar and the food?" He was obviously trying to get us to leave, but after he realized that we weren't going to, we actually had a pretty good conversation about the issues.

The police finally came but they basically waited us out. It was too much trouble for them to cut through our lockboxes, so they waited until we decided to unlock ourselves. And we were willing to do that as soon as we knew that the meeting wasn't going to happen that evening. And it didn't. We stayed until we were sure they weren't going to be able to meet that night and then we unlocked ourselves and the police took us off to jail. But nothing really happened as far as charges went, probably because Sikorsky didn't want publicity.

That was a great . . . it was a really powerful action. Not only were we interact-ing directly with the corporation, but there were almost one hundred people sup-porting us outside the building. They were from the SOA Watch Spring Lobbying action, and they told everybody who walked by what was happening inside and how important it was. That was really beautiful.

Then that Oberlin group wanted to continue in the struggle, so after school ended, we all went back down to Georgia to protest again at the base. We planned an action that I guess I'd call ritual theater or street theater. We actually drove into the base and right up to where the School of the Americas is. (This was before they had a fence around it or checkpoints.) Again, just another ban-and-bar letter.

[Becky crossed the line at SOA two more times without being charged. One was another lockbox protest.]

Becky: For some reason, I was Teflon. They just didn't want to charge me. The *coup de grâce* was in July of 2002, at the trial for the folks who crossed the line in

November of 2001. (Thirty-seven of them went to trial and another six had their charges dismissed.) I was working with SOAW at the time, helping them with legal questions and facilitating meetings.

I decided I wanted to do an action that would force the army's hand. Because one of the things that's so powerful about the SOAW is the effectiveness of civil disobedience within that struggle. Through the prison witness, it grew from just one man to tens of thousands. So after the trials were over, I went alone to the new front gates of Fort Benning on a Saturday morning. I unlocked them and then locked them closed again with Kryptonite locks, so nobody could get in or out. I put a banner on the gate that said, "Lock up the SOA, not the peace makers," and then I locked myself to the gate, with the lock around my neck. I was there for about three hours before they cut me out.

It took them a while to get ready. First a military officer tried to talk to me, and then the Catholic chaplain came out from the base. It wasn't easy for them to figure out how they were going to cut the lock, with it being also around my neck. The fire department eventually got me unlocked, and I really appreciated how concerned they were about my safety.

I was taken to the military police station and they wanted to officially charge me with something and take me to Muskogee County Jail to wait for an arraignment the next morning. But! The Muskogee County Jail was too full, so they let me go. Again!

Finally I was charged and stood trial with others in the winter of 2003 and got six months in prison and a $1,000 fine. And off I went that day, straight into my prison adventure. I stayed in the county prison for a month and after some flying around, I got to Alderson.

Being in prison . . . See, I tend to be rather silly. My mother tells me that I have a Blondie side and an Ernie side. The Blondie side doesn't take anything seriously and can't sit through a church service without giggling. My Ernie side is the part of me that's continually trying to learn, and the Ernie part thinks about getting it all right, figuring everything out, working with the tensions [between] effectiveness and faithfulness. I want to . . . I really have to be perfect. These two sides to me live fairly well together, and don't come into conflict very often. But it's important for me to see joy wherever I go, and to celebrate what I've done, even if it's not perfect.

In the county jail, I spent a lot of my time writing motions to judges for women who didn't write very well, or correcting spelling, or trying to figure out with my lawyers how to help this woman who had been raped by a guard. I was just constantly *doing* things, and I was the only person there who could do them.

Once I got to federal prison, that wasn't the case most of the time. The women there knew their way around, and I was the new person. So I had this real crisis and I didn't know what to do with myself. I even went to "Sweating to the Oldies," can you believe it?

Then I got a grip and started entertaining myself. I developed a "gratitude" for every day I was there. I looked through the library shelves and tried to name all the books that I thought the prisoners of conscience had left there. I found an old half-broken violin. Now, I have no idea how to play the violin, but I'd go in [this room] and try to play "Twinkle, Twinkle, Little Star." I just tried to have fun and let my Blondie side out.

Learning something new also made me feel I was still me. At work, I'd ask my boss if I could try to fix one of the lawnmowers instead of just mowing. I volunteered for weird things and listened to tapes to teach myself Spanish. I went to a weaving class and to ceramics class where I painted little peace bugs. I made a chocolate cake in the microwave and had an impromptu party. That's one of the great skills you learn in prison—how to make anything in a microwave.

I had to reclaim these moments of joy, or else I would've been *so* depressed! If I hadn't done those crazy things, there would have been no Blondie side, and I wouldn't have been able to be present to where I was. Does that make sense?

Also, at Alderson, you can actually hug visitors and have long conversations. I'd have these joyful conversations with my mom, where I'd tell her all the weird happenings. She's the one who taught me to be an activist, really, and we once even did an action together, so she was always extremely supportive, even though she worried. And my grandmother flew all the way from New Mexico to visit me.

Ro: Have you done any more of this "technical direct action"?

Becky: Yes. I did an action at the [New York] National Republican Convention with a loosely affiliated organization called Operation Sybil. We wanted to do a "framing action" that made it clear to the mass media what binds together all the protesters. So we decided to drop a banner on the front of the Plaza Hotel, a banner with a very simple message: an arrow going in one direction that said "Bush" and an arrow in the other direction labeled "Truth." We wanted to convey that no matter what solutions were proposed, what we all had in common was a deep mistrust of Bush.

Banner drop at the Republican National Convention, 2004. (Photo courtesy of Jesse Wegman.)

We had lots of support in New York and raised the money for the climbing gear through individual donations. Students who were artists designed and sewed this *gigantic* banner, which weighed eighty pounds and was something like eighty feet wide by sixty feet long. It was all stuffed in a very specific way into one big back-pack, so we could take it down the ropes with us and unfold it easily.

We rented a room at the Plaza for the night. It wasn't hard to get out on the roof because the door was unlocked and open, so we just walked out. We had two climbers and two people who set up the anchors for them and protected those anchors from anybody—including the police—who might want to cut the ropes or something. I was one of those anchor protectors, so I set up my climber's anchor, and then she went over the side.

We set up a different rope for the bag to go down on. It was quite a feat of climbing and technical skill, and it took us five hours from the time we got to the roof, but it all worked! The banner came right down the front of the building, and it was centered beautifully. It was up for just a few minutes before the cops told us to come in and they pulled the climbers in through a window. But it was hanging plenty long enough to get the picture taken and long enough for people in the street to all turn around and look up.

Ro: But before that, nobody stopped you?

Becky: No. Several people saw us, actually, including window washers on the build-ing next door, and people coming in and out of the Plaza Hotel. People in their hotel rooms even saw the climbers go down past their windows. But I think . . . we all had on bright yellow helmets and we looked very official. And who would be climbing on the side of the Plaza Hotel if they weren't official? You can do lots of things if you look like you know what you're doing.

It takes so much to create safety when you're climbing. You don't want police going down after the climbers, because that can create a dangerous situation for both the police and the climbers, so our goal was to get our banner up and then cooperate fully, and that's what we did. We went into jail that afternoon, and the next morning we had our bond hearing, and were released right after that. I think the charges were eventually dropped with only a small fine, or something. The hotel sure didn't want the publicity, obviously.

The banner was beautiful and the picture went everywhere. But unfortunately, the publicity was marred because a police officer had injured himself while he was on the roof. He cut his leg on a piece of glass and most of the publicity was about his injury, which was really upsetting for all of us. Because everything that we do in these actions is done to create safety for everyone involved.

The whole reason that we had people on the roofs was one, to protect the climbers, and two, to protect anyone else who comes up there because you can trip over climbing ropes and hurt yourself. So it was really unfortunate that this man cut himself on a piece of glass. He's fine. But the media picked up [on] his injury and also our being charged with assault because of it. They dropped that felony charge, though, when they understood that we didn't do anything to create the situation for that police officer to cut himself.

Ro: Becky, why do you do all this complicated stuff?

Becky: Well, it's important for me to ask where my obligation lies. I try to live by this quotation: "Don't ask what the world needs. Ask what makes you come alive, and go do it. The world needs people who have come alive."[5]

It's important for me to be working from my own life and my own space, as a white woman in this culture. I have the power of class, I have the power of race, I have the power of education. In my life, I have the power of love, with a loving and supportive family. I just have so much power, so much privilege, in a culture where so few people have that. I have an obligation to the God I hear inside me, but the way I interpret that obligation is wrapped up in my experience of privilege. And with that, how do I meet my obligation to people who don't live from that place? That's the big question of my life right now: Where do those meet, and where does my duty to the world lie?

[When Becky and I talked, she had been exploring these questions at the Starr King School, part of the Graduate Theological Union in California.]

Attorney Steve Downs had been quietly investigating judicial misconduct for most of his professional life, as a member of the New York Commission on Judicial Conduct. One day he wore an antiwar T-shirt in a shopping mall.

Steve Downs

> *"What we've done, essentially, is to privatize our marketplaces. What used to be a place of free exchange of ideas—bad ideas, angry ideas, hostile ideas, good ideas—has now been essentially taken away from us and we're told what kind of ideas we can exchange."*

As commission members, we try to observe the same rules governing judicial conduct that the judges are expected to observe. So for most of my life, I lived in the same kind of protected cocoon that the judges live in—that is, we didn't engage in political activity or any sort of raucous protest. We lived sober lives and certainly tried to avoid controversy.

Then along comes December of 2002, and the drum beat for war. It got me on a very gut level. I felt the president was lying—that he didn't know what he claimed to know—and that we were being manipulated into war.

[Steve heard about a group who had been asked to leave nearby Crossgates Mall because they were wearing peace T-shirts.]

Steve: The guards actually walked them out into the parking lot and made sure they didn't come back in. I said, "Boy, that sounds crazy!" But I kept thinking about this and about the war and by the first of the year, I felt somehow I had to publicly go on record. I didn't want it to ever be said that I sat by and did nothing when I felt this huge injustice—this outrage of a war—was about to happen.

Now, my work at the commission put me in an awkward position. I didn't want to engage in demonstrations or do things I felt judges probably shouldn't be doing because they might have to hear cases involving the war, and they'd be biased and then . . . you know, all the problems associated with judges getting involved.

But wearing T-shirts at the mall. It was so simple and innocent. That you'd simply walk around with words that called to mind our most basic values, the things that we hold up at Christmastime as being at the core to who we are. So why are we now abandoning them? Go back to who we really are. Believe in peace on earth.

It was a very minimal kind of protest, but it was the best I felt I could do, given my situation. I'd go to bed at night with this idea in my head, and I'd wake up in the morning and the idea would still be there. Periodically during the day it gives me another kick in the back. Now I've never had a religious calling, so I don't know what they would be like. But I can imagine what it must be like to constantly have a voice in the back of your head, suggesting something. Mine said, "Buy the T-shirt, put it on, walk around the mall."

My response to this, inevitably, was, "I don't want to do that! I hate the mall! I don't *want* to get involved in this! I don't want to cause a problem with my job!" But this idea would *not* leave me alone. I'd been talking about it to my son, Roger, and finally I told him, "All right, I've got to do it. I'll buy this T-shirt, walk around the mall for fifteen minutes and then go home, and that'll be it. I won't have to do it again."

So he went with me and that's what we did. We had the T-shirts made up at the mall. I had "Peace on Earth" on one side and "Give Peace a Chance" on the other. Roger thought [my pair of sayings] wasn't very edgy, so he chose "Let inspections work" and "No war in Iraq" or something like that. So anyway, we put on the T-shirts and after about fifteen minutes when almost no one said anything, we went to the food court to get something to eat.

[The security guards first called an outside police officer and then rather reluctantly arrested Steve. (Roger had decided to remove his T-shirt.)]

Steve Downs, 2004.
(Photo courtesy of
Lynne Jackson.)

Steve: I don't remember much about this part. Even though I'd been kind of re-hearsing it in my mind, I guess when it actually happened, I was kind of in shock. As a lawyer for twenty-five years, of course I should know all of this, but when the roles were reversed, it was confusing, as though I was watching it happen to some-body else. I have to say, though, that the officers and all the security guards were very nice. They were, I think, genuinely embarrassed by this whole thing.

The guard's reasoning was that the mall was private property, like somebody's home, and I'd gone into that home and done something to offend the host. Under those circumstances, wasn't it completely reasonable that the host didn't want me there, so I should just get up and leave?

I said, "Well, no, this isn't somebody's house, it's a marketplace, where not only are goods and services sold but also ideas. And I think as a person in a public marketplace, I have a right to express who I am and what's important to me."

So we had this philosophical back and forth and eventually they gave me a ticket for trespass. When I wouldn't promise not to [come] back into the mall, they took me to the town court for an immediate arraignment.

The judge . . . It was kind of funny. He was supposed to inform me of the charge and read me my rights, but instead he just kind of looked at me, and goes, "So?" Then I go, "So?" and he goes, "*So?*"

Now, I know that as a defendant you're just supposed to be arraigned and not say anything, but I explained the whole thing to him and said I was pleading not guilty. He didn't set bail, so Roger drove home with me. We both kind of looked at each other and said, "Boy, was *that* weird."

Well, things rapidly got much weirder. The next morning, I had to tell my boss, and I think he was just thrilled by it. (I mean, he hated the war as much as I did.) I think he somehow got it out to a newspaper in New York City. And it wasn't just one newspaper, it was on all the wire services. How it got there, I've never really figured out.

Anyway, about two days later, the phone woke me up about 6:00 a.m. A radio station in Pennsylvania. I confirmed that the story was true. Then immediately another call—a radio station in Louisiana. I did eight live radio calls before I'd even had breakfast. I got to the office, and the secretary was just going nuts! My desk was piled with calls—just a huge mound of paper. So many had come in that it shut down the phone system. They just didn't stop! The phone lines were clogged for an entire week, and I couldn't get through to a soul, not even a lawyer who wanted to represent me.

There were calls from all over—from Australia, from the United Kingdom, from my parents-in-law in the Netherlands who read it in their hometown paper. There was something about it that the Europeans loved. Of course they missed the nuance that it wasn't the US government that was shutting me down, but the mall. But it didn't matter; it sort of confirmed everything they were feeling. "Somebody with a T-shirt that said 'Peace on Earth' had been arrested. That's how bad it's gotten in America."

I became [a victim] of a crazy feeding frenzy. Television cameras and crews would be in my driveway when I'd get home at night, and I guess the same thing happened with the Crossgates Mall. (Or at least that's what I've heard.) Protest groups would show up and walk around with everybody wearing a T-shirt that said "Peace on Earth." They'd try to get arrested, but they didn't, because Crossgates backed way off. The incident generated just a huge amount of bad publicity for them, so they hunkered down and waited for it to pass.

In the end, it doesn't look like they've changed at all, though. For instance, a couple of months ago, some kid was walking around the mall with what was described in the paper as a Gothic T-shirt. The security guards told him to take it off or leave, and when he refused, they shot him with a Taser! So I don't have the sense that they've backed down at all, and I think if I went up there wearing a peace T-shirt, I might very well be arrested again.

It all comes down to whether or not a mall is a marketplace. And that issue has *got* to be addressed because what we've done, essentially, is to privatize our marketplaces. What used to be a place of free exchange of ideas—bad ideas, angry ideas, hostile ideas, good ideas—has now been essentially taken away from us, and we're told what kind of ideas we can exchange.

Now, maybe we want an antiseptic society in which nobody is allowed to say anything but nice things to each other. But I don't think we want that. If we don't, we have to be willing to accept the fact that in a marketplace, we're going to have some very nasty and even horrible ideas thrown at us. If the neo-Nazis and the Ku Klux Klan demonstrate at the mall, it could get difficult, and it would certainly intimidate a lot of shoppers. But that's what a free society is all about.

My T-shirt was so. . . Everybody knows how awful the T-shirts at the mall are.

No one gets arrested for wearing those, but "Peace on Earth"? *That* gets you arrested? So it definitely hit a chord somewhere.

Lots of interesting stories: I heard that a woman, Erin O'Brien, who was head of a coalition of peace groups got a call from a reporter. The reporter said, "Now, come clean! Downs was a member of your group and you put him up to it, didn't you?" Erin said she'd never even heard of me before the arrest.

The reporter said, "Oh, then it's a legitimate story!" In other words, if a group protests in support of their constitutional rights, it's not a legitimate story. If one hapless individual blunders into an arrest, then it is!

The New York Civil Liberties Union tried to get a suit up to the state supreme court saying that wearing a message-bearing T-shirt at the mall was a free speech right. Finally, in late 2010, the New York Appellate Division dismissed the suit, holding that the mall was private property and there wasn't enough state involvement to impose free speech requirements. Steve wrote me:

> We appealed to the Court of Appeals and the court refused to hear the case on the grounds that there was no substantial constitutional issue involved. (If the Court could not find a constitutional issue in a case that involved only constitutional issues, it has to be a pretty clear rejection of our theory.)
>
> But I think we may have won in the court of public opinion. A friend recently took a state exam to be accredited as an elementary teacher. She was asked the following question (roughly from my memory of what she told me). "In 2003, Stephen Downs was arrested in a shopping mall for wearing a T-shirt that said 'Peace on Earth' which he had bought at the mall. What *constitutional section* [emphasis added] is involved in this arrest: a) the commerce clause, b) the war powers clause, c) the first amendment?" So the Court of Appeals would have answered "none" and presumably would not have qualified to become elementary school teachers. The moral of the story, I think, is that I lost in the law courts but won in the court of public opinion. That may be more important in the long run.

First Amendment constitutional issues remained in the forefront for Attorney Downs, and he retired from his state position a few years after our 2005 interview. He then cofounded both Project SALAM (*www.projectsalam.org*) and the National Coalition to Protect Civil Freedoms. Project SALAM supports and advocates for Muslims who may have been unconstitutionally targeted after 9/11. The Coalition gathers together national groups such as NLG and the Center for Constitutional Rights to address such problems as thought crime prosecutions, manufactured charges, racial profiling, and inhumane treatment of prisoners.[6]

Steve now speaks throughout the country about how the US constitution has been undermined since 2001.

Unlike Steve, Kathy Kelly has been practicing resistance in the Midwest for years. In 1996, she founded Voices in the Wilderness, a community that protested the UN sanctions against Iraq by bringing medicine and material aid to the Iraqi people. Eventually the group was fined $20,000 for their activities, a fine they refused to pay.

Kathy remained in Baghdad with Ed Kinane and others during the 2003 invasion so aptly named "Shock and Awe" by the US government. In 2005, she began a new resistance community—Voices for Creative Nonviolence—which is committed to active nonviolent resistance, particularly in Afghanistan, where they see the results of the unmanned drone bombings. A veteran of many arrests, her longest prison sentences have been for the Missouri Peace Planting in 1988 and the School of the Americas Watch (SOAW) protest in 2003. She begins her interview by describing her arrest at that protest.

Kathy Kelly, with Father Joe Mulligan, SJ

"Every person who enters into a circle that resists this culture of war and consumption does what they can, but everyone should do something."

Kathy: When I was in Baghdad during the "Shock and Awe" bombing, I remember talking with some of my Iraqi friends late one evening and realizing my challenge to militarism had to be taken to a higher level. Because of what I had seen the Iraqi people endure. So the next fall, I crossed the line at the School of the Americas.

For me, it was accompanied by a certain rhetoric. In Iraq, US soldiers trespassed onto the territory of a sovereign country, based on the theory—proven unfounded—that Iraq had weapons of mass destruction. In contrast, if you cross two feet onto government grass at Fort Benning, you're crossing into an area where terrible destruction has been both planned and prepared for. And the evidence is all there. It's not a theory, it's not an argument.

Every November for years, the protests have happened, all very organized, all very nonviolent, and in some ways very predictable. And of course, the military base certainly plans for the arrests. The School of the Americas literature says they train the Central and South American soldiers to have the same respect and regard for human and civil rights that US military police have. Well, I certainly got a new perspective on that!

When we were arrested, we were handcuffed, told to kneel down, and then loaded onto a bus and taken to a big warehouse to be processed. In my experience, this booking procedure is normally not unlike passing through security at an airport. We were taken in one at a time, and I was told to go to Station J where they pat you down. Five soldiers were there. One of them—a woman—was quite brisk and shouting at me.

I was doing what she said: "Spread out your legs, raise your arms." Well, because she was shouting at me, I suppose my high school teacher part came to the fore, and I turned to her and said, "Could you just let me understand. Why are you shouting?"

Well, more shouts. "Look straight ahead! Don't say anything. Keep your eyes fixed on the officer in front of you. Raise your arms higher. Raise your leg higher!" Then started the most aggressive search I've ever experienced. Jabbing, squeezing, pushing hands inside of clothing.

When I was told to raise my other leg, I kind of lost my balance, but then I think I got my moral balance back, and I thought, "I'm not going to go along with this. This is dehumanizing! It's unnecessary, it's intimidating. We're a peaceable protest that's never had a hint of violence in all these years." So I just very quietly lowered my arms and said, "I'm sorry, I can't cooperate with this any longer."

Bam! I was thrown to the floor! (Had a black eye from that.) My wrists were cuffed, my ankles were cuffed. My wrists and ankles were tied together, and one soldier was kneeling on me, referring to me as "this fucker." I'm face down, with my wrists and ankles tied together. I was saying, "I can't breathe. Somebody please help me! I can't breathe."

Nothing was happening. I literally couldn't get a full breath. And oh, it hurt! I kept saying, "Please help! I can't breathe." Finally I managed to get out, "I've had four lung collapses," and then the person kneeling on me got off rather quickly.

Now, I weigh 105 pounds and I'm five foot two. I'm fifty-one years old. So if this is what they'll do to a graying woman, in full view of priests, nuns, witnesses . . . It made me think a lot—think about how these soldiers are trained. "Brook no dissent. Tolerate no exception to your rules." I guess they were thinking they might get in trouble if they didn't do exactly what the manuals say. Somewhere in the manual it must have told them to do exactly what they did to me.

Joe Mulligan: I was arrested with Kathy, and I'd just been brought in the door when I heard some muffled groaning or crying off to the side. But I couldn't see anything, because a cluster of military police were standing in a circle. Then all of a sudden they were picking up Kathy Kelly. They had hog-tied her! Now, she's such a tiny thing, and it was all so totally unnecessary! And totally excessive force. At my trial for the SOA action, I asked the soldiers if they'd learned anything about ethics, how to determine what's right and wrong in the military, or do they just obey any order that a commanding officer gives? Basically, they replied, "Yeah, you just have to obey. You obey whatever order you receive."

Kathy: Two things come to mind about this. One is an article by Nicholas Kristof about a training that happened in Baghdad, a simulation prepping for what they'd do if an Iraqi insurgent came into their barracks. One American soldier had to be the "insurgent" and he was told to go under the bed. Now, the other soldiers weren't told that this was an American. They were just told there was an Iraqi insurgent under the bed.

Well! They pulled him out and taped his mouth so tightly that he couldn't say the agreed-upon code word. And then they began to do just what I described. They hog-tied him, they kneeled on him, and they also beat him. He suffered brain damage, because he couldn't get oxygen to his brain. And this is *training*!

[Kathy continued with a heartfelt story of a time when she lost her temper with her own father in his infirmity. She concluded with a wry observation: "None of us are wired to always be patient."]

Kathy: If you train people to say the word "Kill!" three thousand times a day . . . And if you train people to be on hair-trigger alert, and then if they're in a far-away place and afraid, they . . . the whole cycle is set in place to create further antagonism and hatred.

In Iraq, to hog-tie someone in front of their families, and to pat down a woman if you're a man, to put your foot on another human being, to parade people naked—all the horrible stories that came out from Abu Ghraib . . . I think in that one telescoped moment of being hog-tied myself, I learned a great deal. Of course, the most important thing is to try to understand what's happening to those young soldiers and how they're trained with that "Kill! Kill!"

But I have to remember to tell the whole story. When I was carried hog-tied to where the pictures were to be taken, a young fellow who was carrying me said, "Ma'am, in order to take your picture, we're going to have to move the hair out from in front of your face." (I was handcuffed and couldn't do it.) And he asked me very gently, "Is it all right if I do that now?" I said yes and then—I think I was trembling—he gently squeezed my shoulder and said, "Ma'am, I know these cuffs are really tight. We'll get them loose as soon as we can." I was just so thankful for that kindness, that sign of basic humanity.

After that, they took me to the fingerprint station, and one very large soldier who had been part of the group of five surrounding me said to me, "Since you've been combative . . ." And I was still hog-tied. [*Laughs ironically.*] "Since you've been combative, if you don't follow every instruction we give you when we uncuff you, we will pepper spray you."

Again, this is all coming out of the manual. This was practice, to learn how to "do it right." Finally, I was untrussed and went back with the others, and after that it was all pretty normal.

You know, a new book has come out by a reporter who was embedded with the soldiers during the invasion of Baghdad. It's called *Generation Kill*.[7] But it's not

Kathy Kelly in the Dahiya area of Beirut, 2006. (Photo courtesy of Farah Mokhtareizadeh.)

a good idea for us to point our fingers at any soldiers on any base, because who's paying for all of this?

Ro: Yes. We all have bloody hands. Where did you serve your SOA sentence?

Kathy: I was sentenced for three months at Pekin Minimum Security Prison, which isn't far from Chicago. Before I went in, I was lucky to get some insight from women resisters who had served time there. They told me about Kim Lagore, who was there in the prison and whose son had been killed in Iraq. They said I might want to be a little quiet about my Iraq experience, until I got to know Kim, and that was great advice. Also, I didn't want to bring in a lot of experience that might separate me from other women. So, in a way, I set aside my role as a peace activist when I went in. It was very, very interesting to experience myself as stripped of any kind of notoriety or any sort of purposefulness. Stripped of identity.

At one point, a woman I liked a lot said to me, "Kathy, you are a very quiet woman, aren't you?" And I thought, "Well, that's a new one!" But by the end of my second month, I finally felt I could relax into something more like my usual personality.

Kim Lagore had been told by other prisoners that I'd been to Iraq and that she might want to talk to me sometime. And finally she came to me, and she brought me a picture of her son and talked about him, in just one conversation. We held each other, crying and sharing in common our grief over that war. That was a marker event, to get to know her and to understand the futility of that loss. She still hasn't learned anything other than that he was killed in a training exercise in

Baghdad. It could have been a training exercise where somebody had to get under the bed as an insurgent. Who knows?

Ro: The obedience: as Catholic women, we were both raised to obey, to see obedience as an absolute virtue, like the army teaches. When did you learn that wasn't true?

Kathy: I think it was primarily from Karl [Meyer].[8] When I was younger, resisting an unjust law and going to court and prison had seemed pretty exotic, to be honest. But when I got to know Karl and heard the resistance stories of other people who came to visit us, it began to seem more of a likelihood for me.

Then the timing: I'd already decided that I wasn't going to become a biological mother. I was no longer governed by the fears of my birth family, and was trying to nurture them along to understand. But even if you've got all these kinds of issues resolved in your life, I think it's a good idea to start civil disobedience with something pretty small and manageable, so you get a feel for the process of arrest and at least the brief imprisonment until you're processed. And very importantly, to feel confident about going up in front of a judge without being intimidated by the courtroom. (It can be almost religious in the way that everything's focused on the judge, and if you have low self-esteem, you might feel like a little ant.)

You just obey. "You've misbehaved. You've caused an awful lot of trouble." At my first arrest, Karl sort of nurtured me through the process. My lips were quivering and my knees were knocking and I was very, very ill at ease and frightened. But after that, I don't remember ever feeling nervous in front of a judge. In fact, I feel I'm a teacher there and have a responsibility to help the judge understand something.

Ro: What were the circumstances of that first arrest?

Kathy: Oh, my! It was way back in 1980. Draft registration had just been reinstated and Karl and I and others were arrested for singing peace anthems outside the post office where the young men were delivering their draft registration forms. The charge was disturbing the peace, and I represented myself. When the judge ordered me to pay a fine, I said that I couldn't pay as long as people were hungry and homeless. I remember that my mother was in the courtroom and I think she felt equal doses of bewilderment and pride.

Karl got an acquittal! He asked the officer who arrested him if anyone had complained to them about his singing, or if they themselves were disturbed. He answered no, giving Karl the chance to then ask how he could have been disturbing the peace.

Ro: Karl should have been a lawyer! Now, your first long time in prison was for the Missouri Peace Planting, wasn't it?

Kathy: Yes. It was summer of 1988. Fourteen of us fanned out to the nuclear missile silo sites that surrounded Kansas City, Missouri. (At that time, 150 nuclear missile silo sites were surrounding Kansas City, and a total of 1,000 were spread throughout the heartland.) We either climbed fences or broke locks and entered the sites and planted corn on top of the silos. With that action, we hoped we could communicate with farmers that this was their land, the breadbasket of the world, and that it should be used to grow corn instead of store nuclear weapons. You don't sow razors through a loaf of bread.

We were arrested, of course, but they let us go, and so the next day several of us went back. Every time they let us go, we'd take two days to write a new press release and regroup and go back out to the missile site. So I finally had five charges for trespasses and some also for breaking locks. I was sentenced to one year in prison for that. At Lexington, Kentucky, in a maximum security prison.

Ro: Did you ever get sent to solitary when you were there?

Kathy: No, not there. I did spend three weeks in solitary in Alderson when I was there in transit, though, and I loved it because it was quiet. I was lucky, too, because Jean Gump was there—on her third year for the Plowshares sentence—and she was able to get me books. And cookies in a tin and hand-knit booties and a pencil and paper, too. Such wonderful gifts! I was able to watch the sun coming over a mountain every morning, and . . . so it was fine.

But there was a lot of cursing in "the alley," as we called solitary, and I didn't like listening to it all day long, so I asked the women if they wanted to learn how to type. Some of them said yes, so I said, "Draw your hand." And then, "Draw your other hand." And then I had them label each finger, A-S-D-F-G, and then the other hand too. They thought it was funny, to have typing class in solitary. It didn't stop the noise for very long, though.

Ro: How did you feel when you got out of Lexington, that last stint in prison?

Kathy: Well, the most wrenching day was just before I left. I hid in the laundry room and just sobbed and sobbed. Because I felt such deep regret and remorse that I was leaving the women. And also leaving that "scene of a crime" and there was nothing I could do about it. I thought about all the women I had come to know. I . . . It's hard to explain. You want to take the place apart, brick by brick. To go to the nearest courtroom and shout to people about the racism and the futility of it all, and how close we are to the reenactment of fascism. There's no way we'll ever make up for all the wrong that's being done to them. No way!

I felt the same when I walked away from the barefoot children in the Iraq hospitals. You can murmur, "I'm sorry, I'm so sorry," but how can you ever restore to people what they've lost? And yet, you *do* bear a big responsibility, because you've been there, and you *are* a witness. To Iraq and to the prisons. I have some teaching capacity that other prisoners won't have. So I have a big responsibility.

Ro: How do you decide what to do, what to teach about?

Kathy: You know, I'm really grateful for audiences that sort of nurture me into figuring that out. Some people say I'm only preaching to the choir, but I find that it's by being with the choir, particularly when I'm coming back from Iraq or coming out of prison, that I get to know the dynamic of the teachable moments, the teachable stories, if you will. I kind of feel like I'm just the piano.

Every person who enters into a circle that resists our culture of war and consumption does what they can, but everybody should do something. I think that's the bottom line. What each person will choose to do will be quite different, but if everybody does *something*, maybe—and it's a big maybe—maybe there's a chance that human life on this planet can survive. I'm not at all sure of that. I don't think right now that we're going to be able to create the revolutionary socialism that's needed—a nonviolent one, in my book.

Nevertheless, I think we still can try to live differently and encourage others to live differently and not to see ourselves as being trapped by "the system." The system itself is a huge prison that everybody sort of . . . I can't believe how obedient people are in this society, you know. As they plan their weddings! As they plan their children's education, as they plan their housing. People just obey, obey, obey. Obey dictates that are ridiculous and that don't make them very happy, either. To resist that, I think it's a very good exercise to go up against the so-called criminal justice system and say, "You think I'm a criminal? Well, I'm not going to accept that."

Camilo Mejia said as he was leaving military prison in 2005, "I was a coward not for leaving the war but for being part of it in the first place."[9] Camilo had served most of a one-year prison term after having his request for CO status denied and being convicted of desertion. He was the first peace resister who had served in Iraq.[10]

Camilo Mejia

> *"I'd been against the war from the beginning, yet I didn't act upon my conscience. I didn't do what I should have done."*

I joined the military in part because of the college tuition benefit, but I think . . . uh, mostly because it was a difficult time in my life. I really needed to have a sense of belonging and camaraderie, and the army seemed like the perfect place to get that. I served for almost eight years and was slated to get out in May of 2003. That January, though, I was stop-lossed and extended until the year 2013 with a minimum three-year activation. A couple of months later I was deployed to the Middle East and then two months after that, to Iraq.

I was a staff sergeant in an infantry unit for the Florida National Guard. Stationed first at Baghdad International, then at Al Assad and Hadithah and then to Ar Ramadi. Our unit's first mission there was to run a POW camp and basically to sleep-deprive detainees. We created fear in their hearts through loud noises, depriving them of light, staging mock executions. Not letting them sleep for up to seventy-two hours. It basically amounted to torture. After that, our job was to do patrols and to enforce the curfew and to raid homes and buildings, to set up traffic control points, and to respond to any attacks by the Iraqi resistance.

I didn't question the concept of war itself at that time, but I'd been against the Iraq War from the very beginning. On a very political basis. I didn't buy into the whole weapons of mass destruction rationale or the Al Qaeda connections. But even though I was against it, the war was rarely discussed in my unit.

When I came home on leave, my questions were becoming more broad, and I was beginning to question the concept of war itself. A number of things on the ground made me reject it. I learned that much of what happens in a war really has next to nothing to do with the politics, but more with greed and personal ambition. Like commanders wanting to get promoted and lieutenants wanting to excel, and so going out of their way to arrest people and kill civilians.

For instance, we made ourselves predictable by following the same routes every day, doing the same missions over and over without changing anything, so we gave them all the information they needed to attack. All to try to get a promotion. We had leadership who'd been in the infantry for twenty-five years and had never seen combat, so in order for them to move up the ladder, they had to provoke and instigate firefights. Then they could say they'd killed so and so many insurgents and so and so many of their soldiers were killed or injured that day.

When I first came home I'd talk about this and about my feelings, but I was really afraid of the army, so I didn't do it openly. I gave underground interviews under a fake name. I came home in October of '03 and didn't go back at the end of my two-weeks leave. Instead, I lived underground until I surrendered in March of '04. That was hard, even though my family and friends supported me. On the one hand, I was dealing with the guilt of not going back to my unit. I didn't want to be rejected by my peers and I didn't want them to feel that I had abandoned them. On the other hand, I knew I shouldn't be running and hiding from the military. I didn't go back because *we* were committing crimes, because we were torturing people and killing civilians. I'm not the criminal here. So there were those contradictions.

[Camilo didn't think he could get CO status at first, because he'd served in combat. He finally applied for it at the same time he surrendered.]

Camilo: The CO is something that I felt I had to do, whether it helped with my criminal prosecution or not. For one thing, it might help convince people in the military that they can do the same thing, that they don't have to witness and participate in the commission of war crimes. In fact, you have a *duty* not to commit war crimes. It says, "You have a conscience and the CO procedure can help you get out, so apply for it."

I was born Catholic, you know, and in applying for the CO my religious background might have helped me in my position, but in essence I think it deals more with the humanity in each of us, whether you're Catholic or Protestant or Buddhist or Muslim. My parents taught me that, too. (My mother was a Costa Rican national who was involved with the Sandinista movement to overthrow the Somoza dictatorship in Nicaragua. We lived in Nicaragua during the eighties, through the entire period of the revolution, and then moved to Costa Rica and then to Miami.) The things that turned me into a conscientious objector apply to anyone who follows their conscience.

While I was underground, I knew what was happening in Iraq needed to be told. The media . . . They were saying that the morale of the soldiers was high, and actually it was very low. We were oppressing the people of Iraq, raiding homes and arresting people and basically disappearing them without due process into the network of military jails. For the media here to say that we're doing all these great things and are happy to be there . . . I . . . I felt I had to speak out, had to undo some of the damage we'd done in Iraq.

An organization called Citizen Soldier helped me tremendously. Tod Ensign there knew a number of attorneys who understand GIs in a court of law. My lead counsel, Louis Font, had been a conscientious objector and war resister in the Vietnam War. Other organizations helped, too, particularly toward the end of my underground period, when I became more public. One of them was Lewis Randa from the Peace Abbey in Boston where I surrendered. I believe they told people from Amnesty International about my case, and Amnesty put out an alert when I was court-martialed and then declared me a prisoner of conscience when I was convicted.

The military trial was really something. They restricted entry to the base and barricaded the entire block around the courthouse, with military police patrolling the area. Partly, I guess, because they knew a lot of people were coming to support me, and partly to give the impression that I'm some hardcore criminal, you know, who needs to be guarded.

Ro: And yet you turned yourself in.

Camilo: I turned myself in three times! When I first surrendered to a military base, they basically didn't know what to do with me, so they just verified my unit and gave me a plane ticket. I surrendered the second time to my unit, and they gave me

Sergeant Camilo Mejia looking at a gravestone commemorating civilian casualties, Peace Abbey, Sherborn, Massachusetts, 2004. (Photo courtesy of Norma Castillo.)

a direct order to report to an active duty base, the one where I was later tried. On my own, I again surrendered a third time, so obviously I wasn't a flight risk. Yet they went out of their way to put up all this security.

Ro: What was the actual trial like? Were you able to speak your piece?

Camilo: Not really. I was . . . it was pretty fraudulent from the beginning, I think. Military trials have a 98 percent conviction rate. They're basically a way to enforce discipline. You're guilty until proven guilty and you can't do anything about it. During the pretrial motions, they effectively struck down all our witnesses and all the meaningful defense arguments and kept out all our evidence so we were basically crippled. After three days of trial, with only twenty minutes of deliberation, they convicted me and sent me to jail for a year.

All during the trial, it felt like we were just going through the motions of justice. For instance, right after the sentence, my mother and an army friend of mine went to my barracks room to get my things, and they'd already packed everything up and had wiped my room clean. Now, there was no way they would've had time to take all my belongings away unless they knew ahead of time that I was going to jail. So . . .

I went to Fort Sill, Oklahoma, which is a medium security jail with only 120 inmates. No COs there and not very many deserters. Most were thieves, some were child molesters, some murderers, some sexual predators. For me, prison was an essentially good experience. I'd been through a lot of stress, you know, with the underground period when I was doing all those interviews with a fake name. And then the media attention after my surrendering, and the lawyers and the judges and all the pressure from everywhere . . . After that, being in jail was peaceful.[11] I was able to think and reorganize my thoughts and get in touch with my feelings. I kept a prison journal and wrote acceptance speeches for a couple of awards I received.[12] I could communicate with my attorney, and family members and friends came to visit me, including even my daughter once.

I didn't have to serve the whole year. Getting out three months before the end of the sentence is standard procedure; if you're well behaved, they give you time off on good conduct. Then you're able to earn more time off by doing extra work and stuff like that. For the most part, I was a pretty peaceful, nonproblematic inmate. (Well, maybe problematic in a political way, but not in a behavioral way.)

A couple months after I got out, I started my book and began to work here in Miami with veterans who suffer from trauma.[13] People tell me that I provide a good point of reference, that I did something that they wanted to do but couldn't because they were too afraid. And I understand that because I was, too. In fact, that was the worst part—overcoming my fear of what would happen. Because I'd been against the war from the beginning, yet I didn't act upon what my conscience. I didn't do what I should have done. But now, I'm able to say that I'm the master of my own destiny. I make my own decisions, and I have to follow the dictates of my conscience, whatever the consequences.

EPILOGUE

It was the winter of 2003. The voice of the people had not been heard in the land and Baghdad had been bombed and occupied. Shivering in the Michigan cold, Saginaw resisters continued to vigil—night and day for over a week—braving the newly vociferous flag-wavers to say, "Not in our name. We continue to resist." One of our group, Morgan Guyton, wrote:

Winter Begins

It does no good to scream;
with one wet syllable,
winter can white out your words.

"Move! Move!"
The ghost baton
finds all the skin
that it needs.

"War's not worth the weight of sleet,"
shrug the trees.
"Just drop your leaves and go."
The wind will not negotiate;

The wind will not negotiate;
it speaks through a bullhorn:
"Don't stop; don't look at me;
do you want your eyes to bleed?"

The snarls of ice-dogs
slice through thickets
of squatting families.

The panic bells are drawn
and bugles begin
to carpet the landscape.

A million trembling hands
fiddle with new uniforms;
the march begins—

Snow too thick for horizons,
steps too quick to leave footprints,
hands concealed,
eyes only on the boots ahead.

If only the snowdrifts held their history . . .
If only we had a compass . . .
"We need a fire!" somebody shouts.

So you gather the forest's bones
into an altar;
from spittle and sneers,
the arms of a cedar
shield the young kindling.

Yes, you blow
through cracks too small for *No*,
and soon a new mother
has laid her first coals.

In time, the young furnace
gains a voice.
Other fire-starters
signal you through the god.

A crowd has gathered—
watching till we're warm enough to sing;
singing till we're soft enough to cry.

As courage opens our lungs,
we shout over the blizzard;
more people stop.

Winter screams over louder,
lashing the legs of the curious:
"Move along! Just move along now!"

But now our forest blaze
has stopped the flow of traffic,
Our bodies form a barricade,
for which winter reads us our consequences:

We will get sprayed
till the frost holds open our eyes;
our ears will bleed;
our lips will seal shut;
we may lose fingers.

But if we all stand close enough
and cover the hope with our hands,
if our smiles become mirrors
and our eyes become torches,

if we wipe each other's cheeks
and tie our sweaters together,

Then we can refuse to march this winter.[1]

"Tie our sweaters together." I've never forgotten that line. If I've learned a lesson in compiling this book, it's that only in community can we continue to work, to hope, to fight the fear that causes a disabling cynicism, to continue to pull at the taproot of violence. So find a community or create your own. Find sweaters to tie together as you continue the work.

AFTERWORD

Law does not equal justice. The people in this book stood up for gigantic justice issues and were jailed for violating small laws. They are not as famous as Martin Luther King Jr., Susan B. Anthony, Dietrich Bonhoeffer, or Gandhi, but they stand squarely in the same historical tradition—people who were jailed for trying to stop injustice. Whether they describe their actions as civil resistance or civil disobedience, the people in this book will be raised up for centuries whenever people of conscience search for those who resisted the gross injustices of our time.

I helped some of these fine people try to make the legal system open up to deal with the injustices they challenged. But the gap between law and justice was unable to be bridged in court. Despite their inspiring actions, they paid the price of prison for their beliefs.

The United States has a long tradition of people risking jail to take action highlighting injustices. Many women seeking the right to vote, untold numbers of workers fighting for the right to form unions, and thousands of African Americans struggling for civil rights were jailed in their campaigns for justice.

As I write this in the fall of 2011, thousands have been arrested just since President Obama was elected, protesting against the injustices of Guantanamo, nuclear weapons, the tar sands pipeline, police brutality, the many wars the United States is engaged in, mountaintop removal by coal companies, human rights violations by our military, illegal roundups of undocumented families, Wall Street economic injustices, and immigration and deportation policies.

The people in this book resist the powers of death with courage and determination. Each paid a real price for their stand. Our political and legal systems were unable to respond to their cries for justice, so they were arrested, tried, convicted, and jailed for months, sometimes even for years.

Dozens speak about how and why they challenged war, nuclear weapons, and gross human rights violations. Mothers, fathers, priests, religious sisters, married couples, and singles, each spent considerable time in prison.

We must ask ourselves: why were these people jailed when they acted for peace? National and international laws are violated repeatedly in the cause of war. Why are there no presidents in jail? No generals? No secretaries of state or defense? No war profiteers? Why just these people acting for peace?

Despite the years in jail, these are stories of hope. St. Augustine told us that hope has two beautiful daughters, anger and courage. Anger at the way things are and the courage to do something about it. The hope of the people in this book give us all reason to think more deeply about what we can do for justice and peace and the courage to do something about it.

I end with a poem I wrote when a friend went to prison because of an act of conscience.

Yesterday My Friend Chose Prison

Yesterday my friend walked freely into prison
chose to violate a simple law to spotlight the evil
of death squads and villages of massacred people that we cannot even name
mothers and children and grandparents butchered buried
and forgotten by most, but not by my friend

Yesterday my friend stepped away from loves and family and friends
was systematically stripped of everything, everything
and systematically searched everywhere, everywhere
was systematically numbered and uniformed and advised and warned
clothes and underwear and shoes and everything put in a cardboard box,
taped and mailed away

Yesterday my friend joined the people we put in the concrete and steel boxes
mothers and children and fathers that we cannot even name
in prison for using and selling drugs
in prison for trying to sneak into this country
in prison for stealing and scamming and fighting and killing
but none were there for the massacres
no generals, no politicians, no under-secretaries, no ambassador

Yesterday my friend had on a brave face
avoiding too much eye contact with the stares of hundreds of strangers
convicts, prisoners, guards, snitches
not yet knowing good from bad
staying out of people's business
hoping to find a small pocket of safety and kindness and trust in the
weeks ahead

Last night my friend climbed into bed in prison
an arm's length away from the other prisoners

laying awake on the thin mattress
wondering who had slept there last
wondering how loved ones were sleeping
awake through flashlight bed checks
and never-ending noises echoing off the concrete floors and walls
some you never ever want to hear

Yesterday my friend chose prison over silence
chose to stand with the disappeared and those who never counted
chose to spend months inside hoping to change us outside
chose the chance to speak truth to power and power responded with prison

Though my heart aches for my friend in prison
no one on this planet is more free.

—Bill Quigley
Loyola University New Orleans, College of Law

APPENDIX A

Brief Biographies of the Narrators

Does not include biographies of those whose older interviews appear in
"Roundtable on Resistance" that concludes Chapter 4.

Genevieve (Mickey) Allen (1919–2008)   The late Mickey Allen was an army
nurse in Italy during World War II. After raising nine children, she became a peace
activist with Pax Christi and the Hartford Catholic Worker (CW). Her first arrest
was at age sixty-five. "Grandma Mickey" became a favorite with the arresting officers, but not with her old friends from the local parish. She told me she wanted her
tombstone to say, "Here lies Mickey. She did her damnedest."

Teri Allen   One of Mickey Allen's daughters, Teri is married with small children.
As she reminded me, she has the luxury of bowing out of public life when conditions work against her responding. "People in war-torn countries don't have that.
The women in Iraq with their babies, they're in the same spot every single day,
always dealing with the reality of war." A multimedia artist, her altered billboards
call the people of New Haven to new understandings.

Chris Allen-Doucot   Chris is Jackie Allen-Doucot's husband and a frequent public speaker for the Hartford CW. Deeply thoughtful and articulate, he's sometimes
able to persuade the judge in favor of clemency for nonviolent protest, even once
for pouring blood on a federal building. He has faced death both in Darfur and on
the streets of New Haven, but doesn't let fear stop him.

Jackie Allen-Doucot   One of Mickey Allen's daughters, Jackie participated in
the Griffiss Plowshares action in 1983 when she was only twenty. After her second
Plowshares action, she married Chris Doucot and together they founded the Hartford CW. They have two children, Micah and Ammon.

Micah Allen-Doucot   Micah started going to protests in a stroller. When he was
twelve, he traveled to the Sudan with his father, Chris, delivering food and soccer
balls to a refugee camp. He says he wants to live in a Catholic Worker house when
he grows up.

Steve Baggarly and Kim Williams   Steve and Kim are one of many couples who
learned to live resistance at the Los Angeles CW. Now they and their two boys have
a house of hospitality in Norfolk, Virginia, one of the most heavily militarized cities
in the world. Steve often spends months behind bars, but their interview shows that
stay-at-home mom Kim does the hardest time.

Father Dan Berrigan, SJ   Dan was born in 1921 and ordained a Jesuit in 1952. Radicalized by his brother, Phil, during the Vietnam era, he participated in the second draft board raid and then thwarted the FBI for months by going underground after his sentencing. A poet and a pastor to the nonviolent peace movement, he continues to critique US warmaking.

Frida Berrigan   Frida graduated from Hampshire College in Amherst, Massachusetts. Recently married to Patrick Sheehan-Gaumer, she is active with the War Resisters League and in the campaign to close the prison for suspected terrorists at Guantanamo.

Jerry Berrigan   Several years after graduating from Kalamazoo College in Michigan, Jerry and his wife, Molly Mechtenberg, started the Kalamazoo Quaker CW, with their friends Jen and Mike DeWaele. The two couples and their several children provide tutoring, after-school mentoring, and a safe outdoor play area for neighborhood children in their East Side community.

Kate Berrigan   After graduating from Oberlin, Kate moved to Oakland, California, where she works with adults who have developmental disabilities and is preparing for graduate school in physical therapy.

Willa Bickham   In 1968, Willa and her husband, Brendan Walsh, started Viva House Catholic Worker in Baltimore. An artist and a pediatric nurse, Willa has long supported resistance work, particularly by providing hospitality to activists.

Darla Bradley   Darla was the youngest member of the 1986 Silo Plowshares action. She was sentenced to eight years plus five years probation and $1,680 restitution. Darla told me in 1989 of her painful decision to pay the restitution. In 2007, when I was collecting material for this book, she e-mailed a thoughtful postscript.

Dan Burns   Offspring of a political family in upstate New York, Dan led a fast life in the film industry before coming to the Ithaca CW and a life of resistance. He's one of the St. Patrick's Four, the first resistance group to be prosecuted in federal court after the Iraq War started. Their state jury trial on a "criminal mischief" charge couldn't muster enough guilty votes for a verdict. A later federal felony trial saw their charges reduced but resulted in four-month incarcerations.

Joan Cavanagh   Joan's been an activist since high school. Today she's the New England staffer for the War Resisters League.

Mark Colville   Mark and his wife, Luz, founded the Amistad CW in New Haven, Connecticut. They feel Mark has an obligation as a father to do serious resistance, which has included two Plowshares actions, a dramatic action against Blackwater in North Carolina, and an attempt to bring medical supplies into Gaza.

Frances Crowe   While Frances and her radiologist husband raised their children in Northampton, Massachusetts, she worked for the American Friends Service Committee (AFSC) in the basement of their home. A draft counselor during the Vietnam War, a community activist, and a tax resister, she's in her nineties now and still going strong.

Annette (Nettie) Cullen   Nettie is a registered nurse and the mother of twelve. She speaks poignantly about the challenges of marriage to a Vietnam activist.

Michael Cullen   Cofounder of Casa Maria CW in Milwaukee, Mike was an enthusiastic and compelling sixties activist who inspired others across the country. After his prison term for the Milwaukee Fourteen draft board raid, he and his family were deported to Ireland. They weren't able to return to the States until 1991. Eventually he and Nettie settled in Barron, Wisconsin, where Mike serves as a deacon.

Father John Dear, SJ   A Jesuit who writes about resistance and practices what he preaches, John was most recently on trial for protesting the unmanned drones that fly out of Creech Air Force Base.

Jim and Shelley Douglass   Jim and Shelley were among the founders of Ground Zero in Poulsbo, Washington. They now serve families at Mary's House CW in Birmingham, Alabama. Jim's a prolific writer, with *The Nonviolent Cross* frequently mentioned as a source for faith-based activists. A recent book is *Gandhi and the Unspeakable: His Final Experiment with Truth*.

Steve Downs   Since the interview, Steve has retired from his position on the New York Commission on Judicial Misconduct. Working with Project SALAM and the National Coalition to Protect Civil Freedoms, he speaks throughout the country on issues of pre-emptive prosecution.

Robert Ellsberg   Influenced by helping his father, Dan Ellsberg, copy the Pentagon Papers, but forging his own way, Robert left Harvard for several years and became one of the last of the young men mentored by Catholic Worker cofounder Dorothy Day. He participated in actions with Clamshell, an antinuclear alliance in New England, and at Rocky Flats in Colorado. Today he's publisher of Orbis Books and has edited Day's diaries and letters for Marquette University Press.

Jim Forest   Jim was a member of the Milwaukee Fourteen draft file burning. A prolific writer, he now lives in the Netherlands but frequently travels to the States to speak on topics such as Dorothy Day, Thomas Merton, iconography, and the Orthodox Peace Fellowship, which he founded.

Paul Gallagher   Paul studied to become a lawyer but became a member of the St. Jude CW instead. I spoke with him just hours before his first trial, where he faced six months in prison for "crossing the line" at Offutt Air Force Base near Omaha.

Sister Carol Gilbert, OP   Carol is the youngest of the Dominican triumvirate imprisoned for the 2002 Sacred Earth and Space Plowshares II action in Colorado. Earlier work with Sister Ardeth Platte in Saginaw, Michigan, precipitated a move close to two SAC [Strategic Air Command] bases, where they vigiled and protested until the bases closed. Then they joined the Jonah House community in Baltimore.

Mike Giocondo   Mike was a key member of the Camden Twenty-Eight draft board raid in 1971. For years after the surprising trial and acquittal, Mike worked as a reporter for the *People's Daily World.*

Ana Grady Flores   Ana's the granddaughter of Theresa Grady and John Grady, the architect of the Camden Twenty-Eight draft board raid. She and her mother, Mary Anne, are active in the Ithaca CW. While still a minor, Ana was arrested and tried for an action at a Marine recruiting center during the build-up to the Iraq War.

Mary Anne Grady Flores   Mary Anne was one of John and Theresa Grady's children and vividly remembers the Vietnam protest times. She continues her peacework today by working with the Ithaca Catholic Worker and other peace groups in upstate New York. Her e-mail list helps to connect peace groups around the world.

Jean and Joe Gump   Jean and Joe were influenced by the Catholic Family Movement, taking its "Observe, Judge, and Act" to heart and working first against racism and then against militarism, with separate Plowshares actions at the Missouri missile sites when many of their twelve children were grown and married. They served overlapping sentences for these Plowshares actions, with Jean spending more than three years at Alderson.

Anne S. Hall   Anne is pastor of the Lutheran Church in the San Juans, a group of islands near Seattle. The mother of two grown sons, she and her husband, David, continue to be active in the Ground Zero Center for Nonviolent Action. At her first arrest, for sitting on the tracks as the White Train brought Trident components into the Kitsap naval base, she realized that "if everyone who was opposed to those weapons would sit on those tracks, there's no way the missiles could be put together."

Sister Jackie Hudson, OP (1934–2011)   Jackie knew she wanted to be a sister when she was in second grade and, like the women with whom she's often arrested, became a Grand Rapids Dominican. As a nun, she was also a teacher, a piano tuner, a private detective, and a county bus driver. Before her death, shortly after being released from jail for an action at the Oak Ridge nuclear weapons plant, Jackie lived and worked with her partner, Sue Ablao, at the Ground Zero Center for Nonviolent Action.

Becky Johnson   Becky graduated in environmental science from Oberlin College in Ohio and was in an affinity group there with Kate Berrigan. At the time of our interview, she was matriculated at Starr King School, part of the Graduate Theological Union in California.

Father Carl Kabat, OMI   Carl has spent upwards of fourteen years in prison for Plowshares and other actions. In 2009, again vested in his clown costume, he entered a Minuteman III nuclear missile silo in Colorado, hung banners, and then knelt and prayed. He told me he's never felt he fit into "the normal priesthood."

Tom Karlin   While he was in the navy, Tom worked at Bangor Naval Base. Years later he worked to prevent it from housing nuclear submarines. He and his second wife, Laura, are members of the extended community of the Tacoma CW.

Barb Kass, Mike Miles, and Ollie Miles   Barb and Mike founded Anathoth Peace Community in Wisconsin. In three separately recorded interviews, Barb, Mike, and Ollie talk honestly about the tensions when one member of a family—father Mike—takes a public jail-going stance, daughter Ollie grows up differently than her small-town peers, and mother Barb holds it all together.

Brian Kavanagh   Brian joined the Hartford CW in 1993 as one of its founding members. He's an artist who is often called upon to add names of the deceased to the house's "Cloud of Witnesses" cross.

Kathy Kelly   Now a forceful voice for world peace with Voices for Creative Nonviolence in Chicago, Kathy taught school before beginning her life in resistance. She's been imprisoned several times for nonviolent campaigns, including those of the Missouri Peace Planting and the School of the Americas Watch (SOAW). Kathy was in Baghdad as a peacekeeper during the Shock and Awe bombing campaign that began the Iraq War.

Ed Kinane   Ed's a career activist, with years of commitment to rural Africa, Peace Brigades International, SOAW, Voices in the Wilderness, Voices for Creative Nonviolence, and his local peace group, the Syracuse Peace Council. One of his contributions to the peace movement was a comprehensive training manual for protesters at the School of the Americas. He's married to Ann Tiffany.

Katya Komisaruk   Born in Detroit, with a post-prison law degree from Harvard, Katya concentrates her practice on human rights and the legal issues of civil disobedience. Her first arrest was in 1982, along with 1,400 others, protesting nuclear research at Lawrence Livermore Labs in California. After several years of intense activism, in 1987 she did a solitary Plowshares action at Vandenberg Air Force Base. She was sentenced to five years in prison but paroled after two years in what she describes as a record-keeping mistake.

Rae Kramer   Rae went to prison for an SOAW action when her sons were teenagers. She transformed the prison with the same humor and creativity she uses in her work with the Syracuse Peace Council and the Jewish Peace Fellowship.

John LaForge   John has long been on the staff of Nukewatch, a Wisconsin-based nuclear watchdog and environmental action group. He's served more than four years in jail or prison for nonviolent actions against nuclear weapons and the war system. In 1987, he and Barb Katt traveled to all one thousand of the US land-based intercontinental ballistic missile sites (ICBMs), completing research for the 1988 Nukewatch book, *Nuclear Heartland*.

Tom Lewis (1940–2008)   Tom was an artist and resister for his entire adult life, beginning with civil rights protests and the first two draft board actions. He worked closely with Baltimore's Viva House CW as well as the Mustard Seed in Worcester, Massachusetts, and spent more than four years in jail for resistance actions. When asked what sustained him, he said simply, "My faith and my art."

Father Tom Lumpkin   Father Tom is a priest in the Detroit archdiocese. He cofounded Day House CW in Detroit and was active in Michigan resistance during the eighties.

Brad Lyttle   Brad was born in 1927 and has lived much of his life in Hyde Park, Chicago. He started peacework in the 1950s, working first with American Friends Service Committee (AFSC) and then with the Committee for Non-Violent Action (CNVA). Brad organized several long peace walks, including one to Moscow. In 2010 he was arrested both at Creech Air Force Base, protesting the drones which fly from there to Afghanistan, and at Y-12, the nuclear weapons plant at Oak Ridge, Tennessee.

Andy Mager   Andy learned how to organize by resisting the current draft registration law and was one of the few sentenced to prison for refusing to register. Today he continues his activism in Syracuse, with one of his projects a group called Neighbors of the Onondaga Nation (NOON), which works to reclaim tribal lands.

Liz McAlister   Liz and her husband, Phil Berrigan, raised three children at Jonah House. Since her husband's death in 2002, she has continued as a mainstay of that community, planning and participating in Faith and Resistance Retreats and other actions.

Joan (Joni) McCoy   Joni became radicalized when her youngest was in high school. She protested at Wurtsmith Air Force Base in Oscoda, Michigan, and her convictions eventually ballooned into three months in federal prison. She has traveled three times to Palestine with the Michigan Peace Team. She's a leader in local peace groups and in 2011 coordinated a walk from Saginaw to the state capital as part of Michigan Moveable Peace.

Camilo Mejia   After serving in the military for almost eight years, Sergeant Mejia found he was unable to return to Iraq. He went to prison for almost a year after having his request for CO status denied and receiving a conviction as a deserter. Upon release, he worked for several years with Iraq Veterans Against the War.

Sister Anne Montgomery, RSCJ (1926–2012)   Born to a military family, Anne joined the Society of the Sacred Heart and began a life of peacework after teaching for several years. She took part in the first Plowshares action as well as six others, including the Disarm Now Plowshares in 2009 at the nuclear submarine base in Bangor, Washington. She also traveled to war zones with Christian Peacemaker Teams and would say that taking a risk "is what the religious orders were set up to do."

Harry Murray   Harry lived in several Catholic Worker communities before entering graduate school and writing a dissertation on Catholic Worker hospitality. Now he's a family man and civil resister who teaches sociology at Nazareth College in New York, and takes his students to vigils in DC and at the SOA in Columbus, Georgia.

Michele Naar-Obed   Michele and her husband, Greg, live with their daughter, Rachel, and others at the Duluth CW in Minnesota. As a member of the Christian Peacemaker Teams, she spends part of each year in the Kurdish north of Iraq. Like many other resisters, she sees this accompaniment work as important to her resistance life.

Hattie Nestel   Hattie raised her children in Brattleboro, Vermont. She's been a resister for years and still goes on long peace walks. A few years ago, Hattie walked eight hundred miles from the Oak Ridge National Laboratory in Tennessee to the UN building in Manhattan. The lab is reputed to enrich uranium and plutonium for nuclear weapons.

Sister Ardeth Platte, OP   During the Vietnam era, Ardeth protested the war while she was still wearing the habit of the Grand Rapids Dominican order. She directed Delta College's inner-city center in Saginaw, Michigan; served several terms on the city council; and then became a full-time peaceworker. She and Carol Gilbert founded the Home for Peace and Justice, and later moved to Oscoda and then to Michigan's Upper Peninsula, close to two SAC bases. When both bases were closed, the nuns moved to Jonah House in Baltimore and became Plowshares activists. Ardeth served forty-one months in prison for a 2002 Plowshares in Colorado and in 2010 was arrested at the Oak Ridge nuclear plant.

Bill Quigley   Bill is Riley Distinguished Professor of Law at Loyola University, New Orleans, where he also directs the Law Clinic and Gillis Long Poverty Law Center. He frequently contributes his services to represent or counsel activists on trial for nonviolent civil resistance.

Chuck Quilty   Chuck left his job at the Rock Island Arsenal to start a Catholic Worker house in Rock Island. In the 1990s, he worked with Voices in the Wilderness to end the UN sanctions against Iraq.

Kathleen Rumpf   Liz McAlister once dubbed Kathleen a "one-woman crime spree," and truly, she's been all over the country, protesting nuclear weapons, massacres by SOA graduates, and prison conditions in her town of Syracuse and at Carswell FCI.

Claire and Scott Schaeffer-Duffy   Claire and her husband, Scott, have been doing resistance together since before they opened Saints Francis and Thérèse CW in Worcester, Massachusetts. Their resistance takes different forms, including traveling to war zones and writing as well as imprisonment for peace actions. Their four children are now all teenagers or beyond.

Brian Terrell   Brian is a lifelong practitioner of nonviolent civil disobedience and frequently spends months at a time in jail or prison for protesting the Pentagon, STRATCOM, the prisoners kept at Guantanamo, the drones that target Afghan civilians, and other abuses of the military-industrial complex. His jail experiences complement the life he and his family lead on a small farm in lonely southwest Iowa, where they raise goats and vegetables, weave rugs, and make cheese and beer. Brian sees it all as resistance.

Ann Tiffany   Ann has a long and strong interest in Central American isues and has visited Colombia at least six times. She's married to Ed Kinane of Syracuse and together they make a good activist team. As a community health nurse, Ann had to report her arrests and convictions when renewing her license. Threatened with a letter saying she was guilty of "unprofessional conduct," she took her case to the New York Board of Regents and won!

Marcia Timmel   In the eighties, Marcia and her husband, Paul Magno, lived at Dorothy Day Catholic Worker in DC and then at the Olive Branch CW. She participated in two Plowshares actions, the second one a solitary action at an Arms Bazaar, a month after I interviewed her in August 1988.

Dick Von Korff   Born in 1916, Dick decided as a young man that war was foolish, and with the support of his wife, Jane, he refused to serve in World War II. He was sentenced to eighteen months in Sandstone Prison, although he was released on parole after six months. Then he finished his education with a PhD in chemistry and began a career that finally took him to the Michigan Molecular Institute in Midland. Dick was one of the few World War II resisters pardoned by President Truman.

Kim and Bill Wahl   The Wahls are a professional couple from Seattle who spent years resisting the deployment of Trident nuclear submarines at Bangor, Washington. Kim was part of the flotilla of small boats that met the first sub as it came into the Oak Canal. Bill joined her in resisting the haunting White Train, which carried nuclear ammunition from Pantex to the Bangor naval base.

Judith Williams   Judith is a member of the Catholic Worker community in Waukesha, Wisconsin, where they have an ongoing peace vigil. She is a jail minister and has been arrested as a resister many times over the years, both here and in Honduras.

Robert (Bob) Wollheim   As a student at Reed College during the Vietnam War, Bob refused induction into the armed forces and was sentenced to federal prison. Later, he went to law school. He was admitted to the Oregon bar in 1983 and became a judge on the state court of appeals in 1998.

Lenore Yarger and Steve Woolford   Lenore and Steve lived at the Rock Island CW with the late Chuck Trapkus, before founding a similar community in North Carolina. The consistency of their lives is a tribute to his spirit; the optimism with which they face the future speaks with hope to his frustration. Steve first went to prison before the birth of their daughter, Geneva.

APPENDIX B

For Further Reading

Ackerman, Peter, and Jack Duvall. *A Force More Powerful: A Century of Nonviolent Conflict*. New York: Palgrave, 2000.

Adams, Judith Porter. *Peacework: Oral Histories of Women Peace Activists*. New York: Macmillan, 1999.

Alpert, Rebecca T., ed. *Voices of the Religious Left: A Contemporary Sourcebook*. Philadelphia: Temple University Press, 2000.

Appelbaum, Patricia. *Kingdom to Commune: Protestant Pacifist Culture between World War I and the Vietnam Era*. Chapel Hill: University of North Carolina Press, 2009.

Berrigan, Daniel. *And The Risen Bread: Selected and New Poems 1957–1997*, 2nd ed. New York: Fordham University Press, 2008.

———. *The Trial of the Catonsville Nine*, 4th ed. New York: Fordham University Press, 2004.

Berrigan, Philip. *Fighting the Lamb's War*. Monroe, ME: Common Courage Press, 1996.

Boyle, Francis. *Defending Civil Resistance under International Law*. Dobbs Ferry, NY: Transnational, 1987.

Brock, Peter, and Nigel Young. *Pacifism in the Twentieth Century*. Syracuse, NY: Syracuse University Press, 1999.

Chernus, Ira. *American Nonviolence: The History of An Idea*. Maryknoll, NY: Orbis, 2004.

Cooney, Robert, and Helen Michalowski, ed. *The Power of the People: Active Nonviolence in the United States*. Philadelphia, PA: New Society Publishers, 1987.

Day, Samuel H., Jr., ed. *Prisoners on Purpose: A Peacemakers' Guide to Jails and Prisons*. Madison, WI: Nukewatch, 1989.

Dear, John. *Peace behind Bars*. Kansas City: Sheed and Ward, 1995.

———. *Put Down Your Sword: Answering the Gospel Call to Creative Nonviolence*. Grand Rapids, MI: Eerdmans Publishing, 2008.

DeBenedetti, Charles. *An American Ordeal: The Antiwar Movement of the Vietnam War*. Syracuse, NY: Syracuse University Press, 1990.

Douglass, James W. *The Non-Violent Cross: A Theology of Revolution and Peace*. Eugene, OR: Wipf and Stock Publishers, 2006. First published 1968.

Elmer, Jerry. *Felon for Peace: The Memoir of a Vietnam-Era Draft Resister*. Nashville, TN: Vanderbilt University Press, 2005.

Epstein, Barbara. *Political Protest and Cultural Revolution: Nonviolent Direct Action in the 1970s and 1980s*. Berkeley: University of California Press, 1991.

Foley, Michael S. *Confronting the War Machine: Draft Resistance during the Vietnam War*. Chapel Hill: University of North Carolina Press, 2003.

Frisch, Michael. *A Shared Authority: Essays on the Craft and Meaning of Oral and Public History*. SUNY Series in Oral and Public History. Albany, NY: SUNY Press, 1990.

Kelly, Kathy. *Other Lands Have Dreams: From Baghdad to Pekin Prison*. Oakland, CA: AK Press, 2005.

Kisseloff, Jeff. *Generation on Fire: Voices of Protest from the 1960s*. Lexington: University Press of Kentucky, 2007.

Komisaruk, Katya. *Beat the Heat: How to Handle Encounters with Law Enforcement*. Oakland, CA: AK Press, 2004.

Kosek, Joseph. *Acts of Conscience: Christian Nonviolence and Modern American Democracy*. New York: Columbia University Press, 2009.

Kurlansky, Mark. *Nonviolence: The History of a Dangerous Idea*. New York: Random House Modern Library, 2008

Laffin, Arthur J., ed. *Swords into Plowshares: A Chronology of Plowshares Disarmament Actions, 1980–2003*. Washington, DC: Rose Hill Books, 2003.

Lynd, Staughton. *Nonviolence in America: A Documentary History*. Rev. ed. Maryknoll, NY: Orbis, 1995.

Masse, Mark H. *Inspired to Serve: Today's Faith Activists*. Bloomington: Indiana University Press, 2004.

McCarthy, Colman. *All of One Peace: Essays on Nonviolence*. East Brunswick, NJ: Rutgers University Press, 1994.

McCarthy, Ronald M., and Eugene Sharp. *Nonviolent Action: A Research Guide*. New York: Garland Press, 1997.

Meconis, Charles. *With Clumsy Grace: The American Catholic Left, 1961–1975*. New York: Seabury Press, 1979.

Mejia, Camilo. *Road from Ar Ramadi: The Private Reflections of Staff Sergeant Camilo Mejia*. New York: New Press, 2008.

Nepstad, Sharon Erickson. *Religion and War Resistance in the Plowshares Movement*. New York: Cambridge University Press, 2007.

Norman, Liane Ellison. *Hammer of Justice: Molly Rush and the Plowshares Eight*. Pittsburgh: PPI Books, 1989.

O'Gorman, Angie, ed. *The Universe Bends toward Justice: A Reader on Christian Nonviolence in the U.S.* Philadelphia: New Society, 1990.

Polner, Murray, and Jim O'Grady. *Disarmed and Dangerous: The Radical Lives and Times of Daniel and Philip Berrigan*. New York: Basic Books, 1997.

Schell, Jonathan. *The Unconquerable World: Power, Nonviolence, and the Will of the People*. New York: Henry Holt, 2003.

Sharp, Eugene. *Waging Nonviolent Struggle: 20th Century Practice and 21st Century Potential*. New York: Porter Sargent Publishing, 2005.

Smith, Christian, ed. *Disruptive Religion: The Force of Faith in Social Movement Activism*. New York: Routledge, 1996.

Solnit, Rebecca. *Hope in the Dark: Untold Histories, Wild Possibilities*. New York: Nation Books, 2005.

Tracy, James. *Direct Action: Radical Pacifism from the Union Eight to the Chicago Seven*. Chicago: University of Chicago Press, 1996.

Wilcox, Fred, ed. *Disciples and Dissidents: Prison Writings of the Prince of Peace Plowshares*. Athol, MA: Haley's, 2001.

———. *Uncommon Martyrs: The Berrigans, the Catholic Left, and the Plowshares Movement*. Reading, MA: Addison-Wesley, 1991.

Zinn, Howard. *A People's History of the United States*. New York: HarperCollins, 1980.

———. Introduction to *The Power of Nonviolence: Writings by Advocates of Peace*. Boston: Beacon Press, 2002.

Prison Conditions

Alexander, Michelle. *The New Jim Crow: Mass Incarceration in the Age of Colorblindness*. New York: New Press, 2009.

Christianson, Scott. *With Liberty for Some: Five Hundred Years of Imprisonment in America*. Boston: Northeastern University Press, 1998.

Churchill, Ward, and J. J. Vander Wall, eds. *Cages of Steel: The Politics of Imprisonment in the United States*. Washington, DC: Maisonneuve Press, 1992.

Drucker, Ernest. *A Plague of Prisons: The Epidemiology of Mass Incarceration in America*. New York: New Press, 2010.

Dwyer, Joel. *The Perpetual Prisoner Machine: How America Profits from Crime*. Boulder, CO: Westview Press, 2000.

Elsner, Alan. *Gates of Injustice: The Crisis in America's Prisons*. Saddle River, NJ: Prentice Hall, 2006.

Parenti, Christian. *Lockdown America: Police and Prisons in the Age of Crisis*. New York: Verso, 1999.

Rathbone, Cristina. *A World Apart: Women, Prison, and Life behind Bars*. New York: Random House, 2006.

Talva, Silja. *Women behind Bars: The Crisis of Women in the U.S. Prison System*. Berkeley, CA: Seal Press, 2007.

NOTES

Preface

1. Jim Wallis, "From Protest to Resistance," *Sojourners* 13, no. 2 (1984): 4.
2. According to the United States Strategic Command website (*www.stratcom.mil*), "USSTRATCOM combines the synergy of the US legacy nuclear command and control mission with responsibility for space operations; global strike; Defense Department information operations; global missile defense; and global command, control, communications, computers, intelligence, surveillance and reconnaissance (C4ISR), and combating weapons of mass destruction."
3. My first oral history was *Voices from the Catholic Worker* (Philadelphia: Temple University Press, 1993), published under Rosalie Riegle Troester, and hereafter cited as *Voices*. My second was *Dorothy Day: Portraits by Those Who Knew Her* (Maryknoll, NY: Orbis, 2003).
4. Stephen Kobasa, interview, Catholic Worker Archives, Raynor Library, Marquette University, Milwaukee, WI (hereafter cited as Marquette Archives).

Introduction

1. Some illuminating overviews of nonviolence and war resistance in the United States include Staughton and Alice Lynd, *Nonviolence in America* (Maryknoll, NY: Orbis, 1995); and Ira Chernus, *American Nonviolence: The History of an Idea* (Maryknoll, NY: Orbis, 2004). For a broader history of religion and radicalism, see Dan McKanan, *Prophetic Encounters: Religion and the American Radical Tradition* (Boston: Beacon, 2011).
2. Richard Francis, *Fruitlands: The Alcott Family and Their Search for Utopia* (New Haven, CT: Yale University Press, 2010).
3. Helpful studies of nonviolent resistance in the nineteenth century include Peter Brock, *Freedom from War: Nonsectarian Pacifism, 1814-1914* (Toronto: University of Toronto Press, 1991); Carleton Mabee, *Black Freedom: The Nonviolent Abolitionists from 1830 through the Civil War* (New York: Macmillan, 1970); Dan McKanan, *Identifying the Image of God: Radical Christians and Nonviolent Power in the Antebellum United States* (New York: Oxford, 2002); and Valarie Ziegler, *The Advocates of Peace in Antebellum America* (Bloomington: Indiana University Press, 1992).
4. Illuminating studies of American nonviolence from World War I to the 1960s include Patricia Appelbaum, *Kingdom to Commune: Protestant Pacifist Culture between World War I and the Vietnam Era* (Chapel Hill: University of North Carolina Press, 2009); Scott H. Bennett, *Radical Pacifism: The War Resisters League and Gandhian Nonviolence in America, 1915–1963* (Syracuse: Syracuse University Press, 2003); Anne Klejment and Nancy L. Roberts, ed., *American Catholic Paci-*

fism: The Influence of Dorothy Day and the Catholic Worker Movement (Westport, CT: Praeger Publishers, 1996); Kip Kosek, *Acts of Conscience: Christian Nonviolence and Modern American Democracy* (New York: Columbia University Press, 2009); Marian Mollin, *Radical Pacifism in Modern America: Egalitarianism and Protest* (Philadelphia: University of Pennsylvania Press, 2006); Murray Polner, *Disarmed and Dangerous: The Radical Lives and Times of Daniel and Philip Berrigan* (New York: Basic Books, 1997); James Tracy, *Direct Action: Radical Pacifism from the Union Eight to the Chicago Seven* (Chicago: University of Chicago Press, 1996); and Walter Wink, ed., *Peace Is the Way: Writings on Nonviolence from the Fellowship of Reconciliation* (Maryknoll, NY: Orbis, 2000).

Chapter 1

1. For the brief summary of twentieth-century peace activism in this chapter, I am indebted to *The Power of the People: Active Nonviolence in the United States,* edited by Robert Cooney and Helen Michalowski from an original text by Marty Jezur (Philadelphia: New Society, 1987). This profusely illustrated book chronicles in great detail nonviolent activism from 1650 through the early 1980s.
2. Ibid., 92.
3. Ibid., 95.
4. Schulz was the executive director of Amnesty International USA from 1994 to 2006.
5. Von Korff was lucky. Only selected CO resisters were pardoned, with 90 percent having a felony conviction on their records (Cooney and Michalowski, 111).
6. "Atomic Bomb," *Catholic Worker,* November 1945, 2. While the article is unsigned, the phrasing echoes Dorothy Day's sentiments in "We Go on Record" in the September 1945 *Catholic Worker.*
7. The 1949 Alien Registration Act, commonly known as the Smith Act, made it illegal to advocate overthrowing the government by force. It was used against political organizations on the left.
8. The "Velvet Revolution" is the name given to the nonviolent events in the fall of 1989 that caused the Czechoslovakian Communist government to fall (*www. prague-life.com/prague/velvet-revolution*). Other Eastern bloc countries also eventually gained their freedom from Communist rule, including Estonia with "The Singing Revolution" and Poland with the success of the Solidarity movement.
9. According to the National War Tax Resistance Coordinating Committee, war tax resistance is the "refusal to pay some or all of federal taxes that pay for war. While it is possible to legally refuse by lowering one's taxable income to zero, war tax resistance often involves an act of civil disobedience." During the Vietnam War, Brad organized over a million people in a low-risk action of not paying the federal telephone tax, which had been instituted to pay for past wars. Few were prosecuted. See *www.nwtrcc.org/what_is_wtr.php.*
10. Kathy Kelly, interview, Marquette Archives.
11. Oak Ridge Environmental Peace Alliance, "Day Five Sentencing: Steve Baggarly and Brad Lyttle," September 20, 2011, *www.orepa.org/ day-five-sentencing-steve-baggarly/*.
12. Cooney and Michalowski, 183.
13. Ibid., 184.
14. The National Lawyers Guild is a "non-profit federation of lawyers, legal workers,

and law students [who use] the law to advance social justice and support progressive social movements" (*www.nlg.org*).

15. Francine du Plessix Gray, "The Ultra-Resistance: On the Trial of the Milwaukee Fourteen," *New York Review of Books* 13, no. 5 (September 25, 1969). Also available at *www.jimandnancyforest.com*.

16. Ibid.

17. "Fire and Faith: The Catonsville Nine File" (*c9.mdch.org*), a website maintained by the Enoch Pratt Library of Baltimore, contains photos, primary documents, and an extensive bibliography on the action.

18. Portions of this narrative were published in a different form in *Voices*, 42–46 and 215–16.

19. Joe Tropea writes that the "openly hostile" Judge Edward Northrop sentenced Lewis and Berrigan to six years in prison, with Eberhardt receiving three years and Mengel scheduled for sentencing but never sentenced ("Hit and Stay: The Baltimore Four and Catonsville Nine Actions Revisited," *Baltimore City Paper*, May 14, 2008, *www2.citypaper.com*). Tropea's essay provides excellent detail about both actions, although it sometimes conflicts with Tom's memories.

20. Dan Berrigan, statement at the trial. Reprinted at *www.tomjoad.org/catonsville9. htm* and other places. (*Added to interview by author.*)

21. Father Richard McSorley, SJ (1914–2002), was the founder of St. Francis Catholic Worker in Washington, DC, a prolific writer on nonviolence, and the director of peace studies at Georgetown University.

22. See Art Laffin, ed., *Swords into Plowshares: A Chronology of Plowshares Disarmament Actions, 1980–2003* (Washington, DC: Rose Hill Books, 2003), for descriptions of all Plowshares actions before 2003.

23. Marian Mollin, "Communities of Resistance: Women and the Catholic Left of the Late 1960s," *Oral History Review* 31, no. 2 (2004): 48.

24. Bob Graf, one of the Fourteen, maintains a website about the group at *www.nonviolentworm.org*.

25. For several years, Mike and Nettie ran a charismatic youth camp on the grounds of Clonfert, which was also the site of one of the most beautifully preserved of the Irish Romanesque twelfth-century cathedrals. His memories of the walk to Belfast can be found in Michael Cullen, interview, Marquette Archives.

26. Therese Cullen, interview, Marquette Archives.

27. Lakota Pine Ridge Indian Reservation in South Dakota has a national memorial to the 1890 Wounded Knee massacre. Michael might have traveled to the reservation in sympathy with Native Americans who were campaigning for compensation for the families of Wounded Knee victims and for other rights denied them by the US government.

28. The Catholic Charismatic Renewal is a movement within the Roman Catholic Church that features lively Masses and prayer meetings where one hears testimony of the gifts of the Holy Spirit, including the ability to heal and to pray in tongues. It's similar to the charismatic movement in mainline Protestant churches as well as in some Pentecostal churches. Michael continues to bring his gift of preaching to the Charismatic Renewal.

29. Devlin was a Catholic socialist republican in Northern Ireland.

30. These interviews of Lewis, Quilty, and Timmel were conducted in 1989. Versions of these interviews were also printed in *Voices*, 210–11 and 308–10.

31. Jim Douglass, "Marriage and Celibacy," *Harmony: Voices for a Just Future* 1, no. 6 (1988): 26.

32. Laffin, 40.

33. Allan M. Jalon, "A Break-In to End All Break-ins," *Los Angeles Times*, March 8, 2006. Also available at *www.commondreams.org*.

34. Anthony Giacchino directed a documentary on the group in 2007. See *www.camden28.org*.

Chapter 2

1. Dan Berrigan, "Georgetown Poems (7): The Trouble With Our State," *And the Risen Bread: Selected Poems, 1957–1997* (New York: Fordham University Press, 1998), 239. "Less Than," *And the Risen Bread*, 393–94.

2. A similar passage occurs in Micah 4:3.

3. These retreats, with their speakers and liturgies and community-building, have provided models for similar retreats throughout the country.

4. Excerpt from "Count It All Joy," *Catholic Worker*, December 2010, 8.

5. "Eqbal was an unindicted coconspirator in the Harrisburg Conspiracy trial and a close friend of the family. He helped to orchestrate Dan Berrigan's time 'underground.'" (*Added by Frida at transcript review.*)

6. *Voices*, 183.

7. Kalamazoo College has an extensive program of student-designed experiential education, with frequent off-campus study.

Chapter 3

1. Laffin lists 150 such actions, including those called "disarmament actions" because they don't arise specifically from the Biblical prophecy (2). Others who keep count list ninety-three Plowshares actions as of August 2010, but Sister Ardeth Platte told me that number is also probably inaccurate, as it's hard to keep track of the European actions (e-mail to author, August 20, 2010).

2. In an interesting aside on the name "Plowshares," Irish writer Harry Browne told me: "I did a piece [on the Pitstop Plowshares] for the *Dublin Review*, and the editor changed the name to 'Shannon Five,' as did much of the media in Ireland. He had a particular sort of . . . uh, a pedant's problems with [the title] 'Plowshares' because, as far as he was concerned, they weren't the plowshares, they were the hammers. So maybe that's something the whole brand has to address" (interview, Marquette Archives).

3. See Sharon Erickson Nepstad, *Religion and War Resistance in the Plowshares Movement* (New York: Cambridge University Press, 2007).

4. Details from *GlobalSecurity.org*. The website says it's "the leading source for reliable news and security information" (*www.globalsecurity.org/wmd/agency/351mw.htm*). To find out where the remaining nuclear missiles are, see the Nukewatch site (*www.nukewatchinfo.org*), which says it presents "news and information on nuclear weapons, power, and waste, and nonviolent resistance."

5. *Voices*, 225.

6. Laffin, 2.

7. Laffin, e-mail to author, December 9, 2010.

8. Laffin, *Swords into Plowshares*, 14–15.

9. *Voices*, 223.

10. The six men were Dean Hammer, Elmer Maas, John Schuchardt, Phil Berrigan, Father Carl Kabat, and Father Dan Berrigan.

11. Laffin, *Swords into Plowshares*, 14.

12. The website of Christian Peacemaker Teams (*www.cpt.org*) says it is a group that "places teams at the invitation of local peacemaking communities that are confronting situations of lethal conflict. These teams seek to follow God's Spirit as it works through local peacemakers who risk injury and death by waging nonviolent direct action to confront systems of violence and oppression."

13. A longer version of this interview appears in *Voices*, 217–30.

14. "Tiger cages" were cramped cages where the South Vietnamese government housed political prisoners.

15. Since this interview, Griffiss Air Force Base has closed, and the site now houses an air force research park. Currently, upstate New York protesters are concentrating on the New York Air National Guard Base at Hancock Field. From there, MQ-9 Reaper drones fly over Afghanistan, armed with Hellfire missiles and laser-guided bombs.

16. An interview with LaForge that describes Nukewatch activities in detail is available online through the Minuteman Missile National Historic Site of the National Park Service, *www.nps.gov/mimi/historyculture/oral-histories.htm*.

17. Eighth Day Center for Justice (*www.8thdaycenter.org*) is a multi-issue social justice center in Chicago, supported and staffed by laity and thirty congregations of nuns, priests, and brothers.

18. It was 8:15 a.m. on August 6 in Japan when the bomb was dropped.

19. Father Jerry Zawada is a Franciscan priest and longtime activist now concentrating on Central American issues (Jerry Zawada, interview, Marquette Archives). Samuel H. Day Jr. (1926–2001) edited the *Progressive* for years; he was also a founder of Nukewatch and a creative Midwest activist who was frequently imprisoned for resistance actions. In 1989, he and Bonnie Urfer published *Prisoners on Purpose*, the story of the Missouri Peace Planting. It was a series of actions where participants climbed over or cut through fences, entered the nuclear missile sites, planted sunflowers, sang songs, hung banners, and waited for arrest. Sam served six months for these actions; others served shorter terms. See Martin Zellig, "If You're Considering Going to Jail . . ." (review of *Prisoners on Purpose*), *Peace Magazine*, February–March 1990, *archive.peacemagazine.org*.

20. Father Larry Morlan told me the divorce rate among prisoners is over 50 percent (interview, Marquette Archives).

21. A longer version of this interview is in *Voices*, 211–15.

22. At the time of the interview, Darla was still paying restitution.

23. Philip Berrigan, "Letter from a Baltimore Jail," in *American Religion: Literary Sources and Documents*, ed. David Turley (London: Routledge, 1998), 536.

24. Because he testified to that line in court and graphically showed how he saw Liz throw the blood in an arc on the wall, that particular trial resulted in a rare acquittal (Liz McAlister, interview, Marquette Archives).

25. John Dear, *Peace behind Bars: A Peacemaking Priest's Journey from Jail* (Kansas City: Sheed and Ward, 1996).

26. NAVSTAR is an air force global positioning system. Its satellites provide first-strike navigational guidance signals to nuclear submarines and missiles as well as to the Star Wars system.

27. Lawrence Livermore Lab, managed by the University of California, is a major research center for the production of nuclear weapons and was the site of frequent large-scale protests in the last half of the twentieth century.

28. The White Rose was a nonviolent resistance group in Nazi Germany, consisting of students from the University of Munich. They distributed anti-Nazi leaflets for eight months, from 1942 to 1943, before being apprehended. A 1982 movie about the group is still widely available in both Germany and the United States.

29. Jean Holladay, a "grandmother and nurse from Massachusetts," participated in Plowshares Number Four (Laffin, 17).

30. Leonard I. Weinglass (1934–2011) "was perhaps the nation's pre-eminent progressive defense lawyer," according to his obituary in the *New York Times* (Bruce Weber, "Leonard I. Weinglass, Lawyer, Dies at 77; Defended Renegades and the Notorious," March 24, 2011, *www.nytimes.com*).

31. Katya Komisaruk, *Beat the Heat: How to Handle Encounters with Law Enforcement* (Oakland, CA: AK Press, 2004).

32. Segment by Joan Cavanagh, copyright Joan Cavanagh.

33. Some segments here from the first interview were printed in *Voices*, 36–37 and 196–97.

34. Laffin, *Swords into Plowshares*, 63.

35. Jackie did not live to see my project completed. She became ill while incarcerated for an action at the Oak Ridge Nuclear Security weapons plant and was released after a quickly coordinated e-mail campaign to prison officials demanded that she receive medical treatment. She died in Washington State on August 3, 2011, with her brother by her side and surrounded by members of the Ground Zero community.

36. On October 10, 2008, the *Washington Times* reported that a secret Maryland State Police file had classified them as terrorists.

37. This segment combines words taken from several sources: a phone interview with Sister Jackie in 2007; two interviews with Sister Ardeth and Sister Carol together, in 1996 and 2007; individual interviews with Carol in 2005 and 2007, and with Ardeth in 2007; and Ardeth's handwritten response to my questions, mailed from FCI Danbury.

38. Laffin, *Swords into Plowshares*, 62.

39. *Rahman* and *Rahim* are two of the ninety-nine sacred names of God in Islam. Dr. Paul Meyer of Saginaw corrected my spelling, and in his note he added, "The roots of both *Rahman* and *Rahim* are from a word which means 'womb' so this is about reaching deep inside and giving birth to a divine quality."

40. NORAD (*norad.mil*) is the North American Aerospace Defense Command, a United States and Canada bi-national organization with "missions of aerospace warning and aerospace control for North America. It includes the monitoring of man-made objects in space."

41. Laffin, *Swords into Plowshares*, 79–80.

42. Brenda Truelson Fox filmed *Conviction*, a documentary about the action and trial, assembling an amazing array of opinions about the sisters and providing context with details about the continuing arms race. It is available from Jonah House.

43. The sisters had worn the Dominican black-and-white habit during their early years in the order.

44. Carol asked that I turn the recorder off whenever she talked about her prison friendship with Martha Stewart.

45. For two years, Stephen Kobasa and Anne Somsel and their teen daughters Clare

and Rachel traveled from New Haven to Danbury twice a month to visit Ardeth (Stephen Kobasa, e-mail to author, January 2006).

Chapter 4

1. To learn more about the Catholic Worker, visit one of the houses or farms, explore the Catholic Worker Archives at Marquette University, and go to *www.catholicworker.org*, which contains up-to-date information as well as searchable online versions of Day's writings.

2. Actually, Dorothy's words were even stronger than the phrase normally quoted. In the September 1956 *Catholic Worker*, she wrote: "We need to overthrow, not the government, as the authorities are always accusing the Communists 'of conspiring to teach to do,' but this rotten, decadent, putrid industrial capitalist system which breeds such suffering in the whited sepulcher of New York" (6).

3. Dorothy Day, "On Pilgrimage—July/August 1957," *Catholic Worker*, July–August 1957: 1, 3; available at the Dorothy Day Library on the Web, *www.catholicworker.org/dorothyday/*, document 724.

4. The Rocky Flats Plant was a weapons production facility of the Atomic Energy Commission, not far from Boulder, Colorado. It was in operation from 1952 to 1988, managed first by Dow Chemical Company and then by Rockwell International, and produced plutonium warheads for nuclear weapons. Controversy remains over whether the Superfund cleanup of the site was adequate.

5. Chuck Matthei (1948–2002) carried his noncooperation into arrest, trial, and incarceration, going limp, fasting, and refusing to obey prison regulations. A lifelong activist, he was instrumental in the community land trust and community loan fund movements. In 1991 he founded Equity Trust, Inc., based in Voluntown, Massachusetts.

6. The Silk Hope CW answers calls from the GI Rights Hotline for forty hours every week. This hotline is a network of nonprofit, nongovernmental organizations that provide information to service members.

7. Ammon Hennacy (1893–1970) was one of the most colorful Catholic Workers. An anarchist and pacifist who was jailed for refusing to serve in World War I, he often fasted and picketed alone, carrying a provocative sign. His second book was called *The One-Man Revolution.*

8. Brian is a Benedictine oblate, associated with the Benedictine Sisters of Perpetual Adoration in Clyde, Missouri.

9. Rabbi Heschel (1907–1972) was an American Jewish theologian.

10. Here, at Judith's request, I removed a story of a former prisoner she had counseled.

11. In addition to being the chronicler of Plowshares actions, Art Laffin is a long-term member of the Dorothy Day CW in Washington, DC, and himself a committed nonviolent resister.

12. The School of the Americas (SOA) trains soldiers from Latin America at Fort Benning in Georgia. The School of Americas Watch has coordinated a campaign to close the school, which includes lobbying Congress.

13. Portions of this narrative are from his original transcript in the Marquette Archives. Two paragraphs are reprinted from *Voices*, 203 and 515–16.

14. Howard Zinn, *A People's History of the United States* (New York: HarperCollins, 1980).

15. See Cooney and Michalowski, 107.

16. Portions of these have been printed in *Voices*, 183–217.

17. "We have all known the long loneliness and we have learned that the only solution is love and that love comes with community. It all happened while we sat there talking, and it is still going on." Dorothy Day, *The Long Loneliness* (New York: Harper, 1952), Postscript.

18. Witness for Peace (*witnessforpeace.live.radicaldesigns.org*) was founded in 1983 in opposition to the US support of the Nicaraguan contras. Since then, it has widened its scope to other Latin American and Caribbean countries.

19. Tina is referring here to Father Carl Kabat and Helen Woodson, who were sentenced to eighteen years for their Silo Pruning Hooks action in 1984. They did not have to serve the complete sentence but Helen remained in prison for a subsequent action until September 2011.

20. "Our deepest fear is not that we are inadequate. Our deepest fear is that we are powerful beyond measure. It is our light, not our darkness, that most frightens us. We ask ourselves, who am I to be brilliant, gorgeous, talented, fabulous? Actually, who are you not to be? You are a child of God. Your playing small doesn't serve the world." Frequently quoted as a speech by Mandela, the text was written by Marianne Williamson and first published in *A Return to Love* (New York: HarperCollins, 1992).

21. This interview was conducted in 1988. Paul now manages the Catholic Worker bookstore and serves as finances and operations manager for Witness for Peace.

Chapter 5

1. The following Ithaca interviews are available in the Marquette Archives: Peter DeMott (deceased), Mary Anne Flores Grady, Neil Golder, Clare Grady, Ellen Grady, and Theresa Grady. Narrators Ana Grady Flores and Dan Burns are included in Chapter 7.

2. Father Bourgeois was asked to leave the priesthood in 2008 for his public support of the ordination of women in the Roman Catholic church.

3. Available in the Marquette Archives are three other Syracuse interviews: Dan and Doris Sage, who entered prison at the same time for an SOA action; Jerome Berrigan, the oldest of the famed Berrigan brothers; and Bill Cuddy, who founded Slocum Jail Ministry and as a Catholic priest often presided at liturgies at Griffiss Air Force Base.

4. Betty Brink, "Static," *Fort Worth Weekly*, December 20, 2006.

5. Bread and Puppet is a politically radical puppet theater, active since the 1960s and currently based in Glover, Vermont. They participate in demonstrations for social change and frequently give workshops on stilt-walking and creating papier-mâché puppets.

6. For more on George Richmani's work, see *www.sirajcenter.org*.

7. The nation's bloodiest prison riot occurred at the Attica Correctional Facility in Attica, New York, in September 1971. Led by a small band of political revolutionaries and based in part on a demand for better living conditions, it resulted in at least thirty-nine deaths, including ten guards and civilian employees. Frederic Wiggins, "The Truth about Attica by an Inmate," *National Review*, March 31, 1972.

8. Mickey's name was added to the cross in 2008.

9. The phrase was originally coined by Richard B. Gregg in 1934. In 1973, Gene Sharp

proposed a generalization, "political jiu-jitsu." See Brian Martin, "How Nonviolence Works," *Borderlands* 14, no. 3 (2005), *www.borderlands.net.au/*. Sharp's work has been credited with inspiring the 2011 Arab Spring. See Sheryl Gay Stolberg, "Shy U.S. Intellectual Created Playbook Used in a Revolution," *New York Times*, February 16, 2011, *www.nytimes.com*.

10. Founded by Chicago resister Kathy Kelly, Voices in the Wilderness campaigned against the Iraq sanctions.

Chapter 6

1. I interviewed Kim and Bill separately, although Bill was in the room when Kim and I spoke. In this segment, I've combined their words.

2. I was able to interview Grace's daughter, Amy Baranski-Jewitt. Amy said the government had told the coast guard workers that the protesters were terrorists, "so that's how they treated them" (Marquette Archives).

3. "I made a movie of her first White Train blockade. Took it with Super 8 movie film. Then I made another one in 1984 and began to see myself as documenting the campaign. Then Mike Johnson came in with one of the first video cameras and began to document all the actions around the train. We've turned all of this over to the University of Washington archives, where they have all the Ground Zero material." (*Aside by Bill.*)

4. At Kim and Bill's request, I've excised personal details here about a family illness and the waning of their Bible study and resistance group.

5. Words of Jim Douglass, copyright Jim Douglass.

6. Jim Douglass, "Tracking the White Train," *Sojourners Magazine*, February 1984, 15.

7. Ibid.

8. Lyrics for "There's a Train," copyright Jim Strathdee. Reprinted by permission of Desert Flower Music. Copy license 03262011-P1.

9. The man the marshals arrested was Larry Cloud Morgan. He had violated the terms of his probation for the 1984 Silo Pruning Hooks action by traveling to Georgia for this protest (Laffin, *Swords into Plowshares*, 24).

10. See *anathothcommunityfarm.org*, especially "About the Farm."

11. "Dorothy economics" is a "God will provide" economic philosophy that was practiced by Catholic Worker cofounder Dorothy Day.

12. For many years, the Jonah House community supported itself by painting houses.

13. The Honeywell Project began in 1968 and worked nonviolently to convince the Honeywell Corporation to convert their weapons manufacturing to peaceful production. Large numbers of people were arrested in civil disobedience actions. In 1990, Honeywell formed a new company called Alliant Techsystems. Many of the Honeywell Project people now protest against Alliant Tech. Minnesota Historical Society, "The Honeywell Project," MN150 wiki, *discovery.mnhs.org*.

14. Alliant Techsystems of Medina, Minnesota, is the Pentagon's largest ammunition producer and its sole provider of small-arms ammunition for rifles. It also manufactures uranium weapons, land mines, and cluster bombs. Minnesota's Alliant Action seeks a conversion of Alliant Tech facilities to peaceful products and has mounted a campaign of weekly vigils and occasional civil disobedience. Some of their trials have resulted in acquittals. See *www.alliantaction.org*.

15. Project ELF (Extremely Low Frequency) was a transmitter system built to send one-way messages to submerged British and US submarines around the world,

allowing Trident ballistic missiles to get close enough to targets to launch a nuclear first strike. After years of legal protest and civil disobedience by thousands of activists in both Wisconsin and Michigan, Project ELF was closed in 2004. For a concise history of actions against these miles of transmitter wires, see Nukewatch, "Project ELF Closes," *Nuclear Resister* 135 (October 15, 2004), *nuclearresister.org*.

16.   Before beginning Anathoth, the family spent several years living in and renovating a house at Hunky Dory Farm resort.

17.   For several years a colorfully painted "Wheels of Justice" bus toured the Midwest, its passengers speaking at schools and churches about war and occupation in Iraq and Palestine. Mike would frequently be the driver and organizer. In 2008, the bus developed expensive mechanical problems and the tours were suspended. See *justicewheels.org*.

18.   There are five colleges in the area—Amherst, Hampshire, Mount Holyoke, Smith, and the University of Massachusetts. The schools collaborate with each other on many endeavors, including transportation.

19.   Juanita and Wally Nelson worked for civil rights, resisted war taxes, and in 1948 cofounded Peacemakers, a radical pacifist group whose members pledged draft and tax resistance. The Nelsons lived much of their long lives in Deerfield, Connecticut.

20.   Joni has traveled three times to Palestine as a member of the Michigan Peace Team (*www.michiganpeaceteam.org*). While there, the team works with nonviolent Palestinians in efforts to protect their homes and lands from Israeli settlers and militia.

21.   Faith-based peace groups frequently schedule actions on August 6 or 9, as reminders of the dates when the US dropped the first atomic bombs, decimating two populous cities in Japan.

Chapter 7

1.   For a long (yet still incomplete) listing of peace groups, see the "Resources & Links to Current Peace Organizations & Groups or Individuals" page at the Swarthmore College Peace Collection website (*www.swarthmore.edu/library/peace/index.htm*). The Swarthmore College Peace Collection provides valuable resources for researchers and activists alike.

2.   Schuchardt is an attorney who participated in the first Plowshares action and remains active in the movement.

3.   Peter DeMott, interview, Marquette Archives.

4.   Elmer Maas (1935–2005) participated in the first Plowshares action with Sister Anne Montgomery. In a remembrance she wrote of him, she noted that he gave up the security of college teaching to work for the peace movement, joining with the War Resisters League, the Atlantic Life Community, and, "at the heart of everything, the Plowshares movement to realize Isaiah's command" (*www.jonahhouse. org/archive/MontgomeryElmer.htm*).

5.   The words are by Howard Thurman (1899–1981), a civil rights leader and a theologian at Howard University. (*Added by Becky at transcript review.*)

6.   Muslim Legal Fund of America, "MLFA Helps Form National Coalition," press release, January 19, 2011, *www.mlfa.org*.

7.   Evan Wright, *Generation Kill* (Berkeley, CA: Berkeley Caliber, 2005).

8.   Karl Meyer, Kathy's former husband, is a longtime Catholic Worker peace activist, known particularly for his tax resistance.

9. Camilo Mejia, "Regaining My Humanity," *CommonDreams.org*, February 24, 2005.
10. "Democracy Now," August 5, 2009.
11. Father Joe Mulligan visited Camilo in prison. Perhaps because he works in Guatemala, Joe feels a special connection to Camilo through his father, Carlos Mejia Coday, a well-known Nicaraguan musician who composed the *Misa Campesina* (Peasant Mass). Joe wrote, "We had a wonderful visit. He is a very thoughtful person and eloquent speaker. He has said that he feels a deep peace about his decision and that he is a free man who is able to follow his conscience" (quoted from Father Mulligan's prison journal, which includes the first few days after his release from Harris County Jail for an SOAW action, in e-mail to author, December 2004).
12. Refuse and Resist gave Mejia its Courageous Resister Award and the Peace Abbey its Courage of Conscience Award. The City Council of Detroit also presented him with a commendation for his antiwar stand.
13. Camilo Mejia, *Road from Ar Ramadi: The Private Rebellion of Staff Sergeant Camilo Mejia* (New York: New Press, 2007).

Epilogue

1. Morgan Guyton, "Winter Begins," used by permission of the author.

Index

Note: Within this index, the terms "jail" and "prison" are used interchangeably except in the actual names of facilities. The names of individual narrators and pages referring to their words are in **bold**; pages referring to photographs are in *italics*.